Cast No Shadow

ALSO BY MARY S. LOVELL

Straight On Till Morning: The Biography of Beryl Markham

The Sound of Wings: The Life of Amelia Earhart

The Splendid Outcast (with Beryl Markham)

A Hunting Pageant

Cast No Shadow

THE LIFE OF THE AMERICAN SPY
WHO CHANGED THE COURSE OF WORLD WAR II

Mary S. Lovell

PANTHEON BOOKS
NEW YORK

Grateful acknowledgment is made to the following for permission to reprint
previously published material:

Rosalind Montgomery Hyde: Excerpt from *Cynthia* by H. Montgomery Hyde.
Copyright © 1966 by H. Montgomery Hyde. Reprinted by permission of Rosalind
Montgomery Hyde. Rights in the British Commonwealth administered by Hamish
Hamilton Limited, London.

Library of Congress Cataloging-in-Publication Data

Lovell, Mary S.
Cast no shadow / by Mary S. Lovell.
p.   cm.
Includes index.
ISBN 0-394-57556-3
1. Pack, Amy Thorpe.   2. Spies—Great Britain—Biography.
3. Spies—United States—Biography.
4. World War, 1939–1945—Secret
service—Great Britain.
I. Title. D810.S8P335   1992
940.54'8641'092—dc20

[B]   91-52625

Book design by Fearn Cutler

Manufactured in the United States of America
First Edition

To Geoffrey Watts
who now knows better than to write to authors

I have done the state some service, and they know 't;
No more of that. I pray you, in your letters,
When you shall these unlucky deeds relate,
Speak of me as I am; nothing extenuate,
Nor set down aught in malice: then, must you speak
Of one that loved not wisely but too well.

Shakespeare, Othello

Betty

She had a force, or magnetism, to a terrifying degree. It leapt like light from the whole of her, not just from her green eyes or wide smile. Many a man, I think, read this force as warmth; as a concentrated and passionate interest in himself. The trick of making a man feel he is her entire universe is an old feminine wile, but "Cynthia" had it to the *nth* degree. I felt the impact at once.

Harford Montgomery Hyde
(Former colleague at British
Security Coordination New York, 1941)

It would be difficult to overemphasize the importance of her work. . . . Her security was irreproachable and her loyalty to her employers complete. She was not greedy for money but greedy only to serve a cause in which she believed. In fact she was paid a small salary which represented little more than her living expenses, although the value of her work to Britain could be assessed, if at all, in millions.

BSC Official History (p. 153)

Contents

Introduction

The legend of Betty Pack is simple enough. She was a beautiful American spy who worked for the British Secret Intelligence Service (SIS), and later for the American equivalent, the Office of Strategic Services (OSS), during World War II. Her method of obtaining information from and about the enemy was equally basic. She singled out top men and seduced them. In only one instance did she mistake her quarry, and on that occasion she was able to use the influence of another man whom she had previously "turned" to mitigate the damage.

Recruited by British Secret Intelligence in Poland in 1938, she was active until 1944 when her cover was compromised. During that time she was able to acquire, consistently, information that her spymasters considered of great value to the war effort. Within days of the North African landings, Colonel Ellery Huntington—her former controller and subsequent commander of the OSS Detachment in North Africa—told her that information she had provided, which had been used during the landings, had "changed the whole course of the war."[1]

There have been, inevitably, comparisons with Mata Hari. But Betty was not simply a beauty allowing her body to be used. She was, according to her brother, "highly intellectual," and while this assessment may not be regarded as objective it is borne out by official SIS documents and her colleagues. Marion de Chastellaine of the British Security Coordination, Betty's contact with HQ in 1941–42, also told me:

> Of course Betty enjoyed the *glamour* of the thing. She had got herself involved in Poland and came into the service of her own volition. . . . I think she came across some information and then set about finding someone to pass it on to. . . .[2]

More often than not it was Betty, herself, who targeted her male subjects. She was intelligent enough to know what information they were likely to possess and she used all her skills, including sex, to extract it. To a certain extent she regarded her work in the bedroom as mere expediency. Asked by a friend if she ever felt any shame over her *modus operandi*, she replied:

> Not in the least! My superiors told me that the results of my work saved thousands of British and American lives. Even *one* would have made it worthwhile . . . wars are not won by "respectable" methods. . . .

During the course of my research I learned variously that Betty was: a *femme fatale*; very sweet; a nymphomaniac; a romantic; extremely beautiful; rather ordinary; electrifying; and highly intelligent. A friend who knew her for thirty years said of her, "She was one of the most courageous women I ever knew."[3] Another said, "She was a delightful, intelligent companion, and there was a restlessness that gave the impression that there was something of the wild—untamed, I mean—animal about her. It was an irresistible combination."[4]

Clearly this was a fascinating woman in every sense. Filled with restless energy, she was at her best when channelling its force into supporting her through situations that were fraught with physical danger and adventure. Her exploits extended beyond the bedroom: from burglary and safecracking to posing as the step-daughter of an interned senior official of the Vichy government whom she joined in captivity. From wandering around, alone, in Spain during the civil war searching for an imprisoned lover to running medical supplies across the border to Franco's "insurgents," contravening the direct orders of her ambassador. Her talents ranged from speaking several foreign languages with absolute fluency to an acknowledged ability as a journalist. In addition she was an accomplished hostess in the diplomatic world.

The ingredients alone would make a good novel, but there is nothing fictional about Betty Pack. This is her story.

Cast No Shadow

Chapter 1

1910 - 1929

O n a cold spring morning in March 1938 Betty Pack, wife of Arthur Pack, His Majesty's Commercial Secretary in Warsaw, drove out to a country club on the outskirts of the city. Arthur had recently suffered a severe stroke and Betty had gone with him to England to arrange his convalescence at home. She then returned to Warsaw with the intention of collecting their three-year-old daughter and rejoining her husband.

Betty was a twenty-seven-year-old American. Physically she was beautiful: slightly over medium height and slim with amber blond hair, patrician features and large green eyes. There was a sweetness in her nature, and a sirenlike quality to her soft voice that instantly attracted people of both sexes. Women did not stay attracted very long. Most men stayed too long. Although she was enthusiastic in her passions, she was not naturally garrulous and the aura of calm, serious sympathy she exuded invited confidences; especially from men, who found themselves sharing their problems, hopes and disappointments.

One of these men was Edward Kulikowski, a young man in a senior position in the American Section of the Polish Foreign Office. On her return to Warsaw Betty met the Polish diplomat at a party at the Hotel Europejski and the two began an affair. It was casual and friendly, both using it to assuage the painful after effects of previous serious relationships which had failed. Most evenings Betty would join Kulikowski in his bachelor apartment furnished with fur rugs, a large comfortable divan and a grand piano. An accomplished pianist, he would play Chopin, and afterwards they would stretch out on a fur rug before the fire and sip vodka before making love.

Since Betty also moved in the narrow diplomatic community they had many mutual friends and concerns. Their discussions centred around these, and on the burning issue of the day—Hitler's avarice and the threat of war it posed. On the evening before her drive to the country club, as they lay together before the fire, Kulikowski casually let slip a piece of information that Betty knew, intuitively, was important. Her husband's previous posting had been Spain during the civil war, and she had had occasion to provide items of minor intelligence to British Military authorities. If they had been interested in details of rationing and the gossip of the worried citizens of Madrid, how much more interested would they be in what Edward had just said to her? Yet what was she to do with it?

One of her friends at the British embassy was the Passport Control Officer, Jack Shelley. She telephoned him the next morning and said she needed to discuss a matter of importance. He suggested they play a round of golf together that morning.

The Passport Control Office was a thinly disguised cover within British embassies for British Intelligence operatives, and though Betty was not aware of Shelley's particular role in these operations she knew that he

2

would be able to pass her information on if he considered it as valuable as she did.

Betty told Shelley what Kulikowski had confided to her on the previous night: Hitler's next victim was to be Czechoslovakia and Poland's foreign minister, Colonel Josef Beck, had agreed to condone this aggression in return for "a bite of the cherry." Shelley, the senior officer of the Secret Intelligence Service (SIS) in Poland, was probably already aware of Hitler's designs on Czechoslovakia but he needed as much detail as he could obtain on Poland's position. He told Betty of his connection with SIS and asked her to "Go back and get any more stuff on that that you can. . . ."

Soon she was providing Shelley with regular typed reports of her conversations with Kulikowski, which Shelley passed on to London. As a consequence, Shelley was instructed to recruit Betty as an agent. Apparently happy to abandon her plans for rejoining her husband, she agreed. Her assignment was to make as many friends as she could among senior officials of Polish diplomatic and political circles. To cover the costs of entertaining she was provided with a monthly sum from SIS funds.

There was an unspoken agreement between Betty and her controller that, if necessary, she would sleep with her contacts to gain information. Within weeks she had met one of the most important men in the Polish government and as part of her commitment to SIS goals, slipped naturally into the role of seductress. The role had a six-year run. In the end she may have been one of the most successful women spies of World War II.

Amy Elizabeth Thorpe was born on November 22, 1910, in Minneapolis, Minnesota. Her mother's sister, Aimée, lived with the child's parents from time to time, and it was perhaps to avoid confusion with Aunt Aimée that from her first days the baby was known as Elizabeth, and more often, Betty. Although she would be known by many names in her short and adventurous life, she generally called herself Betty until after World War II, when the diminutive came to be regarded, perhaps, as faintly undignified and she began calling herself Elizabeth.

Her father, George Cyrus Thorpe, was a captain in the United States Marines. The son of a farmer, he had joined the United States Marine Corps in 1898 at the age of twenty-two as a second lieutenant, serving on the USS *Yale* in the Santiago campaign during the Spanish-American War. He was present on the first Puerto Rican expedition.

With countless skirmishes occurring in various parts of the world, those were good times for an ambitious young officer. Within eighteen months his distinguished service and gallant conduct earned him a promotion to captain during the Philippine insurrection.[1] Over the next ten years his service included a spell as Fleet Marine officer of the European Fleet, until he took part in the 1903 American expedition through Syria. In the following year he commanded a marine expedition through Abyssinia to make a treaty with Emperor Menelik II, by whom he was decorated with the Star of Ethiopia. By 1906 George was involved in the war of Cuban pacification, where he helped to quell the election troubles in the new republic. At the time of Betty's birth Captain Thorpe had just finished an extended period of leave from military service, during which he had earned both a bachelor's and a law degree from New York University.[2]

Cora Wells, Betty's mother, was the daughter of State Senator Harry H. Wells. Despite her handsome looks and obvious intelligence she was regarded by some members of society as a bluestocking spinster. A haughty coldness in her manner, which she never lost, may have accounted for this. If Cora did indeed behave with a certain aloofness towards her upper Midwest neighbours, she may have seen herself as having just cause: she had been graduated with honours as a bachelor of arts from the University of Michigan, Ann Arbor, and followed this with postgraduate work at Columbia University, New York, the Sorbonne in Paris, and the University of Munich. But if other suitors were intimidated by such a world-educated woman, the equally well travelled Captain Thorpe seems not to have been.

Cora's family lived in a style far removed from that of the Thorpes. Not for them the huge farmhouse kitchen and a life tuned to the passing seasons. Her father, who left his native Canada to settle in Morris, Minnesota, as an eighteen-year-old clerk, was an ambitious entrepreneur. Within seven years he had married Clara Wolff, daughter of the owner, and was running the business. By the time he was thirty, he had bought out his father-in-law, set up numerous other business ventures, founded a bank and had been elected to the state legislature.

George Thorpe and Cora Wells were married on April 8, 1908. A few months before the birth of Betty, George returned to active service as commander of the naval prison at Portsmouth, Maine, an assignment coupled with promotion to the rank of major. The family lived in Maine until 1914, during which time two more children were born; a second daughter, Jane, in July 1912 and a son, George, in July 1914.

As an adult Betty wrote of her first memories, describing all as having been "built around aloneness." The earliest went back to the age of four, when she would contrive to spend a part of each day in the pine woods that were some distance from her home. She recalled lying among the bluebells and listening to the wind that soughed among the tall trees and the faraway sound of motor boats on Maine's Casco Bay. This search for solitude not unnaturally caused some anxiety in those charged with her care, for she often disappeared for long periods. Fortunately, the neighbourhood policeman soon came to know the child's hiding places and would go and collect her in the evenings and take her home. However, the contentment she found by withdrawing into seclusion at that early age became a pattern; towards the end of her life she claimed that much of the satisfaction she had derived in her life came from this ability to be comfortable in her own company.

Throughout her childhood she never had what is called a "best friend" and apart from her diary she had no confidant.[3] This does not suggest a happy relationship with her parents, or more particularly, since her father was often absent, with her mother. Cora was not a woman who could display love or emotion easily. Added to this was Betty's own strong character, which even at an early age predicted inevitable personality clashes between the two. In those days when adults believed that "children should be seen and not heard," Betty's response to the stresses of her relationship with a highly directed mother took the form of escape into a private world.

Despite the fact that a world war was raging in Europe, Betty's father continued his search for education; his biographical records show that he was graduated from the Navy War College at Annapolis in 1915 and the following year received his M.A. at Brown University in Providence, Rhode Island. During this period Cora and the three children lived in Newport, Rhode Island, moving to Washington, D.C., in 1916.

In 1917, George Thorpe, as chief of staff of the Second Marine Brigade, was posted to Cuba, where he earned praise for his work in capturing a notorious bandit despite having received a serious bullet wound. With his previous record this new achievement ultimately brought him to the rank of colonel. In the winter of 1917–18 Cora took her three children to Cuba, only to find that her peripatetic husband had been sent to South America. She remained on the island until early 1919, when she retreated to Florida to await the return of George, who had received a home posting. Young Betty had a natural facility for languages and in the interim period picked up the rudiments of Spanish. Years later she could recall from this time intricate memories of visits to plantations and the bright social life of off-duty service personnel. The family was reunited in Florida and shortly afterwards returned to Washington, D.C. George's next posting was to the General Staff College.

Thus Betty was already well travelled when at the age of nine she started keeping a day-by-day diary in a large bound volume presented to her by her grandparents at Christmas. Daily she recorded the details of what seemed a remarkably crowded social life for a nine-year-old: ". . . it was a beautiful but sad play about Lincoln." "Today after lunch we all went to our old dressmaker, Miss Mills. . . ." "Went to the Library of Congress, it is all marble and paintings. . . ." "Today Nana [her maternal grand-mother] took me to see Pavlova . . . she danced wonderfully well." On a visit to George Washington's home at Mount Vernon she wrote a vivid description of the house, decorated with the child's memory of the sur-rounding green hills, and the white sails of yachts against the blue of the Potomac viewed from the front lawns. She had developed a writer's knack of observation, though at times one gets the impression that she is too much echoing the style and sentiments of her elders.

The society columns of the *Washington Star* indicate that her parents moved easily in top circles of the city's political and diplomatic milieu. One diary entry engagingly describes a party given by her mother that day for Vice-President and Mrs. Coolidge. Another gives a special insight into the distorted sense of *noblesse oblige* Washington society tried to instil in its children, telling of a late-afternoon party in 1921 when she was taken with her smartly dressed companions onto a balcony where, in the gathering dusk, they "threw pennies to the darkie children."[4]

As an adult she was to write, not altogether sympathetically, that her mother was a passionate believer in the discipline of good manners and the rituals of "society." Betty might have been turned into the artificial, polished creature that her mother would have admired. Instead, as she became conscious of the hypocrisy of society, though she did not rebel openly she became instead a cynical observer noting that good manners were "actually rather useful to hide behind." Tall, slender and blond, her gamine appearance as a pre-teenager now hid a "rather sombre and wild" personality which had already developed twin passions:

> . . . one to be alone, the other for excitement. Any kind of excitement—even fear. Anything to assuage my terrible restlessness and the excruciating sense of pressure (that came from where or what I never knew) that was only released in action, in doing, in exhaustion. I remember when we were very young and running races I always ran past the finish line and ran and ran and ran until I dropped half strangled when my endurance ran out. I just couldn't stop before that. There seemed no sense in running unless I ran myself practically to death. My brother George used to go mad. "You're crazy, you're crazy!" he'd shout as I raced by. "Why don't you STOP?"[5]

When George Thorpe was given command of the marines at Pearl Harbor in 1921 the family left home on June 17 and travelled across country by train in easy stages, visiting relatives in Minnesota and Oregon. In late August, they sailed from San Francisco for Hawaii.

In Hawaii, Betty's parents began writing articles for magazines. George wrote about legal matters and Cora specialized in European cities. Betty also began writing. She wrote an article about her family background called *Days Bygone,* which consisted mainly of a description of a ball given by the King and Queen at Buckingham Palace in 1903, attended by Betty's father. This was followed by a small book entitled *David,* which was much admired within the family. For her next literary project, *Fioretta*, her father commissioned an illustrator and had the story privately printed.

It was a mature book for an eleven-year-old to have written. It must also have been well accepted by the public beyond family and friends, for when the first small run was sold, another edition was printed and distributed by the publisher.

An introduction was written by the governor of Hawaii, W. R. Farrington, in which he talks of the author's hitherto "vagabond existence" and his own acquaintanceship with her:

Betty is a "real little girl" just as her younger brother is a "real boy." She plays with her puppy Eno-san with childish glee; rides her pony with the alarming abandon of confidence in a good seat, and dashes through the the surf of Waikiki with the easy grace of a polynesian sea urchin . . .

The first chapter begins:

Little Fioretta sat at the large-paned window waiting for her father. The sun had not yet cast its sunset robe over Naples but it was sinking fast behind that ancient piece of beauty, Vesuvius which nature had so thoughtfully bestowed upon the earth. A faint pink blush trembled in the softly tinted opalescent sky over lilac mountains and the gorgeous sapphire harbour lay silently beneath the spell of its beauty. The only sound was the low moan of the waters as they met the shore and the soft song of the deep, blue Mediterranean. . . .[6]

It was a romantic tale of a girl slightly older than Betty, living alone with her blind father. She has a wonderful voice and when her father falls ill Fioretta takes to singing on the streets of Naples to earn enough to feed them. Heard by an impresario who provides voice training, she ends up as a famous soprano. The most telling theme about the story, the blazing love of the young girl for her father, clearly mirrors the author's feelings for her own father.

In the autumn of 1922 George Thorpe began to experience some sort of physical problems, apparently resulting from an old injury. He retired from the USMC after twenty-four years of distinguished service.[7] The family sailed for California on January 23, 1923, aboard the SS *Cambra*. They arrived in Washington in March and by late April had left for Europe on the grand tour.

Travelling slowly, from Paris through Avignon, Grasse, Nice and Monte Carlo, the party made their way to Italy, where after Rome Betty at last reached Naples and the setting for *Fioretta*. She was desperately anxious to see how accurate her descriptions, both imagined and those culled from travel books, had been. That evening she stood on the terrace "gazing across a bay so blue that the azure Hope Diamond is pale beside it. Vesuvius rising tall and stately in a robe of violet with the silver thread trailing gently into a soft sky of ambers and crimson, and Capri a line of mulberry in the twilight haze. . . ."[8] It was far more beautiful than she had guessed.

After a short time in Germany, Betty spent three months studying French at the Institution des Essarts, housed in a gaunt chateau perched above Lake Geneva.

its garden ringing with the sound of children's voices, and at other times —before they take possession—silent as a deserted world. With its tiny winding stone steps moss-grown and the tall black cypresses rising against the stormy skies. The songs of wood thrushes or larks, and the little wood birds fluttering in the sighing elms as they rock to and fro with the soft sad lullaby of a lake wind hushing the silence brings out a joyous thrilling note into the gardens, loneliness.[9]

By October, Betty's French was almost flawless. With her quick intelligence, she readily absorbed new ideas and concepts. There was never any need for tutors to repeat things to her, and she became easily bored when her classmates could not think at her own rapid pace. She found the rigorous routine of the *école* over-strict and was in several scrapes with the principal before she and Jane left "joyously" at Christmas to rejoin her mother and brother in Paris en route to the United States. Back in Washington in the New Year she slipped easily into the old routine of school and visits to the ballet and opera. Her descriptions of what she saw are now more adult and discerning, but the overriding theme is that she misses Europe.

9

While at various private schools over the next few years her diary constantly echoes this keening for Europe. Her special intelligence, along with the enormous breadth of experiences already crowded into her short life, served to isolate her from her school fellows. She was never a sharer of secrets, and her preference for solitude, for her own company over that of her school friends, was alien to the other girls of her age. She excelled in her studies without ever having to exert herself, and though her companions respected her, even admired her in a shocked sort of way when she flouted rules, they recognized that she was not really one of them. Despite the veneer of exquisite manners, the loner and unconventional young animal she had become did not invite close friendship, and her friends responded in kind. "She was always trying to prove that she could tackle almost anything we funked doing, and that usually meant getting into some kind of mischief. We always felt it was a reaction against her mother who was terribly conventional," said a school friend.[10] But now the picture of that perfect porcelain child that she had always presented to the doting adults around her began to show its flaws. She was asked to leave at least one school for flouting rules and setting a bad example.

Each summer the Thorpes took a house in Newport, Rhode Island, for the season. Colonel Thorpe raced a chartered sailboat and the family's social life centred around the exclusive yacht clubs. Cora had her own reason for enjoying Newport; a good part of Washington and New York "high society" gathered there in the summer months. Busy in the role of hostess in which she both revelled and excelled, she relaxed her chaperonage of Betty, who quickly caught the eye of a young man, "as lonely and desperate" as herself. Betty never revealed the name of the man except to say that he was of an Irish family. "[He] was 21, and belonged to a well-known family whose names often appear in the Social Register. I imagined myself in love with him, for at that age you cannot go to bed with anyone without feeling love. We were both lonely and we met only twice before the 'love affair' was over. . . ." Betty was fourteen.

Betty claims she was seduced on that first occasion, but a school friend, interviewed years later, thought it unlikely. "If anyone did the seducing it would have been Betty."[11] Awakened to the joys of sex, sophisticated and mature beyond her years, Betty delighted in her power to attract men, particularly older men.

That summer of 1925 Betty's diary was untouched from March 28 until November 18, when she confided in perfect French:

> . . . so many things have happened to me since March 28th. So many affairs of the heart, so many thoughts, ideas and changes in me that I have sometimes thought I was a different person and have not always been in charge of my emotions. I have not written every day because I know I can never relive the feelings and experiences . . .
>
> . . . My looks are better than I hoped, God was kind in that at least, and I have strong emotions [though I fear] I have too much love. I love and love with all my heart, only I have to *appear* cool. The men are the ones who change . . . I know that if I love too much at the start I risk losing their respect and admiration for they only seek the joy of telling of a conquest.
>
> Life is but a stage on which to play. One's role is to pretend, and always to hide one's true feelings. *Plus tard!*[12]

After their European tour the family moved to Washington, where George established a law practice specializing in maritime cases. He and Cora were prominent members of the capital's society. Betty found herself a minor celebrity in certain circles. Her book *Fioretta* had somehow found its way to the Italian embassy and the ambassador, Martino Nobile, and his diplomats made a pet of her.

The Italian naval attaché, Commander Alberto Lais, then in his early forties, was particularly charmed by the sophisticated teenager. When he was working in Boston, and Betty was at boarding school in Wellesley studying music, the two would often meet for tea.[13] He called her his "little golden girl" and though it may be that nothing untoward happened between the diplomat and the teenager, Betty's *outré* behaviour in entertaining the handsome Italian was the basis for much gossip and speculation among Betty's classmates.

Lais was not the only diplomat to take more than a passing look at Betty. Her youthful, tanned body stretched out, Lolita-like, beside the pool at a Washington country club transfixed Arthur Joseph Pack, a Commercial Secretary at the British embassy. Years later he confided that he never forgot that first sight of her. And there was an erotic moment with a young Spanish aristocrat, not much more in reality than a few burning glances exchanged during a tennis match at the same club where Betty was spending the last day of her Easter vacation before going back to boarding school. The Spaniard was with a group of lively people, all members of the young diplomatic set, and by smiling seductively and fixing him with a special look Betty tried hard, but in vain she thought, to entice him to approach, for he departed with his large party of friends without doing so. But before leaving he stopped before her and saluted her with a graceful bow. The mysterious stranger with classically beautiful features came to embody all Betty's teenage romantic and sexual fantasies. Eventually he, too, was destined to play a role in her adult life.

Cora could hardly have failed to notice the effect her daughter had on men. Still, Betty was a daughter to be proud of. Slim and poised, she had developed into a beauty with superb colouring—a light, glowing complexion, amber blond hair, green eyes, and particularly long eyelashes. There was nothing to give the impression that she was fast; indeed, there was something almost "above it all" in the cool way she often seemed to be standing quietly apart from everyone, simply observing them thoughtfully.

It seems odd that coming from parents who had placed such a high priority on their own college careers Betty appears not to have been pressed to complete her education. There is no question that she had the ability.

In November 1929, a day before her nineteenth birthday, Betty was presented to Washington society. Cora hosted a tea dance for a number of prominent Washington hostesses and a flock of "sister debutantes," whom the society correspondents referred to as "buds."[14] Unquestionably, she expected Betty to attend the right parties, behave well and simper to prospective husbands. It was what Betty had been educated for: to achieve the right sort of marriage. What else was there for a well-brought-up girl at that time? This was what the gifted Cora, a product of her time and upbringing, almost despite her educational success, had done with her own life. One must suppose she was satisfied with such an end for a talented woman with drive and energy, for she was clearly attempting to impose it on her daughter.

Betty's resentment of this is apparent in her memoirs:

> She was mad about society. Good society, I must admit, but to a degree I thought silly and slavish, and she also loved money and titles and labels for things. It was a superficial life she lived, with an energy and discipline that could have run a government. . . . She disapproved of me and I disapproved of her.

According to a former British diplomat Betty was both emotionally and mentally ahead of all this;

> she was an exceptionally adult girl with a mind of her own . . . there was always about her that look of challenge, something that seemed to be permanently daring one to do something with her whether it was to play polo, go on a midnight picnic or just leap into bed with her. . . .[15]

She was passionate, polished, shrewd and sensitive; and she possessed that indefineable questioning confidence that is perhaps peculiar to well-educated American women.

Over Christmas Betty was involved heavily with an unnamed man to whom she wrote a short poem in her diary on January 4:

> *I think I cannot quite understand*
> *The depth of wanting unfulfilled desire,*
> *And hating you to touch my hand*
> *When embers die where once there was a fire.*

This man might have been Arthur Pack, for Betty had known him throughout November, and he had been a guest to a small tea party at her parents' home in Woodley Road on November 18.[16] Whoever he was he seems to have been the father of Betty's child born on October 2, 1930, nine months to the week after the date of this diary entry.

Chapter 2

1930-1935

A rthur Joseph Pack and Betty were fellow house guests at a weekend
party in November 1929, and when Arthur retired to his room
on the second night of their stay he discovered Betty, naked, in
his bed waiting for him.[1]

Arthur was a large man, over six feet in height and broad-shouldered;
he had a beautiful baritone voice with which he readily entertained his
companions when invited to do so. He appears to have been as drawn to
younger women as Betty was to older men and indeed had recently proposed to a woman only slightly older than Betty, and been rejected on

the grounds that their age difference was too great. At thirty-eight, he was almost twice as old as Betty.

Betty had had an eye on Arthur as well. He went about with a set of rich embassy colleagues and wealthy Americans,[2] a glittering circle of eligible men and beautiful women who belonged to the right clubs, dined in the best restaurants and were *personae gratae* with the top hostesses.

To all external appearances Arthur was a comfortably off, successful diplomat with a good future ahead of him. But in reality he spent far beyond his means on outward appearances, to disguise his modest origins and to help further his diplomatic career.

Arthur was born in 1891 into a family of limited means and had worked very hard to reach his present position as Commercial Secretary at the British embassy. After attending grammar school he joined the Civil Service by passing a highly competitive examination. He chose a difficult path for an ambitious man with modest beginnings. In those days virtually the only way to gain promotion to senior levels in the British Civil Service was through the influence of some highly placed connection. Without that influence, the only route open to him was sheer hard work. One year after his appointment as a clerk to the General Post Office his diligence and exemplary behaviour earned him his first promotion; he became an officer of His Majesty's Customs and Excise.

There is a clue to Arthur's character in that all this career planning and hard work was merely a safety net. His first ambition was to become, ultimately, an opera singer, and any money he could save after helping his family went for music lessons, though there was little to spare. With war brewing he joined the Civil Service Rifles, and went to France in the first weeks of the war in 1914. In January 1915 he was commissioned, and shortly thereafter, having been in the trenches for over a year, granted home leave.

As it turned out his leave was compulsory medical leave, for he caught a chill and this turned to double pneumonia.[3] He was seriously ill and was lucky to survive, but the illness put an end to his hopes for a career as a singer. Although his voice remained beautiful, rich and rounded, his lungs were permanently damaged and no longer capable of providing the stamina required of an opera singer.

16

While he convalesced in England he was commissioned captain in the Machine Gun Corps. The United States had entered the war by this time and Captain Pack was sent to America, seconded to the U.S. Infantry as a machine gun instructor. He accompanied this regiment to France in the last months of the war and was fortunate enough to escape injury or further illness.

After the war, Arthur went first to the Government Laboratory and then passed an examination for entry into the Foreign Service in 1920. Once again his diligence and determination paid off, though it irked him to see younger men who worked less hard than he promoted over his head purely because of some influential connection. This became a source of bitterness that stayed with him throughout his life. Despite his apprehensions, in 1925 he did receive an overseas posting as acting Commercial Secretary in Washington. In the Foreign Service this is regarded as a junior position, but to Arthur it represented a significant leap. He was delighted, and perhaps his only regret was that it meant leaving his friend Eleanor with whom he was somewhat smitten.

Eleanor was sixteen and they had met at a country house party which she attended with three school friends. She recalled that she was surprised that Arthur should pay her any attention.

He was asked to sing, as he always was, and he sang the Victorian ballad *Eleanor* at me, positively *at* me. I was a bit embarrassed but he meant it as a compliment. He did it several times after that and I got used to it. To my surprise he seemed to take me seriously despite the age difference between us. At first I thought him a bit stiff—not withdrawn, perhaps it was shyness or reticence. But he was great fun with a nice sense of humour and he could be very jolly.[4]

Over the following years, Arthur often used leave time to visit Eleanor at her family's home in Cheshire. In 1928 he learned that she was in Italy and somehow contrived to get himself sent to Rome to deliver a special diplomatic message so that he could spend a few days with her. When he visited her at Oxford a year later and proposed to her, Eleanor considered the proposal seriously. She ultimately refused, pointing out that as an undergraduate she could not marry anyone. "But my main

17

concern," she recalled in the summer of 1990, "was that he was so much older than me."[5]

A few months afterwards Arthur formally met Betty in November 1929. They were horseback riding together in a Washington park when he proposed to her only weeks later. She accepted.

It has been suggested that the proposal, or at least the acceptance, was occasioned by the fact that Betty was pregnant. However, at the time that the engagement was announced on February 8, probably days after the proposal itself, Betty was barely a month into her pregnancy and it does not seem likely that she could have been aware of her condition so early.

But why Arthur? Even if Betty thought herself ready for marriage, there was for her no shortage of beaux of her own age. Whatever she sought in bed with adult men was part of a search for something she had not found in her relationship with her parents. There seems to have been little loving affection exchanged with her mother. Betty was scathing in her denunciation of Cora's slavish concern for "society" and its values. As for her father, Betty adored him, but he was always too busy with his own career. Betty's preference for older men may have been rooted in this neglect. The teenage Betty was an emotionally lonely person with parents who, well-intentioned or not, failed to provide her with the kind and level of love she needed.

Yet it may be too facile to say simply that she accepted Arthur because she was looking for a Captain Thorpe to call her very own. If so, if she was looking for a man already formed in his ways, able to cope with her own headstrong and impulsive nature, why one such as Arthur? It may be simply that she saw him and wanted him, and that being a person who wanted what she wanted when she wanted it, she was not going to agonize over the pros and cons of this life-altering decision before going ahead and saying yes. Once she decided she wanted him, why not seduce him? And once he proposed, why not say yes? Marrying a man twice her age, one whose work would very likely take her back abroad, in a wedding that would likely be the high point of the Washington social scene, must have seemed exciting enough adventure for the moment.

But why Betty for Arthur? If he did not know she was pregnant, why did he propose? Here surely was a man able to plan for his future. Whether or not Arthur was the child's father will always remain a mystery; and he was certainly to have his own doubts in later years. But he must surely have known that in Betty he was not getting a conformist to match his own respect for convention, and that he would have on his hands a bit more than a typical young debutante who had sown a few wild oats. Speaking many years later of his first encounter with Betty, Arthur asked his sister, ". . . there she was in my bed. What could I do?"[6]

From Betty's own words we can guess that to persuade the convention-bound Arthur to make love to her she had to do more than simply make herself available, that she had to assure him she was not a virgin. She later told a friend that Arthur once protested that "If it hadn't been for that boy in Newport I never would have touched you. . . ."[7]

Still, it appears that at the time Arthur saw this intelligent, talented and beautiful young woman of fine family as a matrimonial "catch," and he wrote with pride about his fiancée to his family in England. Nor could he resist writing to Eleanor that he had become "engaged to an American girl," pointedly adding "my fiancée is even younger than you," though the difference was only a year. As a wife for an ambitious diplomat in Arthur's circumstances Betty had everything, including those society connections he had long lacked. Her Protestant religion was a minor drawback; Arthur was a Roman Catholic, as was his ambassador, Sir Esme Howard, who later interviewed Betty and persuaded her to take instruction from a Catholic priest. She promised that she would carefully consider embracing the Catholic faith.

And so Arthur was beside himself that this lovely, glowing girl who had connections, intelligence and personality had agreed to become his wife. If in her search for excitement she tended to stretch the rules a bit more than made him comfortable, well, that seemed a small enough price to pay for all that he was getting.

"Washington Debutante to Wed British Diplomat" the headlines trumpeted on the society pages of the *Washington Post*, while a more restrained report appeared in the *New York Times*.[8] Arthur had just been advised of promotion to a senior grade and seemed destined for higher office in his chosen service. As a measure of what Cora wished for her daughter, it should be noted that when the couple broke the news to her she was delighted. Betty was the first of the season's crop of "buds" to marry and the fact that Cora's future son-in-law was of her own generation apparently created no problem.

In Arthur, Cora saw a man who was socially acceptable and who intended to go places. Refreshingly, the fact that Arthur did not come from a family of established wealth meant less to Betty's parents than his clear ambition. One wonders what Cora would have thought had she been aware of precisely what it meant to be in Arthur's circumstances— that he not only had no money of his own but that he lived on an annual salary of £1,000 plus £1,200 a year rent allowance.

Years later, Betty would accuse Cora of pushing her into the marriage, but there is no contemporary evidence that Betty was, or could have been, pushed into such a marriage.

At the start the couple planned an early summer wedding but within a few weeks Betty was aware of her condition and the matter became one of more urgency. At what point Betty confided in her mother is not known, but she told Arthur in March. He was horrified. Many years later she wrote that Arthur had panicked and encouraged her to try to provoke a miscarriage by horseback riding at a disunited trot for long periods, jumping off walls, skipping rope and running hard. She co-operated with his suggestions, to no avail; she took baths so hot that she almost fainted. At length she made herself ill and her mother forced her to consult a doctor, who not only confirmed her condition but told her that she must take things easy if she were not to endanger her life.

Arthur was a Catholic; doctrinally, the soul of the unborn child should have been important to him. Many years later when Betty's recollection of his response to the news of her pregnancy was revealed, his family was shocked by, and would not believe, the accusation that Arthur had tried to provoke a miscarriage. A previous writer also had doubts, commenting that "it is hard to think of [Betty] . . . strong, vivid [Betty] submitting to this bullying."[9]

But then again, that writer further ventured, she may have been made vulnerable by pregnancy, leading her to fear Arthur, whom she was already beginning to perceive as "cold, complex and a little cruel."[10] According to Arthur's many friends this characterization of him is unfair; he found it difficult to display emotion, certainly, but he was unfailingly kind, and cruelty would have been totally uncharacteristic.

In any event, Arthur had no wish to lose Betty, though he would have been only too aware that a child born within five months of their wedding, to a woman so much younger than himself, would reflect very badly on him. Within that narrowly circumscribed world of the Foreign Service, it would almost certainly affect his career prospects if indeed it did not result in a direct request for his resignation. It is not implausible, given his ambition, that he might have been sorely tempted to encourage Betty to try what she claimed he did. Clinical abortion, a difficult matter to arrange, was seen as sinful as well as illegal under most circumstances. Better an encouraged accident that required a little help from fate, the rationalization might have gone, than a deliberate and sinister act allowing only one outcome.

The wedding date was moved forward to April 29, 1930, by which time Betty was almost four months pregnant. Fortunately her condition was not yet visible.

Arthur gave Betty a fur coat as a wedding present. She thanked him nicely but privately described the coat as rather inexpensive and not up to her own standards.[11]

Heralded by Washington papers as "the first International Wedding of the year," the ceremony was performed at the Church of the Epiphany, which had been lavishly decorated with palms and lilies, and British and American flags. The large number of guests, described by journalists as a brilliant company, included a clutch of foreign ambassadors, numerous senior diplomats representing fifteen countries, the attorney general, the sister of the vice-president, six senators, senior State Department officials, several titled persons and many noted personalities. In short, anyone who was anyone in Washington.[12]

Arthur was supported by his best man, Captain J. T. Godfrey, naval attaché at the embassy, and half a dozen fellow diplomats. None of Arthur's family were present, but Cora had no difficulty in filling the groom's side of the church, and the whole affair went off with great aplomb. Betty, who never smiled in photographs, looks pensive even after the ceremony, but she undoubtedly made a lovely bride in her high-waisted gown with train of ivory silk taffeta and her long rose-point veil held in place by a circlet of orange blossoms.

Mr. Pack and his bride will spend their honeymoon in Europe. They will be abroad for about five months, returning to Washington in October after making visits to England, Scotland and on the continent. For her travelling costume Mrs. Pack wore a smart ensemble of chartreuse green trimmed in mole, with a blouse of gold metal cloth. Her hat was a close-fitting turban of chartreuse and mole ribbon.[13]

Arthur's plan was to have the child placed in foster care for a few years and not tell anyone of its existence. He must have reasoned that a career posting would inevitably take them overseas at some point when it would be possible to fudge dates. This was not such a cruelly outlandish plan as it seems today. In those days the personal columns of the London *Times* were littered with advertisements offering fostering for small children; parents posted to the British colonies did not always wish to subject their offspring to the rigours of travel nor the risks of foreign diseases. Betty went along with this plan, though she privately thought Arthur exaggerated the risks to his career prospects. However, Arthur knew Sir Esme as a very stern moralist, and was probably correct in his judgment.

The couple visited mainland Europe for a month in June, then travelled to Scotland for a few weeks before taking a rented house in Bignor, a small village near Petworth in Sussex. Here an abiding memory for both was long walks on beautiful Bignor Hill and the tranquillity of the little churchyard with its birdsong and great yews, from where they would sit and look through summer haze towards the South Downs and the English Channel. In late September they went to London for Betty's confinement and on October 1, two weeks earlier than expected, she went into labour and was rushed into Wellbeck Street Clinic where her son was born with a minimum amount of fuss in the early hours of October 2. They called the child Anthony George.

No announcement of the child's birth was made and in the statutory notification to the Registrar, Arthur was economical with the details of his occupation and address. Arthur Joseph Pack, Economist, residing at Westminster, is all one can glean from the birth certificate. At some point, however, Arthur had placed a discreet advertisement in the personal columns of a national daily newspaper asking for applications for the post of foster-mother for a baby whose parents were posted abroad.

The advertisement was seen by Mrs. M. B. Cassell, a doctor's wife who lived in the Shropshire village of Dorrington, a few miles from Shrewsbury. The arrangement was intended as a purely temporary one and she answered it thinking she could earn a little pin money. Dr. and Mrs. Cassell had a child of their own, Margaret; but she was fifteen years old by that time. Mrs. Cassell seemed to be everything Arthur hoped for; well mannered, well educated, but unlikely to know anyone even remotely connected with diplomatic circles. When Anthony, or Tony as he became known, was ten days old Mrs. Cassell took the train to London and collected the baby from Wellbeck Clinic.[14]

In her memoirs Betty recalled being passionately upset about the loss of her baby, but this was not apparent to those who saw her in the week after her discharge from the hospital. Eleanor (now Lady Campbell-Orde), Arthur's former girl friend, was one of these and called on Arthur and Betty at their rented flat in Queen Anne's Gate. It was her first meeting with Betty and she was interested in meeting the girl who, despite being younger than Eleanor herself, had married Arthur.

> They were over here on honeymoon and Betty told me that she had just been in hospital but it was not until many years later that I found out it had been to have a baby. She was a ravishingly lovely creature, very tall and slim and fair. I could easily see why he fell for her. Her colouring was superb and she was quite extra-ordinarily pretty. She had great charm and poise and a slight American accent.[15]

That week Arthur also took his nineteen-year-old bride to see his family in Forest Gate before returning to the United States. The Pack family had met Betty briefly in the first weeks after they arrived in England and just as they were immensely proud of Arthur's achievements so they welcomed Betty and were proud of her too. Arthur's sister, Rosina, had niggling reservations about the suitability of the marriage but she kept these to herself for a long time. Years later she would reveal that though she loved her brother and was immensely proud of him, she "felt sorry for Betty who was so lively and passionate, married to Arthur who found it difficult to show emotion." It wasn't the age difference, she said, "but there were large sexual and emotional differences."[16] No mention of the baby was made to Rosina, or indeed to any other family members.

"We were all bowled over by Betty," Arthur's niece recalled. "I remember very little of her personality—I just remember her exquisite beauty and great elegance, and perhaps a romantic seriousness in her manner."[17]

When they returned to America, Arthur was temporarily posted to New York, where he had taken charge of the Commercial Secretariat for eighteen months prior to meeting Betty. According to Betty's memoir they returned to Washington in April 1931, just after Arthur had been told he was to be transferred to Santiago, Chile. The couple do not appear in the society pages or city directories during 1931. It may be that during that year they were dividing their time between New York and the nation's capital. In August the London *Times* announced Arthur's promotion and in September he was pictured on the front page of its "Imperial and Foreign Supplement," featured as an up-and-coming young diplomat.[18]

According to Betty's recollections they lived well, always in good houses and with servants. As a wedding gift Betty's parents had given her a dowry which she said later was £2,000 (worth approximately $80,000 in current values). This was Betty and Arthur's sole savings and they dipped into it whenever an emergency arose. Betty was a good manager, however, and ran their home with a flair belying her youth, usually managing to make ends meet.[19] She was a little shocked to learn how much Arthur spent on outward appearances compared with how little money he actually had. But he convinced her that his entertaining and show of casual comfort was necessary to support his career prospects, and she went along with it. Indeed, before long it was she who comforted him when he had occasional depressions about what would become of them if they were faced by a real emergency, "a rainy day," as Arthur phrased it.

Still, the marriage seemed successful. If, as she states in her memoirs,

Betty no longer pretended to herself that she loved Arthur, she liked him, respected him and was comforted by his maturity. She was touched by the story of his early struggles and supported his ambitions by subtly working to promote his interests. Through his previous postings he seemed to know many people in the international set wherever they travelled, and she enjoyed this and the position that her marriage to him provided. In September of 1931 they sailed from New York for Valparaiso, and from there travelled to Santiago, Chile's capital, by train.

Those were the days of elegant travel for those who could afford it. No woman could travel light when she was expected to dress for dinner every night, and the Packs were accompanied by an enormous amount of luggage. However, Arthur's diplomatic status assured them of courtesy and service at each port of entry, where there were waivers of customs formalities, all pre-arranged by embassy administrative processes. So the boat journey was fun and interesting, providing a relaxing opportunity to meet new, perhaps influential friends over cocktails or a game of bridge; and the train ride through the foothills of the majestic Andes was an unforgettable experience for Betty.

Soon after they arrived and settled in Chile Arthur gave a birthday party for Betty. She was twenty-one that November and it seemed a good excuse for a party and an opportunity to meet new people. As usual, they both made friends quickly and soon were an active part of the social set. Both already had rudimentary Spanish, and with Betty's facility for languages within a year she spoke Spanish as she spoke French, without an accent. Arthur's Spanish was less pure than Betty's, but he was virtually fluent and could discuss business easily with local leaders in their own language. In Santiago he headed the small Commercial Office, and was able to run it in his own way. Two months after their arrival the London *Times* noted in an article headed "British Trade with Chile":

The Commercial Secretary to the British Embassy, Mr Arthur Pack, gave a luncheon today to a large number of local businessmen and representatives of the press and made a speech pointing out the necessity of

25

confidence in the future and drawing attention to the fact that the services of the Commercial Secretariat at the Embassy were at the disposal of those in any way concerned in commerce with Great Britain. . . . Mr Pack has only recently been appointed to Chile and his undoubted initiative in thus making himself acquainted with the business interests of the country has won very favourable comment.[20]

Arthur was in his element, but for Betty, left alone for the most part of each day and often during the evening too, with little to do but join the other embassy wives in the endless round of coffee mornings, teas and cocktail parties, the time was not as satisfying. Surrounded by much older embassy wives, full of restless energy, she was bored and lonely. The only available physical outlet was riding.

She was a superb horsewoman. Before long, encouraged by male friends at the Santiago polo club, she could be seen playing in club chukkas. Not many women played polo in Chile—few were good enough riders and even fewer possessed the necessary coordination of hand and eye—but Betty quickly became a popular member of the practice teams. When she was not off riding in the hills she was inevitably to be seen practicing stick and ball at the polo ground. This was somewhat frowned upon by the Chileans, whose women were not encouraged to ride hard lest it should affect their child-bearing capabilities. The English were less critical; in the African and Indian colonies it was not unusual to see women making up settlers' teams.

It was at the polo club that Betty met a wealthy industrialist whom she calls, in her memoirs, Alfredo. He had made his money in nitrates and owned a large ranch where, among his many activities, he bred polo ponies. He was much older than she, attentive, generous and kind. It was almost inevitable that before long the vivacious Betty would become infatuated by this charming and powerful man, and that they would become lovers. Betty was soon convinced that she was in love and later recorded in her memoirs that she poured into this new relationship all the thwarted passion she had been unable to express in her marriage to Arthur. It was as well a time of great loneliness. Deprived of her child, she was made even more vulnerable. She basked in Alfredo's adoration of her, the joy spoiled only by a niggling guilt at her first marital infidelity.

The affair lasted a few months, until at a party Betty ran into her lover accompanied by a beautiful Chilean woman. When her enquiries revealed that she had been his mistress for some years, Betty was devastated. When she next saw Alfredo she tore into him. Though he swore that it was Betty he loved, she felt angry, cheapened and rejected; she immediately ended the affair.

Hurt and somewhat wiser after the affair with Alfredo, she threw herself into helping Arthur's career; despite her youth she could hardly have been a better hostess. Encouraged by his wife's enthusiasm Arthur blossomed as a host and invitations to dinner at the Packs' charming terraced apartment were much sought after. It is not unreasonable to assume that Betty's contribution helped Arthur earn the Order of the British Empire in the next New Year's Honours. If so, her efforts were rewarded, for Arthur was granted home leave and the pair sailed to England in the spring. In London Arthur received his O.B.E. from the hands of King George V and Betty made her curtsy when she was presented at a court levee. The photograph taken of her on this occasion in her formal gown and headdress shows a beautiful young woman. She is not smiling and there is a wistful light in the large eyes and a generosity of spirit in the set of her full lips.

While they were in England, Arthur and Betty paid their first visit to Dorrington to see Tony. By then the little boy was two and a half and Betty had apparently set her heart on taking the child out for the day with Arthur. Though she had been looking forward to this meeting, she clearly had little experience with children. The Cassells had done their best to explain to the little boy that his mummy and daddy were coming to take him out in a car, but it was not clear to him precisely who these strangers were. Almost as soon as they arrived they picked him up and walked out to their car without giving Tony any time to get to know them. Mrs. Cassell's daughter, Margaret, recalled the moment: "He was terrified and immediately started screaming and screaming. It took ages to calm him down. After that he developed a stammer which I always thought stemmed from that incident. . . ."[21]

Despite her later assertions that she missed her son so much that it had

27

made her deeply unhappy during the previous two and a half years, this would remain the only visit Betty paid to the boy until he was almost five years old. Betty and Arthur were in England for sixteen weeks in 1933, yet they made no further attempt to see him during that time. It might be argued that she worried about further upsetting the child, but a week or so spent at Dorrington with Tony might have been all that was required to establish a trusting relationship.

To Mrs. Cassell Tony had already become the son she and Dr. Cassell had long wanted and never had, so she was relieved that the Packs showed no inclination to remove their son from her care. There was little practical reason why they could not have done so. They could have taken him back to Chile and prevaricated about his precise birth date, had they wished to have him with them. Or at any time during their stay abroad they could have introduced the fact that they had a son in England, so that at some time in the future he could have joined them without exciting comment. But they continued to keep his existence a close secret.

The Packs returned to Chile at the end of October, stopping en route in the United States for a week,[22] and paid a brief visit to Betty's parents in Washington. It was while she was there that she told them about Tony, impressing upon her mother that nobody outside the family must know about the child. This conversation indicates that Cora was not aware of her daughter's condition at the time of the marriage.

Back in Santiago the trip seemed to have brought the Packs closer together, and no one was surprised when Betty became pregnant in the following spring. Her daughter, Denise Beresford, was born on New Year's Eve, 1934.[23]

It was an exciting time for them, for Arthur had just been told he was to be transferred to Spain, his first senior appointment, and Betty looked forward immensely to living in Europe. She wrote:

It was a big thrill when . . . my husband was appointed to the British Embassy in Madrid. It seemed to me to be "going home" [for Spain] had an almost mystic attraction. I had learned the language well (the Chilean variation of the mother tongue) and felt prepared for this realisation of a long held dream.[24]

28

Because Denise was so young the couple made their way to Europe in easy stages. Accompanied by a children's nurse they sailed to Havana in early March, spending a few days there before flying on to Miami, Florida, where they took the train to Washington to introduce the baby to her grandparents.[25] After a week in Washington they travelled to New York and sailed for Spain.

Chapter 3
1935-1936

A rthur was at work in his new post within days, while Betty looked for a suitable apartment and wandered, charmed, around the old city. For the moment they made the best hotel in town their home, but Betty quickly found an apartment in a pleasant residential quarter of the city near the Prado. It was within a short walk of the city's centre, railway station and huge park. The rooms in Castellana 63 were high-ceilinged and the walls so thick that with the windows thrown open to catch the slightest breeze it was deliciously cool. Arthur approved of the place and Betty gave it white walls, white carpet and white soft furnishings, and relieved it of starkness by adding antique oak dressers and wine-coloured curtains and cushions.

In the first months they seemed happy together. Arthur was proud of his baby daughter and loved to show her off, as he loved to show off his beautiful wife. Their circle of friends was composed for the most part of embassy colleagues and wives, and young Spanish diplomats with whom they played golf at country clubs, picnicked in the Guadarrama mountains, played bridge and shared "unforgettable intimate evenings, which usually ended up at Meyer's, a tiny night-club with a pocket-handkerchief dance floor."[1] The pianist, a Scotsman named Jimmy Campbell, had a good repertoire of modern romantic dance tunes that he was happy to play until dawn and the club became known as "Jimmy's Place."

But just as she had in Chile, Betty quickly became bored with the life of an embassy wife; she found relief from an unexpected source. One day, she drove to the exclusive Puerta de Hierro country club to pick up Arthur where he was playing golf with an old acquaintance from his days in Washington. The golf partner, a handsome auburn-haired man, had a certain familiar arrogance to his graceful movements. When she tried, at first, to recall who he was she found him "hidden in my yesterdays," but after a moment or two, she realized to her astonishment that it was the young Spaniard she had once flirted with from afar at her father's Washington country club, the man of the dramatic bow and around whom she had subsequently spun so many teenage fantasies. Señor Carlos Sartorious remembered Betty, too, and was charmed and flattered that she should have remembered him from that brief moment.

They laughingly explained their earlier meeting to Arthur, and Carlos related how, on the following day, he had returned and inquired about her. Before he could track her down, he explained, he was recalled to Spain. He now introduced his wife, Carmencita, and for some months the two couples made a regular foursome. Betty expressed a wish to learn about the "real" Spain, not the Spain known to visitors and tourists, and Carlos willingly brought the Packs into his exclusive circle of friends, taking them bull-fighting and shooting.

Betty was now almost twenty-five years old and probably close to the height of her dazzling beauty, but concealed beneath the outward allure

32

and gaiety was an internal wariness. She and Carlos initially adopted a light flirtatious attitude towards each other, apparently not resented or even acknowledged by their respective partners. Almost as a natural fulfillment of her girlish dreams, Betty found herself physically drawn to Carlos, very strongly so. For all his Latin temperament, it took Carlos a while longer to recognize what was happening, or to admit what he would be risking and make the jump. The passion, when it was finally unleashed, both his for her and the level of emotion he evoked in her, came as a revelation for Betty; she had never before known lovemaking like this. Betty would probably say she was genuinely in love on two occasions during her life; the affair with Carlos was the first.

Arthur had never been a passionate lover and though he was not a cold man it is almost certain that his sex drive was not strong. This is not to say that the couple were unhappy in their marriage but their needs were so very much different, and this unreconcilable difference led, almost inexorably, towards unfaithfulness on Betty's part. Without any wish on her part to injure Arthur emotionally she was physically unsuited to exist within a marital relationship that fell so far short of her emotional needs. She could not resist what Carlos had to offer her, but for Arthur's sake she resolved to be discreet.

Betty embarked upon her love affair in the full knowledge that it could never amount to anything more than a transient relationship. Carlos was a scion of an aristocratic Roman Catholic family and there could never have been any question of divorce on his side. Nor is it likely that Betty had ever considered it, for divorce would destroy Arthur's career, which had become almost as important to her as to her husband. So, by taking the attitude that if they behaved discreetly no one would be hurt, Carlos and Betty were able to enjoy a relationship that lasted almost a year.

Handsome, well educated and rich, Carlos had attended public school in England and was a senior officer in the Spanish air force. His upbringing gave him a confident air that intoxicated Betty—a far cry from Arthur's private agonies of insecurity, at times amounting almost to paranoia, as when promotions were granted to colleagues for reasons of obvious favour.

Carlos introduced Betty to a world of culture and nobility to which she took with ease, absorbing new information and ideas without effort. He also lived with the intensity that Betty had always found natural, making her former existence in the United States, and even Chile, seem tame. In Spain she found the elements of splendid romance: a tempestuous people with a proud history, a magnificently harsh landscape accented by the lonely sweep of a hawk against a flawless Murillo sky, set in contrast to the exquisite tinkle of a fountain in a quiet courtyard in a gracious old hacienda. The untamed soul of the country appealed to the wild streak in her nature, a streak that she always ascribed to the Irish in her ancestry.

Betty's excellent Spanish became faultless and her increasing absorption of Spanish culture served to give a sense that this had always been intended, that she had been drawn to Spain as a sort of spiritual home. She and Carlos were too handsome a couple, however, and despite their discretion it was only a matter of time before their relationship became the subject of speculation in the narrow diplomatic community, though their respective partners seem to have remained unaware of the extent of their involvement with each other.

After a few months Carlos borrowed a penthouse apartment of a friend. Situated on the outskirts of the city it was quiet and secluded with its back to Madrid, overlooking the mountains. The couple met there several afternoons a week to make love. In January 1936 Betty made a trip to London to undergo a minor unspecified operation recommended by her gynaecologist. She took Denise with her, arranging in advance with Mrs. Cassell to leave the baby at Dorrington while she was in the hospital, an arrangement that would give her an opportunity to see Tony. She travelled in company with a group of embassy staff returning on leave and altogether it was a gay interlude during which she dined often with Lord Castlerosse at Quaglino's. She had met the aristocratic journalist on the journey and he had been attracted to her and her lively ways, even to the extent of using one of her amusing asides, about the strikes in Spain, in his daily newspaper column. In turn she enjoyed his company and the circle to which he introduced her, which included Lord Beaverbrook.[2]

At Dorrington the Cassells were surprised that Betty did not wish to have her son with her permanently now that she was in any case bringing up a daughter, but they kept it to themselves. Margaret had her own ideas:

"Nothing was ever said to me but I always suspected that Tony was not Arthur's son. . . ."[3]

Loving the little boy as they did, Dr. and Mrs. Cassell did not ask too many questions. Tony was a well-made little boy, tall for his age, slim and fair-haired with his mother's aquiline features, large, deep-set green eyes and long, thick eyelashes. Like his mother when young he was "crazy about horses." Betty's own descriptions of him at this time are full of loving admiration, yet it must be observed that she seemed quite content to leave the boy with his foster-parents. He did seem by then, it might also be noted, to be more of their family than hers.

Before leaving Dorrington, Betty promised to send Tony a toy gun. All Tony's little friends had guns and he eagerly awaited his. But even here Betty was forced to disappoint him. After she returned to Spain, Mrs. Cassell received a note from Betty saying that Arthur disapproved of giving children weapons to play with and had forbidden her to send the gun.

Back in Spain Betty decided to adopt the Catholic religion. It was a decision she had long considered, dating back to her promise to Arthur and his ambassador, Sir Esme Howard, at the time of her marriage. It was not altogether an inexplicable decision, for she had now lived for five years in Chile and Spain, both Catholic countries, and a large number of their friends were Catholic. But how she accommodated this decision to commit herself to such a demanding faith with her continuing affair with Carlos she never revealed. It may be that her passion for him had palled slightly by this time, despite her later claims that he remained the centre of her existence until they were forced apart.

Her religious instruction coincided with Carlos's absence for some weeks on military manoeuvres. The political situation in Spain was extremely volatile in those early months of 1936 and the Air Ministry intensified training programmes. Meanwhile one of Arthur's senior colleagues, George Ogilvie-Forbes, the embassy counsellor and a leading Catholic in England, offered to help Betty in her preparations and act as godfather at her baptism.

It was on one of these evenings, as he was escorting her down to her car, that the lift came to an abrupt halt as the result of one of the many strikes prevalent in the city. The lift was tiny and Ogilvie-Forbes a very large man. Working out that no one would come to look for him until he failed to turn up at the Chancery on Monday morning, and that in all probability the strike would last at least that long, he settled down to wait in the extremely cramped conditions for what promised to be a long wait. Arthur was away from home and her servants would not look for her, but Betty was not at all resigned to the prospect of remaining in the lift for over twenty-four hours and at her companion's suggestion knelt down and prayed for deliverance from her plight while he said a few rosaries.

In the event, it was Arthur who came to their rescue (though Betty's companion thought it a fast answer to the new convert's prayers). Arriving home earlier than expected, Arthur became worried when Betty failed to return by 1:00 A.M. On reaching Ogilvie-Forbes's apartments he found the lift unserviceable and a short investigation revealed his wife's plight. He called the fire brigade, who helped Betty climb through a hatch in the roof of the lift. Ogilvie-Forbes, however, could not get through the escape hatch and had to be supplied with various comforts until he could be released on the following morning.

After her baptism Ogilvie-Forbes secured the services of a young local priest who agreed to visit Betty every day for an hour in her apartment to help her spiritual growth.

In 1936, the battle lines for the Spanish civil war were being drawn in domestic terms, between what were called the Popular Front and the Nationalist Front. The latter, headed by Franco, comprised defenders of the old order, represented by the Roman Catholic Church, money, aristocracy, diehard monarchists, and the party of Spanish fascism, the Falange. In the Popular Front (also known as the Loyalists and the Republicans) were parties of widely diverse political credos, ranging from middle-class liberal reformers, to socialists with their strong labour-union backing, to the Soviet-dominated Spanish Communist party.

The electoral victory of the Popular Front earlier in the year brought to power a government with a strong communist influence, but it proved unable to govern. In the first half of the year there were over 200 political murders and 160 churches were burned to the ground. When church leaders denounced the new government, those in religious orders (there were over a hundred thousand monks, priests and nuns in Spain) were publicly vilified as agents of the reactionary forces being organized under Francisco Franco. There was growing anger at the clergy, and priests began disappearing into prisons.

In this divided world, Betty chose not merely to side with the Church but to join it as an active communicant. On the other hand it was not unnatural for Betty to place her strong loyalties with those Spaniards who, as the wife of a diplomat, she would have regarded as her friends.

Priests were in a particularly precarious position, and so it came as no surprise to Betty when her priest asked her one day to meet him at another address. It was an apartment in a part of town she did not know but had heard of as an area "where wealthy Spaniards were in the habit of taking their girl-friends for an hour or two's love-making in the afternoon."[4]

Once there Betty found her priest not only in civilian clothes, but in the guise of something other than spiritual advisor. "Somehow," she wrote in her memoirs "we found ourselves in each others arms," and he confessed that he had fallen in love with her.

. . . it was more than the flame of religion that was kept alive in my breast. The priest was a good looking young man . . . and [there] followed a series of secret meetings once or twice a week at the apartment . . . as he was poor and the cost of the rooms high I was always happy to help him out with the bill.

One day he failed to turn up and I went round to his church to enquire what happened to him and was told that he had been arrested the night before and thrown into prison, following the stepping up of the Republican Governments anti-clerical policy and the burning of many churches in Madrid. With the help of Sir George [George Ogilvie-Forbes was knighted in 1937] I found out which prison he was in and with the help [of the papal nuncio] secured his release. . . .

[Due to the political situation] we judged it best for him to go underground and this he did. I visited him from time to time in his hiding place. He said he wanted to give up the priesthood and marry me but I told him this was impossible. Subsequently he decided to try to make his way to the north-east of the country where Nationalist forces were massing in an underground movement and where he felt he could forget about me and pursue his vocation. . . . Of course I did not allow this relationship to interfere with my affair with Carlos which continued right up until the moment when the Ambassador and his staff and their families were evacuated from Madrid.[5]

This is not the only occasion when Betty would enjoy an extra-curricular affair outside her main emotional relationship. The fact that this particular one was with a Catholic priest does add a certain novelty, to be sure, but perhaps its importance is in the indication that here was a woman who would not allow her life to be constrained by the trappings of a dying Victorian morality.

This is not to imply that she entered into her physical relationships in a calculating manner, merely as a means of satisfying sexual urges. Her memoirs show that in each affair she ran through the entire mating ritual: the flirting; the chase; the professions of deep, undying love; the secret meetings; the insecurities; the jealousies. She possessed the same attitude towards love and personal relationships that—formerly, anyway—only male heroes were permitted. In this instance of her affair with her priest Betty does not even bother to condone or attempt to explain her affair set against her professed "great love" for Carlos. Nobody, and certainly no social constraints, would hitherto be allowed to dictate to Betty who, how and when she should love, be loved or make love.

By this time civil war was imminent. Every day brought new hardships and "the vortex of chaos that was leading to catastrophe," Betty wrote. "Communist infiltration abetted the very poor masses and there were endless strikes and towards the end the enormous, awful spectacle of burning churches spread across night skies."[6]

The climax was triggered by two assassinations, of an army officer on July 12, and of a right-wing politician on the following day. Within days army rebellion had spread throughout Spain and the government issued orders which armed the civilian population to fight the military insurrectionists.

On July 13, three days before war broke out, Arthur and Betty left Madrid to travel north to Biarritz, just over the border in southern France. The British ambassador, Sir Henry Chilton, had considered it expedient to move virtually his entire staff to the "summer Embassy" at San Sebastián in the north of Spain just a few miles from the French border, leaving only George Ogilvie-Forbes and the consul in the embassy at Madrid. The Packs were among the last to leave and their apartment was shuttered and locked. The studded timber entrance door was affixed with the impressive Embassy Seal, upon which hung a message to the effect that the contents of the apartment were under the protection of His Britannic Majesty's Government. On the previous night Betty had taken a passionate and concerned farewell of Carlos. He had tried to make light of their parting, promising to fly up to Biarritz to visit her, but she had a premonition of bad times to come. Now, Arthur, Betty, and Denise, accompanied by a children's nurse, Juanquita (whose own daughter was a month or two older than Denise), set out to drive to their rented villa at Biarritz.

Until they reached the Pyrenees the Packs encountered no problems and were unaware that a war had begun. The sky was a deep cloudless blue as they drove unhurriedly towards the French border through sleepy villages along quiet roads bordered by fields of golden grain splashed with red poppies. In the evening they reached the Spanish border town of Irún and here had to join a long queue of cars and other vehicles driven by refugees trying to leave the country, most of whom were sympathizers of General Franco and his Nationalist forces.

Once across the border, Arthur and Betty settled into their rented seaside villa while keeping a wary eye on the troubles which were, in fact, almost worse in the northwest than they had been in Madrid; Biarritz and Saint-Jean-de-Luz on the French side had become a refuge for many Spaniards of "rightist' tendencies. In mid-July General Mola, commanding the Nationalist forces, attacked San Sebastián with the aim of taking the city along with pro-Republican Irún and thus capturing and isolating the pro-Republican Basques from their French brothers over the border.

On Monday, July 21, a diplomatic message from the U.S. embassy at San Sebastián advised the State Department of the situation there:

> Rumoured attack on San Sebastián thus far false alarm although civilians armed by local authorities still leaving town in automobiles and trucks in direction of Pamplona apparently with purpose of defending city. Shooting in the streets continues . . . have assembled staff in Continental Hotel which houses Chancery. No definite information obtainable as to success of revolutionary movement but it has been quelled in Madrid and government radio bulletins optimistic. [Rumours are] that Burgos, Vitoria . . . and Pamplona in hands of insurgents.[7]

All roads from San Sebastián were barricaded and all those venturing forth in cars found themselves stopped at frequent intervals by excited and nervous groups of armed peasants and workmen who pointed guns at the occupants and demanded they explain their presence on the road; accidents happened and there were innocent fatalities. The American consul trying to reach his ambassador was forced at gunpoint to go to the local "Casa del Pueblo" or Proletariat Headquarters. There he was given a safe-conduct, good for one day only, and warned to stay indoors after that. This pass was delivered to the ambassador at Fuenterrabía who hurried to San Sebastián only to find the men at the barricades in an ugly humour, warning that rebel troops were coming and they would be "killed like flies."

By then the Continental Hotel had also become the temporary home of the British and Norwegian embassies, Sir Henry Chilton having driven over from his house at Zarauz with Lady Chilton. Inside the hotel (which had been officially conceded as having international and diplomatic character), pandemonium reigned. The hall was like a railway station; the atmosphere of the dining room, the ambassador reported, "could be cut with a knife, the windows having been closed for five days owing to the danger from bullets, and to the fact that the sight of food might have excited the proletariat." Four civil guards were posted to protect the diplomats from the constant sniping which had increased considerably, due mainly to Nationalist machine-gun nests which presently became punctuated by the cannon shells from their gunboats offshore landing within yards of the hotel. A general strike began and the armourers' shops in the town were looted by workmen aided by police. Private cars were requisitioned and raced around the town at high speed, crammed with excited civilians and "bristling with armaments." Also, Sir Henry noted, "there was much loose potting at windows [and] . . . the whole town was in alarm."[8]

He attempted to get help by visiting the Casa del Pueblo in the civil governor's offices

I imagine that anyone who had experience of Russian administration in the early days of the 1917 revolution would have found those conditions faithfully reproduced in the "Casa del Pueblo."

A small group of men, unshaven and short of sleep, but fired with enthusiasm for their cause, issuing orders, which must have lacked coordination, by telephone and in writing and improvising transport, commissariat and munition arrangements to meet the needs that were constantly brought to their notice by loud voiced individuals all armed with revolver, shot-gun or rifle. . . .[9]

By July 20, the San Sebastián area was under siege by General Mola's forces and all communications with the outside world had ceased.[10] Arthur became increasingly worried about the fate of his embassy colleagues. He had no actual knowledge of what was happening, and though officially on leave, tried to contact his ambassador. When this failed he contacted the Foreign Office in London by telegram and was asked to investigate and report back with his recommendation for relieving those embassy staff caught up in the fighting. From Biarritz to San Sebastián was four hours by car and on the morning of July 21 Arthur told Betty and Ann Chilton, the twenty-five-year-old daughter of the ambassador, who was staying with them,[11] that he would drive over there and return that night.

At the frontier Arthur met Mr. Goodman, British vice consul, and the Netherlands minister and his secretary who were all trying to reach San Sebastián. All four spent the following forty-eight hours waiting for safe-conduct passes, but by the evening of the twenty-third had reached the French embassy at San Sebastián, having been stopped and threatened countless times en route; only the British and Netherlands flags calmed the agitation of those manning the barricades. As darkness fell they could go no further and had to spend the night on benches in the French chancery. Fortunately Arthur found the local telephone service still working at times and managed to talk to his ambassador and advise him of his situation.

It was not until late afternoon on the following day, despite an expired safe-conduct, that he managed to reach the Continental Hotel on foot, having run the gauntlet of machine-gunners between the French embassy and his objective. On the previous day Sir Henry had tried to cable the Foreign Office in London requesting the presence of British warships in order to protect and evacuate British nationals from San Sebastián. The governor "demurred at the request asserting that it would be derogatory to the prestige of Spanish authorities."[12]

When Arthur had failed to return to the Biarritz villa as planned, Betty grew worried. Or possibly her anxiety was as much suppressed excitement and annoyance at having been left out of what promised to be an adventure. But when word reached her that Arthur had been killed,[13] she discussed the matter with Ann Chilton and decided to try to get to San Sebastián to see for herself what was happening. She set out early on the morning of July 23, with her young chauffeur, stopping briefly at a seafront hotel to beg the loan of a Union Jack. To placate the communists, who she believed were in ultimate control of the area, she managed to scout up a square of red material of similar size, and attached both flags to the front of the car.

At the border town of Irún she was suspected by the Republican guards of being one of Franco's spies attempting to cross the border with forged papers. After a long wait she was interviewed by the commandant, an unsavory man who was not too careful about personal hygiene. He had long unkempt hair, four days' growth of beard, and wore a bandolier packed with bullets across his greasy waistcoat. He drank continuously while interrogating Betty and with each gulp became more agitated and less willing to listen to her explanations. Eventually he ordered her to be detained and despite her alarm and vigorous protests she was led away by two youths armed with machine guns to a basement room crowded with male prisoners captured in heavy fighting on the previous day.[14]

Some were wounded, some half-drunk, some half-naked. The smell of cigarette smoke was suffocating and the fetid atmosphere with its human and verminous population both repelled and worried her. Nobody would miss her except Ann Chilton and even she would not be surprised if Betty did not contact her for a few days; and now there was an additional anxiety. Several of the men were casting meaningful glances in Betty's direction. She decided that the best way of dealing with this new problem was to pretend she had not noticed. Yet she was deeply concerned. The thought of having to spend a night (or perhaps longer) with her fellow detainees was unpleasant, to say the least, but her appeals to the guard to be allowed to speak again with his superiors were met with rude indifference.

After a while a man got up and left the room, passing by the guard with apparent ease. When he returned some time later he took one of the few vacant seats, on a bench opposite Betty. Reasoning that he must have some influence to be able to move freely in and out of the prison, Betty decided to see if she could persuade him to help her. She fixed her large green eyes on him in what she hoped was mute appeal. He came over to sit beside her to ask if there was something he could do to help. She pleaded with this stranger to help her secure a release so she could return to her baby daughter in France.

It worked. Much to her relief, after a further anxious half-hour, she was released and her car and chauffeur were returned to her. The two men with machine guns escorted her back across the frontier and she returned to Biarritz. Here she told Ann Chilton the story of her adventures, and after a discussion between the two Betty telephoned a Mr. Greene at the Foreign Office in London.

Nothing had now been heard from the ambassador or his staff for over forty-eight hours, and according to her memoirs Betty suggested (having agreed this with Ann Chilton) that the Foreign Office should ask the Admiralty to send a destroyer to San Sebastián to evacuate the embassy staff by sea. Meanwhile, she said, she would try again to get to San Sebastián during the next few days. Whether it was as a result of this conversation or of Sir Henry's earlier request to Spanish authorities in Bilbao asking that they relay his request to London, or of other requests altogether, ships HM *Verity* and *Veteran* were dispatched that evening.[15]

Betty set out again two days later to attempt to cross into Spain. This time the guards, who recognized her from the previous occasion, were more polite to her. Nevertheless she was again taken before the commandant. To her relief it was a different man, this one more intelligent and courteous, as well as sober. He did his best to dissuade her from crossing the border and putting herself into certain danger, but she pleaded utmost concern for her husband's welfare and eventually the commandant provided her with a precious one-day pass for herself and her chauffeur, Eusabio, and for an escort he provided her with two armed militiamen.

The party experienced the same sort of shelling, sniping and constant stops at road-blocks described by fellow travellers (at every village the car was stopped and surrounded by armed men, women and boys), but four hours later, to the astonishment of the British contingent, Betty drove up to the front of the Hotel Continental.

She found Arthur safe and well and a general sense of relief among the beleaguered members of the embassy and the growing number of British residents now that the *Verity* and *Veteran* were anchored only three-quarters of a mile offshore.

The ambassador complimented Betty on her actions and questioned her about conditions outside of San Sebastián. They decided that with the pass and the two militiamen she stood a good chance of being able to return to Biarritz that day.

Betty was given information to pass on to the Foreign Office, including the fact that several Spanish friends of the Chiltons had been shot despite the fact that they had taken no part in the fighting but simply were known to be of one persuasion or the other. "The Scarlet Pimpernel," Sir Henry was fond of saying, "would be of great use in Spain today."[16]

After her interview with the ambassador, Arthur let Betty know that he was less than pleased to see her in San Sebastián—having assumed she was safely in France with their daughter. But Betty was clearly enjoying the experience; before she spoke to Arthur she had been plotting in the lobby with five young Franco supporters who had asked her to help them get from San Sebastián to Fuenterrabía, where they could join the revolutionary forces. There was a fierce battle raging at the edge of town, and the hotel was close to an area being shelled by a rebel Spanish gunboat.

Food was running very low and the guests of the Hotel Continental were already on very short rations.[17]

Still, it seemed only a matter of hours before the remaining military barracks committed to the rightist side within San Sebastián would be overrun, and the five Nationalists were convinced that they would be summarily executed if discovered by the Republican forces.

When Arthur learned about Betty's plan to take the men with her he absolutely forbade it. For one thing, he pointed out, the government militiamen would not permit it. Arthur, like Betty, personally sympathized with the Franco side but he was not prepared to let her risk her life over a fight that was not theirs. Added to his anxiety was the fact that he could not accompany her back. He had to stay to accompany a convoy of refugees across the French border on the following morning. As soon as she was clear of the border, he directed her, she was to go straight to Biarritz and stay there until he was able to rejoin her.

There was a major difference between Arthur and Betty in this emergency situation. Arthur was clearly worried while Betty revelled in the sheer excitement. However, he was too busy to spend his time ensuring that she acted as he had instructed.

When Arthur left her, Betty provided her personal militiamen with enough credit at the bar to get them drunk. When they returned to the car, Betty airily advised them that the five men crowded into the rear had to be dropped off on the way to Irún. They paid little attention and the crowded vehicle left while Arthur was still with the ambassador. The return run was less eventful and they were not stopped once. The five passengers were dropped off in the mountains and Betty returned to the Republican border where she made a point of thanking her "protectors" and the commandant.

Back in Biarritz by 8:00 P.M., she exulted that she had probably saved the lives of the five men. Nerve-racking the incident had been, but Betty knew for the first time the flow of adrenalin and the post-climactic rush of a dangerous mission that would eventually become so familiar to her. She found it as intoxicating as a secret love affair.

Her exhilaration was quickly stemmed by a cable from her mother. Her father had died at the Naval Hospital in Washington of lung cancer.

George Thorpe had been ill for some time but only in the last few weeks had his condition given real cause for anxiety. She did not record her feelings at this time, and her letters to her mother on the occasion have not survived. However, Betty's memoirs make explicitly and implicitly clear that she worshipped her father, and so his death must have been a severe blow to her.

Meanwhile Arthur had been dispatched with a party of twenty British nationals back to the border with instructions to return the following morning to escort another lot. After three such dangerous trips (which took longer than anticipated because every member of the party was thoroughly searched by the guards), it was considered too dangerous to make any further trips by road, and Arthur made his last journey out of Spain by sea, aboard the USS *Oklahoma* with sixty-one refugees.[18] He took with him the papers of the British embassy and had been instructed to set up a temporary embassy in France to receive the ambassador and his staff who were to be evacuated by British warship a few days later. During this entire crisis period Arthur worked tirelessly, hardly sleeping for days on end and spending money out of his own pocket to ensure the safe dispatch of his charges.[19] For this work he was mentioned several times in the ambassador's dispatches to Anthony Eden.

> On our arrival at San Jean de Luz [*sic*] we were met by Mr Pack, who throughout the crisis, could not have worked harder both there and at Bayonne in dealing with the many hundreds of persons evacuated from Northern Spain by H.M. ships and upon whose shoulders rested the task of obtaining accommodation for the members of the Embassy at Hendaye-Plage and of discovering a suitable place for the Chancery. He succeeded in finding a small office in a house at Irún on the Spanish side of the International Bridge, where the Norwegian and Netherland Ministers also have rooms so that "officially" we may be said to be still in Spain. Actually the Chancery is situated on the French side of the bridge nearly opposite the railway station at Hendaye-Ville.[20]

At the makeshift embassy at Hendaye, situated a hundred yards from the bridge dividing France from Spain, the diplomatic staff received terrible stories on a daily basis of atrocities and summary executions coming out of areas in control of the government forces.

As the Nationalists gained ground the battle moved to the border town of Irún. Fierce fighting raged through the last week in August. Finally, on September 3, the Republicans, recognizing certain defeat, set fire to the town before escaping over the border bridge to France. Betty, who was in Hendaye in late August and early September, sat on a French hillside across the river from Irún and watched as the town burned throughout the night. Later she wrote to Rosina, Arthur's sister, in England:

> We do not know how much longer we will be here . . . and are only waiting to get back to Madrid, which we will do as soon as the "Whites" take it. What a dreadfully heart-breaking and tragic three months this has been. My beloved Spain being so ruthlessly tortured, and many of one's friends butchered and assassinated. My priest was still alive a week ago (he is hidden in Madrid) but his safety is a constant source of anxiety to me . . .

Shortly after this letter was written Betty's priest did manage to get to northern Spain and join Franco's forces. She continued, castigating the "Reds," repeating stories of atrocities said to have taken place on the other side of the country:

> Some of their atrocities are beyond the bounds of imagination. For example in Barcelona they split open the abdomens of pregnant women and put these women in shop windows saying "these women were nuns." In one province little children were hung by their feet head downwards and left to die of hunger and thirst. And there are many other such crimes to their infamy. It is a *nightmare*. Someday when I see you I will tell you much that I cannot write.[21]

Arthur and Betty's Spanish friends tended to be supporters of Franco and their own sympathies lay strongly in that direction. But as Italian and German planes started bombing Spanish cities, many in the Western democracies started to see the prospects of a fascist victory, and soon sympathies among these Western democracies started to shift. But the real dilemma for the governments of these democracies was that they were opposed to both the Soviet communist sponsors of the Republican government *and* the German and Italian fascists supporting Franco. Eventually Arthur would be severely criticized for too obviously supporting the Nationalist cause, though surviving correspondence in the Foreign Office archives reveals that the Packs were not unusual among British diplomats in their attitude. The British, in particular, naturally tended in private to be supporters of the monarchy, who were on the side of the Nationalists, though their dreams of restoration would not be fulfilled with the eventual Nationalist victory. Betty, however, felt everything so strongly that she could not resist continuing to argue the Nationalist cause at every opportunity; she particularly spoke out against the widespread execution of fellow Spaniards by the Republican government. Much of her anguish may have been related to her deep concern over the fate of Carlos, of whom she had had no word since leaving Madrid. But her outspoken criticism of the government that Britain still recognized as the legitimate government of Spain came to the ears of Arthur's superiors and was considered inappropriate for a diplomat's wife.

After one dinner party Arthur was warned to instruct his wife that if she could not revise her opinions then she must curb her tongue. Although many years later she wrote that she regretted having spoken so hotly, at the time she fretted miserably over the constraints of being a diplomat's wife. When George Ogilvie-Forbes visited Hendaye from Madrid she asked him if he had heard anything of various friends, including Carlos, but he was not able to give her any information. She also told Ogilvie-Forbes of her frustration; she wanted to *do* something. Anything. He had just been appointed chargé d'affaires at Madrid and was alone there with the consul, John Milanes. While counselling caution he promised to give the matter some thought to see if he could think of some way in which she could help in an active way. In the meantime, she was to write:

The life to which we settled down was one of waiting but in other respects it was a dramatist's dream. It resembled a cross section of humanity that only war could have brought together in such a confined area. There were rightists and aristocrats from every part of Spain, there were foreign diplomatic missions that had been in Madrid, there were journalists and observers, valued secret agents and ordinary spies and every kind of adventurer and arms smuggler. There were courtly courtesans, half price harlots and casanovas. There were luxurious villas, casinos and *chambres d'amour* and everything for anyone who loved Spain and her people. The only thing was that she was being torn by war . . . and that almost every day one heard of a friend who had been killed or was in prison or shot by the communist infiltrated Republican government.[22]

After a few months the Packs moved from Biarritz to a small house in Saint-Jean-de-Luz, and Betty did her best to support Arthur, whose job had become very demanding. Apart from his normal work he was busy dealing with claims from British nationals and British-owned companies, such as Rio Tinto, whose properties had been damaged or otherwise affected by the activities of "the insurgents." The British officially continued to recognize the Republican government,[23] but in March Sir Henry received a telegram from the Foreign Office instructing that Arthur should attempt to establish a commercial office in Nationalist-held Burgos province of northern Spain. By then the entire northwest of Spain, including the French frontier, was under Nationalist control and this area was too large not to have some British commercial representation. Franco had a commercial agency in London and although this was not accredited, the Foreign Office had obviously decided to turn a blind eye to its operation.

Arthur questioned the cable, since it required him to make a direct approach to Franco's cabinet for permission which would in turn raise the question of some form of recognition for the Nationalists from His Majesty's Government. He also stated that due to war conditions it was out of the question for him to take his wife and child to live in Burgos. He suggested that, initially at least, he should merely conduct enquiries during regular visits to Burgos of two or three days at a time. Safe-conduct passes were now more easily obtained from the Nationalist military authorities now controlling the border, and his working in this way might not invoke a request for a *quid pro quo* from Franco.[24]

Arthur made frequent trips back into Nationalist-held Spain throughout the winter months and during this time he established close working relationships with Franco's brother—and right-hand man—Nicholas.[25]

Betty accompanied Arthur on a few occasions, acting as his secretary, but nevertheless she found herself with a great deal of free time. When in late February George Ogilvie-Forbes visited Hendaye and suggested that Betty return with him and work as his secretary, she leapt at the idea. She wished more than anything to have some active involvement with Spain's internal fight.

The eastern parts of Spain were at this time the last secure strongholds of Republican control—though Madrid itself was still in government hands, the front line wrapped around the capital to the north and west —and one wonders why Betty would have wanted to submit herself to the authority of these people whose ways she found so repugnant. It all became academic when Sir Henry Chilton vetoed the suggestion. When Arthur learned of it he was appalled that Betty could even consider it, knowing of the conditions there. The incident and the reaction of both Sir Henry and her husband must have borne in or her that if she were to "do" anything it would have to be in secret. In any case, a few weeks later Ogilvie-Forbes was transferred to Berlin.

Thus, when Betty received a visit from an old friend from the pre-war days, Viscount Augustín de Altamira, and he suggested a visit back into Spain she did not tell Arthur. Altamira's motive was to join Franco in Burgos, but when he told Betty of the horrific conditions in the makeshift hospitals behind the lines she wondered if she might be able to help in some way, by obtaining medical supplies. Arthur was just about to leave for London to discuss a number of complicated commercial matters and would be away for two weeks.[26]

It was an ideal opportunity for her to take a few days to see what was going on. Altamira agreed to collect her on the morning that Arthur left.

In the meantime the Packs had had another visitor—Carlos's wife, Carmencita. Starving and without money, indeed possessing only the clothes in which she stood, she had made her way with great difficulty through the fighting lines to Arthur and Betty, hoping that they might be able to work some diplomatic miracle. Carlos, known to be a Franco sympathizer, had been arrested one night in early February, together with a number of fellow officers. Despite her enquiries Carmencita had not been able to find out where he had been taken by the Republicans or

50

even whether he was still alive. Many people so arrested were simply executed without trial; therefore his death was a distinct possibility. Long-term incarceration in one of the dank Republican prisons with their sparse food and lack of light and exercise seemed only a marginally better alternative.

Carmencita was fed and cared for and sent on to relatives in France, and Arthur made tentative enquiries through diplomatic channels.

Betty decided to use her forthcoming trip to Burgos to make her own enquiries.

Chapter 4

1 9 3 6 - 1 9 3 7

F rom Burgos to Irún is about 170 miles, and the day Arthur left for England, Augustín Altamira collected Betty and drove her into Spain. They had no trouble getting through the frontier. This was quite unlike other recent experiences; when Betty had accompanied Arthur, acting as his secretary, she had always been searched thoroughly.

At Burgos, Altamira—a colonel in Franco's forces—introduced Betty to Dr. Luis Valero, head of the Spanish branch of the International Red Cross. She told Dr. Valero that she had heard about the shortage of medical supplies and asked him to tell her what was most needed, suggesting that perhaps she could raise funds among her friends and deliver the items to him. He recommended that she accompany him to the hospital and see for herself. "What I saw was heartbreaking, even for a field hospital," Betty later wrote. "In makeshift conditions, wounded and dying in every stage of suffering lay on the floor, their bandages improvised from any kind of paper at hand." The shortages list given to her by a baleful Dr. Valero consisted mainly of disinfectants and basic dressings —bandages, gauze and cotton wool—but she thought his request for twelve dozen pairs of surgical gloves "a mute comment on his expectations."

Back in Saint-Jean-de-Luz some days later she talked a wealthy Spaniard into providing all the items on the list. She then returned to Burgos where her supplies were received gratefully by Dr. Valero.

During this second visit to Burgos Betty spent some time making enquiries among Altamira's contacts about Carlos. Her presence was made known to Franco's first foreign minister, Vizconde de Santa Clara Avedillo, who asked her to meet him. She appealed to him to give her any news he might have had of Carlos's whereabouts. He was able to confirm the news of the arrest by the other side, but he could tell her nothing new. Both knew there was a strong possibility that Carlos had been executed, but the lack of news strengthened rather than defeated Betty.

Avedillo also gave her a sealed envelope to deliver to Sir Henry Chilton. In the course of their discussions he expressed his gratitude for the work she was doing for the Nationalist cause and his hope that she would continue. He added that she could help a lot more by trying to persuade the British ambassador to formally recognize Franco, the message of the letter he had given to her.

Betty's dealings with Avedillo have to be viewed as astonishingly indiscreet. It is almost inconceivable, given her experience as the wife of a diplomat and her quick intelligence in sizing up things, that she could not see how her actions—consorting against the recognized Republican government with a group whom the British government saw as rebels— would sit with the ambassador. True, Arthur had been instructed to open negotiations with Franco's administration for commercial cooperation through diplomatic channels; but Betty's behaviour might easily have compromised Arthur's bargaining position in these discussions.

I left Burgos and drove to Hendaye. It was evening when I arrived and the lights were still on so I went in. Someone on the staff told me my husband had returned from his trip and was very angry about my absence but I did not want to be scolded then as I had first to see the Ambassador and give him the envelope. . . . As it happened when the Ambassador had finished with me, nothing my husband added subsequently mattered. I went back to Biarritz, delivered Dr Valero's second list and lay down on my bed and cried.

Betty does not reveal what the ambassador said to her but it must have been a severe interview to have reduced Betty to tears. She was subsequently made well aware by Arthur that her outrageously indiscreet behaviour had placed his career on the line. One only has to look through the Foreign Office archives covering the period to understand how delicate a matter was the decision on whether or not to recognize Franco's regime. It was discussed by the Cabinet in that very week and Chilton was receiving, daily, long confidential reports on the matter. To have the wife of a member of his staff waltz blithely through all this red tape and appear with a direct message from the "insurgent's headquarters" must have brought Chilton close to apoplexy.

Notwithstanding the displeasure she had incurred, however, when Betty received a phone call two days later, telling her that another consignment of medical supplies was ready to be delivered, she did not hesitate for a minute. She picked it up and took the now familiar road across the frontier. "The sentries knew my car and had previously waved it through, but this time they stopped me and said I was wanted in the *comandancia*." There, to her surprise, Colonel Altamira met her. He appeared greatly excited and said he had orders to arrest her on a charge of espionage; the order had come from General Franco's military Headquarters.

I replied "It cannot be true Augustín, someone has made a mistake. You know me. The only possible thing to do is to phone Headquarters and ask them to check. Tell them I am here and have got to get on to

Burgos and make my delivery to Dr Valero. If they want to arrest me there they can." He put in the call and when it came through he beckoned me to the telephone and invited me to listen in.

The voice from Headquarters said there had been no mistake. The charge against me was formal and that if I remained in Spain I was to be arrested and this would lead to a diplomatic incident. In conclusion I was to be over the border within half an hour and should be given an escort to ensure that this was carried out.

So I gave my supplies to Augustín who kissed me goodbye saying that someone had obviously "denounced" me. "And I think we both know who it is . . ." During the following weeks I was able to satisfy myself as to the identification of the person who had denounced me to the Franco authorities. It was indeed a woman who did not like me and had used her influence in high quarters; she said that as a member of the "red" British Embassy, which did not give official recognition to Franco, my visits to Spain were an altruistic cover simply for purposes of espionage.[1]

The woman, said Betty, a Spanish woman living in Biaritz, "had a cause to be jealous of me," but she reveals neither the identity of her denouncer nor the reason she might have had for taking such an action. One wonders about this person who was powerful enough to communicate with Franco's cabinet and what she said to convince her contacts that Betty's humanitarian, clearly helpful, activities were non-friendly. Betty made an odd comment in rounding off this story in her memoirs: ". . . in any case my usefulness there had ended." Why the words "in any case"? Had she not been "denounced" her runs to Burgos, the only "usefulness" that she revealed, could easily have continued. And why the peculiar use of "denounced" with its implication that the informant was imparting a truthful fact, rather than the more doubtful "accused"?

At this stage Betty was supposed to be, and always maintained that she was, working in a purely free-lance capacity, driven by her concern for Carlos and her fierce support of the Nationalist cause. However, the staff at the British embassy were not all career diplomats. There is always a military intelligence presence in embassies, especially in troubled zones. In fact there is evidence that even at this stage Betty had been recruited in an unofficial manner to watch and report on prevailing conditions,

56

and perhaps—because of the circles in which she moved—conversations with important Nationalists. The name of her contact within British Naval Intelligence is not known but we do know that she provided "useful information" during the course of several visits into Spain during the civil war. The late Commander Don Gomez-Beare, a Gibraltarian who became a British naval attaché at Madrid during World War II, confirms this:

> Betty was *even then* [emphasis in original] a powerhouse of ideas and information . . . there is little doubt that her activities had been reported back to MI6 headquarters in London and that she had . . . been used as a useful informant . . . to British Naval Intelligence.[2]

This was not the first time—and certainly not the last—that Betty's life was thrown off course by the actions of a jealous, often a wronged, woman. However, it was all too easy to qualify for the term "spy" or "Red" in those desperate days, with the end too often an overcrowded prison, a travesty of a trial and the firing squad. The membership of the Nationist party was as broad in type and class as that of the other side, and there are many incidences of summary execution for minor offences, such as failing to give the Nazi salute. Extreme brutality existed in both camps.

However, it was not only Betty's association with Franco's foreign minister that threatened Arthur's career. Arthur's own political views displeased his superiors. In the Foreign Office records there is a cable from the head of the Foreign Office, George Mountsey, to Sir Henry Chilton:

> It has unfortunately come to our ears that Pack . . . while in London has created the impression both in official and unofficial circles that his attitude over the Spanish conflict is strongly biased in favour of the Franco regime.
>
> This in itself is not unnatural but it is obviously more prudent of any representative of HMG to be cautious in this respect. Unfortunately I don't think Pack has been cautious and has, moreover, led some people to believe that he was expressing the views of HMG, and has thus clearly though perhaps unintentionally let it be understood in certain quarters that His Majesty's Government are quite determined that Franco must win this war.

He has, I fear, been indiscreet in other respects but it is this association quite unjustifiably—even if unintentionally—of his own views with those of His Majesty's Government in his conversations with business and city people which has caused the most mischief here, and I fear that it may be partly in consequence of such indiscretions that the Government have during the last few weeks been pilloried in certain circles as being pro-Franco and even pro-Fascist in their sympathies. . . .

Arthur had expressed his "indiscreet" views during a dinner attended by the directors of Rio Tinto, a company which had good cause to be grateful to Arthur's work on its behalf. It was through the chairman, Sir Aukland Geddes (formerly president of the Board of Trade) that the gist of Arthur's conversation was relayed to Mountsey. The thirteen-page letter goes on to suggest that Pack be given a firm and friendly caution, but even that would not be the end of it.

But we doubt whether this is really either a final or satisfactory solution. . . . Pack holds strong views, which he is temperamentally unable to conceal; and though . . . it is not his business to harbour or express any views on local political issues it is much easier for us to say this than for him, built as he is, to subscribe in practise to the line of restraint that we would impose upon him. . . .[3]

The letter concluded that the only solution appeared to be to move Arthur to another post, preferably where there were "no live internal political issues to distract him," though it was recognized in London that this would cause "serious embarrassment to you, as his wide experience of commercial affairs, his knowledge of the Spanish language and character, and the good relations he has established in Spain . . . are assets of which it is hard to deprive you. . . ." This was especially so in view of the fact that Franco was seeking recognition of Belligerent Rights and that Arthur, because of his earlier contacts, was the one person indicated for the unpleasant job of trying to obtain commitments from Franco, personally, without offering anything in return.[4]

The ambassador was as upset about the affair as Mountsey knew he would be. Chilton attempted vainly to change the minds of his Foreign Office chiefs but eventually he conceded defeat, permitting himself one last grumbling comment on the subject: ". . . it is a great pity that Pack, who knows the ropes and everyone [in Franco's administration] should be transferred just at a moment when it looks as though some results may be expected."[5]

Poor Sir Henry—only a few months later he too would be the victim of tittle-tattle that would ultimately lead to his, too, having to leave Spain.[6]

By then, according to Foreign Office records, Chilton had experienced several long interviews with a pained Arthur who, probably to spare his feelings as much as to protect the London informant, had been told only part of the truth. Arthur reacted predictably. At home, overcome with anger, bluster and wounded pride, he laid into Betty, placing on to her a great deal of the blame for speaking too freely of her sympathies for the Nationalists, and included references to her poorly timed recent adventures in Spain. Her behaviour, he stormed, had cost him the reputation carefully built up over years of hard work.

The outcome, he raged at his wife, was that he had been given four months in which time he had to tie up any loose ends and introduce his replacement, Cecil Jerram, to all aspects of his work. Betty would have to pack up and transfer all their possessions to his new post at Warsaw.

Betty recorded this domestic uproar without any comment on whether Arthur's anger at her was justified or not. But it has been suggested to me by several people who formerly worked within SIS that Arthur's transfer was merely a trumped-up excuse to enable Betty to be moved to an arena where her particular abilities could be of more value to the intelligence service. According to Betty's published memoirs, she was working in a purely personal and unofficial capacity in Spain and was not recruited by SIS until almost a year later.

But there is no doubt that there is something strange about Arthur's transfer. He was, perhaps, indiscreet. But no more indiscreet than many of his colleagues, and senior politicians at home, who shared his views —before long even the British government would come to regard Franco as the lesser of the two evils in Spain. A strong reprimand, enabling Chilton to retain Arthur's services in the sensitive diplomatic exchanges with Franco, would seem a more appropriate solution to his misdemeanor.

If his (or his wife's) conduct was viewed to be so serious as to require virtual expulsion, why was he given *four months* to clear up his affairs? Surely, had he been creating sufficient diplomatic embarrassment to warrant a transfer, he would have been moved immediately—or sent on convenient leave while a replacement was arranged. And assuming his transfer *was* for indiscretion, why send him to Poland? Why not Africa or South America or some other less volatile posting where his opinions would not cause diplomatic ripples? In the summer of 1937 Poland, of all places, was a posting where diplomats required coolness and discretion.

There is no doubt that by this time Betty's skills in passing through lines and her ability to make friends of highly placed men had come to the notice of SIS. It is more than a possibility that it was considered she could be more valuable in the eastern territories adjacent to Hitler's Germany than she could ever be in Spain, which was becoming a *non sequitur* to the British. And it is more than a possibility that to this end the Foreign Office were persuaded to move Arthur to Warsaw. Undoubtedly SIS worked in this way; strings pulled, favours repaid, a word in the ear of an old school chum at a chap's club. It is all perfectly possible; finding corroborative proof of this in public archives is another matter.[7]

Eventually, Arthur calmed down. Betty decided to return to Madrid before they left for Poland. Having decided on one more attempt to help Carlos, she had given the matter a lot of thought and concluded that the best way to track him down was to begin at the scene of his arrest.

She told Arthur that she intended to return to their apartment to collect some of their more valuable belongings. In particular, she said, she had no intention of abandoning items of sentimental value such as the few heirlooms and paintings she had brought to their marriage. Although he appreciated and sympathized with her practical reasoning (they had left their Madrid apartment with only the items they could pack into their car, equipped for a "long vacation" rather than a permanent move), Arthur firmly vetoed what he saw as an ill-timed suggestion. Republican-held Madrid was under constant siege by the Nationalists and conditions were known to be extremely dangerous there.

She did not argue with him, deciding to return to her old pattern of subterfuge. She knew he had several long visits to make to Burgos with Cecil Jerram and simply awaited her opportunity. Meanwhile she obtained written permission from the Spanish embassy in Paris to obtain a visa from their office in Bayonne and bought her air ticket.[8]

In the light of her "denouncement" in northern Spain her decision can only be construed as either foolhardy or very brave. Although Madrid was hundreds of miles away there was more than a possibility that senior officers operating from Burgos at the time of Betty's visits there could be transferred between battle arenas. Such a striking woman as Betty was easily recognizable. Either this did not occur to her, or she ignored it after weighing the odds.

There is an element of farce here. Betty had been denounced to the Nationalists as a Republican spy, though in fact she had incurred the wrath of her ambassador for carrying messages for the Nationalists, not the Republicans. Arthur was being sent into exile for having been too cozy with the Nationalists, a relationship the Republicans apparently saw as inimical to their interests. As Betty made her way through Nationalist territory into Republican-held territory either side might find cause to arrest her as a spy for the other.

Her opportunity came during the first week in June. Arthur was to leave on a mission on June 7 but he was to attend a stag dinner on the night of June 6. He was hardly out of sight before Betty began to pack a small suitcase for herself. She left a note and gave it to the maid with strict instructions that it be given to Arthur no earlier than nine the following morning. Leaving Denise with her nanny, Betty borrowed a friend's chauffeur and travelled to Toulouse to take the plane to Valencia from where she hoped to organize transport to Madrid.

The diplomatic post in Valencia was quartered in a dilapidated building in the centre of town and gained some dignity by being referred to as "the Chancery." John Leche was chargé d'affaires there with a small clerical staff and, because of the prevailing conditions, rather more autonomy than he might otherwise have expected. He was an astute, no-nonsense man, but any hint at brusqueness was tempered by a wry sense of humour. His previous assignment had been in Buenos Aires and within days of arriving in Valencia his pithy report had been cabled to London. It did not stop at the political situation but gave a thumbnail sketch of the flotsam of humanity he encountered in the war-torn city:

I have not yet got over the idea that I have landed in a lunatic asylum
. . . every crank and busybody in the world, amongst them, I regret to
say, a great many British, seem to be gathered together and hold forth on
Spain and the Spaniards on the strength of a short stay without for the
most part knowing a word of the language. Every kind of fisher in troubled
waters of both sexes seems to be collected. Some of these people are sincere
no doubt, some are not, and some are doubtless frankly here out of
curiosity.[9]

Leche had spent the previous two days trying to arrange transport for
British women *out* of Spain when Betty appeared in his office at the
makeshift Chancery on June 7. In describing her first meeting with the
beleaguered chargé d'affaires she recalled that he had "snarled" at her,
"dark with displeasure" that Hendaye should have approved the visit, and
ordered her to take the next plane back to France.[10]

Swiftly disabusing him of any notion that she had the approval of
anyone at Hendaye, Betty hotly retorted that she was going to Madrid
with or without his help. Leche had been in Madrid only a few weeks
earlier, but his arguments that Madrid was under constant heavy shelling,
that the embassy there was closed, that there was an acute food shortage,
that the city was not as she remembered it but dirty and disorganized, his
recitation of the huge daily casualty figures, and finally the flat statement
that if she went and was killed he would be placed in an intolerable
position, made no impression whatsoever. Betty was stubbornly determined, and he soon saw what he was up against. When she got up to
leave to look for overnight accommodation he offered her a room for the
night.

Each evening the embassy staff drove to a beach house between Perelló
and Las Palmeras, some 15 miles south of the city, which was the target
of heavy bombardment every night.[11] This "night-time embassy" looked
like a film set for a Somerset Maugham novel: a large, ramshackle house
on a deserted stretch of beach, the seaward-facing rooms opening directly
on to the sands. Leche's invitation was followed by a gruff recommen-
dation that since the staff regularly took an evening swim in the sea before
dinner she might try to acquire a swimsuit.

She spent the afternoon making enquiries about how to get to Madrid but learned only that the road between Valencia and Madrid was so dangerous that she could not hire any transport. Still, she had already come too far to turn back. That evening she sat next to Leche at dinner and noticed with interest that his staff referred to him as H.E., the abbreviation for "His Excellency" normally reserved for those holding the rank of ambassador. Leche was not an ambassador but chargé d'affaires holding the imposing title Minister Plenipotentiary, but in any case he was quite unlike any British ambassador she had ever met. In appearance he was the embodiment of a Gypsy fortune-teller's "tall, dark, handsome man" and he dressed quite informally in an open-necked shirt and slacks with fisherman's espadrilles on his tanned feet. Yet Betty saw at once why such a prestigious name had been given to him, for along with his Gypsy-like, dissolute looks, he had a powerful aura about him.[12]

She decided that her best course of action was to set out to charm him:[13]

I told him he had been kind to invite me and he made some cynical remark about having little choice in the matter. I then pleaded with him to give me some sort of official clearance to get me as far as Madrid, adding that I would be happy to absolve him of any blame should anything happen to me. He gave me no reply but next day he called me into his office and with an impatient air, and ferocity in his voice he handed me a free-transit pass from the office of the Republican Government's Secretary General.[14]

He also advised her that he had arranged a car and driver to take her to Madrid or as close as they could get. After that, he said, she was on her own in "this foolish business."[15]

During the day Betty returned to Valencia to make enquiries about Carlos, without any success, and at the appointed time she returned to the Chancery where a car was waiting for her. In addition to the chauffeur there was young English officer who introduced himself as Captain Lance. They left immediately and drove through the night. The drive itself was through large areas of open countryside where there were no military objectives, but about two hours before they reached Madrid, just before dawn, they had to drive through heavy aerial bombing from Nationalist planes and Betty and her companion spent a good deal of time on the floor of the car while the chauffeur attempted to dodge the worst of the explosions.

They reached the British embassy building soon after daylight. Captain Lance bade her good luck, placed her suitcase on the pavement and drove away. Betty suspected that he was probably an intelligence agent; although she never saw him again, many years later she discovered that he had been captured and imprisoned at Figueras near Barcelona and while there lost his sight.[16]

Almost immediately, a number of planes appeared overhead and starting bombing. Betty sought shelter in the deserted embassy and was admitted by the Spanish caretaker. During the raid she wandered around in the entrance hall looking at the paintings of the king and queen, remembering the many occasions she had been there prior to the conflict. "It seemed to me that I had come into a graveyard where white-shrouded pieces of furniture were tombstones among which the ghosts of the past played . . ." she recalled.[17] When the bombing ended she walked out into a city strewn with debris from constant barrages. She decided that her first move should be to try to get to her apartment, to sleep and freshen up before pursuing further enquiries. She picked her way through the littered streets, shaken at the changes which had occurred to the familiar route since her departure.

The appearance of the once prestigious building of Castellana 63 also came as a shock to her, its elegant courtyard filled with bomb debris and refugees who had sought the shelter of the high walls along with their bundles of personal belongings, mattresses, chickens and goats. Despite the Embassy Seal on the front door, the Packs' apartment had been broken into and some silver had been stolen. Most of the refugees were peasants, sad but philosophical. One of them, an old man called Enrique, helped her to make the apartment secure again. Some days later he also traced the thief, but the items had already been disposed of. "Enrique seemed to gain satisfaction in protecting me, though from what I shall never know."[18]

She slept for a while and was wakened by the embassy caretaker knocking at the door. He had brought her a message from a Miss Jacobsen of the Scottish Ambulance Unit in Spain, a group of well-funded, surprisingly efficient idealists who were operating under the auspices of the International Red Cross. If Betty wished to stay with her during her time in Madrid, wrote Miss Jacobsen, she was welcome to do so. Although Betty never discovered how her presence in Madrid had become known, she suspected that John Leche or Captain Lance had a hand in it. She was probably correct. Leche had recently been constructive in arranging for the release of two ambulance drivers who had been arrested while in the act of rescuing wounded soldiers from a battlefield, and Foreign Office archives reveal that he was in regular contact with Miss Jacobsen, who ran the unit.[19]

With no one else to turn to, Betty made her way to the unit's headquarters, where she was made welcome by the small Scotswoman dressed in uniform and wearing a Red Cross armband. Briefing Betty about their work of distributing food and other supplies to the hospitals around Madrid and rescuing wounded, she seemed pleased when Betty offered to help during her stay, and introduced her to her "boys." Betty had the advantage of knowing her way around the city and for the next weeks spent a lot of her time accompanying drivers as navigator. She also toured hospitals and reception centres, questioning in an oblique manner anyone she thought might give her news of Carlos. She felt that a direct approach to the few government contacts she had might place Carlos in even greater danger, so her enquiries were kept discreet.

Between times she concentrated her energies on packing up the contents of her apartment, the ostensible reason for her journey. The government authorities gave her a permit to obtain lumber and she hiked around the city trying to find wood, which she then persuaded a local coffin-maker to turn into packing cases. John Milanes, the British consul, gave her a stack of old newspapers for packing filler but it was not enough so she went to a shop that made horsehair mattresses and bought two large burlap sacks of the stuffings, which she dragged across the city at night to her apartment. She kept her money in a pocket sewed into her girdle and was worried that because of inflated prices she would run out of cash before her work was finished. Every night she accompanied the ambulance men as they toured the streets, dodging bombs, to rescue wounded civilians and take them back to the headquarters. "It was . . . good training in keeping cool . . . the Scottish boys set many examples which helped me during my later life."[20]

Conditions were appalling. Bombing raids were not confined to darkness and Betty became accustomed to darting into doorways and alleys while death rained down from the skies. Like her contemporary, Martha Gellhorn, she got used to seeing "crazy-eyed children running through the streets in hope of shelter, and . . . old people who could not run."[21] Food was almost impossible to get and long queues, mostly of peasant woman, faces drawn with hunger and anxiety, formed outside bakeries each day at dawn.[22] For Betty though, her biggest problem was the inability to obtain cigarettes. There was a kiosk in the city centre which issued rationed supplies each Tuesday, but she had been a heavy smoker since before she married Arthur and the shortage was a serious nuisance to her. Eventually, "the boys" showed her how to make her own cigarettes using lavatory paper.

When all the transportable effects of Castellana 63 were packed, Miss Jacobsen again came to Betty's aid, agreeing to allow the packing cases to go to Valencia on the unit's trucks on their weekly journey to the coast for medical supplies. At this point Betty thought it might be a good idea to telephone Arthur and give him some encouraging news, hoping to defuse his certain wrath. She obtained permission from the government authority in charge of communications, but they warned her that her calls would be monitored and that she should restrict what she had to say to purely personal matters.

Arthur seemed pleased that things were working out well. He told her to have the packing cases shipped to the Polish port of Gdynia. When she said she would be returning home shortly, he assured her that she need not bother to hurry back. She suspected sarcasm, but when she heard music and voices in the background she realized with surprise that he was serious.

By June 22 Miss Jacobsen had received word from Valencia that a large shipment had arrived there for the unit and that their trucks would have to go and collect it. Betty was still without word of Carlos, and so her business in Madrid was unfinished. She considered staying on but the bombing was increasing in its ferocity and the apartment building stood a real chance of being blown up. Moreover, Franco's troops were advancing, so that there was a possibility, if she stayed, that she might be trapped in the middle of a battle for the city. In a piece of brinkmanship, fate resolved her dilemma. Enrique arrived at the Scottish Ambulance Unit's flat to tell her that he had heard that Carlos was still alive, and was imprisoned somewhere near Valencia.

She clearly had no alternative but to press on, confident as usual that she would be able to persuade someone at the embassy in Valencia to help her. With four friends from the Scottish Ambulance Unit she drove eastward and in late afternoon Valencia shimmered into view through waves of dust and summer heat. She asked to be dropped at the Chancery but hardly had she stepped out of the truck with her suitcase than she saw the tall, dark figure of John Leche coming towards her.

To her surprise Leche greeted her with a smile and invited her up to his office. There he poured a generous gin and tonic, commenting that she looked thin. How had she managed for food? Where had she stayed? He had only just returned from a three-day reconnaissance tour himself and knew exactly how bad conditions could be.[23] Furthermore, during his absence a cable had been received from the ambassador asking for a report on Betty's whereabouts and instructing Leche to arrange her immediate return on the next available destroyer.[24]

They were interrupted briefly by a colleague of Arthur's from Hendaye, Angus Malcolm, who was en route to Madrid to report on conditions there. Betty needed little encouragement to tell him all about her time in Madrid, what the bombardment was like, the fighting spirit of the people, and how half a million people were living on a diet of lentils, beans and rice. Betty asked him what people at Hendaye were saying about her and whether the ambassador and his staff were still angry with her for the way in which she had left. He replied with a rueful grin, "Not really, dear girl. We got used to you a long time ago."[25]

After Malcolm left she remained chatting with Leche. She could only marvel at the apparent change in his disposition towards her, but when she stood up to leave he said that he must be thinking about getting her home. Betty bridled, first because at last she felt that she stood a real chance of locating Carlos in Valencia, and not least that she had been mistaken in believing that Leche had come to enjoy her company. She asked him why he was so keen to make her return to France and begged him to allow her to stay even if only for three or four days.

Leche calmed her, telling her not to be so blind and stupid. He hadn't meant *her* home, he said. He meant *his* home at Las Palmeras. During her absence, Leche had clearly become attracted to her. Why or how this transformation had taken place will never be known. Perhaps it had been her determination in the face of massive opposition that impressed him and the fact that she was more than just another pretty embassy wife. Or had Leche learned from someone—Angus Malcolm perhaps—that Betty's activities *were* more than the actions of an empty-headed romantic out for excitement? This time he drove her to the villa, alone:

> On the way to Las Palmeras he took my hand and asked me to tell him what I was thinking. "You aren't going to evade me any more are you?" he asked. I knew exactly what he meant. "No John," I said. "I won't avoid you if you don't fight me." Then I told him about Carlos and my search for him and my hope that I could help to have him freed.[26]

Leche questioned her about Carlos and whether her feelings for him ruled out any other man in her life. Betty told him that Carlos was the only man she had ever cared for deeply. They did not discuss Leche's wife, Helen, who—when Leche received his Spanish posting—had returned to her family in Philadelphia.

That evening there was the usual routine of swimming, cocktails and supper during which, despite the casual dress, normal embassy formalities were maintained. Supper, to which all the embassy staff came, "was served at a huge table in a long room and there was decent food and good Spanish wine."[27] The only drawback to the place, Betty recalled, was that due to a heavy blackout the windows had to be kept shuttered and this resulted in the dining room becoming very hot and stuffy, especially after diners had lit cigarettes.

When they left the dining room Leche suggested that they go for a walk along the beach and watch the huge fireworks display of bombs bursting over Valencia. After a while they sat on the sand in the warm night air and talked about the situation in Madrid and then about themselves—telling each other the innumerable things people who are just discovering each other will find to tell. Both were reluctant to bring the tête-à-tête to an end but at last they rose and Betty gave "H.E." her hand to bid him goodnight. He caressed her fingers and, reaching out, stroked her hair. "I don't know how to let you go," he told her.

She walked back to her room and as she closed the door she saw that he was standing as she had left him, with his back to her, staring out to sea. Her memoir recalls:

I don't know how much later, but sometime in the night I wakened from a deep sleep to an exquisite anguish that I did not, at first, understand. My body had been moved and I lay wrapped in H.E.'s strong arms. We were both naked and his mouth was covering my face and throat with kisses that he pressed into my flesh as though to seal the contact. He was taller than I and my body fitted his like a built-in part of it, making us one welded substance in which I completed him from his shoulders down to his thighs.[28]

He told her he wanted her, that he had fallen in love with her and that despite her love for Carlos he knew he could bring her to love him; he wanted her completely. Sadly, she told him that she could never love anyone "completely," and that she did not share his feelings. "I am 26 already and the thing you mean is never likely to happen to me. . . ." However, she admitted that she liked him and was physically attracted to him.

He gathered me to him then so utterly that we seemed to have no relation to anything except that which was happening between us and which continued to be our only world until the sun came up, long afterwards, over the rim of the Mediterranean and brought us back to one of reality.

We made love every night after that, almost for as long as I remained in that part of Spain, and in Valencia where we spent the daytime H.E. made changes to his routine that would allow us to be alone together at least twice before returning to Las Palmeras. . . . He was a passionate man, very tender and kind.[29]

She did not attempt to justify this affair played out against her proclaimed great love for Carlos, but there is perhaps an explanation in her statement that Leche was never condescending or censorious; "rather he was a companion, and peaceful to be with when I wanted peace."

He was some twenty years older than Betty but older men had always played a large part in her life; had, in a sense, moulded her without ever intimidating or dominating her. She seemed to need in her important relationships some element of her first love, her father, and she needed too the sense of safety provided by a figure whom she could respect and upon whose reliability she could depend while she herself flitted from adventure to adventure. And yet the relationships, once established, often disapointed her, for she seemed to grow inside the union while her partners did not.

While Valencia, far back from the front lines dividing the two armies, was a good deal safer than Madrid had been, it was nevertheless a war zone, subject to aerial and naval bombardment and the internecine violence that marred Spain during most of its civil war. Only a few days before Betty's arrival, Leche had reported that "for the city of Valencia itself the figure spoken of is 23,000 murders out of a normal population of roughly 275,000." When the embassy staff drove into the city each morning they became accustomed to seeing the results of the previous night's "bumping-off party."[30]

Despite the risks, she continued her enquiries into Carlos's fate. At the end of June she wrote to Arthur:

> *British Embassy, Valencia*
> *June 28th 1937*

Dearest Arthur,

A courier is leaving in a few minutes by destroyer and will post this to you from Marseilles so I am enclosing the list that I have compiled of the furniture and pictures so that if need be you can check with the shippers. As I told you on the telephone in spite of the Embassy Seal on the door our flat was broken into and three items were taken: Denise's pram, the silver inkstand and two silver plates (why not all?). With the help of my faithful watchdog, Enrique, I ran the thief to earth, but his confession and apologies did not do much good as he had already sold the things. He was was one of the innumerable refugees at Castellana 63.

The furniture and pictures are here awaiting shipment and should leave any day by ship. The Scottish Ambulance people were wonderful and brought it down in their supply trucks—three lorryloads. The bombs have chased us out to Las Palmeras at night but we come to the chancery in the morning. It is a hectic life, but the Ambassador is trying to have me evacuated by destroyer next week.

I hope you are all flourishing and not casino-ing too much! Hasta la Vista and much love to everyone,

ETP

P.S. General Fuqua sends his best. He is having a grand time . . . one would think he was running both sides of the revolution.[31]

Stephen Fuqua was an old family friend of the Thorpes whom Betty, much to her amazement, had run into one day while wandering around Valencia, dispirited because she had just gone through the lists of prisoners in four prisons where people suspected of being pro-Franco were held and had found no mention of Carlos. She had begun to wonder if Carlos were really still alive or whether he had been shot. It was quite a surprise to come across a friend from her childhood in such a place and at a time when everything seemed so grim. Fuqua, a vigorous, active man, was listed among the guests at Betty's wedding as Major General Fuqua, but he signed his intelligence reports from Spain during the Spanish civil war "Colonel Stephen Fuqua."[32] He was nearing retirement and Betty had last seen him before she and Arthur left Madrid where he had been military attaché at the United States embassy.

They retired to the bar of a nearby hotel and in response to his questions she began to tell him about her adventures and her search for Carlos. As part of the diplomatic community in pre-war Madrid Fuqua had known Carlos and now he interrupted her to say that he knew exactly where Carlos was—in the huge military prison outside of Valencia on the Barcelona road. The prison, he told her, was impregnable and she must not try "any pimpernel stuff there" or she'd find herself leaving in a hearse. There was only one way for a visitor to get in and that was with a pass from Indalecio Prieto, the minister of national defence.

Prieto was probably the most powerful man in the Republican government and certainly the only one with any international standing. In one of his regular reports to London Leche had written recently, ". . . the only outstanding man is Prieto, most of the rest appear to be nothing but windbags."[33] Betty told Fuqua that that she needed time to think about what he had told her and to plan her strategy.

Later she related the whole story to John Leche. She told him that she needed to see Prieto and asked him to help her. Leche agreed to use diplomatic channels to arrange for her to see him, provided she made it quite clear to Prieto that her visit was a purely personal one and had nothing whatever to do with His Majesty's Government. In return, he said, she could help him to effect the escape of a prisoner from one of the temporary city gaols, a converted civic building. The prisoner in question was the Marqués de Arueza, Luis Villada, a man who, coincidentally, had been a dancing partner of Betty's in the old days of "Jimmy's place." He had recently been arrested on suspicion that he was a Franco sympathizer.

The plan was simple. Villada was ill but capable of walking and able to be visited. The prison regime was apparently low-key and the building was large and not well guarded. Using his diplomatic pass Leche could easily gain access for them both driving the car into the courtyard. Once inside they would pretend to be members of the man's family and Betty was to take on the role of his sister. The prisoner's hair was fair, unusual for a Spaniard, almost the same colour as Betty's in fact, so they could easily be taken for brother and sister. All three would walk out into the courtyard and while Leche distracted the guards she was to walk slowly and calmly to the car with the prisoner; they would drive away, adopting the status of a diplomatic party again when the car reached the outside gates.

Betty's memoirs tell how Leche fooled the guards; the ministerial car carrying diplomatic plates and flying the Union Flag was not hindered as they drove confidently into the courtyard and out of sight of the guards on the gate. Everything went according to plan and the only hitch was the absolute bewilderment of the prisoner when they were shown into his cell. Betty leaned close to kiss him on the cheek and said rapidly, "Luis, I am your sister and Papa and I have come for you. Just come along calmly and if things go wrong stay near to me, the guards won't shoot close to a woman. . . ." Leche, a tall, charismatic man, found it easy to engage the guards in loud, confident conversation, so that all attention was on him while Betty and the prisoner sauntered to the car holding hands. After a short time Leche simply walked calmly away from the guards and got into the car, and they drove out of the gate. The rescued man was left in a hiding place until he could be shipped to France aboard a destroyer.[34]

Exactly why John Leche should have engineered this escape is uncertain—though Betty wrote later that the man was a family friend of Leche's. His previous monthly report to London had carried the cryptic paragraph:

> As you know for some time the questions of exchanges has been handed over to the Red Cross to be dealt with in bulk and the government absolutely refuse to consider the exchange of individuals. Exchange of whole lists containing hundreds of men, obviously presents great practical difficulty. I have, however, a faint hope of getting through one special case.[35]

Two days later, Fuqua drove Betty to her appointment with Indalecio Prieto. In her handbag she carried a piece of paper given to her by Leche, on which were listed the names of seventeen additional former air force pilots, all suspected of being pro-Franco, who had been captured and who were being held in the same prison. Advising her not to mention them unless Prieto seemed well disposed towards her plea on Carlos's behalf, Leche had, nevertheless, asked her to use her best efforts for them if she judged it right to do so.

She felt nervous now that the day "for which I had worked and schemed for so long" had at last arrived; and she worried that she might say something which could harm Carlos.

So much depended upon the person one had to deal with, or rather on the mood of the moment and on heaven knew what combination of circumstances. I prayed that [Prieto's] decision . . . would be made on a plane well removed from the influences of daily harrassments. . . .[36]

As the car stopped in front of the forbidding old *palacio* that was the headquarters of the minister of national defence she had a sudden uncharacteristic attack of stage fright. Fuqua hectored her contemptuously, reminding her that she was her father's daughter, and this bolstered her as she entered the building.

Nor was her new confidence shaken when the weary-looking minister appeared in the room where she had been asked to wait, and introduced himself quietly with a single word, "Prieto." Betty began her rehearsed speech, stressing the fact that she had come to him in a purely personal capacity, though it was with the full knowledge and approval of the British chargé d'affaires. When he questioned her further about her interest in the matter she decided that the best way of handling the matter was to make him her confidant. She told him of her love for Carlos and said that for this reason she knew him well enough to be certain that he would never have done anything against Spain or the Spanish government. If the minister would only investigate the events surrounding the arrest she knew he would discover that no evidence existed to support the accusation.

Prieto reflected quietly for a while before speaking. At last he said that he could give her no immediate decision and could "do nothing capricious" but that he would consider her plea. But he had not dismissed her petition and she took the opening, going on to tell him of her search for Carlos in Madrid and her plans to return to France, soon, by destroyer. He approved of this, saying that it was a wise plan, the alternative being to travel via Barcelona. Conditions there were so bad, he told her, "I wouldn't dare go there myself!" Just before taking her leave Betty also asked him to consider the plight of the seventeen airmen on her list and he agreed to do so. Almost as an apparent afterthought she asked if it would be possible to see Carlos. She must have judged Prieto nicely for he agreed and provided her with the necessary pass to visit Carlos for an hour.

With Fuqua as her chauffeur, Betty set off immediately for the prison some miles out of Valencia on the Barcelona Road. The huge, surrealistic building in which Carlos had spent almost six months was awesome, but the guards were equally awed by Prieto's pass and treated Betty with immense respect and courtesy. Two chairs were placed in a corner of a long gallery with a guard stationed at the other end, out of earshot. With a minimum of delay Carlos was brought into the gallery and the two lovers were able to embrace each other for the first time in a year. To Betty's relief he had not been badly treated and apart from looking paler and thinner, and sporting a long auburn beard, he appeared unchanged.

She told him her news: of Carmencita's journey and that she was safe; of Prieto's promise to review the matter of Carlos's imprisonment; everything, in fact, except her relationship with Leche, and that she was due to leave for Warsaw with Arthur within a matter of weeks and that this meeting might be their last for a long time. There were no tears when she left after their hour together.

It was a bittersweet meeting and certainly there must have been mixed emotions within her, for this was the time when her relationship with Leche was at its height of passion. Her recollections of this period, where she wrote of her love for Leche with the same intensity as of that for Carlos, indicates that by this time she had cooled towards her former "great love." Possibly it was inevitable that the passage of time would blunt the edge of such intense emotions, or it may be that her vividly defined sexual experience with Leche, crammed as it was into a very short, stressful period of time, was easier to recall than the carefree year spent with Carlos prior to the outbreak of war. Certainly Leche satisfied some strong need in her, for she remained in Valencia a further sixteen days after her visit to Carlos.

But even where she had replaced one lover with another, she remained a fiercely loyal friend, prepared to risk her own life and liberty for someone who had once meant something special to her. And it was not false hope she now gave to Carlos; he was released some months later. One wonders if the seventeen airmen released with him ever knew how much they owed to one brave woman they had never met, for there is little doubt that without Betty's intervention Carlos and the other airmen would have remained in prison, possibly for the remainder of the war, living with execution a daily possibility.

In the succeeding days she spent with Leche several cables were received at Valencia from Hendaye urging Betty's return. Leche did his best to field them but it must have come as a relief when the Admiralty advised him on July 11 that due to unavoidable circumstances only two ships were available for the entire Eastern Section until the end of the month. This meant that they would not be providing the transport previously arranged to take refugees out.[37] Towards the end of July Betty told Leche that the time had come for her to leave. Leche protested and taking her in his arms proposed that she stay with him despite the consequences to them both. Her reminder that the scandal would ruin his career brought forth the reply "I don't give a damn about that." But she knew that time had run out for them; their affair, fulfilling as it had been in its wartime setting, was over as surely as her affair with Carlos was over. She persuaded Leche that she could not live with him in the idyllic way he envisioned unless she could disentangle herself from her obligations, and she assured him that if after three months apart they still felt as strongly she would somehow find a way for them to be together.

On the following day he took her to the port where a launch was waiting to take her to the destroyer. Betty could not bear to look back as she rode out of his life.

She travelled home full of sadness at her parting from Leche, and in baleful anticipation of the unpleasant reception she expected from Arthur. To her surprise, Arthur was strangely uninterested in interrogating her when he met her at the quayside. Later he told her he knew of her affair with Leche; it had apparently been leaked by a member of Leche's staff and was common knowledge at Hendaye. Instead of making this an excuse for an angry tirade about this new damage that she had inflicted on his career he merely told her that he did not wish to discuss the matter further, and that Leche's name was never to be mentioned between them again. At first Betty felt only relief but later wondered about such uncharacteristic behaviour; it was not long before she discovered the reasons behind Arthur's oddly quiescent acceptance of her unfaithfulness.

Her "unemotional" husband had fallen in love with another woman.

This began shortly after Arthur's arrival in Biarritz during the previous summer; she was the wife of a junior colleague whom Betty calls Ralph in her memoirs. The woman's name is given as Maude in one draft of Betty's manuscript and Barbara in another. When Arthur told Betty his story it became obvious to her that at least some of his many absences over the past months had been engineered so that he could spend time with Maude.[38]

The interview in which Arthur told Betty this story was extremely painful for him. He was careful to make it clear to Betty that his feelings were not mere infatuation but that he loved Maude deeply. However, as they were both married and there were two careers to think about they had decided that they should part. Their forced separation when Arthur moved to Warsaw would help them both get over it. Betty, still feeling the pain of her severance from John Leche, understood his anguish and was sympathetic. It is clear that there had been no physical love between Arthur and Betty for some time, but she liked him and respected him, and a deep friendship had survived their many troubled times together. Arthur had given her an easy exit route had she wanted to take it. She chose not to grab at it, and now, instead, she shared heartbreak with him, though the heartbreak of each was for another.

In mid-August John Leche wrote to Betty telling her he was coming to Hendaye, but the ambassador told her shortly afterwards that he had denied permission for the visit. It was made clear to her that she was not to see Leche again. She never did.

Chapter 5

1 9 3 7 - 1 9 3 8

*I*n September 1937 Betty, two-and-a-half-year-old Denise, Denise's nurse, Juanquita, and Juanquita's daughter, a few weeks older than Denise, were met at Warsaw Station by a secretary from the British embassy who escorted them to a hotel. Shortly before she was due to leave, Betty learned with concern that Arthur had been feeling ill for some weeks, suffering from headaches and blurred vision. A local doctor diagnosed overwork and the couple decided that Arthur should not directly follow her but should, instead, take some leave in Paris.

Before leaving Saint-Jean-de-Luz Betty had made some enquiries of

Cecil Jerram (Arthur's predecessor at Warsaw and successor at Hendaye), and from him had learned that his old apartment at Ulica Frascati might still be available; she went at once to see it. She liked the apartment and the immediate neighbourhood was home to many British and foreign diplomats. With her flair for organization, enhanced as it was with her special ability to obtain co-operation from men, she redecorated the apartment and had it ready for occupation in a matter of a few weeks. She took possession early in October. By then the packing cases had arrived from Valencia and soon the rooms were arranged with the furniture from their Madrid apartment in her favourite scheme of white and claret.

Not expecting Arthur to arrive until November, Betty spent her time looking up old friends and making new ones. The number of continent-hoppers was very small in those pre–jet set days, and those in the diplomatic service made up the only other international group who regularly travelled around the world.

Betty was now almost twenty-seven. Chic and vivacious, she made friends easily, mostly easily with men. She did have a few women friends too, but in the main women tended to be wary of her. She was also acquiring a reputation. Stories of her adventures in Spain (not to mention her affair with Leche) had leaked from Hendaye, where she had been a subject of gossip for months.

Robin Hankey was first secretary at the British embassy in Poland in the autumn of 1937 and happened to mention to two acquaintances from the Polish Foreign Office that the new Commercial Secretary was Arthur Pack. He thought that as the acquaintances had both been at the Polish embassy in Washington in the early 1930s they might have known the Packs, but their reaction surprised him. They rubbed their hands and said, "Betty's coming here? Oh boy, Oh boy! Now we'll have some fun. . . ." Led by this to expect a glamorous vamp, Hankey reports that he was a little disappointed when he met Betty to find her "rather ordinary, really."[1]

One finds so many attestations to Betty's great beauty and overwhelming charm in recollections of first meetings with her that this represents an off-note in the pattern. Lord Hankey's mild "I didn't think her particularly glamorous, but she had dangerous curves, if you know what I mean," suggests that Betty may have been aware that gossip about her activities in Spain had created new threats to Arthur's career prospects and kept herself tightly in rein in those first meetings with embassy people.

If so, it was a new and not very natural side to Betty. This is how she recalls her feelings at the time:

> I was . . . full of fun and the spirit of adventure with which my exciting experiences in the Spanish Civil War . . . had whetted my appetite. I felt instinctively drawn towards the Poles with their keen zest for living and consummate sense of artistry. I liked their alternate fits of gaiety and sadness which accorded closely with my own. . . .[2]

She was disappointed with life in Warsaw during the first few weeks there when her social contacts were limited to British embassy staff. The ambassador, Sir Howard Kennard, Betty described as "a real sourpuss who disapproved of any kind of gaiety and confined himself to the purely formal diplomatic entertaining that his duties required." However, it must be said that this description was written in retrospect when Betty had no good reason to recall him kindly.

Lady Kennard was an American who was not at that time living with her husband, so the role of hostess was more often than not played by Mrs. Clifford Norton, the wife of the counsellor, who, though her Christian name was Noel, was known as Peta. "For some reason I could never understand," Betty wrote, "Mrs. Norton took a strong dislike to me and I must say that feeling was reciprocated on my side."

There was one member of staff whom Betty really liked—the Passport Control Officer, Lieutenant-Colonel John Patrick "Jack" Shelley. He was engaged to a young Austrian girl, Sophie Wagner, and the couple were kind to Betty, often inviting her to accompany them to parties and dinners in her first weeks at Warsaw. Jack was an Anglo-Irishman from Cork and though Betty had to go back to her father's grandfather for a fully Irish forebear she identified strongly with the Irish. Her memoirs are peppered with people of whom she says "he was Irish" (her first lover, and Arthur, for example), as though that explained an invisible attraction for her. When describing her nationality she inevitably claimed she was "Irish-American."

In early November Arthur arrived from Paris and their first day together was depressing. He gave no indication of being pleased to see her when she met him at the railway station. Arthur was extremely displeased with the apartment Betty had found. It was too small, he said, and not at all what he had wanted or expected. When she told him that the only alternative had been a large and very pretentious house vacated by the wealthy counsellor of the United States embassy, he was furious that she had not chosen that instead of the apartment. Her argument that they could not have afforded the house only prolonged his anger.[3]

Arthur's medical tests had shown that he had a mild diabetic condition and was suffering from dangerously high blood pressure, possibly exacerbated by his work during the Spanish civil war. The emotional pressures created by his feelings for Maude and his concern about his career should he follow the dictates of his emotions and divorce Betty to marry Maude could not have helped. His innate sense of duty to his marriage vows no doubt was a factor as well.

Betty also found him to be deeply unhappy and in several long talks he confessed that he found the idea of permanent separation from Maude "intolerable." He had even discussed the matter with Maude's husband, Ralph, who refused to consider the matter of divorce. Ralph and Maude had been transferred to Rome; Arthur told Betty that a vacancy would be opening up there in a few months and that he had decided to apply for it. Meanwhile, he eased himself into his job at the Warsaw embassy. A former colleague, Robin (now Lord) Hankey, recalls:

> He was a huge bull of a man . . . I would say he was a nice man, I liked him and he had a good sense of fun. I remember that he used to go most evenings down to the Hotel Bristol [the best hotel in the city] where there was a dance band. Arthur would inevitably get himself up onto the rostrum with the band and sing an aria or two. He had a wonderful voice and it used to bring the house down. . . .[4]

Betty and Arthur naturally joined in the social life of the embassy—it was a duty as much as a pleasure—and Betty quickly developed a genuine interest in Polish political problems, seeing how uneasily the country was poised between Hitler's Germany and Stalin's Russia. However, when she discussed the matter at a dinner party, Arthur—perhaps as a result of several painful interviews on his own and his wife's indiscreet championship of Franco in Spain—scolded her and told her that she must not abuse people's hospitality by asking questions about political matters.

December 31, 1937, was Denise's third birthday. The Packs gave a children's tea party in the afternoon and were invited to a New Year's Eve party at the French embassy that evening. Arthur had complained of headaches all day, but accompanied Betty to the party as planned. Shortly before midnight he collapsed. As the party was only a very short distance from their apartment he was carried home unconscious, put to bed and a doctor called. The diagnosis was serious. Arthur had suffered a stroke.

For two weeks Betty nursed him with great concern and devotion. That she still cared for him is evident in a letter she wrote to Arthur's family which they have kept:

Warsaw
January 24th 1938

Dearest Family,

It is 4 a.m. and I wanted to write earlier but had a mountain of business correspondence to attend to so this will be only a note to give love to you all and to say I will write individually when I can. Dear Rosie, please pass this on to Mother and Dad to whom I hope to write soon with a postscript in Arthur's own hand!

He is better. I push him into "the den" twice daily where he sits in an armchair and looks at picture magazines and has his lunch and supper. His diabetes is well under control, I've got all kinds of sugarless jams and starchless breads and flour from England. I hope to take him to London by train (and of course, stretcher) in a fortnight as he cannot get well here. This is a sad, grey place and I'll let you know when our plans are more concrete . . .

I'll leave Arthur at Osborne House [Isle of Wight], look for a cottage, return to Poland for a few days to pack up and collect the "family" (besides

Denise we have a Spanish child), then on to the Isle of Wight to be as near as possible to your son and brother and to my husband.

He is such a darling, patient, brave man. I love courage and Arthur has it. . . . Please do not worry. ARTHUR IS GOING TO GET WELL. I am a demon of determination, I've never yet failed in something I really wanted and I'm so determined about him. I'm giving him everything I have in me . . .

To you all, our love. Your letters have been a joy . . . please keep on writing. Your loving daughter,

Betty

Betty took Arthur to England in early February and to all appearances she presented the very model of a devoted, caring young wife. She fussed to ensure that Arthur was always made comfortable and that he suffered as little distress as possible given the difficulty of the journey in a North European winter. She stayed only briefly in England, as planned. Arthur was most concerned that she return to Denise and remain in Poland at least in the short term as an indication that he would be returning to his post. From the day of his collapse Maude was never mentioned again between the couple.

So Betty returned to Warsaw alone; a "grass widow" is how she described her status. Within a few weeks she embarked on an affair with the handsome young Pole, Edward Kulikowski, who lived in an apartment across the street from her own. It began as a congenial friendship with loneliness, as much as anything, drawing them together, and was never serious. Betty makes it clear, in her memoirs, that through this period she still missed John Leche a great deal.

Kulikowski, a young, ambitious diplomat who held a reasonably senior position in the Polish Foreign Office, was himself on the rebound. As a member of the staff at the Polish embassy in Washington he had fallen deeply in love with an American woman from a leading family. She had borne him a daughter whom he was not allowed to acknowledge. Betty never identified her but in 1963 wrote cryptically that she had subsequently "married a man who became the stepfather of a *Very Important Person* in the United States today."[5]

After formal dinners or receptions Edward and his friends would invite Betty back to their houses and—free of Arthur's restraining influence—she was able to give full rein to her curiosity and full expression to her opinions about the political situation. The discussions, in French, went on long into the night and soon Betty felt they were treating her not as the wife of a foreign diplomat but as one of themselves. There is a certain naïveté in her assessment of the political situation and she reveals an ignorance of just where the Ukrainian and White Russian minorities lived within Poland, but displays an eagerness to understand the problems of the day in a historical context.

The crux . . . lay in the fact that for over a century the country had been partitioned between three powerful neighbours, Germany, Austria and Russia. When eventually Poland appeared on the map of Europe in 1919, the peace treaties gave her more than her fair share of territory as well as an addition to her native population of some 8 to 10 million who were not Poles at all but belonged to the minorities such as Germans, Ukrains and White Russians. This portion was cut off from the rest by a strip of territory known as the Polish Corridor which had been given to Poland so she could have an outlet to the Baltic.[6]

These discussions would continue when Betty joined Edward in his bachelor quarters, which consisted of a small apartment, its living room comfortably but sparsely furnished with a large divan, a grand piano and a number of furs and skins scattered about on the polished wooden floor. After a supper of caviar and vodka, an hour of Chopin (Kulikowski was an excellent pianist), they would stretch out on the tiger-skin rug and drink and talk of whether there would, or would not be, a war. It was only natural, Betty wrote, that after they had enjoyed each other's company so much they should enjoy each other physically as well, and they would retire to the broad, low divan to make love. Later on, as spring sunshine warmed the Polish landscape back to life, they would drive into the country and find a secluded spot on the banks of the River Vistula where they could sunbathe naked and make love alfresco.

More often than not their talks were about the ominous political problems. In such manner she learned from Edward about a German proposal for partitioning Czechoslovakia, which he explained in detail. "It was top secret information at the Polish Foreign Office but Edward shared it with me as casually as he did other things," Betty recalled in her memoirs. Germany's occupation of Austria (the Anschluss) in March 1938[7] provoked a great deal of discussion. Betty's friends saw it as proof that Hitler had embarked on a course of aggression that might soon threaten Poland. On the evening after the Anschluss Betty and Edward were talking about this when he casually told her that he had positive information that Hitler did have further plans for annexation. His next victim was to be Czechoslovakia. "What is more," Edward said, "Poland intends to take a bite of the cherry!"

In her memoirs Betty tells how, during a game of golf on the following morning, she told Jack Shelley of her conversation with Kulikowski. She claimed Shelley reacted immediately by telling her of his association with the SIS and commissioning her to get more information for him. It does not seem plausible that Shelley would have shed his cover with Betty on the strength of this single piece of information that she had stumbled onto and small inconsistencies suggest that her memoirs tell only part of the story. This is not surprising, for when she was writing her memoirs many years later she got Shelley to "clear" what she wrote about the Polish episode (it was at his suggestion that she identified him as Jack Wordsworth). A more likely scenario, assuming that she had not been deliberately *sent* to Warsaw, is that on the strength of her reputation in Spain she had been approached shortly after her arrival in Poland (possibly the reason she had seen so much of Shelley in those first weeks), had already been passing on 'useful' information, and that this was the first important piece of intelligence which had come her way. There is little doubt, however, that from March 1938 she was actively working for the Secret Intelligence Service.

After her meeting with Shelley, Betty arranged another romantic tête-à-tête with Edward. He was quite unconcerned at her curiosity and talked freely. Having seized Austria, Hitler now turned his gaze towards Sudentenland, a mountainous part of Czechoslovakia containing some 3.5 million Germans. Edward explained to Betty that Hitler was proposing to annex Sudentenland through political agitation and threats of war. This would not only deprive Czechoslovakia of an area of her country but would as well strip her of important border defenses, for it was in Sudentenland that the Czechs had placed their modern fortifications.

In return for Poland's acquiescence in this first key step in the destruction of Czechoslovakia, Poland would later be allowed to annex a small piece of Czechoslovakia which the Czechs themselves had taken from Silesia in 1919 while the Poles were fighting the Russians It was an old sore to the Poles, and was the "bite of the cherry" to which Kulikowski had earlier referred. At the Munich conference in September 1938 the French and British gave Hitler their own acceptance for his annexation of the Sudetenland in return for a document which Chamberlain used to announce that he had secured "Peace in our time." Thereafter events did unfold very much as Kulikowski had told Betty they would.

After an ultimatum delivered to Czechoslovakia in early October, German units marched on Czechoslovakia and the Polish army began occupying a tract of land called Teschen (Trans-Olza). Participation in the dismemberment of Czechoslovakia cost Poland a great deal of sympathy in the Western democracies. Poland was a country that had herself suffered partition; it was difficult to condone her taking part in a similar act against a defenseless neighbour.

Betty's obtaining this information from Kulikowski and her delivering it to Jack Shelley established a pattern of work that was to continue for many years. London, once informed of the source of information, instructed Jack Shelley to recruit her as an agent. It was a role for which she was ideally suited in some ways, with her lack of fear in potentially dangerous situations, her love of adventure, her ability to mix and speak well with those people in high places who would have valuable information. Not least—given her *modus operandi*—was her talent to captivate men. On the debit side, she was untrained and had already demonstrated that she could be indiscreet. On her own admission, too, she was apt to become emotionally involved with her subjects.

The Secret Intelligence Service (SIS) operated on an extremely small budget pre-1939, under the nominal control of the Foreign Office. Its task was to gather intelligence, partly by espionage. Agents were recruited and sent off around the world under a variety of covers to do the best they could with the particular talents they already possessed. Jack Shelley, a former Guards officer, was typical. As for screening new recruits, it was usually enough that a prospective agent was known to and trusted by an existing agent. This often meant that the recruit had been at school or university with an agent and that his (or more rarely, her) family background was known. In this respect Betty had an important asset that she neglected to mention in her memoir. The best man at her wedding had been Captain John T. Godfrey, military attaché at the British embassy and a member of the free-spending set to which Arthur had belonged in Washington between 1927 and 1930. The military attaché at Warsaw in 1938 was none other than the same John Talbot Godfrey. Betty's family background was doubtless known and respected.

From her first reports British Intelligence must have known the methods Betty was using, but if there was any bridling or coyness back in London about what His Majesty's Government was condoning in employing her, the controller did not mention it. For her part Betty relished the idea of working for a cause—it gave her a *raison d'être*—and she especially liked the idea of being an agent for the British.

The instructions given her were simple. She was to cultivate the friendships of men in high positions in the Polish government, just as she had been doing, and encourage them to give her information. Jack Shelley primed her about particular subjects to listen for. To widen her circle, she was to do some entertaining, and was provided with a small allowance[8] so that her husband, who must not be told about her work, would not question the additional household expenditure.

None of this seemed difficult. Edward had already introduced her to many important diplomats and she delighted in feeding Shelley information in the form of regular typewritten reports.

Her new career took an important turn when at a dinner dance at Warsaw's American embassy she was seated next to the tall, elegant Count Michal Lubienski, who told her that he was *chef de cabinet* to Colonel Joseph Beck. Betty understood immediately that this meant Lubienski ran the foreign minister's office, and that he would have sight of all secret and confidential papers passing through the office. Had he been as ugly as sin here was a man she would have to have charmed, but happily no sacrifice was necessary. Not only was he good-looking but he had the engaging old-world courtliness of the Polish aristocrat: a charming man to charm.

The American ambassador to Poland, Anthony J. Drexel Biddle, and his wife were a rich Washington couple, well known to Betty's mother. Everything they did was on a lavish scale, and the dinner party in Warsaw on that romantic early summer evening was no exception. The light from massive chandeliers flashed on silver and crystal, red diplomatic sashes bestrewn with jewelled orders adorned formal evening dress for men. Rubies, diamonds and emeralds glittered on beautifully dressed women. After dinner an orchestra played in the flower-bedecked ballroom and Michal and Betty danced the evening away. During the last waltz the count whispered to Betty that something was happening to him that he did not understand (it is a fair guess that Betty understood it) and that he must see her again. He arranged to telephone her on the following day.

Next morning a large bouquet of roses was delivered to her apartment, and when Michal telephoned she agreed to have dinner with him. He came to her apartment where they had drinks and went out to a restaurant. Michal's wife had taken their children away for a holiday and would be gone for some weeks, so he was in no hurry to get home. Lubienski could not hide the fact that he was deeply attracted to her. Betty was a delightful dining companion, intelligent and sympathetic to Poland's difficulties; she entertained him with femininity and humour and yet managed to present herself as lonely and vulnerable due to her husband's enforced absence. The couple spent the night together.

After that, Betty wrote in her memoirs, they were inseparable. So that his servants would not gossip, Michal spent each night at his own home, but he arrived at Betty's apartment each morning at daybreak, letting himself in with the latchkey she had given him. While they lay together she encouraged him to talk about his work. After work he would call in for drinks before he returned to his office at about seven to see if any important cables or messages had come in, then they would go out to the theatre or to dine or to dance or sometimes simply to sit and drink at one of the innumerable open-air terrace cafés where music from string orchestras provided a backdrop to the sounds of conversation and laughter, as Warsaw's lights came on each evening.

As the days went by Michal showed Betty the Old City of Warsaw with its baroque charm, twisted porticoes and crooked steps. He introduced her to the thick honeyed mead served in taverns in the city's "Painted Square," and lunches of bright red fresh-water crayfish at riverside cafés. Small wonder in this romance-drenched atmosphere that Betty's professional interest became entangled with a deepening emotional involvement.

SIS was interested in the Polish Foreign Office because the London office suspected that Foreign Minister Beck was not playing entirely straight with them. Michal, a thoroughly loyal Pole, was himself troubled by the devious line in politics and diplomacy that Beck was taking and spoke freely to Betty about his concerns. Betty is very critical of Beck in her memoir, but it has to be said that through this period neither the Western allies nor the Soviet Union had shown much inclination to take on Hitler for the sake of the smaller countries of central and eastern Europe, and Beck's attempts to play both sides has to be understood in this context.

The information that Betty acquired and passed on to Jack Shelley provided SIS with evidence that Beck was indeed trying to make his best deal with Hitler while asking for British and French guarantees of Poland's territorial integrity. She was able to provide full details not only of Beck's contacts in Berlin, but also of his day-to-day secret communications within the Foreign Office and even with the prime minister. But it was even broader than that. No area of information was overlooked, from political to military intelligence, from industrial to economic facts. Even rumour and gossip circulating in the Polish Foreign Office were reported. It must be said that at least some of this material may have been available to SIS from other sources as well, but it is in the nature of intelligence work that the more sources providing confirmation of acquired information, the more reliable the information can be regarded, especially when the means of access of the several sources are disparate. Indeed, one reason why Betty's information did not prove even more useful was related to the fact that confirmation was not available for much of what she provided.

At this time Britain's intelligence coverage of Poland was very weak; Betty was virtually the only agent in Poland providing on a regular basis intelligence classified as "important" rather than merely "useful," and it was almost impossible to confirm much of what she passed on, especially those subjective reactions of Michal to Beck's motives that she learned about in Michal's arms post-coitus. Today the evaluation of intelligence data is far advanced, and the way Betty's information had been generated would likely render it especially credible, for those receiving the information could be sure at least that it had not been delivered to a known agent by someone who might benefit from its falling into the hands of British Intelligence. But in the late 1930s, Betty's methods, rather than lending an air of credibility to her information, cast a shadow of suspicion over it in the minds of many of those charged with the responsibility of protecting Britain.

The prime minister of the time, Neville Chamberlain, was one of those who discounted intelligence obtained through such distasteful methods. But Winston Churchill would soon prove less prudish, snobbish or squeamish about accepting whatever help might be useful in defeating Hitler. He had many clandestine contacts who passed on to him information such as that provided by Betty. Major Desmond Morton (a close friend and neighbour at Chartwell) simply took secret papers from Intelligence files and supplied them to Churchill. Churchill used the contents as ammunition for his famous harrying speeches that urged "the government of cowards" to action.[9]

In her memoirs, which were written in 1963, Betty did not disclose precise details of the information she obtained from Lubienski but she was connected, by others, with providing early intelligence reports on what is now regarded as the greatest secret of World War II—the German cipher machine known as Enigma, on which a team of Polish engineers was working at the time of her affair with Lubienski.[10] It is probable that Betty never realized the true value of the material she provided about this project. Her notes about this period merely stated how easy she found it to make highly trained, professionally close-mouthed patriots give away secrets in bed, and I swore to close my mind to everything confidential on our side. The greatest joy is a man and a woman together. Making love allows a discharge of all those private innermost thoughts that have accumulated . . . everything is released. I just never dared to learn our own secrets . . .

Ironically, this great secret—Enigma—had started life as a commercial venture in the 1920s, marketed openly as a "secret writing machine" that could transmit messages in unbreakable cipher. It was envisaged as a commercial rather than a military tool and only the Germans seem to have recognized the ultimate military potential of such a machine at this stage. Although the American military attaché in Berlin did arrange to have one sent to Washington in 1928, nothing came of this; the new secretary of state, Henry Stimson, firmly announced it as his opinion that "Gentlemen do not read each other's mail" and closed the cryptanalysis department.[11]

For some years prior to the American acquisition of this one machine, however, the small highly trained and motivated German army under General von Seeckt had been using a military variant of Enigma. In 1926, Poles in the Biuro Szyfrow (cipher bureau), monitoring German transmissions, first encountered a mechanically produced cipher that their finest cryptanalysts were unable to break. After obtaining several early models of the commercial Enigma the Poles understood what they were up against and in 1928 a team of brilliant young mathematicians—Marian Rejewski, Jerzy Rozycki and Henryk Zygalski, working under Major Maksymilian Ciezki, head of the German section of the Polish Secret Service—were set to work on the problem. They made good progress, for by 1933, with the aid of documents (provided by French Intelligence)[12] giving a list of the keys (settings) used over a period of two months in 1931, and thousands of unsolved German intercepts, they succeeded in decoding a series of Enigma messages. The main problem was keeping up with the regular changes introduced by the Germans, made possible by Enigma's unique design.[13]

The machine itself looked like a primitive typewriter. An operator pressing—for example—the letter A would find that the machine printed another letter, perhaps Z. So far this is similar to other cipher machines. But the riddle of Enigma lay in a complicated arrangement of three interconnecting wheels which carried the code letters, a variety of methods of setting up the machine and the random way the machine made frequent changes of these settings.

The act of pressing the letter A generated an impulse through Enigma's highly complicated wiring which caused the wheels to revolve through a series of permutations so intricate as to be thought by the Germans to be beyond calculation. If pressing the letter A produced a printed Z the first time, it was impossible for this to happen twice, for on the next occasion different contact points were now in touch with each other, and the electrical impulse would pass through a different section of the wheel's internal wiring. What is more, each of the three revolving wheels (which could be inserted into the machine in different positions thereby producing almost incalculable variations of possible combinations) could also be replaced by "spare" wheels containing yet further sequences of letters and alternative wiring schematics. It was only by retyping the ciphered message into an *identically set* Enigma machine that the message could be decoded.

The main difficulty for the Poles was that new settings (keys) were introduced on a daily basis. Even had they obtained an up-to-date machine it would have been almost useless without these daily settings. It has since been estimated that the possible number of permutations to discover the correct method of setting up one of these machines, without access to the daily key, was "not far short of one hundred and fifty million, million, million."[14] So the problem was not that the Enigma cipher could not be broken (as some British cryptanalysts thought), but that it could not be broken *consistently* without the aid of a sophisticated electro-mechanical device to establish the keying. To help them in this, the Poles developed a high-speed calculating machine. Compared to today's desktop computers the Bomba was primitive, but with it the Poles were able "to tackle some of the problems posed by Enigma at speeds beyond the scope of human thought."[15]

It is not the purpose of this book to fully explain or chronicle Enigma. It is mentioned here only in the context that by 1938 the British (who were well to the fore in the field of cryptology but were foundering as far as Enigma was concerned) were starting to suspect that if the Poles were not already reading German Enigma traffic they had reached an advanced stage in learning how to do so. There was concern that, should Poland be overrun—which was almost inevitable—this work would be lost. Jack Shelley had established contact with Polish Intelligence, but the Poles were not inclined to share the results of their work (as the British had nothing to give them by way of exchange), or even to discuss the subject. A further impediment to British-Polish co-operation was the fear that some in Britain were trying to court the Soviet Union as an ally against Hitler and that the price Stalin would likely demand in return would be a piece of Poland.

British Intelligence had information from elsewhere that Enigma machines were being built by the thousand, making it obvious that the German military forces were whole-heartedly committed to Enigma as a method of message transmission. If this project was so important to the Germans it became vital for SIS to learn more about it, and the Poles were the possessors of all the knowledge that existed outside of Germany.

This was the information which Shelley hoped that Betty would be able to acquire through her relationship with Michal Lubienski. And according to several sources this is exactly what she did. It was natural that Foreign Minister Beck should take a personal interest in the important project to break Enigma and because of this he was kept informed of progress in the form of regular secret reports. Not only did Betty produce information that the Poles had been able to read Enigma traffic but she was able to supply details of the Polish "Enigma" cryptanalysis unit, its location in the Kabacki Woods some 10 kilometres to the south of Warsaw near the town of Pyry, their manufacture of a small number of machines, and other information, such as their co-operation with the French secret service.

At least one writer has suggested that she obtained information that the Poles were working on a "portable" version of Enigma but it seems more likely that this was a reference to the new models introduced in September 1938, when the Poles learned that the Germans had upgraded the machine by adding additional wheels, thereby increasing the possible permutations.[16] It was not until January 1939 that the Poles admitted Britain into their discussions on Enigma when Commander Alistair Denniston headed a British delegation at a secret conference of Polish, French and British cryptanalysts that convened in Paris. Even there the Poles did not admit the fact that they had the ability to read German messages, though the British were now aware of this fact. It was in August 1939, seventeen days before the outbreak of the war, that the British actually got hold of a machine.[17]

The entire Enigma story was the most closely guarded secret of World War II, and indeed intelligence documents on the subject are unlikely ever to be released (though some of the results—_Ultra_ decrypts—are available in the Public Record Office at Kew). Histories written directly after the war made no reference to Enigma or to the role that British access to its secrets played in defeating Germany, causing historians to go back and rewrite their histories when the story became known in the 1970s.[18] It is therefore not surprising that so little has been written of Betty's role in getting information to the British about how far along the Poles were, even by Betty in her own memoir. So valuable was the source (by 1942 the British were decrypting 84,000 items of German traffic a month—including high-level strategic information) that the defense of the secret became the main task of "C," head of the British Secret Intelligence Service:

> In the end he became a prisoner of the secret, for he could not reveal it even in his own defense. Such a secret did it become, indeed, that at the bars of history Churchill felt compelled to dissemble about it, even 20 years later.[19]

But if Betty never spoke of her connection with the great secret (and John Shelley certainly never did), how did such information finally reach the public arena? One source is Sir William Stephenson. Stephenson (who will be discussed at greater length later in this book) was a rich Canadian industrialist, later identified as the world-famous superspy codenamed Intrepid. During the thirties he used his frequent travels in Europe, and his engineering and industrial contacts, to provide useful items of information of varying degrees of interest to Churchill's friend (and later his personal intelligence advisor), Major Desmond Morton.

As a radio expert Stephenson first became interested in Enigma for purely commercial reasons and claims to have made a basic investigation of its potential in the 1920s, but found it of no particular interest to his companies. He claimed that he learned of the military use of Enigma through his important commercial contacts, of whom he had many (such as Fritz Thyssen, the German steel manufacturer who poured millions into Nazi party coffers, until 1938 when he "lost control" of Hitler), and Charles Proteus Steinmetz, a Jewish scientist who had fled from Germany. Stephenson first heard of Betty Pack at this time because her reports dovetailed with the information he was supplying to Morton.

Sir William (he was knighted after the war) revealed the story of Betty's work to his biographers Harford Montgomery Hyde (a former intelligence officer who worked for a time in Stephenson's organization and knew Betty) and William Stevenson (no relation).[20] Both writers had access to documents supporting what Stephenson told them and many of these documents survive although, since the death of Hyde, some have been closed by the Foreign and Commonwealth Office. Sir William may or may not have been the source for other writers such as David Kahn (a leading cryptologist), John Costello and Nigel West, who also wrote about Betty's role in obtaining Enigma intelligence.[21] Richard Deacon, a prolific writer on the subject of espionage, interviewed a member of the intelligence team involved in the early days of Enigma, who told him that Betty had persuaded Michal to remove documents from Beck's office which she then copied before returning them.

At first we couldn't believe our eyes. Here was the missing link in the whole chain of our intelligence on Enigma. You see capturing the secrets of the Enigma machine was a major intelligence operation in itself, involving many people and many departments—SIS, the Admiralty Intelligence, the War Office etc. What Enigma did, to put it in terms the layman can understand, was to turn messages into an unintelligible scramble before transmitting it in Morse.

Many people played a role in obtaining these secrets, getting a detail here and another there. . . . The trouble was, you see, that there had been several variations of Enigma over the years, with new models coming out just to cause more headaches for the "I" boys. And that is where [Betty] came in with the most unexpected results . . . .[22]

I, too, was able to speak to someone who was in Poland in 1938, knew of Betty and her work and confirmed to me that Betty was passing Polish Foreign Office documents, on the subject of the Polish Biuro Szyfrow, to Shelley. In exchange for this information I offered anonymity, but wish to make it clear that I was entirely satisfied with the probity of my informant and information.

There is one additional important source that Betty was connected with Enigma that so far as I know has not previously been revealed. On July 3, 1990, William Stevenson (biographer of Sir William Stephenson) wrote to me:

> In 1971 or 1972 (I will have to check) General Sir Colin Gubbins spoke of Betty in 1938 in connection with Enigma after receiving a cable from Sir William to talk freely to me. . . .

That Gubbins (who became the head of SOE) was in contact with Shelley at that time is historical fact; the two men were to tour Poland together in the following year. Gubbins told Stevenson that Betty had discovered that the Poles were in possession of the vital "keys" to Enigma. But, as with Betty's work in Spain, unless the British Foreign and Commonwealth Office open SIS files to public researchers, it is unlikely that the *entire* truth in all its details will ever be confirmed.

No one, of course, suggests that Betty played the sole or even a leading role in the British acquisition of Enigma; many people were involved in the events leading to this. It may be that the information she obtained merely confirmed that which had been obtained from elsewhere. But that is the game of intelligence. It hardly ever happens that a single agent supplies an earth-shattering or unique piece of information; rather, the picture is pieced together from many isolated scraps of information, sometimes seemingly unrelated, often seemingly uninteresting in their own right, often duplicated by several agents, some from highly regarded sources and some from very doubtful sources. In this respect nothing may be disregarded, for the most trivial comment might provide the important link between two apparently unrelated items, thus supporting the authenticity of an item that might have been under suspicion of having been planted by the enemy.[23]

Intelligence sent to London was classified by MI6 under one of the following descriptions:

A. Very reliable (inside source)
B. Fairly reliable
C. Uncertain reliability
D. Doubtful reliability

1. At first-hand
2. At second-hand
3. At second-hand uncertain
4. Rumour[24]

Using this rule, intelligence gathered by Betty through her contact with Lubienski could only be classified as A1; though, her liaison with her Polish lover was starting to cause distress among many in the diplomatic corps, especially among the other embassy wives. Lubienski was not the only channel by which information leaked out from Beck's office, however. Beck was a persistently heavy drinker and on one occasion (prior to 1937), Franklin Roosevelt was informed by an agent that the foreign minister's dispatch case containing secret papers had been stolen from him by a woman while he was drunk.[25]

The summer of 1938 was glorious for Betty and made especially heady by the freedom she enjoyed over the long course of Arthur's absence, the *frissons* of excitement created by her work as an agent, the passion of her affair, with its half-sad overtones due to the inevitability of parting; and not least by the gaiety of Warsaw with its outdoor cafés; dancing by moonlight and always, music, laughter and stimulating conversation. Her ability to shut out the most dismal prospects for her future and enjoy only the pleasures of the present allowed her to feel that for the first time she was living life to the full; draining every last ounce of essence from it. For a few short weeks she was happy beyond her imaginings.

In the background of this happiness hovered the shadow of Hitler's military escalation. In August Germany called up 750,000 men for military service and almost immediately began a series of "manoeuvres" near the Czechoslovakian border. Emboldened by Hitler's support, Konrad Henlein, the leader of the Sudeten German party, rejected every one of Czechoslovakia's settlement proposals, and Britain and France had to face the fact that unless they encouraged the Czechs to give in to all Henlein's demands, a new world war might be about to break out.

But what were Hitler's real intentions? The information Betty had from Michal made gloomy reading, but how accurate was it? Was Hitler bluffing? Were his threats of war simply a negotiating tool to get the Sudeten Germans a better deal from the Czechs, as some were saying? Would he back down if the Allies held firm? At the Nürnberg war crimes trials we learned that Hitler was promising his generals that he had no intention of marching on Czechoslovakia unless he was "firmly convinced" that the British and French would not intervene on Czechoslovakia's behalf,[26] but the British had no way of knowing at the time about the assurances that Hitler was giving his generals. And of course, everything he said was designed to convince the Allies that unless the Czechs gave in to Henlein's demands, he intended to march no matter what the Allied response might be.

When Poland was invited by Hitler to send a representative to the Nazi Party Day rally at Nürnberg on September 13, Beck did not wish to appear to other countries as being a cohort of Hitler's by sending a senior member of government; nor did he wish to offend Hitler by sending a nonentity. He solved the problem by sending his *chef de cabinet*, Count Michal Lubienski.

When Betty learned of Michal's mission she invented a reason to accompany him, at least part of the way. He was to travel via Berlin where he had some business to take care of, Michal told her. Betty had a good friend in Berlin; her godfather, Sir George Ogilvie-Forbes, was counsellor at the British embassy there. What better excuse to give Michal than that she had intended for a long time to visit her godfather? It was not difficult to persuade him that they should travel together by train to Berlin; they spent two days there before Michal left for Nuremburg, having arranged to meet up again for the return journey. Betty then went on to Czechoslovakia, ostensibly to visit old family friends, the Wilbur J. Carrs at the American embassy in Prague.

Early in September Michal had told Betty that he believed Hitler had set a date for his invasion of Czechoslovakia for later that month. London already had this information from another source, but Betty was instructed to stay as close to Lubienski as possible and extract as much information as she could. Perhaps he would have more to tell her on the return train journey. Meanwhile, Betty set off for Prague and another mission as British Intelligence agent.

Chapter 6

1938-1940

*T*he Honourable Wilbur J. Carr, head of the American diplomatic mission in Prague, Czechoslovakia, like John Leche, was a minister rather than an ambassador and held the grand title of Envoy Extraordinary and Minister Plenipotentiary. At sixty-nine years of age he was nearing retirement after a period of service of over forty-seven years with the[1] Department of State.

He and his wife had known Betty since she was a teenager in Washington and were delighted to welcome her as their guest, even at this time of great concern over their host country's future. Rich and popular, they were an ideal cover for Betty's assigned task, for they were able to introduce her to everyone of importance in Prague, and she hoped to meet a member of Konrad Henlein's staff.

Henlein, the youthful leader of the Sudeten Germans in Czechoslovakia, had his office in Prague. A physically attractive man (suspected by some of being homosexual) and a persuasive talker, throughout that summer of 1938 he had busied himself trying to charm Czechoslovakia's allies into supporting him. In an interview with Churchill he had tried to persuade the great man that he would try to restrain Hitler in respect of Czechoslovakia and limit the demands of the Sudeten Germans to "autonomy." In reality he was totally in the pay of the Nazis and reported back to Ribbentrop on all these meetings. On September 1, 1938, he met with Hitler to finalize plans for German accession of Sudetenland.

In order to stave off a German invasion, Czechoslovakia had by then met almost all of the Sudetenlanders demands, but talks were broken off by Henlein on the pretext that the concessions had come too late. By September 14, the day after the Nürnberg Rally, peace was already teetering; having ordered the British fleet to alert status, Chamberlain flew to Berchtesgaden to talk to Hitler. Henlein chose the day of this summit to make open demands for immediate German accession of Sudetenland and then fled to Germany to escape arrest.

Betty's task in Prague was to obtain any information that might add to what SIS already knew about the German plans for the invasion and dismemberment of the country.[2]

Originally she had intended, through the Biddles, to meet highly placed individuals, but when she learned of Henlein's flight she met her contact in Prague, another member of British Intelligence, and they conceived an alternative plan.

Tantalizingly, the exact sequence of events and the name of her companion were not mentioned in her memoirs, and she wrote elsewhere that she was unable to reveal these details. Presumably Shelley could not allow it because of other agents involved. What is known is that not only was Henlein's office burglarized but Betty came away with a number of highly sensitive documents, at least one of which (Hitler's plans for annexation of middle Europe over the next three years) she copied and retained after passing the original on to Shelley. She used it to good effect in a newspaper article she wrote sometime later.

On the train from Berlin to Warsaw she encouraged Michal to talk about his work in Berlin, which included a meeting with Hitler. One important fact she learned was that Hitler had promised full German support for Poland in her territorial demands on Czechoslovakia. This information was passed to Shelley immediately—possibly even before Michal had a chance to report to Beck.

We now know that Hitler was feeding the Western Allies information to confirm their worst fears—that if he did not have his way on the Sudetenland he would plunge the continent into a new war. Others in London, Churchill for one, believed that Hitler could still be persuaded to be reasonable if only he were convinced that the West was prepared to go to war. From German papers captured at the end of the war, we now know that this latter group was right. But we do not know who in London in 1938 really believed which possibility, and by passing along what she learned on this trip Betty may have unknowingly served Hitler's plan.

Betty's return to Warsaw saw an end to the emotional happiness she had enjoyed over the past months. Not only had Michal's wife and children returned to Warsaw but Michal was also desperately worried that Beck would take Poland into an alliance with Germany. Their meetings became fewer and were less relaxed. Betty had always known that she would have to return to Arthur eventually but it was becoming obvious to her that the time of her parting from Michal was imminent and—quite apart from professional considerations—this was something she was reluctant to face. On the day after Michal's return to his office he told Betty that he had confessed to his wife and had told her that he wished to obtain a divorce and remarry as soon as Betty could divorce Arthur. In a recent interview Mme Lubienski could not recall her husband's ever telling her about this affair with Betty, nor his requesting a divorce. Quite naturally this is not the sort of memory a woman would want to hold on to dearly. But then again it does not seem the kind of thing one could forget. One must face the possibility that either Betty or Mme Lubienski was not being entirely truthful in her account of the incident; Mme Lubienski did, unwittingly, drop the information that Beck had actually written to Kennard complaining of Mrs. Pack's behaviour. But there is another possibility as well—that Michal had not yet told his wife, but that, knowing Betty well, he was testing for her reaction before going home and ending his marriage.

In this same conversation, Michal revealed to Betty that he had also told Beck about his plans; his superior had been appalled and had stated that he could under no circumstances countenance such a proposal. In the current political crisis Michal's divorce and remarriage to an American woman who had been married to a British diplomat was unthinkable and could only result in a forced resignation and the ruin of his career.

Betty listened to Michal's revelations and when he had finished she told him that she was equally appalled. She loved Michal but had never planned a permanent liaison. She would not be able to live with the thought that she had been responsible for the breakup of his marriage or the ruin of his career. There was also the fact that she had come to regard her personal freedom quite highly, and finally, felt a gnawing apprehension that Michal's actions might have alerted Beck to the possibility that there was more behind the relationship than a mere love affair.

As Betty talked, Michal became aware that he was about to lose her for good and his Polish sense of tragedy overcame him. He seemed obsessed with the thought that when war started they might be "on opposite sides." His wife was out for the evening so he took Betty home with him and made her walk round his study, like Madame Ranevska, touching everything, his books, pipe, favourite chair and other personal items, so that there would always be something of her presence there.

A few days later Michal telephoned Betty during the day. He seemed very nervous and told her that Colonel Beck was most anxious to talk to the British ambassador, Sir Howard Kennard, but had been unable to reach him. Attempts to talk to Clifford Norton and Robin Hankey had also failed and he was telephoning her to ask if she knew where any of them were. Since the ambassador had only just left her apartment, having tried and failed to persuade her to leave Poland (all the other wives except Mrs. Norton had already gone), Betty was able to tell Michal that he had just returned to the embassy.

That evening Michal went directly to Betty's apartment after leaving his office and asked her if the ambassador had said anything to her about his subsequent conversation with Beck. She had not seen Kennard since he left her earlier in the day and asked Michal if he knew what the "flap" was all about. He was very strung-up and tense and ignored her question, saying that perhaps the ambassador was right, war seemed inevitable and it would be safer for her to leave Warsaw. Betty told him he was talking nonsense.

He stayed only half an hour and shortly after his departure, Mrs. "Peta" Norton arrived. The two women had never been friends and had hardly even made a pretence of liking each other. Mrs. Norton was very forceful and said that the ambassador was now insisting that Betty leave Warsaw within forty-eight hours. Immediately after Mrs. Norton left her, Betty telephoned Jack Shelley who promised to look into the matter and do what he could. Betty then telephoned Clifford Norton.

Norton had formerly been private secretary to Sir Robert Vansittart, the permanent under-secretary of the Foreign Office from 1930 to 1937 and a man well known to have been a prime supporter of SIS when the political leaders of the day were less inclined towards an intelligence service. When SIS's meagre resources proved inadequate, Vansittart built up his own "private detective agency" in Europe, particularly in Germany, to gather intelligence which was passed through Liaison Heads in the Foreign Office to SIS's Broadway HQ.[3] Clifford Norton, too, believed strongly in the value of intelligence and he played an active role in its transmission despite the lack of interest from his political masters; until the outbreak of war he was a channel for information leaving Poland. Knowing that Betty was supplying Shelley with intelligence of a superior grade, he too said he would do what he could, though as the embassy counsellor he must have been only too aware of the diplomatic dilemma involved.

Betty's final desperate attempt to stay in Warsaw was a plea to Robin Hankey who lived across the street from her in Ulica Frascati. "She telephoned and said she was in awful trouble and could she come and see me. Then she sat on my sofa with her head on my shoulder and cried buckets. She said I must save her. . . ."[4]

Hankey promised to talk to the ambassador in the morning and there was nothing further for Betty to do but go home and wait in the hope that her friends could help her. Next morning both Norton and Shelley came back with negative answers. Despite all their arguments, the ambassador was adamant. Mrs. Pack must leave immediately. Shelley appeared very angry and thought it a strange situation that their best agent should be sent away and at such a time. There was "more to it than meets the eye," he ventured.

In her memoir Betty said she had never found out why she had been "expelled" from Warsaw and concluded that it was due to the jealousy of Mrs. Norton because of Betty's friendship with her husband. Further, Mrs. Norton made no secret of her irritation over Betty's relationship with Michal Lubienski. Admitting that she and Michal had perhaps not been very discreet and that their affair had become known about, Betty wrote: "[Mrs. Norton] had considerable influence with the Ambassador and may have put it into his head that I was leaking secrets to the Poles. . . ."[5]

Robin Hankey told me what he knew of Betty's summary dismissal:

> Yes, . . . there was quite a scandal. Beck had called Kennard and complained about Betty who, he said, was trying to break up the Lubienski marriage. Lubienski is dead now so I don't mind telling you this . . . Anyway Mme. Lubienski couldn't see why her marriage should be broken up by Betty.
>
> Perhaps in an attempt to handle it in the most diplomatic way Kennard got Peta Norton to see Betty. But the two women never got on and so when Betty refused to go I had to phone her and tell her she had to go. I was very harsh with her and told her she had to leave within 24 hours; her servant and child would have to follow on later . . .
>
> I certainly didn't know what she was up to with Jack Shelley . . . and saw her merely as a rather dangerous person to have around in a diplomatic environment . . . though equally she was a highly intelligent person.[6]

It seems inconceivable that Betty could not see that Kennard had no alternative, now that Beck had formally complained of Betty's affair with Lubienski. Poland was involved in a major crisis and one of its most important men was emotionally involved with the wife of a representative of another government. On the face of it Kennard had absolutely no option in the circumstances, no matter how valuable the information she was supplying. Nothing Jack Shelley could have said could alter this. But the revelations could, in any case, have made things very hot for Betty had she been allowed to stay on. How long would it have been before Beck suspected that his *chef de cabinet* might have confided in his mistress, if—indeed—he had not already recognized the possibility?

There is every reason, in fact, to believe that Shelley saw the potential danger at once and may have been responsible for putting out a cover story that would help kill any suspicions that Betty had been connected with British Intelligence. The cover story, passed through Peta Norton, was that Betty had been passing information learned at the British embassy to Lubienski and to pro-Nazi contacts at the Polish Foreign Office. This was a widely accepted fact throughout the diplomatic set in Warsaw, who felt that Betty had been shockingly indiscreet but—a plausible story after all they had been led to expect of her.

On the morning of September 27, Michal and Jack Shelley drove Betty to the airport where she boarded the plane for Helsinki. On the following day she flew to Stockholm and checked in at the Palace Hotel, recommended to her by Michal. Hardly had she reached her room than Michal was on the telephone begging her to return, saying that he had straightened everything out with Beck. Later she contacted Hallett Johnson, an old friend from Madrid and Saint-Jean-de-Luz days, who had just been moved to Stockholm as American consul general.

Johnson, who assumed that Betty had been sent away from Warsaw because of the potential danger of war, advised her to return to Warsaw if she wished to. The immediate danger had passed, he told her, and there was to be a summit meeting of Britain, Germany, France and Italy at Munich later that day. Betty telephoned Clifford Norton and begged him to see the ambassador and tell him that she needed to return to Warsaw to collect her child and pack her belongings. There was no reason, now that agreement had been reached at Munich, she said, that she should not be allowed back. Norton expressed grave doubts of being able to persuade the ambassador and later that day Betty received a cable to the effect that Kennard had refused permission for her return. Shortly afterwards, Ambassador Biddle would report to the State Department of

a stiffening, in the form of a drastic decree . . . Polish citizens who associate with persons on behalf of a foreign government or international organization against the interest of the Polish State [will be] subject to severe penalties. In [the event] of war these penalties [will] carry a death penalty or imprisonment for life. . . .[7]

Frustrated and disconsolate, Betty flew to London where she had a brief meeting with her mother who was on a tour of Europe. Mrs. Thorpe had just visited the Cassells at Dorrington to see her grandson. The Cassells thought her a frightful woman, loud and complaining, snobbish to a degree and with a grating voice which condemned everything she saw. "Nothing was good enough for her, the cars were too small, the roads were bad, the houses too cold . . ."[8] Nevertheless Cora took to Tony, who

used to balance on the footboard of my bed . . . and then with a flying leap, dive into my pillows looking for shillings. I loved him like my own son.[9]

Betty subsequently paid a visit to the Cassells and kept them fascinated with stories of her adventures in Burgos and Madrid during the civil war. "Her stories seemed so fantastic that we hardly knew whether to believe her or not . . ." the Cassells' daughter, Margaret, recalled.[10] Tony was now just turning eight years old, a healthy, lively little boy attending the local preparatory school. It was an unusual year for him, for his father had spent a few weeks at Dorrington earlier in the year after leaving his London nursing home, Cora Thorpe had completely spoiled him during her visit, and then to cap it all his mother turned up just before his birthday. It was not the start of a pattern, however, and his childhood would be behind him before he saw a member of his family again.

Following her trip to Dorrington Betty flew to the south of France to join Arthur who was convalescing in Saint-Jean-de-Luz but had already received news of a new appointment at Belgrade, Yugoslavia, which he hoped to take up in January.[11] She did not tell him about her work as an agent but she did tell him all about Michal. Clearly she placed no importance on the fact that she had been virtually expelled from Poland; she said that she had decided she could not live without Michal and wanted a divorce so that she could be free to return to him, if not to marry him then to live with him.

Arthur, still recovering from the effects of his stroke, refused to give her a divorce on the grounds that he would need her support when he returned to work in a few weeks' time. However, he was sympathetic to her need to see Michal again and also annoyed at the ambassador's cavalier treatment of Betty, which he took as a personal insult. Consequently he fired off a cable to Kennard: "Why will you not allow my wife back in Poland?" Back came the laconic reply: "It is in the interest of the Service that she does not return."[12]

Betty wrote that she could hardly believe the situation in which she now found herself. She knew that the value of the intelligence she had obtained from Michal was important—Shelley had classified it as Top Secret—and yet here she was, being prevented from returning to Poland as a *result* of her liaison with the man from whom she was obtaining the information. In fact, this puts a finger on an inconsistency which undermines her statement that she did not know the real reason she had been ordered to leave. She could not have been innocent of the fact that once it became known about, her affair with Michal was alone sufficient reason. While she was able to justify her behaviour to herself on the basis of the valuable information her liaison had yielded, she must have suspected that others—who did not know of her real work—viewed her as an indiscreet threat to diplomatic decorum.

Shelley's superiors apparently made no attempt to bring further pressure on Betty's behalf. Perhaps the ambassador simply set his face against Betty so strongly that nothing could be done. The Secret Intelligence Service in 1938 and 1939 had limited powers and the information they provided was not regarded highly by the prime minister; they may not have been in a position to force an issue. But it is clear that Betty was finished as an agent in Warsaw; indeed her return there could have been viewed as dangerous from several angles. There was a possible physical danger to

Betty if the pro-Nazis realized what she had been up to and this could in turn have led to identification of Shelley and his other contacts. On the face of it Shelley had no option but to close her down as an agent.

After consideration of her position Betty told Arthur she would remain with him, but made her agreement conditional. He must somehow obtain permission for her to return to Poland if only for a short time. Again she gave as her reason her unwillingness to abandon her family belongings. The resultant pressure by Arthur on the Foreign Office, claiming that it was essential that his wife return to pack up their possessions and collect their child and servant, eventually brought the grudging response that Betty might return for a few days "provided she promised not to see anyone." Betty gave the promise "with my tongue in my cheek."[13] She had no intention of honouring her word and indeed when she arrived at the airport Michal was there to meet her, accompanied by Jack Shelley and Sophie Wagner. After dining as a foursome, Betty and Michal went to her flat where they talked into the night. Both knew that there was only one end, now, to their relationship.

On the next day, as she began her packing, Betty had a call from Robin Hankey who suggested that they meet while she was in the city. She refused, saying that she had been ordered to see no one. Furthermore, she told him, she could not trust him not to go straight to the ambassador and repeat everything she might say to him. Later that day, having arranged to have the remainder of her belongings packed up by a removal firm, she left Warsaw and went with Michal to a country hotel where he promised her they would not be found. Before leaving she met Jack Shelley, who told Betty that her work had been invaluable and that she would certainly be contacted again by "the firm" no matter where she was. Within SIS everyone, from the chief—"C"—downwards, referred to the Secret Service as "the firm," as though it were a commercial corporation.

It was her last meeting with Shelley for some years, though she wrote to him occasionally, as a friend. Shortly afterwards Shelley married Sophie, but the twenty-year-old bride was killed a few months later in a German air raid. The couple were sheltering at military headquarters (in Luków where embassy staff had been sent for safety). Ironically, the embassy was not hit and Mrs. Shelley was the only casualty of the British mission.[14]

Betty and Michal spent a week together in their country hideaway. The autumn weather with its alternate days of bright sunshine filled with woody scents, and others of rain-washed melancholy, mirrored their own emotions of joy in each other's company and despair at the inevitable parting. During one discussion Michal cautioned her not "to go through life playing the role of Scarlett O'Hara," but to get some direction in her life and use her considerable abilities to some end.

Betty was to write that during those days, "we existed only for each other, but at last came the terrible moment when we had to say goodbye, one morning in early November. . . ." Michal drove her to the airport and at their parting was in tears, saying all the things that a heart-broken lover *would* say. "I'll find you again, somehow, someday—if it takes twenty years. . . ."

Staff at the British embassy apparently never learned of this romantic tryst, for when I mentioned it to Lord Hankey he was surprised. "No. I didn't know she'd spent that week with Lubienski; that was one in the eye for the ambassador. . . . As far as I remember we assumed she had returned to Pack within a few days."[15]

Betty recorded in her memoir that she set her chin and boarded the aircraft, again without looking back (she seemed to make a habit of this). "And that," she recalled, "was the end of my first secret service mission, and also the end of my big Polish affair." Michal wrote to her several times but their correspondence soon dried up. Betty thought that to encourage its continuance could only make the separation more painful and increase the physical longing for Michal that she was to experience for many months.

Michal Lubienski went on to make a distinguished career in the Polish Foreign Office. Despite his personal reservations about Beck's policies he was a very loyal and conscientious man. According to a dispatch from the American embassy to the State Department he was the last person to leave the Foreign Office in Warsaw during the German invasion and only then after he had made a huge bonfire of all remaining files.[16] He managed to get to France with his family and then to England where they settled happily after the war. Thirty-five years later Betty was in London, and hearing that Michal was living there attempted to make contact, but he was away from home. They never saw each other again.

Betty's diary does not relate how Denise and her nurse returned to Saint-Jean, or what happened to them while Betty was having her last romantic week-long leave-taking of Michal. She wrote that she travelled to Saint-Jean alone. Presumably the nurse was left to bring the child back alone, by train, possibly staying with relatives en route. Denise had still not joined her parents by mid-December when they set off together for duty at the embassy at Belgrade. Arthur quickly found he could not function there. "It did not agree with me," is how he put it in a somewhat diffident letter to London asking if a transfer to a more agreeable climate would be possible. To his surprise and delight he was advised by cable, almost by return, that he was transferred immediately to his old post at Santiago, where he was to take full charge of the Commercial Section.

The couple returned to France, where they were reunited with their daughter, and sailed for Chile on April 7. Arthur wrote home:

> Things do not look very hopeful in Europe so perhaps it is just as well for my health that I am going to the other end of the world. I am feeling very well indeed and continue to make good progress. . . . Denise and Betty are both very well and we are all together again for the first time in over a year. . . .[17]

A postscript from Betty in this letter tells them that Arthur is not only well but that his morale is very high and that he had made a remarkable recovery from what had been a massive stroke. After his initial spell in Osborne House in the Isle of Wight Arthur had had himself removed to London, where he undertook a course of intensive and difficult physiotherapy to alleviate paralysis down one side of his body. It was not easy for a man of Arthur's temperament to accept helplessness, and a friend wrote: ". . . we saw him struggling to regain the use of his limbs when perhaps ninety-nine people out of a hundred would have resigned themselves to their fate." This friend put Arthur's recovery down to sheer "dogged perseverance."[18]

Arthur's posting to Chile was a step backward in his career, for European postings were considered more important than South American, but as Foreign Office files show, Arthur's health problems played a major part in the decision. However, he had local knowledge and relevant experience. In her memoirs Betty states clearly that by this time she had lost contact with British Intelligence, and that this was a source of great disappointment to her.

At first she picked up her former life in Chile easily, riding, playing polo, and mixing freely in society. But she had been spoiled by her time in Warsaw. She now found the role of embassy wife even less acceptable than previously. She missed the danger and excitement of her work as an active agent and decided to work on an informal basis; keeping her ears open for information which she considered might be useful and asking probing questions. She took due note of the sympathy among many prominent Chileans for the Nazi cause and was alarmed by the new confidence in the German community. She put everything she heard into reports of a professional format, headed with the word "SOURCE," followed by the reliability of the source, an explanation of the situation in which the information was gathered, a summary of what was said, and sometimes concluded with her own assessment of the matter. She signed them E.P. and sent them to the ambassador, who passed them on to London.[19]

Foreign Office archives show that Sir Charles Bentinck did not make a habit of forwarding gossip from the wives of his diplomats to his Foreign Office superiors. He must have been impressed with the lucidity, content and accuracy of Betty's reports to have not only commented on them but enclosed them with his dispatches.

Throughout the summer, Betty's main attentions were engaged in making a home for Arthur and Denise,[20] so she was happy to keep her hand in the intelligence game in this minor way, but by August she had begun to fret. One of the first things she had done on arrival was to make contact with the Polish community in Santiago, and their letters from home kept her in touch with the ominous developments there. She shared the deep concern of her Polish friends for the future of their country. As well, their conversation brought her close to the exciting times she had left behind in Europe. The world was being turned upside down and she was on the sidelines. She longed, passionately, for close involvement.

The anxiety of the Polish community was not misplaced. On August 22, 1939, Hitler delivered a summary of his real design regarding Poland to his top generals. The transcript of his speech was made public after the war and reveals his murderous intentions towards that country:

I have sent to the East only my "Death's Head Units," with the order to kill without pity or mercy all men, women and children of the Polish race and language. Only in such a way will we win the vital space that we need. Who still talks nowadays of the extermination of the Armenians? . . . My pact with Poland was only meant to stall for time. And besides, gentlemen, with Russia will happen just what I have practised with Poland. After Stalin's death . . . we will crush the Soviet Union.

. . . The invasion and extermination of Poland begins on Saturday morning.* I will have a few companies in Polish uniform attack in Upper Silesia or in the Protectorate. Whether the world believes it doesn't mean a damn to me. The world believes only in success. Be hard . . . Be without mercy. The citizens of Western Europe must quiver in horror.[21]

One contact who was useful in bringing her back into what Betty called the "I" game, was Colonel Montagu Parry-Jones, the British military attaché at Santiago. It was through him that she made her initial attempts to contact British Secret Service chiefs in London.[22] She had met the attaché at several parties and marked him down as a target; he was soon hinting that he'd like to get to know her better. While out riding one day her horse shied and tossed Betty into a muddy puddle almost at the feet of Parry-Jones. Her laughter as he helped her to her feet and her remark "Well, we are getting acquainted" remained with him always. He arranged for Betty to work in the code-room at the embassy, and to "snoop a little."[23] What form this snooping took, or where it took place, has not come to light.

Her role as Arthur's wife and hostess provided a good cover for her attempts to gather the thoughts and ideas of Nazi sympathizers, and from all accounts she did this in a gracious, sunny way. But occasionally her need to flout conventionality showed through in her personal life. The

---

* In fact the German invasion was postponed at the last minute and actually occurred on September 1, 1939.

Packs had two very close friends, Reginald ("Rex") and Leslie Doublet. Rex was manager of the Bank of London and South America in Chile, and he and Arthur became close friends. While the two wives never achieved the same closeness, they were casually friendly and liked each other well enough to share shopping trips and tea parties. It is symbolic of the legend of Betty that one of Leslie's most vivid memories of their time together in Chile involved Betty's almost compulsive need to resist useless convention. One day the two women were shopping in the glowering heat of late summer. Seeing a dress Betty admired in a shop window the two women went in so that Betty might try it on. Leslie accompanied her into the changing room and was stunned when in a single movement Betty pulled her dress over her head to reveal that she had not another stitch of clothing on and was stark naked. Leslie's sharp, shocked intake of breath and mild protest that Betty "ought to wear some underclothes" were met with an impatient "Phooey! there's a war on. I haven't got time to worry about things like that."[24]

Although by this time she had attempted through the British Passport Control Officer to obtain some sort of active work she might do for MI6, all she was given was work of a mundane and minor nature in the coderoom at the embassy. But when in early September Hitler attacked Poland Betty felt she could not remain idle. Members of the embassy staff left to return to England to fight, and this made her even more discontented.

One aspect of her life in Santiago that had made her extremely angry in preceding months was the pro-German line taken by one of the leading newspapers in Chile. Consequently she went to see Carlos Prendis, the editor of a rival paper that had taken a neutral line, and suggested that she write a series of articles, free of charge, to present the other side's view. Prendis was not at all happy with the suggestion at first, but once again Betty was expert in getting a man to do her bidding. Before long Prendis agreed to allow her to write propaganda articles for La Nación.

Arthur was very much in favour but suggested that it would be prudent to get clearance from the first secretary at the embassy and this she did. However, after her first article appeared, the ambassador, Sir Charles Bentinck, asked her to come and see him. Such articles, he said, were a potential source of embarrassment to His Majesty's Government and she must not write any more until he had obtained the sanction of the Foreign Office.

If he expected her to submit to this dictum obediently and leave he had the wrong woman. More likely he had some idea that telling Betty Pack what he had decided she must do would not work; that in the past she had waged guerrilla warfare against the Foreign Service to get her own way. He allowed her to negotiate a compromise with him. He would allow her to continue writing under the pen name "Elizabeth Thomas," provided she submitted her articles to him for approval. He made many changes and curbed Betty's inclination to hurl personal insults at the Germans, which irritated her at times and caused her to describe him as a "stuffed shirt," but at least she was again involved and doing something constructive.[25] It is interesting to note that all those ambassadors and other high officials who tried to frustrate her were dismissed with similar epithets of disdain. In Poland the ambassador was a "real sourpuss," Bentinck was a "stuffed shirt," Beck was "the most unpleasant foreign minister in Europe."

Within a matter of weeks "Elizabeth Thomas" also began writing in the English-language paper *South Pacific Mail*. Her first article appeared there on September 21, 1939, entitled "The Polish Corridor"; it was a translation of the first article for *La Nación*, enhanced by illustrations, including a reproduction of the map she had stolen from Henlein's office a year earlier. This map shows clearly Hitler's aggressive intentions beginning with the annexation of Austria and Czechoslovakia in 1938 and 1939, and the invasion of Poland in 1939, events that had already taken place. But what was more interesting to *South Pacific Mail* readers was the purported future plans of Herr Hitler: Yugoslavia, Rumania and Bulgaria in 1940; while in 1941 Hitler planned domination of France, Switzerland, Luxembourg, Holland, Belgium and Denmark, and finally the Soviet Ukraine. Britain was not included in this long-term plan at that stage.

Other articles, presumably edited before publication by Bentinck but carrying the byline "Elizabeth Thomas," thundered under such headlines as "This is my last Territorial Demand"—Hitler's Excuse for Latest Theft:

When Hitler ordered the German invasion of Poland he said that his object was not the destruction of Poland but that he was merely going to change her frontiers. This was entirely consistent with the annexationist tendency of the Third Reich. Let us examine the pretexts used by the German Government for this frontier-changing tendency.

Hitler has created and nourished two theories for world consumption. One was that there must be a restoration to Germany of all the German territories that have been "lost" by her so that there should be "Ein Volk, ein Reich, ein Fuhrer," and the other was that Germany needs more living space. The annexation of Austria and of the Sudetenland were presented to the world under the camouflage of the first theory. The return of Memel to the Reich, said Hitler, was based on the principle of auto determination and was simply the recovery of territory inhabited by people of German origin. Then came the turn of Danzig and the Polish Corridor in the Polish province of Pomorze. How was this accomplished in accordance with either of the Nazi theories?

I was in Danzig after the Nazi propaganda campaign for self-determination and consequent union with the Reich began and I heard the story from both the Danziger and the Pole. . . .

A history of the Port of Danzig follows and a powerful summary of what Hitler had done, and why, summarized the present position:

Briefly, the Nazi objective in the union of Danzig and the Polish "Corridor" with Germany was not, and could not be on any grounds, the restoration of German territory to the Reich. Hitler knew that he must exterminate Poland and this he would have done through economic strangulation and political and military pressure from a completely German Danzig. The frontiers of Poland became intolerable to Germany not only because they were those of a strong independent state (any independent state with tempting territory is "intolerable" to the Third Reich) but also because those frontiers were an obstacle to the Nazi programme of world domination. . . .

It is interesting that Betty felt the need to excuse Poland's behaviour in seizing Teschen, an act which many in the West found unforgivable:

"Poland has committed no aggression. She has only resumed, with the full consent of the world, territory which was hers for centuries and to which the Third Reich had no more right than a robber has to his booty. . . ."[26]

Material for the pieces appears to have come from overseas, so it is obvious that at least in the latter stages of this phase she had outside help and perhaps official guidance as to the content of her articles. In addition it is known that both Arthur and Rex Doublet aided and encouraged Betty in the construction of some of her articles and she undoubtedly had the help of members of the Polish community. Soon her journalistic efforts, their contents and tone, became the most talked-about item in Santiago society.

Under such headlines as "Development Plans which the War has Stopped," "Poland's Economic Vitality," and "The Polish War Machine," she was able to give full vent to her frustrated need to serve a cause. But the German community became so annoyed with the articles that a pro-German journalist was recruited specifically to answer, refute or deny Elizabeth Thomas's assertions. When she received several threats to stop writing "or else . . ." she obtained a revolver from the naval attaché, and to the irritation of embassy officials, and more especially to their wives, practiced firing it in the embassy grounds. She continued to create small jealousies in the close society in which she moved, but this was almost inevitable given that she no longer felt any emotional tie to Arthur other than that of friendship.[27]

Eventually, and predictably in such a small community, the real identity of Elizabeth Thomas became known and Betty received personal warnings from the German ambassador that unless she stopped writing he would make a formal complaint to the Chilean government that she was abusing her position as wife of a British diplomat and request her expulsion from the country. Despite Arthur's partial paralysis his career was proceeding satisfactorily once more and such an occurrence would have undoubtedly affected it. Sir Charles Bentinck had only good reports to make about his Commercial Counsellor,[28] and when in March the ambassador had occasion to travel on a special mission to Bolivia he suggested that Pack should be left in charge pending the return of the first secretary, Richard H. Allen, who was temporarily absent.[29]

The brief spell as chargé d'affaires breathed new life and ambition into Arthur and Betty was quick to back him, for she had plans of her own now that Arthur's recovery was assured. He had put up a "magnificent fight" against his disability and had "obtained magnificent results," she told Arthur's family, and by the summer of 1940 was "well installed in Chile, with his work going well, in a well-run house and with well-trained servants."[30]

Happy in the conviction that Arthur was now independent of her, Betty made arrangements to pursue her own aspirations. These did not include Arthur or Denise.

Chapter 7

F or months Betty had made various attempts to contact the SIS
and find work as an agent. She wrote via the diplomatic bag to
what she called "intelligence headquarters" in London, reminding
them of her past work and asking to be considered for intelligence work,
preferably in occupied Europe. It was not until June 1940 that she had
a positive response. The reply from the War Office in London was worded
somewhat austerely in Betty's opinion and said that should she think of
returning to England she might be of assistance in the war effort. Yet

despite its impassive tone, the letter would turn out to be exactly what she had been hoping for.

She began immediately to make arrangements to travel to London. During the months that she had been writing her articles and caring for Arthur she had worked very hard and had begun to look tired and thin.[1] She told Arthur now that she had to get away for a while and intended to visit her mother while it was still possible to travel easily. She left Santiago on what was ostensibly to be a holiday of several months' duration, but in reality she hoped to be sent into occupied Europe as an agent.

It is worth discussing at this point the part which women of spirit and intelligence such as Betty were starting to play in the war. In today's more cynical era it would be difficult to re-create the climate that existed in 1940. Young people had been brought up believing that something was expected of them; duty was paramount among virtues. The sacrifice of the previous generation (in World War I) was before them, and there had already grown up an almost universal desire to defeat Hitler and permanently reverse Germany's aggressions. This fervour was fuelled by patriotic films, newspaper articles, newsreels and radio programmes, all received unquestioningly by a mass audience brought up to believe what they saw and heard. Not that what they heard and saw was untrue. By mid-June 1940 Hitler's armies had smashed their way through Holland, Belgium and France; they had driven the British army out of France and held Europe in thrall. Winston Churchill had been in office as prime minister for barely a month and prospects looked as grim for England as they would get, when he made the speech that inspired Betty's generation to make their own sacrifices:

> The Battle of France is over. I expect that the Battle of Britain is about to begin. Upon this battle depends the survival of Christian civilization. Upon it depends our own British life, and the long continuity of our institutions and our Empire. The whole fury and might of the enemy must very soon be turned against us. Hitler knows that he will have to break us in this island or lose the war.
>
> If we can stand up to him, all Europe may be free and the life of the world may move into broad, sunlit uplands. But if we fail, then the whole

world, including the United States, will sink into the abyss of a new Dark Age made more sinister . . . by the lights of perverted science. Let us therefore brace ourselves to our duties, and so bear ourselves that, if the British Empire and its Commonwealth last for a thousand years, men will say, "This was their finest hour."

Yet, experiencing the same natural urge to protect home and hearth as any man, and subjected to the same calls to service, women were formally denied an active part in the fight against Hitler. They were not allowed to carry firearms in the armed forces and French women, at the outbreak of war, did not even have the right to vote. An elite core of women who preferred not to be part of prescribed women's occupations, such as the British WAAFS, WRENS and WRAFS, chose—like Betty —to explore alternative avenues of service.

For many this service would lie in resistance movements within their own countries. There are countless instances of women working at all levels, from simply ignoring the stranger who had suddenly appeared next door under the guise of being a neighbour's son but who was more than likely a member of the resistance or even a foreign intelligence agent; to providing shelter, passing messages and equipment, perhaps belonging actively to a resistance cell or organized escape line. In cold print, to a generation brought up vicariously on TV action-women, such activities may not seem terribly exciting, but for those in occupied countries the danger was acute and all the more terrifying because to the woman in-volved home and family, perhaps even her children's lives, were at risk if she were discovered.

For such women living in unoccupied countries, or those who had escaped from occupation, there was another way to make an active con-tribution to the war effort. Service within the Intelligence organization, which for most meant, eventually, within the shadowy Special Operations Executive (SOE). This provided an unusual and often highly dangerous form of personal involvement.

Over the course of the war this agency was to provide immeasurable help to the Allied cause through the supply of men and women who coordinated the underground resistance which was to prove so crucial to the eventual defeat of Nazism. SOE came into being in July 1940 when Churchill sent a brief, handwritten memorandum to the War Cabinet outlining his idea for a new Special Operations unit. Its function, he said, would be "to co-ordinate all action by way of subversion and sabotage against the enemy overseas. . . ." The War Cabinet approved and SOE was born on July 22, and placed within the Ministry of Economic Warfare (MEW) under Dr. Hugh Dalton.[2]

Naturally it was a secret organization, so secret indeed that almost a year later in May 1941, just after the first group of agents was established in France,[3] Maurice Buckmaster, one of the chiefs of the organization, was still encountering problems when he sought help from *within* his own intelligence department (Ministry of Economic Warfare) to fulfil Churchill's instructions to "Set Europe ablaze" using the methods of subversive warfare:

"This is Major Buckmaster, French Section of the SOE . . ."

"Of what?"[4]

But secrecy alone was not responsible for the troubles that beset the embryonic SOE. Inter-departmental rivalry and petty jealousy was rife within the entire intelligence service and did almost more damage than enemy agents who had infiltrated the service (there were some, despite official denials). Churchill's conception of the new force, which crystallized in the weeks following the fall of France and the evacuation of Dunkirk, had at its heart the intention of destabilizing the Nazi foothold from within, in all occupied countries. He reasoned that the best way of achieving this was to send to Europe small highly trained groups of agents to foster the spirit of resistance, to organize and help arm those who wished to fight. Every type of subversion was to be encouraged in this respect: "including industrial and military sabotage, labour agitation and strikes, continuous propaganda, terrorist acts against traitors and German leaders, boycotts and riots. . . ."[5]

Although when originally conceived the ideal agent was thought of as a man, the French section of SOE, in particular, used a significant number of women who formed more than a quarter of the force;[6] it was soon recognized that there were tasks better performed by women than men. Women would be less conspicuous (and therefore less prone to be stopped and questioned) walking about the streets in France, for example, than a man of fighting age who—even the dimmest Axis soldier could reason—should have been either fighting or working. They often tended to be more manually dexterous with radio operation and more patient at waiting for contacts than male counterparts, and SOE's chiefs were quick to appreciate that even these practical considerations aside, the more respected qualities of courage, ingenuity and leadership were by no means confined to one sex. Initially, there was a great deal of debate in the Baker Street headquarters as to whether it was "legal" to use women in this type of work, but Churchill resolved the dilemma by ruling that in the fight against the Nazis no holds ought to be barred.[7] Once this policy was established women were treated almost as equals in the SOE.

Recruitment took many forms and more than one agent became involved simply because she had answered an advertisement for a bilingual secretary. Some women who knew or guessed at the organization's existence actively sought recruitment within the agency. Others, possessing the necessary requirements of service—fluency in a European language coupled with a strong reason for loyalty to an occupied country—found themselves "invited" to present themselves for interview with regard to a way in which they could help the war effort. Their names might have been passed by word of mouth by a personal contact, by a civil servant who noted in one of the innumerable forms one had to fill in during the war for ration books and identity cards that the applicant was half French or half Italian.

All received a vaguely worded letter similar to that sent to Betty, inviting them to the interview at the War Office: "Your name has been passed to me with the suggestion that you possess qualifications and information which may be of value in a phase of the war effort. If you are available for interview I should be glad to see you at the above address. . . ." Those who attended invariably found themselves in a dingy room containing nothing but a trestle table and two hard chairs. The interviewer gave little away at first so that most wondered why they were there at all. It was only at the second or third interview that those who had passed examination were given the briefest information. There was never any attempt to persuade women to join. Indeed, the risks were openly laid out before them. That there was only a 50 percent chance of a safe return (in fact, of fifty-three women agents put into the field by SOE twenty-nine were imprisoned and twelve were either executed by the Germans or died in captivity). That if caught the *best* they could hope for might be death. That they would be working alone (except for local colleagues), and that if they were caught and tortured or otherwise abused, the organization could not extend any help.

Those who accepted the challenge found themselves undergoing SOE's comprehensive training course in one of a number of large country houses. The bucolic settings masked a range of activities ranging from the sinister—how to fight, maim and kill—to the practical: Morse code and wireless operation; the use of codes and ciphers; parachute dropping; fire-arms training and handling explosives, etc. During this gruelling period in which the recruits were deliberately subjected to maximum physical and mental stresses, they were also continuously assessed. Those who passed would be infiltrated into occupied territory by small boat or para-chute (one girl, Josiane Gros, parachuted almost into the arms of her mother who had gone in with an earlier mission and was now heading the local resistance "reception committee") to operate as couriers and "pianists"—the term used for radio operators—and general support, as-signed to a *réseau* headed by a male "organizer."

It is hardly surprising, given the state of excitement, tension, intrigue, close co-operation and mutual trust such work involved, that romances flourished between the men and women thus thrown together. Several women married their organizers; other relationships where one or both parties were already married were invariably doomed to a painful ending. Such liaisons were not encouraged—they made operators even more vul-nerable, especially in case of capture. The best agents left their personal lives at home, but even the best (of both sexes) were susceptible in such unusual circumstances.

To some of these women, service in the SOE meant leaving children—at times no more than babies—at home. This surely, more than any other factor, indicates the high level of motivation driving these women. Vera Atkins, Maurice Buckmaster's right hand in Baker Street, has said that there were as many motives as there were women. It is clear though, that whichever particular passion drove them, the urge to be part of the defeat of the enemy was irresistible to these women and it is equally clear that Betty Pack shared this urge.

In the field most women worked with singular success, some achieving tremendous personal triumph. Pearl Witherington (now Mme Cornielly) is one such woman. In the week leading up to D-Day, she found herself, through the illness of her organizer, leader of nearly 2,000 *maquis* in an area critical to the Germans because it was their gateway from Bordeaux to Paris. German troops were sent in to search for the resistance operatives and a large reward was offered for the capture of Pearl (code name Marie). At one point in that week in June her troops engaged some 2,500 men, the remains of a German division on its way to Normandy; the battle lasted fourteen hours and Pearl escaped only by lying in a cornfield for twelve hours under continuous machine-gun strafing. Colonel Buckmaster believes that this diversion directly contributed to the success of the D-Day landings.[8]

Another woman, Virgina Hall, an American journalist, contacted British Intelligence after she had already set up her own organization in Lyon; thereafter she worked through SOE. From the summer of 1941 until November 1942 Hall worked tirelessly, recruiting and organizing the activities of a large network of agents, sub-agents and resistance fighters. From providing shelter, to finding a new radio crystal or ration ticket, to establishing direct communications with London HQ, she managed, under cover of her nationality and profession (for a good part of this time the United States was not yet at war with Germany and Lyon was in technically unoccupied Vichy France), to evade capture or identification by the Nazis. She appears in cameo in other people's stories, "confident and mysterious . . . a striking figure; tall, red-haired and with a pronounced limp . . . in those early days of SOE's endeavours she flickered through the streets of Lyon and the lives of F Section agents, an *éminence rouge*."[9] She was the first woman to receive the Distinguished Service Cross.[10]

One story about this enigmatic agent is told by Maurice Buckmaster though other, slightly different versions exist. Hall had lost a leg as the result of a pre-war auto accident and, perhaps in a deliberate attempt to deflect unwanted sympathy, always referred to the wood-and-brass replacement leg as "Cuthbert." Forced to escape from Vichy France as the Germans marched in at the beginning of November 1942, she had to cross the Pyrenees on foot. Winter had already set in and it was only her indomitable self-will that enabled her to keep up with the able-bodied male members of the party. On her arrival in Spain she wired London that she was safe and well but that Cuthbert was giving great trouble. The officer who replied (in Buckmaster's absence) was uninitiated as to the identity of Cuthbert and assumed he was a sub-agent; he replied that if Cuthbert continued to give trouble he should be eliminated.[11]

Light-hearted moments were few and far between, however. The reality of war lay in the ultimate fate of such women as Odette Hallows, Violette Szabo, and Noor Inayat Khan. SOE operated on a military basis, never regarding itself as an espionage organization, and the women did not see themselves as spies.[12] But there can be no doubt that they were agents of an enemy power not in uniform and were regarded as spies by the Gestapo. Their mission was not primarily to gather intelligence but they could not avoid collecting "useful information," which was inevitably passed back to base, either by radio or through debriefing procedures. Hallows was betrayed and captured. In an unsuccessful attempt to force her to betray other members of her network, she was put through torture, during which all her toenails were pulled out with pincers, and was afterward imprisoned in appalling conditions. After liberation she married her former organizer, Peter Churchill.

Noor Inayat Khan, code-named "Madeleine," was taken after her *réseau* was penetrated. Operating one of the last networks in Paris she somehow survived for a year, though she took terrible chances and was careless of her own security in the field. It was not surprising that she was eventually captured (after transmitting important data by radio for many months); indeed it is surprising that she was not taken earlier. She, too, survived brutal torture only to die in Dachau shortly before the end of the war. Violette Szabo ("the bravest of them all," Buckmaster told me) suffered a similar fate.

Christine Granville was a former Polish beauty queen and a countess by birth. Half-Jewish, she had ample motivation for the work she undertook as an agent in occupied Europe. Once, when picked up by the Germans for questioning, she bit her tongue until it bled and—coughing up blood—convinced her captors that she had tuberculosis. She worked to great effect in the Middle East and then France under the code-name "Pauline." She was one of the survivors and after the war was awarded the George Medal and the OBE, but like so many women who had tasted the particular freedom that came with responsibility and danger, she found it hard to settle down to ordinary civilian life. She became a stewardess on the South African Line. Always possessed of a mesmeric personality, she attracted more men than were good for her. One, whom she felt sorry for, was a colleague on her ship. A poor specimen, not of her background or intelligence, and schizophrenic, he nevertheless fancied himself in love with her. He eventually murdered her in a fit of jealous rage when she made it clear that she could offer him only platonic friendship.[13] Few women who worked as agents were able to make a satisfactory family life after the war.

The British were not the only force employing women in such roles. After the United States entered the war, American women made similar contributions through the OSS. Virginia Hall returned to the United States to work in and for OSS, having evidently persuaded OSS chief William Donovan that her knowledge and abilities were essential to victory. By the end of the war she was running a network near Nevers for the OSS.[14]

Another American woman working in the field was Lieutenant Jeannette Guyot, an OSS agent who was parachuted into France on February 8, 1944, as a member of the "Pathfinder" mission. As the principal liaison agent of "Pathfinder" she travelled widely over the northern half of occupied France to contact, personally, the agents who were essential to the mission due to begin in April as the first element of the D-Day operation. It needs little imagination to recognize the dangers under which she worked, travelling at this crucial time when everyone, friend and foe alike, was nervous and suspicious of strangers. She performed her task admirably and though she was only twenty-five years old became the heroine and the symbol of the entire operation. [15]

By 1940, Betty had proved that she had all the essential attributes of a good field agent: intelligence, fluency in languages, ingenuity, bravery and ruthlessness to do what had to be done. What is more she had experience in covert operations. Her one fault (in retrospect) seems to have been her habit of falling in love with her subjects, though she never sacrificed her work for her lovers. Nor was Betty prepared to wait until she got to England to start her work as an agent. It was perhaps more than coincidence that the ship on which she booked her passage to New York, the RMS *Orbita* sailing from Valparaiso on July 4, was also carrying a large number of Chilean delegates to the Pan-American Conference in Havana. Betty quickly cultivated two of the delegates, Senator Rodolfo Michels and Senator Rafael Gumucio. As a result of long conversations with them she was able to send from the first stop at Callao near Lima, Peru, a letter and a typewritten report about their mission to Sir Charles Bentinck.

This report, forwarded to Lord Halifax by Ambassador Bentinck, provided information on the political sympathies of the forty-five delegates to the conference, with particular emphasis on six actively pro-German gentlemen, and gave other information such as the points to be raised by the Chileans at the conference, their policy on fifth column activity and their opinions on England's chances of defeating Hitler:

> [The Chilean Government] does not believe that Germans in Chile will take any steps unless Hitler wins the war. On this point, the Government is certain that Hitler will not win, and that if England resists for six months he will be defeated inasmuch as "no army will fight without food." My impression is that the Government is far more preoccupied with the Communist menace in Chile. . . . [16]

Almost as interesting as the ambassador's letter and Betty's report, which are archived in the Public Records Office at Kew, are the remarks scrawled by staff at the Foreign Office in London on the report when it was received a month later: "Mrs Pack is a forceful American lady . . ."; "I quite agree [with Mrs Pack]"; "Copy to M of I (Ministry of Information) and Political Intelligence Dept with Mrs Pack's memorandum attached. . . ."[17]

When the ship docked at Havana Betty's godfather, George Ogilvie-Forbes, was there to meet her. The last time they had met was in Berlin, when Betty was on her way to Prague. Clearly her intelligence background was no secret to him, for he immediately introduced her to the Secret Service representative, "our man in Havana" as Betty gleefully called him in her memoirs. She was in no special hurry to continue her journey for she readily left the *Orbita* at Ogilvie-Forbes's suggestion and remained in Cuba for two weeks before taking another ship to New York. From there she went to visit her mother in Washington.

During the three weeks she spent in Washington she met Sir Charles Orde, newly appointed British ambassador to Santiago on his way out to Chile to replace the man Betty had called a "stuffed shirt," Sir Charles Bentinck. Orde was clearly impressed with Betty, for he mentioned the meeting in a letter to the Foreign Office: "My initiation as Ambassador was a sort of crescendo from the moment I met the Commercial Counsellor's wife in Washington. . . ."[18]

Cora told Betty that an old friend of hers had returned to Washington only a few weeks earlier as naval attaché to the Italian embassy. It was Alberto Lais, the distinguished officer who had long ago paid visits to her at school in Wellesley and created so much excited conjecture among her classmates. Betty had last seen him at her wedding; he was then an under-secretary in the naval attaché's office but was now, Cora told her, an admiral. Betty telephoned Admiral Lais to suggest that they might meet but his response to her call was cool and he told her that as their two countries (presumably he meant Britain and Italy) were at war he thought it would not be possible for them to meet and resume their friendship.[19] If he had been more sensible than romantic he would have stuck to this course.

On September 13 Betty purchased a one-way Pan American Airways ticket from New York to Lisbon at a cost of $318.75.[20] This was not a simple transaction in those difficult times. But Betty had good contacts at the British embassy—one such was Angus Malcolm, whom she had last seen in John Leche's office at Valencia—and using her contacts and the letter she had received from the War Office in London she obtained a transatlantic travel permit from the British embassy. This not only enabled her to purchase the ticket but to obtain a flight within weeks at a time when other passengers had to pull strings to get a flight within three months.

It was a long journey, taking four days to complete, the circuitous route made necessary by the fuel limitations of the aircraft. Flying via Miami and Jamaica to Natal in Brazil, where the Clippers landed before crossing the South Atlantic to reach Monrovia, capital of Liberia; then up the West African coast to Portuguese Guinea before the final leg which set them down on the River Tagus.

When she arrived in Lisbon Betty was met by Colonel Montagu Parry-Jones, the former military attaché in Santiago who had been her riding companion and a good friend; and as he put it later, "we used to snoop a bit together."[21] He was able to secure Betty a "priority" flight to London. Unfortunately the seaplane on which she was to travel developed engine trouble as it began its take-off run up the River Tagus and the flight was aborted. Betty returned to her hotel to wait until repairs had been effected.

When she arrived back at her hotel she found a cable there from Arthur. Clearly her movements were not secret to him. Betty always claimed that Arthur knew nothing of her secret activities and one wonders what excuse she had given him for flying to Europe into an ongoing war. Surely it was not merely that she wanted to see their son, for she had had ample opportunity during peace-time to go and had made no special effort. Arthur may, of course, have learned of Betty's movements through Sir Charles Orde, who arrived in Santiago at about this time and who may have been aware of Betty's application to the Washington embassy for a travel permit to fly to Europe.

Arthur's cable was a plea for her to return to him, at least temporarily. An important British trade mission to South America, headed by Lord Willingdon (a former viceroy of India), was due to arrive in Chile in December and as Commercial Counsellor Arthur would be required to play a major part. He needed her to act as official hostess, Arthur cabled. Would she please return and help him?

It speaks volumes that Betty immediately dropped her plans to fly to England and arranged to return to Chile. Love had been absent from their relationship for a long time, but affection and friendship remained and these commanded loyalty and sacrifice. She was concerned that her return to Chile might spoil her chances of future work in the Secret Service but through Parry-Jones she was able to send an explanation to London of her reasons for postponing her plans, giving her mother's address in Washington as a contact address.

If it was exceedingly difficult to get flights from America to Portugal it was virtually impossible to get flights going the other way. Every wealthy refugee in Europe was ahead of Betty in the queue. With no official reason for her journey she was lucky, even with her diplomatic contacts, to get a berth on an American ship headed for New York. A shipboard romance with a man whom she names in her memoirs only as "Norman W." helped to while away the tedious Atlantic crossing.

Norman did not realize that he was only Betty's shipboard diversion and fell in love with her. Indeed, he proposed marriage. In her impulsive and playfully passionate way Betty enjoyed the romance and went along with it after they arrived in the United States. She booked a passage to get her home to Chile in December and went to stay for two weeks at Norman's opulent home in Newport, Rhode Island. At his request she invited her mother for the weekend. Possibly Norman thought that if he could impress the mother it would have a good effect on the daughter. He had it partly right.

Cora was bowled over by Norman, his home and his wealth, and at his prompting tried to persuade Betty to divorce Arthur and marry this "divine man." When Betty told her that as a Catholic, Arthur would never allow her to divorce him, Cora said she would go to Chile and see Arthur and explain to him that he was ruining a marvellous chance for Betty. Her concluding remarks to her daughter probably helped Betty reach a decision. "Just think of all the wonderful things you could do for me," she said.

Sharply telling her mother that she was "talking like a Madam," Betty told her that even if she were to persuade Arthur on the question of divorce she would never marry again unless she loved the man. Cora never mentioned the matter again.[22]

Mother and daughter travelled to New York to spend a few days there before Betty's ship sailed. Norman was forgotten when Betty met a young naval lieutenant in the Ritz-Carlton Hotel in New York where she and Cora were staying. Lieutenant Paul Fairly was an Irish-American from the Midwest. When Betty met him he was in New York on official business; it did not take Betty long to find out that he was based in Washington and worked in the Office of Naval Intelligence. They seem to have become close very quickly, for having elicited this fact Betty told him that she had worked for SIS in Europe and was trying to return to it. Before she left she had extracted a promise that he would use his contacts to try to help her. Clearly, from subsequent developments, she and Fairly had already become lovers. All the same it does seem surprising that Betty should have been able to extract information and cooperation so quickly from a member of an organization not normally noted for indiscretion. Perhaps it is an indication of how well she had perfected her clam-knife skills.

Betty and Fairly agreed that when she returned to the United States from Chile in January they would meet again. Meanwhile he would keep in touch with her. Cora was introduced to Lieutenant Fairly, and an arrangement was made that she would contact him immediately should anyone try to reach Betty while she was travelling. It is clear that Mrs. Thorpe learned about Betty's activities in the Secret Service very early on in the war—almost certainly at some time she bullied Betty into telling her—but at this stage she seems to have known only that her daughter wished to participate in secret war work.

At the Panama Canal Betty received a cable from Fairly advising that "our friends have contacted your mother and wish to communicate with you." At the next port of call Betty contacted the British consul and asked him to send a message through Fairly advising that once the Willingdon mission departed from Chile in January she would be available for any work they considered suitable.

Her return to Arthur was not without its problems. He assumed that after her "holiday" his wife had now got "all this nonsense out of her system." After the trade mission had departed, he was stunned when Betty told him she was leaving again. Emotionally undemanding himself, Arthur thought that since her return he and Betty had reached a new plateau of understanding and tried to persuade her to stay with him. Knowing that it would hurt him deeply, but unable to find any other way of making a permanent break, Betty told him she had been unfaithful to him with Paul Fairly and was prepared to give him written evidence of her adultery so that he could obtain a divorce should he wish to do so. In fact she had probably just become aware that she was pregnant by Fairly, though whether or not she included this in what she told Arthur is not known. In any event it is clear that Betty had reached the point where, despite her strong loyalty to Arthur as a friend, she was no longer able to remain locked into a marriage that was emotionally and physically unfulfilling. But it is equally clear that the driving force in Betty's life, as 1940 drew to a close, was a fierce determination to take up her work again in what she regarded almost as a holy crusade: the fight against Hitler and the ethics of Naziism. The SIS had indicated that she could be of help; she had reached a point where she was not prepared to allow anything to stand in the way of her participation in this fight. She knew that she had particular skills that could be of assistance: her intelligence and skills in languages, her ability to move freely at all levels of society and her ability to charm important men into confiding in her matters which they would probably never have revealed under torture. She had been told by Shelley and others that her work in Poland during the run-up to war had been of utmost importance. Now that battle had been joined and Hitler's star was in the ascendancy, she was constitutionally unable to stand back and watch the fight from a distance.

When Betty left Santiago Arthur was too upset to see her off. He made an excuse not to accompany her to the train for Valparaiso, but Sir Charles Orde, his ambassador—a relative of Eleanor Campbell-Orde (Arthur's long-ago sweetheart)—was travelling to Valparaisso on the same train and escorted her to her ship.

One may ask about Denise in this domestic upheaval. The little girl was five years old at this time. For the time being she was to be looked after by her nurse, Juanquita, and she would attend the local primary school in due course.

Betty had no particular women friends in Santiago. Her reputation and her forceful manner, not to mention the way in which men seemed to gravitate around her at any social gathering, had not led to popularity within the ranks of embassy wives. But the apparent abandonment of Denise merely to join her mother in the safety of Washington earned for Betty the condemnation of every woman at the embassy.[23]

Chapter 8

*B*etty's journey to New York was enlivened by an incongruous incident. It was normal practice for any diplomat of Arthur's rank to be granted certain courtesies while travelling. The traveller would be provided with special customs clearances and, usually, would be met at each overnight stop by a member of the local British embassy staff and escorted to whatever accommodation had been arranged. As Arthur's wife, Betty was entitled to the same privileges, and the embassy at Santiago had accordingly cabled the minister at the British legation in Peru, Mr. Courteney Forbes, to advise him of Betty's arrival in Lima.

Betty had met Forbes previously, in the company of Arthur, and had not given him much thought. He was an unprepossessing man who made no particular secret of being anti-American, but this had not bothered Betty particularly. Her intention during her short stay in Lima was to contact an old friend from Madrid days, Señor Paradol, who had been the Peruvian minister there. So she was somewhat taken aback when shortly after the ship docked in Callao in the early morning, she got out of bed in her nightgown to answer a knock at the door assuming it was a stewardess, and found Forbes instead. Before she could react he had stepped inside and locked the door after him, following which he stepped forward and threw her down upon the berth. Possibly something of Betty's reputation had preceded her arrival, for His Majesty's minister clearly expected no resistance and when Betty fought him he attempted to rape her. "Evidently," Betty recorded, "the sight of me in my diaphanous nightie was too much for him."[1]

After a short struggle she managed to reach out and ring the service bell, bringing the minister to his senses. By the time the stewardess arrived Betty was standing at the door in her dressing gown. Forbes invited her to lunch, and on the understanding that he behave himself Betty accepted. Meanwhile he was shown to the ship's lounge to wait while she dressed.

Over lunch he told her that he had read all her newspaper articles and was very impressed with her work. When she told him that she had had to stop writing in Chile because of pressure from the German ambassador and was returning to America to work as a journalist, he offered her £100 a month to stay in Peru and work from the legation's Information section to help the war effort. Interpreting Forbes's offer as also including "a stint in the bedroom," Betty politely refused. She was repelled by Forbes; more important, she was anxious to return to real intelligence work.

After lunch Forbes drove her to her rendezvous with Señor Paradol. He also knew the Peruvian diplomat and went in with Betty, gracelessly introducing her with the words, "Well, here's your girl. You know, I think she's a spy. The Germans are after her so she's left Chile. . . ." Betty was able to laugh off the embarrassing incident. She later explained discreetly to Paradol that she had earlier been forced to repel Forbes's amorous intentions, hence his barbed introduction, obviously a nervous attempt at humour. But she was alarmed at the time. Had the person she was meeting been a gossip rather than an old friend and a man of character, her cover could have been blown before she got started.

She took care not to see Forbes again. When the ship was under way she met the newly embarked French military attaché, Colonel Dassonville, and his wife, who were on their way to Europe to join de Gaulle's Free French forces. They were soon friends and told Betty that before they had sailed Forbes had warned them about her, saying "There's a woman called Mrs. Pack on board. She's a spy who had to leave Poland because the Germans were after her and she's also a perfect tart."[2] This remark, when sections of the memoir were published in a Sunday newspaper, became: "She had to leave Chile because the Germans were after her."[3] Was the earlier reference in her memoirs a slip on Betty's part? Were "the Germans" on to her in Poland (perhaps after the Henlein burglary, or as a result of Beck's knowledge of her affair with his assistant), and does this better explain why Shelley did not try harder to retain her services in Europe? It must remain a possibility.

Before long the three had become fast friends and Betty claims she had persuaded Dassonville to give her information on military establishments in Peru, which she promised to pass on "to the right people." This implies that she shared with him the fact that she was also involved in intelligence work; surely an indiscreet thing for her to have done on the strength of such a short acquaintance? There is another small inconsistency that sits awkwardly in her memoirs at this point.

She told Courteney Forbes that she was "on her way to the United States to work as a journalist." According to her memoirs there was no suggestion at this point that she had received any contact from British Intelligence other than the noncommittal letter to her mother in late November. Yet when she eventually arrived in the United States and made contact, she *did* go to work using the cover of "journalist." The explanation could be simply that Betty had already worked this out for herself and that her New York spymasters went along with what was a very good, easily checked cover story. The alternative is that she had already been in contact with Intelligence representatives (other than Fairly), a fact which she chose, for some reason, not to reveal.

After the long journey aboard the SS *Excalibur* Betty was relieved to reach her destination and as the ship nosed into the great waterway of New York Harbor an official launch came alongside. Aboard this launch was Lieutenant Paul Fairly, who had come equipped with the necessary authority to remove Betty and her luggage, waiving customs formalities. Later he gave her the letter which had precipitated his cable to her in Panama some two months earlier.

The letter was addressed to Betty's mother and merely stated that the caller, J. Howard, had been sorry to miss Betty when he called to see her. "Should you have any news of her which you wish to communicate to me, would you kindly ring the above number in New York City. . . ." From her time in Poland, Betty knew that the name "John Howard" was one frequently used as a cover name for SIS agents.[4] So, having checked into her hotel, Betty rang Mr Howard at the telephone number he had provided: Atwater 9–8763.

"John Howard" sounded pleased to hear from her and explained that he had been trying to make contact for months at Lisbon, Washington, Panama and Santiago but she had always been "just ahead of him." He wanted to meet her at her hotel immediately, but Betty excused herself for a few hours saying that she had some urgent business to take care of.

Her urgent business was Paul Fairly for whom she had hungered for the past two months and who, even as she spoke on the telephone, was embracing her. Her diary claims that within a minute of her replacing the receiver she and Paul were in bed making passionate love. An hour later Fairly took his reluctant leave of her and Betty composed herself to meet her new controller.

Howard's real name was John Arthur Reed Pepper. A good-looking, fair-haired, blue-eyed Englishman of about her own age, Pepper had been recruited by William Stephenson (now better known as "A Man Called Intrepid" through the book and film of that name)[5] as a senior aide in the organization coordinating British Secret Intelligence in the Western Hemisphere. Stephenson had the power to recruit superior people from anywhere and his preference was for enthusiastic amateurs who were unlikely to be on enemy files and were free from career ties to the intelligence service. Pepper had been recruited from a London company associated with Stephenson's corporation; his specialty was economic intelligence. He accompanied Stephenson to New York in June 1940.

Betty talked to "Mister Howard" for a long time, telling him her entire history from her family background to her marriage to Arthur, the period she spent in Spain during the civil war to the work she had done with Shelley in Poland, including her *modus operandi*, and her propaganda journalism in Chile. Pepper could hardly avoid questioning her closely about her motives, as an American (and an Irish-American at that), in wanting to help the British. Betty told him that as Arthur's wife she was the holder of a British passport and furthermore her roots as well as her personal inclinations were European. From the questions he put to her it was obvious that he already knew a great deal about her background and was merely seeking confirmation.

From the account of BSC (British Security Coordination) agents recruited at the same time, we have an idea what line John Pepper took at these meetings:

> Our primary directive from the PM [Churchill] is that American participation in the war is the most important single objective for Britain. It is the only way, he feels, to victory over Nazism.
>
> Our best information is that the forces of isolation, a front here for Nazism and Fascism, are gaining, not losing ground. How do you personally feel about these forces, for example the America First movement? . . . Do you feel strongly enough on these matters to work for us in your own country To spy on your fellow Americans and report to us? . . .
>
> . . . Be careful of the FBI, and the Neutrality Act can land you in prison. In this work you cannot register as the agent of a foreign power, as the law requires; it would give the whole show away. . . . And if you are caught, we haven't heard of you. You understand that?[6]

Pepper seemed satisfied with Betty's answers and promised to contact her again soon.

In fact she was contacted again within a matter of days and on this occasion she went to an office in the downtown New York area. It was through this office that she was to report for the next year, sometimes directly to John Pepper and sometimes to another contact, "Marion."

Either would meet her at a pre-arranged time at the Ritz-Carlton Hotel where she would hand over her weekly report. Betty was given the code-name "Cynthia." In general, BSC agents used a version of one of their real Christian names; Harford Montgomery Hyde, for example, used the code-name "Harford," though he was introduced to Betty as "Mr. Montgomery." Betty's usual contact, Marion de Chastellaine, was known as "Marion." There was an existing agent code-named "Betty," but whether there was any other significance in the name "Cynthia" is not known. Later, Betty would use other names.

Her immediate instruction was to go to Washington, rent a house and re-establish her presence in Washington's diplomatic and political society. Her rent and living expenses would be met by the organization. BSC paid its women agents between $300 and $400 a month but Betty asked for somewhat less than this. "Whatever her motives might have been," the BSC official history states, "they did not include money." She would be expected to do some discreet entertaining, Pepper told her. There was no need for him to be more explicit; Betty knew precisely what might be required of her. As her former go-between, Marion de Chastellaine, told me: "She could only get information one way; she used it and got the information. Her contribution was enormous and the information she provided was extra-ordinary. . . ."[7]

Her first real assignment was "to detect and uncover a female agent from a neutral country who was on her way to Britain to make pacifist propaganda for the Nazis." The woman was arrested in Bermuda on May 1 when she was removed from the Spanish steamer *Marqués del Comillas* on suspicion of being a Nazi spy and interned for the remainder of the war.[8] The work involved following the woman for a few days, noting her movements and contacts. It was not very exciting but Betty was not depressed by this; she understood that she was on trial and expected no more.

She learned little about the organization for which she was now working but understood that it was under the direction of William Stephenson, known variously as "The Chief," "Little Bill" and sometimes simply "God"; and operated through a variety of covers ranging from the British Passport Control Office, the British Purchasing Commission and the British Library of Information, to name but a few. The organization operated out of the thirty-fifth and thirty-sixth floors of Rockefeller Center at 630 Fifth Avenue, thanks to an equable arrangement between Stephenson and Nelson Rockefeller, and a small plaque at the main entrance proclaimed that these were the offices of British Passport Control.

Betty called it "British Intelligence" and it would shortly become known as British Security Coordination, a title suggested by J. Edgar Hoover.[9]

[It was] an organization whose power stretched beyond the United States into the whole of North and South America, and its responsibilities covered far more than security matters.

Essentially, BSC was Britain's intelligence window in America, acting as representative of the major British Intelligence agencies concerned with security and intelligence issues, and as their principal liaison in the United States with their American counterparts.

The most important British agency was the Security Executive created by Churchill almost as soon as he became Prime Minister . . . "to find out if there is a fifth column in this country and if so to eliminate it." . . .

Directly responsible to Churchill, the Security Executive, and its work, is still shrouded in secrecy, and its files have never been released. But while then, and now, remaining largely invisible, it was a powerful body that cast a wide net over a host of activities affecting national security; communications, censorship, travel, ports, shipping and the internment of aliens. So far as British Security Coordination was concerned, the Security Executive was the parent body that laid down the guidelines it was to follow.[10]

Stephenson was the representative in the Western Hemisphere for SIS (also known as MI6) and—from 1940 to 1943—for MI5. Moreover, BSC was not simply an extension of SIS but was a unique service which incorporated as well SOE, censorship, codes and ciphers, security and communication. "In fact, nine distinct secret organisations . . . and in the western hemisphere, ran them all."[11] But Betty knew little of these details. It was enough that she could work constructively for a cause in which she believed.

Once in Washington she took care of a matter that had been concerning her for some weeks—she refers to it in her memoir as "a mishap"; she was now almost three months pregnant,

> which might have seriously interfered with my work if immediate steps had not been taken to remedy it. . . . I had learned a good deal since my marriage and made no amateur attempts to get rid of it as I had done before. This time I had an abortion. It cost me quite a lot of money and I was ill for a fortnight but there were no after effects. I never told my lover in the U.S. Intelligence anything about it.[12]

The house Betty rented at 3327 O Street in the elegant Washington suburb of Georgetown was similar to others nearby that were rented and used by the British embassy to house temporary members of staff. Betty's house, though, was rented directly from the owner and was listed under her own name in subsequent city directories.[13] All the houses in the area are Federal in style, elegant variations of Georgian architecture dating from the second half of the nineteenth century and comprise one of the most important single groups of historical buildings in the United States. On the shaded narrow streets finely proportioned houses with English cellars, two stories and attics with shuttered dormer windows butt directly onto the pavements shoulder-to-shoulder, lacking the familiar front lawns and garages of most modern American towns. The area exudes a tranquillity far removed from the bustle of the city of Washington, and Georgetown on a quiet Sunday morning is more reminiscent of a European community than an American one. O Street itself, a few blocks from the Potomac River, is cobbled and tree-lined and down its centre run, still, the disused street-car tracks that were active when Betty moved there in February 1941.

She was pleased with the gracious little house and its high ceilings, polished wooden floors, and aura of old-world charm. It consisted of a comfortably furnished sitting room, with windows onto O Street, which led to a dining room overlooking a small garden at the rear of the house. From the kitchen a door led through a covered porch to a sun deck and the garden; an important feature was a rear entrance to an alleyway which exited onto Thirty-third Street, but could not be seen from the front of the house, which hugged its neighbours on either side. Upstairs the main bedroom and bathroom overlooked the street and there were two smaller bedrooms at the rear.

It was not hard for Betty to ease herself back into Washington society. Her mother, who now lived at 2139 Wyoming Avenue in uptown Washington (an address which would later have great significance for Betty), was still a noted hostess and frequently threw parties for the inhabitants of Washington's Embassy Row as well as for American politicians; she was a great help in re-establishing Betty within the higher echelons of Washington society. Cora's daughter-in-law, Shirlee Thorpe, recalled: "Mrs. Thorpe was a wonderful hostess and threw lots of parties. If you went to a dinner party she was quite likely to have most of the Cabinet in attendance."[14] Cora was only too delighted to find that her daughter had at last developed a real interest in society, and she was probably responsible for Betty's immediate inclusion in the Washington Social Register, the very seal of respectability. Through Arthur, Betty also had the entrée to the British embassy, and in addition she found friends made during her eleven years of marriage in various foreign embassies in the city. But it was Cora who helped Betty with her second assignment.

The Lend-Lease Bill under which Britain could receive from the United States the immense list of supplies Churchill had requested from Roosevelt, without paying cash for them, had gone before the House and Senate on January 10, 1941. Considerable opposition was offered by isolationists and "waverers," according to Cordell Hull in his memoirs, "and those who resented any additional grant of authority to the President." The opposers of the bill believed that even if Germany were to win the war the safety of the United States would not be affected. Why then should the United States involve itself in a war that was not of its making and in which it had no interest? They brought to the

145

stand people of note such as Charles Lindbergh to support their case.

This opposition was led by a number of prominent senators, including Democrat Thomas Connally of Texas and Republican Arthur Vandenberg of Michigan. The president and Cordell Hull knew that somehow these men and others like them would need to be won over if the bill, one of the most revolutionary legislative actions in American history, was to have any chance of succeeding.

Betty's second mission for British Security Coordination was to try to convert the opinions of Senators Connally and Vandenberg into, if not support, a less heated opposition to the bill which literally meant the difference between survival and defeat for the British. Other agents of both sexes were given similar missions with other politicians. Although the full details of how she set about her work have not come to light, it is known that Betty, accompanied by her mother, called on Vandenberg at his home in February 1941 and that Betty saw him on at least one other occasion subsequently. It is thought that Betty worked on this family friend by telling him of first-hand experiences in Europe under the threat of Hitler, and by convincing him that should Hitler succeed in defeating, the British control of the high seas would pass into the hands of those whose ultimate aim was unlimited conquest. With Vandenburg Betty was successful; with Senator Connally, chairman of the Senate Committee on Foreign Relations (which was holding a hearing on the bill), she was not.

Contriving an introduction at a dinner party she told Connally, when asked, that she was a journalist. He immediately spiked her guns by saying "You're an American turned British. . . . I guess that means you are going to try to get us into the war. You're wasting your time, my dear—come over here and sit on my knee instead. . . ." Betty did not record her reply to the senator's suggestion, or whether she saw him again. The Lend-Lease bill was, however, passed with amendments and became law on March 11, 1941. By then Betty was already embroiled in what would become one of her greatest successes as an agent.

In February, during one of his regular visits to Washington, Pepper had visited Betty at her house on O Street to discuss her next assignment. During their conversation he asked if she knew anyone at the Italian embassy and she replied that many years ago she had been a close friend of the present naval attaché, Vice Admiral Lais. * She explained the nature of the relationship and added that she had tried to renew their friendship six months earlier but that Lais had rejected her suggestion that they meet. Pepper said that the admiral was the person in whom he was chiefly interested.

Admiral Alberto Lais had been, from 1937 to 1940, the director of naval intelligence in the Royal Italian Ministry of Marine in Rome. In the spring of 1940 the Italian embassy had advised the State Department that a flag officer of the Italian navy would be appointed to the vacant position of naval attaché in Washington. They subsequently named Alberto Lais. It was the opinion of Pepper and his associates in British Intelligence that this transfer was suspicious. Why should the director of naval intelligence suddenly be transferred to the United States of America as a naval attaché? Lais, with his previous experience in Washington and his American wife, would seem ideal for a Washington assignment at such a sensitive period, and it seemed on the surface a happy arrangement, albeit an unusual posting for someone as important as a former director of naval intelligence.

But apart from this there was an additional reason for their interest. Several months earlier, in December of 1940, William Stephenson, the Chief Passport Control Officer, had been advised by SIS/London that the Admiralty urgently required the Italian naval cipher, a copy of which was known to be in the possession of the Italian naval attaché in Washington. [16] Betty did not need the assignment spelled out to her. She was already an experienced agent with a good track record, and now Pepper was suggesting that she employ the same methods she had used on Michal Lubienski to gain access to the Italian naval ciphers.

Before Pepper knew about her old relationship with Lais, he had merely hoped that she could infiltrate the embassy by making friends with someone who worked there. Now there was a possibility that she might be able

---

* In an aide-mémoire from the Royal Italian Navy to the State Department on August 30, 1940, they took pains to point out Lais's correct rank to the Americans. He was an "*Ammiraglio di Divisione*, a superior rank to that of Rear Admiral, as shown by the fifteen-gun salute to which [he is] entitled . . . and the nearest translation to English would be 'Vice Admiral, Junior Grade'. . . ." NARA 701.65511/970.

to work on the top man. But first she had to get Lais to reverse his decision not to see her again. Betty lost no time in telephoning the admiral. As before, he sounded cool and said she must see that a meeting was out of the question. Betty said that she understood his position but was sorry for it because she had separated from Arthur, was deeply unhappy, and needed to talk to someone she could trust. She ended the conversation by expressing the hope that at some time in the future it might be possible to take up their friendship again.

She did not have long to wait. According to her memoirs, it was only a few days before Lais telephoned Betty at her home in Georgetown to say that he had thought about her suggestion that they should meet again. He now felt it *might* be possible if done very discreetly and provided they were not seen together by anyone. Betty said that if he came to her house after dark she would ensure that her maid was given the night off and no one need know of their meeting. He told her he did not need her address as he had already obtained it from her mother.

The following evening Lais visited 3327 O Street and over a bottle of wine and a light supper Betty poured out her problems: how her marriage to Arthur had been a failure and though she had left her husband, as a Catholic she could not see any possibility of a divorce. Meanwhile, she said, because she could no longer live with Arthur she had lost contact with her five-year-old daughter. She told him, finally, how much in need of old friends she was now that she had returned alone to Washington. She made no attempt to treat him as anything other than a valued older friend or even uncle, but he could see clearly that she was no longer the teenager he had entertained to tea. Lais was almost thirty years older than Betty and perhaps not surprisingly, now, he reciprocated by telling her about the problems in his own marriage. Betty knew Alberto's wife, Leonora, and listened sympathetically as he confided that he had married because she had been suitable, not for love. He knew just how Betty must be feeling, he said.

Within the week the two were lovers of sorts and Lais visited Betty on several subsequent evenings; visits which are confirmed in FBI files only recently released[17]—and for the first few meetings she was careful not to mention anything remotely connected with his work. Instead she concentrated on insinuating herself deeper into his affections by playing the role of "his little golden girl."

She made no demands on him, sexual or otherwise, and their love-making was not, in general, conventional. From Betty's memoirs it would appear that Lais wanted nothing more than to lie next to her and fondle her naked body; their relationship never progressed to actual regular intercourse. Betty reveals that it was their custom after sharing a light supper and a bottle of wine to lie together while he caressed her. Their conversations at these times ranged over many topics, often harking back to the old days when Betty was a teenager. He had admired her even then. Who would have thought, he marvelled, that fifteen years later they would become so close. He told her about his own country and of the sadness he felt that the two countries he loved, Italy and America, were approaching a state of enmity.

He was an extremely sentimental man according to Betty, though her memoir shows no remorse at her ultimate betrayal of him, not for the America he claimed to love as a second homeland, but for Britain, which would have especially humiliated Lais had he ever learned of it, for the Italian politician class of the pre-war period harboured a special enmity towards Great Britain.

In the secret treaty of London in 1915, the Asquith government of Great Britain promised Italy the Italian-speaking areas of the Istrian Peninsula and Dalmatia if she entered the First World War on the Allied side. When, at Versailles, France's Georges Clemenceau and America's Woodrow Wilson moved to leave a great part of the disputed area within the new state of Yugoslavia, the Italian premier, Vittorio Orlando, turned to the British. Lloyd George, now the British prime minister, simply shrugged his shoulders. The whole affair turned ugly when Orlando left the conference. Later, the Italian poet Gabriele D'Annunzio defied the terms of the Versailles Treaty and led an army of 100,000 Italian citizens in the occupation of the port city of Fiume, now called Rijeka. One might think that the Italians would be angrier at the French and Americans, and indeed a lot of anger was focused on Wilson. But most of those in the Italian government principally faulted the British for failing to insist with the other Allies that Britain must honour her word.

Alberto knew of Betty's failed marriage to a British diplomat but nothing about her connection to British intelligence work; clearly he continued to see her as a beautifully grown-up version of the beautiful American teenager he once knew. Eventually he started to tell her a little about his work as a naval attaché but did not provide any clue as to whether or not he had been sent to the United States on a specific mission. Betty filed field reports, stating that she had re-established contact, and setting out the content of her conversations with the admiral. She was instructed to let the relationship continue in its own way, always bearing in mind that the chief requirement of her assignment was to obtain information on the Italian naval ciphers; she was to find out anything she could about these: how they were stored and where; who had access to them; and, if possible, whether there was any way that they might be obtained.

One evening the admiral brought her a gift. He had wanted to give her something he treasured, something that would always remind her of him, he said, and now presented her with a finely worked Italian-silver trinket box. His manner was so loving and sentimental that Betty judged that the time was right to bring up the matter of the ciphers. She records a certain amount of nervousness, so the shy tremor in her voice as she spun her story did not have to be faked. She told him she had a friend in the ONI (Office of Naval Intelligence) and he had told her that the Americans badly needed the Italian ciphers. If he wished to give her something she would really value he could do so and help both America and Italy at the same time.

Lais did not immediately respond. Indeed he must have been taken aback at her request, but eventually he said he would give it some thought. For her request to have any power to it, there must have been an implication that things between them might be spoiled if he rejected her on this, and after he had left Betty fretted that she might have overreached herself, moved too early, or frightened him off. But according to the BSC official history, compiled at the end of the war from official documents and agent's field reports, Lais kept their next tryst and during the evening gave her the name of the cipher clerk in his office, telling her to contact the man directly. Both the official history and Betty's memoirs (which differ only in the sequence of events) agree on this, but also make it clear that Lais had no further role in what followed. There can be little doubt, however, that he knew that Betty would pursue this to its end and chose to close his eyes to it.

According to Betty's memoirs the name Lais gave her was "Giulio," but she did not provide the real name in the margin of her manuscript (it is possible, given the passage of time, that she had simply forgotten it). On the few occasions that she provided only Christian names, research has shown that they were generally the real names of those involved. There were two secretaries called Giulio in the office of the naval attaché; one, a third secretary who lived at the Shoreham Hotel in Washington. FBI and State Department archives confirm that Betty had several contacts with a man (name censored) "at his apartment at the Shoreham Hotel" at this time.[18] Whichever Giulio this was, Betty had no compunction in telling her man that Admiral Lais had given her his name and wished Giulio to be helpful to her. Both Betty's version and the official history agree that Betty was able to negotiate a purchase price with a "relatively lowly-paid secretary in the Embassy," in return for which he produced the cipher books, which were photographed and returned to him within hours. The copies were then sent off to London.

The subsequent fall-out from these revelations is worth exploring. In the BSC official history the Lais affair is given prominence and claimed as a major coup; indeed much of the legend of Betty as a World War II superspy relies somewhat on her success on this assignment. But the validity of the claim rests upon several factors. Dates are not provided consistently in the official history and hardly any precise dates are given in Betty's memoirs, written from memory twenty years after the event (though official documentary evidence is available which confirms many of the incidents). The two versions tally precisely in respect of how the ciphers were obtained but they chiefly divide on one point. In her memoirs Betty recalled that she obtained the ciphers *after* Lais left the United States, while the official history states unequivocally: "After she had obtained the naval ciphers, 'Cynthia' continued to maintain contact with Admiral Lais and obtained from him a quantity of valuable information concerning Axis plans in the Mediterranean."[19]

On the question of chronology it is known that Betty was in Chile while the Willingdon mission was there and that she set out for New York in early January. Allowing twelve days for the boat journey up the Pacific coast of South America, with three stops, through the Panama Canal and up the eastern seaboard to New York, it can safely be assumed that Betty could not have reached New York before the third week in January. She spent several nights in New York during which time she saw John Pepper and Paul Fairly. She then went to Washington to find and rent a house, and successfully carried out her first assignment, tailing a suspected Nazi agent. For two weeks she was ill following an abortion and so (allowing for the unspecified period in which she spent beguiling Lais) the ciphers cannot have been obtained much earlier than late February.

Assuming that the ciphers were obtained within this time span and sent immediately to London, as recorded in the BSC official history, then the official history's claims might be valid.

At that time Britain was still alone, and the Royal Navy was spread thinly over the seven seas. In the Mediterranean the forces available might well have proved insufficient to meet the demands of the situation had they been challenged by the Italian Navy in strength. Yet it is a matter of history that they were never so challenged, and that the Italian Navy was virtually neutralised and failed to win a single battle.

This may have been largely due to the fact that the British had knowledge of the Italian Naval cypher, which provided the means of learning the enemy's intentions in advance and thus enabled the Commander in Chief, Mediterranean, to dispose of his meagre forces to such effective purpose that the Italians were constantly deceived concerning the numbers and strength of British units and did not dare to risk a major engagement.[20]

This is all very impressive and yet the story may not be as straightforward as this history, written for the intelligence service (Winston Churchill was also sent a copy), indicates. When the story of Betty's acquisition of the ciphers was first broken by H. Montgomery Hyde in his 1962 biography of William Stephenson, head of British Security Coordination,[21] the Italian government immediately refuted the story, stating that the claims were a lie and a vile slur on a man of the highest integrity and honour. The Italian Ministry of Defence suggested that if Betty acquired anything it was probably a fake cipher book.[22]

This is a not unpredictable reaction considering the source of the objection, though due to the circumstances the Italians were unlikely to have known the truth of the matter, either way. The admiral would not have recorded the trysts with Betty in his duty log. Certainly, denials of the admiral's marital infidelity may be ignored, since evidence exists within files released by the FBI that he was not involved only with Betty, but that he had previously had an intimate relationship with another woman.[23]

Admiral Lais's family then instituted proceedings against Hyde for bringing the name of the late admiral into disrepute, stating that he would never have betrayed his country (the family's case was later upheld in Italian courts). Again, the reaction was not surprising but not strictly relevant either, since in the circumstances the admiral would have been unlikely to have confided in his family.

Time magazine next stepped into the arena with its statement in Betty's obituary, and used by Hyde on several occasions:

. . . British Intelligence undeniably proved uncannily adept at forestalling Italian fleet movements, notably in the March 1941 sea battle off Cape Matapan, where the Royal Navy crippled Italy's numerically superior force.[24]

Assuming one accepts the accuracy of both the timing given in the BSC history and indeed the document itself, it is certainly possible that the ciphers obtained by Betty could have been in the hands of the British navy in time for the Battle of Cape Matapan on March 28, 1941, off the southern tip of Greece, where the major part of the Italian fleet was gathered.

The main objective of the Italians, under the command of Admiral Iachino, was to attack the British convoys sailing from Africa to Greece carrying a British Expeditionary Force. The British fleet, under the command of Admiral Cunningham, not only "sensed" the planned attack but set a course with such foresight that a scout plane sent off at dawn contacted the enemy squadrons precisely where the admiral had predicted they would be. The British promptly attacked the far larger Italian fleet in the most important naval battle of the European war, deploying surface and air forces, and sinking the cruisers *Pola*, *Zara* and *Fiume*. Two destroyers, the *Vincenti Gioberti* and the *Maestrale*, were also sunk, as well as a battleship of the Littorio class; more than 2,400 Italians were lost. The only British loss in the battle was a Swordfish torpedo bomber airplane.[25] In effect, this action finished the Italian navy for the remainder of the war, and was a major cause for celebration in London.

But what was the material Betty obtained? The Cambridge historian F. H. Hinsley, who worked at GCCS* Bletchley during the war, and who was also the senior compiler of the official history *British Intelligence in the Second World War*, told me that "the main Italian naval cyphers were rarely read after July 1940 and that the cypher that was useful at Matapan was a rarely used one that was briefly readable."[26] This, at least, adds weight to the BSC official history's claim that British Intelligence "were extremely anxious to acquire the Italian Naval ciphers."

However, Professor Hinsley had never seen any documentation relating to Italian ciphers that BSC might have sent to England:

The Italian fleet used an Enigma Machine until the spring of 1941. Apart from that, the fleet cyphers were all book cyphers and were rarely read after July 1940. The C38 Machine was used by the navy, but was used only for convoys; this was read from June 1941. But neither machine would ever have been distributed to the United States Italian offices.

The more I think about it the more I feel [that] . . . if a cipher was obtained in Washington it would have to have been one used by the naval attaché or the ambassador—diplomatic cyphers. I don't think material taken in Washington helped to read these—but it may have done—and . . . [if] it did not help [that] does not mean that it was not taken. . . .[27]

---

* Government Code and Cipher School, centre of British cryptography activities. The best brains in the country were recruited and it is no coincidence that the site was exactly half-way between Oxford and Cambridge.

Given Lais's former position as director of naval intelligence it does not seem beyond possibility that he would have access to the most secret grades of ciphers.

Clearly, Betty obtained documents which trained and *highly experienced* SIS officers at BSC—such as Colonel Charles H. "Dick" Ellis[28]—believed were the current naval ciphers. The BSC official history states: "He [Lais] put her in touch with his own cypher clerk, who produced the cyphers after a suitable financial agreement had been reached. They were photostated in Washington, and the photostats sent to London immediately."[29]

What is beyond question is that a team at Bletchley's GCCS under the leadership of Dillwyn Knox succeeded in breaking the "rarely used" Italian naval code used at Matapan during March; decrypts were made available to Admiral Cunningham before March 25. The timing is crucial here, for Betty had been in contact with Lais for over a month by then. It is therefore not impossible that the ciphers obtained by Betty and sent to London by BSC were of help to the Bletchley team in breaking the rarely used Italian code in time to be helpful at Matapan. It must be said, however, that Professor Hinsley found nothing to substantiate this.

There is one possibility that must always be considered in examining intelligence activities—that the Italians fostered fakes on Betty, that a discontinued set of ciphers was passed over by the enterprising Giulio (with or without the knowledge of Lais). However, Stephenson clearly considered the results of this operation important enough to include the operation as an outstanding success in the official history of his organization written in 1945–46. It follows that he must have had good reason to believe it *was* an outstanding success. Had the ciphers been found to be useless it is inconceivable, given Stephenson's position as head of British Intelligence in the Western Hemisphere, that he would not have been advised and perhaps even requested to try again.

In an earlier chapter the well-documented inter-departmental rivalry that existed between the various departments of British Intelligence, and that sapped the embryo SOE of vital support, was mentioned briefly. British Security Coordination, with its newly recruited, largely Canadian work-force, suffered similarly throughout the war. Indeed the level of ill-will which one still encounters from "establishment" intelligence staff when researching Stephenson's organization is surprising; it is almost as though the two organizations were on opposing sides.

This possibly stems from the fact that when Churchill formed SOE with the brief to use methods such as sabotage, the "professionals" in SIS saw the alarm and counter-measures this would evoke as hampering the smooth and secret gathering of intelligence. Their immediate reaction was that of a sixth-former to a new boy—caution tinged with disapproval. Fuelled by inter-departmental rivalry this caution grew to an almost open enmity. Stephenson's colourful outfit in New York came in for particular scepticism and were regarded by many in the SIS establishment head-quarters at London's Broadway as amateurs playing at spying.

Since it has become fashionable for former intelligence agents to break into print, virtually everything that BSC achieved (for which Stephenson subsequently received a knighthood at Churchill's *personal* recommen-dation) has been publicly depreciated by people who had no formal con-nection with Stephenson or BSC and often little knowledge of what they did.

This attitude may explain why Betty's work has been largely ignored, even refuted by some, and why one eminent historian wrote to me, "As for 'Cynthia', assuming such a person existed, all that can be said about her for certain is that she did not acquire . . . the Italian naval ciphers. . . ."[30] It is not easy to be critical of people who have been helpful during research, but I sensed more than a suggestion of old boy protectionism in this conservation of spy work as the preserve of only those who shared certain ties. Perhaps the detractors see the competition from the BSC amateurs as in some way devaluing their own important work.

Where Betty is concerned such a reaction may be no more than a desire not to see the reputation of their profession tarnished by association with a woman who stole secrets in bed. The Bletchley crowd made no secret of what they thought about intelligence gathered in this manner, for Betty was certainly not the only woman employed by the British Secret Intelligence Service to obtain information during pillow talk. Dr. R. V. Jones, chief scientific advisor to SIS, once wrote a report, "A Scientific Intelligence Service," highlighting the manner in which information could "leak out." There were five ways listed, but first and second were:

1. Accidental indiscretions . . . of which there are always a large number and if these are pieced together a valuable impression may be gained.
2. Indiscretions encouraged by alcohol and/or mistresses. The results obtained by these methods are all that can be expected.[31]

Betty took advantage of both of the above (though she used other methods too, resorting to burglary on at least two occasions). The more important aspect of her work—the seduction of senior officials in order to obtain information—was known at SIS headquarters (Broadway), generically, as "Dirty Work"; and intelligence thus gained was treated with what was considered appropriate suspicion.[32]

But R. V. Jones himself admitted to being the grateful recipient of an "outstanding" report gained in this manner by the woman agent Amniarix. At a crucial point in the war Amniarix seduced a German officer and came away with a detailed account of the Flying Bomb organization at Peenemünde.[33]

What of the other women who used their charms on behalf of His Majesty's Government? There were several well-known agents who employed the same methods as Betty and Amniarix, such as the "beautiful young blonde from His Majesty's consulate at Tangiers who kept an open bed for notable Spanish and Axis officers."[34] To be strictly fair, it does not appear that it was official policy for the SIS to *train* women in the arts of seduction for the purposes of espionage. On the other hand it does not become those who were the recipients—perhaps unwitting—of the advantages gained by such methods to dismiss the source with such self-righteousness. From an objective viewpoint it might seem that the war was won because many people made many kinds of unique contributions to the overall effort.

Those responsible for and with experience in field work—one might call them spymasters—are not so dismissive. Colonel Maurice Buckmaster, head of the French section of SOE, is on record on the subject:

My organization used quite a number of courageous women; they were not called upon to use their feminine charms in the way that "Cynthia" did. But I can well see the advantages of a good-looking woman spy using her feminine charms as an added weapon in seeking information.[35]

Having made, during the course of writing this book, an extensive study of intelligence methods it seems that there was much "dirtier" work afoot than that of an act of love between two consenting adults; and as Betty herself argued, surely her methods were better than killing or torturing to gain information?

To return to the narrative: Betty records that on the evening of Saturday, March 29, 1941, the day after the battle at Matapan, Admiral Alberto Lais was lying in her arms. She stated that he seemed unusually sad and, indeed, at one point was actually in tears. Having read of the British victory in the Mediterranean on the previous day she was not especially surprised that he would be depressed. Nevertheless she displayed sympathy and encouraged her lover to talk. What he told her on this occasion not only surprised her but galvanized her, for she needed to act quickly to make use of the startling information she had just received. Yet she could not appear to be either unduly interested in the news, nor could she immediately think of any reason to suggest he cut short his visit so that she could get to the telephone.

What the admiral told her was that he had that day received orders from Rome to sabotage all Italian ships lying in U.S. ports. This consisted of a sizable fleet, for few Axis merchant ships dared to run the British Atlantic blockade in attempts to get home and many were consequently immobilized in American ports. The orders from Italian high command were undoubtedly issued after realization that the United States would inevitably abandon its neutral position and seize these ships.

Betty quietly asked how he could possibly go about such a task, and he sadly told her that he had already given the orders. Five ships in Norfolk, Virginia, were to be destroyed and sunk, within hours, by time-bombs already in place. Ships in other major ports throughout the United States would be put out of action by extensive damage perpetrated by obedient crews to whom orders had already been dispatched by cable.

Shortly after this astonishing revelation the admiral got up to visit the lavatory. Betty remained in bed thinking furiously about her next move and was surprised when Alberto came quickly back into her bedroom saying that there were two men outside the front of her house and that he suspected they were FBI "G" men. Then, as now, the bathroom overlooked O Street, and idly glancing out of the window he had seen the two men watching the house. Turning out the light Betty peered from behind the curtains to the lamplit street below. Sure enough, there were two men standing looking up at the window, no doubt alerted by the fact that the bedroom light had been switched off.

They would not be from her own organization, Betty knew, so she guessed that the admiral was probably correct in his suspicions that they were FBI agents. She was unaware that the FBI had been monitoring Lais's frequent visits to 3327 O Street for some weeks and had already reported that "Admiral Lais, . . . the naval attaché . . . was on intimate terms" with her.[36] Apparently they did not yet know who was using whom, for Betty herself was the subject of surveillance by the FBI, a matter subsequently personally authorized by J. Edgar Hoover:

To: Special Agent in Charge, Washington, D.C.
Re: MRS ARTHUR PACK (was ESPIONAGE F)

Reference is made to your letter . . . in which you set out certain information concerning subject Pack and request authority to make an investigation of her. It is believed that a discreet enquiry of Mrs Pack may produce valuable information and the same is authorized. . . .

Very truly yours

John Edgar Hoover
Director[37]

Alberto panicked, convinced that his instructions to scuttle the Axis ships were already known and that the men had come to arrest him. Betty, seeing her opportunity, told him that his best course of action was to get back to the embassy, where he could claim diplomatic immunity. There was a way out of the house, she explained, which the two men in the street below could not see. Alberto dressed rapidly and Betty led him to the back of the house, where she opened the window of a small bedroom over the roof of the covered porch. If he climbed out onto this he could drop quietly into the garden. A small door in the wooden fence would lead him into an alleyway which exited onto Thirty-third Street. A few steps would take him to P Street; once there he could easily make his return to the embassy.

Alberto was no lightweight and not a young man, so it must have been an anxious moment as he clambered over the sill and eased himself down out of her sight. A few seconds later she was relieved to hear the subdued click as the latch of the garden gate closed. Returning to her darkened front bedroom, she looked down onto the pavement outside the front of her house. As she lifted the curtain one of the men went to her door and rang the bell. Not knowing that she had been followed for some time, she was reluctant to become involved with the FBI who might hinder what she now had to do, so she ignored the doorbell. After a few further rings the man rejoined his companion and the two walked off down O Street.

Betty telephoned John Pepper in his New York apartment at 410 East 57th Street and then Paul Fairly of the Office of Naval Intelligence at his apartment, telling Fairly (presumably with Pepper's clearance) everything Lais had told her about the location of the bombs and the times set for detonation. The chief site of destruction was Norfolk, Virginia, but other ships were lying in New York, Newark, New Jersey, Philadelphia and Jacksonville, Florida; an attempt was to be made to scuttle one ship in the channel of the Panama Canal.

Her warning was almost too late as valuable time was lost in bureaucratic processing. The United States was not yet at war and action could not be taken with the freedom given to such actions in wartime. So the Office of Naval Intelligence reported the information to the Treasury Department, which has jurisdiction over the Coast Guard. As soon as he was contacted, Acting Secretary of the Treasury Gaston communicated with Secretary Morgenthau, who was vacationing in Arizona. He, in turn, had to obtain approval from the president, who was then aboard his yacht off the coast of Florida. Only then, operating under a 1917 act, could an instruction be given to Admiral R. R. Waesche, commander of the Coast Guard, to carry out appropriate action.[38]

By the time the blue-jacketed Coast Guard patrols boarded Italian ships they found that most of Admiral Lais's orders were in the process of being carried out.

The boarding parties interrupted the cutting of rods and shafts with acetylene torches, the wielding of sledge hammers on engines and equipment, chiselling of bearings, prying down bulwarks with crowbars and the burning of boilers that would have damaged them beyond repair . . . On several ships piles of inflammable waste and scrap were found near cargoes of oil and volatile materials.[39]

Of twenty-eight ships only two were boarded before any damage had been done. Some half dozen had been rendered totally useless and the other twenty would require substantial repairs before they could be made seaworthy. However, it is clear that without this warning from Betty the damage would have been far worse. As it was, half these ships were repaired and in active service for the Allied cause by the end of the war.

The master of one ship, the *Mongolia*, freely admitted that he had performed the act of sabotage and produced for his interrogators written orders from Admiral Lais to do so. Subsequently thirteen similar telegrams were confiscated from Italian crews, who were then arrested. Alberto Lais, of course, was inviolate from arrest, because of his diplomatic status.

The U.S. State Department had only one card to play. The Italian ambassador was summoned to the office of Breckinridge Long (former ambassador to Italy and presently head of a special division of the State Department handling problems arising from the war) on the direction of the president and the secretary of state:

When the Ambassador came in I told him it was necessary to notify him about [the behaviour] of one of my friends who was one of his staff. He asked if I referred to Lais. I replied in the affirmative and started to hand him the note. . . . The ambassador was very downcast and nervous. He did not read the note or open the envelope in my presence. When I remarked that their action in destroying the engines constituted the vessels "obstacles to navigation" in our waters as well as an illegal act he started to say that they were no more obstacles than they were before, either tied to the docks or anchored in the stream, but I promptly dismissed that as legitimate argument and stated they had become like barges, lacking the power to propel themselves and had lost their character as vessels, and that it was a breach of good faith so to act while enjoying our hospitality . . . but the serious part of it was that the act was committed in our ports and was a serious infraction of our laws.[40]

The note read:

> Your Excellency: I have the honor to state that various facts and circumstances have come to the attention of the Government of the United States connecting Admiral Alberto Lais, Naval Attaché of the Royal Italian Embassy, with the commission by certain persons of acts in violation of the laws of the United States.
>
> The President had reached the conclusion that the continued presence of Admiral Lais as Naval Attaché of the Embassy would be no longer agreeable to this Government.
>
> The President has directed me, therefore, to notify Your Excellency that Admiral Lais is *persona non grata* to this Government . . . and to request Your Excellency's Government to withdraw him immediately from the United States. . . .

Cordell Hull

A note on the copies sent to U.S. embassies stated baldly: "For your strictly confidential information the actions mentioned were directions to captains of ships that sabotage be performed."[41]

In reply the ambassador meekly accepted the secretary of state's order, advised that Admiral Lais would be leaving the country on April 25 and requested assurances that the admiral would not, in any way, be hindered by the British authorities as he left the country. He then stated that his instructions were that Captain William Bentley, assistant military attaché for air at the United States embassy in Rome, was declared *persona non grata* and should be withdrawn from Italy immediately.

On the following day, March 31, the United States seized all vessels belonging to Italy, Germany, and Denmark despite loud protests from the Germans and Italians, and from isolationists at home who claimed it was tantamount to an act of war. The Danes, whose sympathy with the Allied cause was never in question, made it clear to the State Department that they were not unhappy at what had occurred.[42]

The resulting media coverage of the admiral's expulsion, accompanied by graphic pages of photographs of the sabotage, and topped by United States seizure of Axis ships, could not have been better for Betty's reputation within the service. The head of BSC, William Stephenson, can only have been delighted at the coverage which amply illustrated the perfidy of the Italians and their Axis associates and provided irresistibly tempting opportunities for editorials on the subject. The chief reason for Stephenson's presence in the United States was to help bring about America's entry into the war. One important goal was to sway American opinion against the Axis powers through the way the media covered the war and portrayed the participants. Thanks to Betty a major point had been made, though of course her role allowing the Coast Guard to save some of the ships could not be made public knowledge. It is unlikely that the ONI revealed their source to the State Department when requesting urgent action to try to prevent the destruction of the ships. There were those at senior levels in the State Department, such as Adolf Berle, who felt strongly that British Intelligence already had far too strong a foothold in the United States. This was no time for drawing attention to the fact that every newspaper in the United States was screaming about an incident which had been exposed by a British agent.

With his world coming down around his ears, Lais continued to pine for Betty. It says much for his feelings for her, and for Betty's ability to communicate absolute sincerity while working her subjects, that he did not even suspect that the orders he gave to the masters of Italian ships were, in so many cases, frustrated because he had revealed them to Betty. While he could not find a way to see her in the intervening weeks, he did want to spend his last night in America with her in a New York hotel. At one point he told her, by telephone, that instead of returning to Italy, he planned to miss his ship and go instead to Mexico where he would "do a job" for his government. This information was duly passed on to the ONI—who had a close working relationship with Stephenson's organization apart from Betty's relationship with Fairly. The ONI advised the State Department, adding pointedly that they believed "there is no

163

Italian Naval Attaché in Mexico at the present time." The State Department, which had recently heard from U.S. ambassador Messersmith in Mexico City that he had learned of an "underground Italian movement which had its headquarters in the city,"[43] subsequently made it clear to the Italian ambassador that they had learned of the admiral's proposals and that such a course of action was absolutely unacceptable.[44]

Betty happily agreed to see Lais in New York. Whether or not she retained any lingering affection for him is not clear; she had, after all, known him for a long time, and he had been a friend before he was her "professional" subject. Many years later she spoke fondly enough of him to a friend, recalling that he was soft and sentimental, with no hardness about him at all.[45]

But once again, Betty showed that she would not let emotional attachment interfere with the diligent performance of her chosen work. While the admiral was out shopping, she examined his luggage and made notes that included full descriptions of each piece, including make, size, colour and the type of locks. The information was hastily forwarded from New York to Bermuda where, despite promises made to the contrary,[46] plans had been made by the British to detain Lais on his arrival there. Betty's last night with Lais followed the pattern of their others with a great deal of fondling and stroking; one is forced to wonder whether the admiral was bizarrely virtuous, had a sexual fetish about younger women, or was merely impotent.

There is no way to confirm Betty's account of what went on between her and Lais in bed. Both are now dead and though FBI agents reported that the couple were "intimate," even they did not get this close. But there is one other possibility that ought to be considered in reading Betty's account of the admiral's sexual behaviour. Betty had a need in her memoir to portray her sexual liaisons—even where not motivated by great love— as arising at the very least out of a natural need for sexual fulfilment. She seems to recoil from any suggestion that what she did could have been viewed as a form of prostitution. In her affair with Norman W., for example, she found little difficulty in revealing that she whiled away the long days and nights of an ocean crossing in bed with him. Yet when her mother advised her to marry him, Betty struck back by accusing her mother of acting "like a Madam," suggesting that she saw sleeping with Norman every night, simply for the advantages that could be gained from such a marriage, as a form of prostitution.

She had slept with Kulikowski and Lubienski, and had used them. But she could tell herself with some conviction that she would have slept with them whether or not there had been anything other than love in it for her. And we know enough about Betty at this point, to know that she would have used them even had there been no love involved.

Now with Lais, the time may have come to give up this last layer of defense. Lais was a weak man, overweight and almost thirty years older than she. Hardly the type of man Betty would have found appealing, and it would seem that he was not the sexual athlete some of her other lovers had been. Moreover, from a deposition signed by Arthur some years later it would seem that Betty was still romantically and sexually involved with Paul Fairly.[47] It is more than possible she used the infrequency of Lais's demands to turn the relationship into something she could more easily live with. This spared her the painful duty of having to describe it as what it was—a young and beautiful woman sleeping on demand with an older man from whom she was trying to get something valuable, an arrangement she would have had difficulty distinguishing from most of her contemporaries' definition of prostitution.

There had been some doubt about whether the admiral's family would be on hand to see him off at New York. His son was already in Italy at the Naval Academy. His nineteen-year-old daughter, Edna, had previously organized a large party for a number of youngsters from the Washington diplomatic set for that same day and there seemed to be uncertainty about whether this could be rescheduled.[48] Signora Lais attempted no explanation to the press for her statement that she intended to remain in the United States when her husband left and did not know whether she would be seeing her husband off; she was, after all, an American by birth. On that last morning the admiral's wife and daughter did arrive on the quayside to see the admiral off but according to both Betty's memoir and the BSC history, the besotted admiral spent his last few minutes with Betty.

In her memoirs Betty also claimed that it was here, minutes before he left the United States, that he gave her the name of his cipher clerk, while the BSC official history states: "The lovesick Admiral spent his final minutes with her and ignored his tearful family entirely."[49]

The SS *Marqués del Comillas* reached Bermuda on May 1 and Admiral Lais was held there for twelve days. Diplomatic messages of protest flew hither and thither but the main thrust of the British reply was that the admiral would be released when the Yugoslav foreign minister and his staff, who were being held in friendly detention in Italy, were on neutral soil. This was accomplished on May 13 and the admiral sailed for Lisbon where in an interview he stated emotionally: "After twenty-five years of close contact with the American Navy I can't help loving them."[50]

The silver trinket box given her by Lais was presented by Betty to John Pepper to pass on to Pepper's son. To remind Pepper of what she called "this most important intelligence operation" she gave him a photograph of Lais taken during the previous year and inscribed to Betty with the admiral's love.[51]

One thing in this part of Betty's memoirs bothered me at first. I was highly sceptical about Betty's "professional" relationship with Paul Fairly; she seemed to share information with him quite freely and used him almost as an adjunct to her controller. Surely John Pepper would never have allowed this informal liaison between Betty and a member of another agency, even though the ONI had well-established links with BSC. I was wrong. Pepper *was* open to such relationships, as related by a fellow BSC agent, Donald Downes. Downes recorded the similar arrangement he made with Pepper on accepting the terms of recruitment.

DOWNES: "I understand [the terms] perfectly, but I make a few conditions . . . One is that I am free to give any of the information I may turn up to any American government agency to which I think it would be interesting. Another is that on a personal, unofficial basis, I am free to inform a friend in Naval Intelligence what I am doing . . ."

PEPPER: "Agreed. When can you start?"[52]

Chapter 9

APRIL - MAY 1941

S oon after Lais's departure Betty heard from Arthur who had problems
of his own, having been the cause of a minor diplomatic scandal.
The subsidiary of a British oil company, Shell-Mex Ltd, had applied
to remit a sum of £25,000 to England and was refused by the Chilean
government. Shortly afterwards the company was approached by a former
employee of the Commission of Foreign Exchange offering to guarantee
the acceptance of their application for a *coima* (illicit pay-off) of 350,000
pesos. [1]

Arthur subsequently wrote a very strongly worded letter to the president of the Exchange Control, accusing former members of the commission of blackmail, and sent a copy to the Bank of London and South America, the bankers involved in the refused application. Arthur's closest friend was Rex Doublet, the bank's manager, so there may have been more to Arthur's attack on the Exchange commission than he formally reported to the Foreign Office; accusations of financial double-dealing had been bandied about and Doublet was innocently involved. The letter that Arthur sent to the bank was somehow leaked and published in the newspaper the next day, unfortunately (due to poor mail delivery) even before the president had received his copy.

As a result Arthur found himself in the middle of a row in which he was described in a complaint to the Foreign Office as "impetuous" and his ambassador, Sir Charles Orde, was accused of being too lenient with him.[2]

In a report ordered by London, however, Arthur was completely exonerated, and described in terms of warmest admiration as a man

who, despite his physical disability is a tower of strength and resource. He is a man, moreover, aggressive and inquisitive, in which I suspect he is much assisted by Mr Doublet, the Manager of the Bank of London and South America in Chile who has something of Mr Pack's own qualities and thoroughly enjoys working out with him ways and means of discomforting the strong local German community. He is a man much overworked and it would seem that Mr Pack's aggressiveness and possibly his tiredness may have created difficulties. . . .[3]

This report was passed around the Foreign Office in London and annotated with the opinions of its readers who were unitedly inclined to ignore the problem, send Pack on holiday and wait to see what happened. Besides, one soothed, "we already know that Pack is liable to occasional gaffes. . . ."[4] As a consequence Arthur found himself invited to Washington for two weeks in early June for discussions with Lord Halifax which would "greatly assist" Arthur in his "Economic Warfare work."[5]

There is little doubt that Arthur supplied intelligence through the Foreign Office to the Ministry of Economic Warfare. The extent of his involvement is not known, though the American consul at Santiago later reported to the State Department that Arthur was possibly involved "in subversive activities."[6] There is a certain piquancy in the fact that this aspect of Arthur's work was not known to Betty, while Arthur, it seems, did not know of Betty's activities in SIS.

Arthur wrote to Betty suggesting that while he was in Washington they should meet and discuss their personal situation. Betty readily agreed but, in the event, it was several months before Arthur was free to make the trip.

At about this time Betty had her first meeting with William Stephenson.[7] He arrived unannounced at her home in O Street one day, introducing himself as Mr. Williams from the New York office. Having never heard of any "Mr. Williams," Betty was at first suspicious of him.

I used to go to New York once a week. The routine never varied. I stayed at the same hotel on Madison and awaited MARION or MISTER HOWARD. They debriefed me, and gave me assignments, and acted as paymasters. They were my only contacts. So I had no way of telling who this "Mister Williams" might be.

I was worried about agents-provocateurs. The FBI was becoming troublesome and was now trying to figure out my game. I knew nothing then about squabbles and lines of command. I didn't want to know. It was enough to be told to deal with the two BSC contacts and—from time to time—anyone to whom they referred me.

It became obvious that Mister Williams was no ordinary man. He looked about forty-five, with the rugged handsomeness that is improved by a small flaw—in his case, what seemed a scar that pulled up one corner of his mouth. This gave him a lopsided grin.

He didn't waste time. He referred to a couple of things I'd done, in a way that told me he *must* be from the New York office. He dropped a couple of remarks that indicated he knew *all* my background—one I remember was a reference to when Cora, my mother, studied at the Sorbonne in Paris. It was a discreet little warning that I had been thoroughly investigated.

They talked for some time about her work in connection with the Italian admiral, and it gradually dawned on her who her visitor was. She asked him for his opinion on "the Chief." "Oh, the Chief," he said

. . . "terrible chap. . . ."[8] Stephenson did nothing without purpose and this occasion was no exception for he had a special assignment in mind and he undoubtedly wished to size her up for the job personally.

> He said he had an extremely difficult job for me. . . . "The New York office needs certain things" was the way he put it. And I knew he meant London, Churchill, the secret armies. . . .[9]

Betty did not exaggerate. Churchill did indeed "need certain things" and had said as much in a memo to "C," head of SIS in London.

> I am not satisfied with the volume or quality of information received from both the occupied and unoccupied areas of France. We seem as much cut off from these areas as from Germany. . . . So far as the Vichy Government is concerned it is not creditable that we have so little information. To what extent are Americans, Swiss and Spanish agents being used . . .[10]

What the description of this meeting between Stephenson and Betty rules out is that they had ever met previously in Europe. That he knew of her work for SIS there and her "free-lance" work in South America is not in doubt. But claims that the two were involved face-to-face in acquisition of information about the Enigma code machines is undermined; as are claims that Betty was already working for Stephenson while she was in Chile. Contemporarily involved in information gathering they may have been, but they certainly had never met before, nor worked together.[11]

Following Betty's success with the Italian admiral, Stephenson now had it in mind that she could repeat the process by making contact with a senior member of the Vichy diplomatic mission. BSC's particular interest in this can be summed up briefly. It was the aim of the Vichy French to keep the United States out of the war, to keep open the vital aid and relief channels between America and France, and to employ every method possible to break down the British blockade of France.[12] These aims were directly opposed to Stephenson's own primary objective, as he claimed Churchill himself had defined it: Bring the United States into the war at all costs.

To this end BSC unashamedly waged a war of propaganda, using "Dirty-Tricks" methods at every turn to discredit, distract and discomfort the Vichy French and other "neutral" pro-axis countries. Winston Churchill had aptly nicknamed his new Special Operations Executive (SOE) the "Ministry of Ungentlemanly Warfare," and there was certainly nothing gentlemanly about BSC's tactics. One of the most common methods used was to discover information of an embarrassing personal nature about important officials and then leak it to the press, along with full evidence to support the charges.

This is where Betty came in. Her instructions (when she received them from John Pepper a few days later) were brief: to find out anything and everything she could about everyone who worked at the Vichy embassy. BSC already had an agent working in the New York consulate who had provided a certain amount of information, but it was hoped that Betty, her social standing making personal introductions to senior diplomats possible, could achieve more.

In particular the matters of greatest concern to the British at that time were the Vichy plans for what remained of the French fleet—which Churchill did not want handed over to the Germans—and the $300 million in gold constituting France's reserves held on the island of Martinique. Clearly any information she could obtain on either subject should be regarded as of vital importance and telephoned to New York with all possible speed, ignoring the normal weekly shopping-trip arrangement.

Lest it be thought that the British were alone in their concern about the Vichy government it should be noted that the Americans were equally uneasy about the French situation. They were under no illusions about the real state of affairs in France and were well aware that the titular leader of the Vichy French government, the octogenarian hero of World War I, Marshal Henri Philippe Pétain, was merely a figurehead. He had been named premier at the time of the French defeat in 1940 in an attempt to lessen the national disgrace. The real power at Vichy was Admiral Jean Darlan, a cynical opportunist who admired the methods of, and collaborated openly with, the Nazis.

With Churchill's secret encouragement, the United States maintained diplomatic relations with Vichy; a major reason for this was the intelligence value of having an American diplomatic presence in Vichy France. Roosevelt nominated the highly regarded Admiral William Leahy as United States ambassador to the Pétain government with instructions to try to stiffen Vichy against granting further concessions to the Germans. In the public outcry that followed, many American liberals suggested a sympathy within the State Department that seemed warmer than necessary for the simple maintenance of diplomatic relations and strategic expediency. But the act enabled the Americans to establish a considerable intelligence force both in Vichy France and in the North African territories under Vichy control. This would all prove invaluable at a later date.

Reports flooding in from these U.S. intelligence sources underscored the importance of filtrating the Vichy legation to the United States. BSC had already accomplished this at the Vichy consulate in New York—also housed in Rockefeller Center. Now Stephenson had plans to do the same thing at the Washington Vichy embassy, in conjunction with Colonel William Donovan and his Office of Strategic Services (in simple terms, the American equivalent of BSC).

There was never any need for her controllers to explain or repeat instructions to Betty; indeed, she found repetition annoying, and made this obvious. The danger inherent in this rapid processing of information that came so naturally to Betty was that she might form conclusions too quickly, possibly before the whole picture had been presented.

A leading British handwriting analyst given a letter written by Betty during this period, but not knowing the identity (beyond her first name) or profession of his subject, stated:

There is virtually no indication of her analysing the information she received—it would be accepted as perceived. In addition she was very inclined to view a situation as she would want it to be, rather than as it necessarily was, and this would tend to reinforce the danger of her coming to too hasty or inconclusive conclusions.

A further concern would arise because her speed of comprehension would preclude her paying attention to the opinions of other people. . . .

Of assistance in her thinking was a strong organizational ability. As information was presented to her she would arrange her own thoughts and plans into proper perspective. She was also very aware of the importance of detail and had excellent powers of observation which would have increased her general awareness.

She set her sights high and this would lead her to enjoy new and untried endeavors. Not only was there challenge in these but it would probably help to satisfy her great need to be well out in front of others. This not only gave her a sense of security but might also help satisfy her need to be noticed as an individual. Supportive of her high goals was an awareness of her ability and confidence that she could achieve whatever she set out to achieve. . . . It was indeed her own goals that were most important and which motivated her, notwithstanding a strong sense of loyalty to what she believed to be right.[13]

The important Vichy personalities in the United States were Gaston Henry-Haye, the ambassador; George Bertrand-Vigne, counsellor, and Charles Emmanuel Brousse, press attaché. Betty's immediate task was to find out what she could about each and try to befriend any she considered likely to assist her. In New York she was able to read résumés on each man provided by Pepper. In Washington she made apparently casual enquiries about them, nervous that she might betray herself and thus her colleagues through overeagerness to achieve results on this assignment she had received from "the Chief." She was well aware of that streak of impatience in her temperament which had often led her into scrapes and she was now torn between the call for urgency and a desire to proceed carefully lest she "let the side down." There was something else new in this assignment. For the first time, she was being asked not to charm a man she already knew—and had likely already started to attract in passing—but to charm a man she had never even met, and she was anxious that she might not be able to establish the necessary relationship of empathy with an absolute stranger.

On May 19 Betty telephoned the French embassy, introducing herself as Elizabeth Thorpe, a journalist sympathetic to France's plight who wished to help by writing appropriately supportive articles. Her initial target was the ambassador himself, on whom BSC had already collected a large amount of unflattering biographical material, among which were indications that he was not averse to dalliance. Her request to interview Ambassador Henry-Haye was granted and on the following day, together with another woman "journalist" posing as her assistant, Betty went along to her appointment at the French chancery on Wyoming Avenue, at two o'clock as arranged. The chancery building was three doors down the street from her mother's apartment. The ambassador was out, at a meeting with Secretary of State Cordell Hull, but the two women were received by Charles Brousse, of whom Betty already knew a considerable amount.

From the personalities file in New York Betty knew that Brousse was forty-nine years old and came from Perpignan in the Pyrénées-Orientales. He had been married a number of times (reports varied between three and six) but his present wife, to whom he had been married for twelve years, was an American woman, formerly Catherine Calhoun Graves of Rome, Georgia, and a great-granddaughter of John C. Calhoun, once vice-president of the United States and states-rights advocate. She had worked as a voluntary nurse in World War I, during which time she was torpedoed three times, and received a British decoration for her service. Brousse was a doctor of laws, a licentiate in letters, and advisor on foreign commerce to the former French government. His record as a pilot in the 1914–1918 war was impressive. As commander of a group of bombing squadrons at the Battle of Saint-Mihiel in which his airplanes supported American ground forces, some twenty of his thirty-two fighters had been shot down. For his own part in the battle he had been awarded the Legion of Honour and croix de guerre and was mentioned four times in dispatches. Two of his brothers were killed in that war. He still held the rank of reserve captain on the General Staff of the Air Army in which, during 1939, he had served as an intelligence officer at Anglo-French head-quarters.[14] President and co-owner of a leading regional newspaper (*L'Indépendant*), he was president of the Syndicate of Regional Daily Newspapers, giving him a certain amount of power over public opinion in rural France, especially in the southern *départements*.

174

Apart from all this he was a thoroughly charming, good-looking and "robust" man and it did not take Betty long to realize that he was considerably attracted to her. He was also impressed with her accentless French, which went a long way towards removing a great deal of the usual awkwardness of a first meeting. She had naturally taken great pains over her appearance for this important rendezvous since she had hoped to make a good first impression on the ambassador, and was wearing a green dress that exactly matched the colour of her eyes.

The ambassador's delay allowed Monsieur Brousse to flirt delightfully, despite the presence of Betty's companion.* As he led the two women to the ambassador's office, an hour later, Brousse expressed the hope that he might see Betty again.

From her research Betty knew something of Henry-Haye's background. He, too, had been married to an American woman and their son was attending school in the United States. Prior to the German invasion of France he had been mayor of Versailles and friend of Marshal Pétain, but he was also known to be friendly with French fascists and in particular with Otto Abetz, then a German spy and later head of the German administration in Paris. Betty had read accounts which placed Henry-Haye high among supporters of the notorious Société France-Allemande (known for its subversive pro-Axis activities), and reported him as having "benefited financially [which was] a *secret de polichinelle* in . . . Paris."[15] Most sinister of all was a report that expatriate supporters of the Free French movement would have their families back in France harassed and prosecuted. This charge (though subsequently denied by Henry-Haye) is supported up by a memo from the FBI that

---

* This woman does not appear in either the series of newspaper articles written by Betty shortly before her death, nor in the biography which was compiled from her memoir by H. Montgomery Hyde shortly after her death. But in the first draft of her memoir she unequivocally accompanies Betty and she is also mentioned in BSC records of the incident. She was probably left out of the articles as a device to allow Brousse to tell her "all about himself" at that first meeting where Betty described him sitting on the edge of a desk deliberately revealing an amount of leg ("of which he was so proud") for her approval and looking at her, provocatively, up and down.

this Bureau has received information that French Ambassador Henri-Haye [*sic*] has received instructions to start collecting immediately all information possible on the de Gaulle movement sympathizers in the United States, in order to begin a merciless prosecution of their families in France. . . .

Yours sincerely,

J. Edgar Hoover.[16]

The ambassador was in a poor mood and considerably ruffled by his interview with Cordell Hull. Secretary Hull never liked Henry-Haye and described him as "a little man with ruddy cheeks and a truculent moustache [who] arrived with the taint of association with Laval and his group." Hull had been firm with Ambassador Henry-Haye, telling him plainly that he regarded Hitler as

the most devastating and all-pervading conqueror and destroyer within a thousand years and therefore we do not propose to say or do one single thing knowingly that would aid or encourage him and his ruthless forces of destruction. . . . It is impossible for the American people to understand why the French Government would hand to Mr Hitler a loaded gun with which to shoot at their best friends.[17]

A week earlier, following French vice premier Darlan's negotiations with Hitler's representative Otto Abetz, Pétain had issued a statement justifying the concessions offered to the Germans by the Vichy government: ". . . if, through our close discipline and our public spirit, we can conduct the negotiations in progress, France will surmount her defeat and preserve in the world her rank as a European and colonial power." President Roosevelt immediately ordered the Coast Guard to take custody of all French merchant ships in American ports.

Henry-Haye had requested the meeting both to protest the seizure of French ships and to complain about press criticism of the Vichy mission in the United States, which he told Secretary Hull was inaccurate and misleading. Cutting across Henry-Haye's protests Hull told him curtly:

You can imagine the astonishment of peoples here and everywhere when they saw Pétain's announcement with its clear, express and implied meanings. The definite belief was created in every nation of the world that the French Government at Vichy has gone straight into Hitler's arms, with all the implications of such a step and that the well-known pro-Hitler officials in the French Government have finally taken control, their first thought being to deliver France body and soul to Hitler. . . .[18]

Arriving back at his embassy the flustered Henry-Haye found two American newspaperwomen. Having heard that they were disposed to be sympathetic, he spent time justifying himself and telling them about his "difficult" mission. "France's future," he said according to BSC records, "requires cooperation with Germany. If your car is in the ditch, you turn to the person who will help you put it on the road again. That is why we will work with Germany."[19] The two women listened attentively in the two-and-a-half-hour off-the-record interview, occasionally making notes for an article which would never be written. Betty, an accurate reporter in any case, was able to recall long tracts of conversation without notes. "He was still smarting when he saw me," she reported, "[and] was full of contempt for American vulgarity and lack of civilized manners. Americans did not comprehend the subtleties of European politics. How dare they judge France when they themselves had never suffered invasion." The ambassador gave very frank replies to a number of penetrating questions and was neither reticent nor particularly cautious; the opportunity to impress an anti-British line upon the American public through these two sympathetic women was too good to pass up.

When the interview was finally brought to an end the ambassador showed the women to the door and told Betty he would be happy to see her any time she cared to visit the embassy. Charles Brousse accompanied the two women out of the embassy onto the street, shaking hands with one and kissing the hand of the other. Betty's hand.

The BSC official history states that both men were to see Betty again. "The Ambassador saw more of her than he would have liked. The Press Attaché saw more than was good for him."[20] And Betty, who was happy that she had achieved her first objective of making contact, felt sure that she would be hearing from one of the two men again. And within a few days. Her judgment was not faulty. The next morning a Georgetown

177

florist delivered a bouquet with a note from Brousse suggesting Betty meet him for lunch at the Ritz-Carlton Hotel.

She wrote that she never forgot that lunch. The attraction which had begun the previous day in more formal surroundings was now fuelled by champagne, and over lunch flamed into open desire.

It started mundanely enough, with Brousse continuing to boast about his background and family. From here he graduated to telling Betty about his innumerable affairs. Betty responded by telling him about her travels as the wife of a British diplomat whom she was now, she stressed, divorcing. This was as well, for Brousse displayed great antagonism towards Britain over the attack on the French fleet off Oran in the previous year, where French casualties had been heavy. Many Frenchman shared Brousse's fury over this and found the act unforgivable.

Prior to the incident Churchill had been concerned that French warships should not fall into the hands of the Germans or Italians and when he received Vichy assurances but failed to see evidence that this would not be allowed to happen he issued the instruction to take into custody all French warships in British ports. The British navy then delivered an ultimatum to the admiral of a large part of the French fleet anchored at Mers-el-Kébir near Oran in North Africa that it must either join the British or proceed to British or West Indian or United States ports to be interned for the duration of the war.[21] When the French admiral refused, the British opened fire, putting all but one of the ships out of commission.* Vice-premier Pierre Laval urged a declaration of war, stating "France has never had, and will never have, a more relentless enemy than Great Britain. All our history attests to it."[22]

In discussing this with Betty, Brousse made it clear that despite his

---

* Admiral Sir James Somerville who commanded Force H, which attacked and sank the French warships, had questioned his orders and wrote that it was the "biggest political blunder of modern times. . . . The French were furious that we did not trust them to prevent the ships falling into German hands. . . . [But] I'd sooner that happened than we should have to kill a lot of our former allies. We all feel thoroughly dirty and ashamed. . . ."

anger at the British he was no admirer of Hitler. He was simply a loyal Frenchman, trying to help France survive a stunning defeat. He felt strongly that France's best chance of survival lay in maintaining friendly relations with the United States. His arguments justifying the Vichy government's remaining friendly with Germany struck Betty as weak.* His family holdings were all situated in that part of France under Vichy control, not the part occupied by Germany. Of course it would have been foolish of the Brousse family to openly oppose the ruling government. All of this boded well for Betty's plans.

These important issues may seem to be unromantic subject matter for the first tryst of Betty and Charles, but in 1941 it was almost impossible for two intelligent and worldly people to meet without discussing world events. Brousse was not entirely anaesthetized by current political problems, however. Much later he was to confide to Betty that it was her voice that first attracted him to her. Others have attested to the alluring quality of Betty's voice, describing it as quiet, well-bred, soothing; in several languages almost devoid of any accent. Her laugh, which flattered many men into believing they were interesting beyond their dreams, was merry and genuine. In short she was an enchanting companion, leaving aside the fact that she was also quite stunningly attractive. She could tell from Brousse's small attentions to her during the meal that the combination of her personality and looks was having the desired effect. What she hadn't bargained for was her own fierce attraction to him.

When he took her hand across the table and caressed it before turning it and gently kissing the palm, she felt not only a thrill of triumph but a

---

* Though many Vichy Frenchmen behaved cravenly through this time it must be said that once the decision was taken in 1940 to surrender to the Germans and take France out of the war (rather than do what Poland did and take the government into exile and from there continue the fight), the French did not have much practical choice other than to go along with the Germans. More than half of France was under German direct occupation and the remainder, the rump country called Vichy France after its capital in Vichy, was left with no army on the long border separating it from German-controlled areas. Any time the Vichy French failed to be sufficiently obeisant to the Germans, German panzer divisions would have poured across the borders and occupied the remainder of France. Indeed, this eventually happened.

sexual *frisson* which, she well knew, made the burgeoning relationship a potentially dangerous one. Nevertheless it was too delicious an experience not to enjoy. He stroked her bare arm with his fingertips, apparently absently, during their long conversations, "as though he were feeling a silken fabric." She deliberately lightened the conversation by telling him anecdotes and stories ("a few naughty ones") about diplomats whom she'd known over the years, and was at her sparkling best as she cast a spell that was to entrance Brousse for the next twenty-odd years. Their talk became more intimate, and by late afternoon when they finally left the table Betty had already started to make plans for capitalizing on what was an obvious conquest.

Previous experience had taught her that the best way of captivating a man was to "play" him for a while, allow herself to be wooed and won over during a period of days or even weeks. This also established the fact that a sexual encounter with her was to be prized, not taken lightly; after all, her ultimate aim was to ask men to betray their countries for the privilege of knowing her fully. Nevertheless she instinctively felt that Brousse was not a man to be trifled with. Rather than lose him by too much coyness she decided to make the game a short one. She would, she decided, capitulate at their next meeting.

Charles had other ideas as he drove her home to O Street, followed (though the couple did not know it) by FBI agents who were adding to their already considerable file on Betty. These many meetings with foreign diplomats, the report concluded, constituted highly suspicious behaviour.

Betty's maid was out and once inside the door Charles lost no time in putting his own plan into operation. After a few passionate kisses in the hallway he picked Betty up and carried her up the narrow stairs. Uttering feeble feminine protests, but with alacrity in her heart, she allowed herself to be carried into the bedroom, where Charles laid her on the bed and began to undress her. He was a skilled lover, ardent and passionate; Betty was only too aware that here was a man she could love—indeed, she was already half in love with him. So her response was not merely rooted in her need to entrap him. She was as thrilled by their lovemaking as he was.

For many women such strong feelings would have spelled a death-knell to plans to "turn" Charles, but Betty saw no reason why the objective she started with should be set aside. Many hours later Charles left, promising to see her on the following day. She sat for a while savouring the memory of the past few hours. Then she telephoned John Pepper in New York to report on her progress.

"It's in the bag," she told him.

Chapter 10

For the next few weeks Betty saw Charles almost every day, and it soon became clear to her that this relationship was special. Her feelings for Charles were stronger than anything she had ever known. Here at last was the "complete" love that she had always thought would never happen to her, and yet she could not forget her duty to the service: the need to extract information from Charles. Quite where it would all lead she could not guess, but for the moment she was intoxicated by the romance. The absolute discretion they employed, which Charles believed necessary to prevent his wife's discovery of his affair, but for which Betty had her own reasons, gave an added piquancy to it. Surprisingly, Betty introduced Charles to her mother, who noted to her daughter-in-law Shirlee that the two could hardly bear to be out of each other's sight. Cora characterized the relationship in somewhat indelicate terms: "They're so much in love I think they go to the bathroom together!"[1]

Shirlee remembers Betty during this period:

> I was very much in awe of her because she was so gorgeous and glamorous, but she was very sweet to me. Her colouring was lovely, green eyes and lovely light auburn hair . . . She had an odd, distinctive walk, not graceful—not clumsy . . . just distinctive. She was good at everything she did. I think I was told pretty early on that she had two children and there was no secret about Tony. I knew that he was at school in England and Betty said to me once, "Why don't you write to him?" so I did.

> I remember once I was in a taxi with Betty just before I married George and she said to me "If you want your marriage to George to succeed you'll have to get him away from my mother." And she was right. [The marriage lasted only three years.] Mrs Thorpe was hard to resist, a very powerful woman. Domineering. All three of them, George, Betty and Jane were adults and yet they behaved like naughty children when Mrs Thorpe was around. None of them was *quite* normal.

> Jane was an alcoholic who later reformed, but once (before Betty met Charles) when Mrs Thorpe had to go out I offered to sit with her as she wasn't to be left alone. After a while Betty arrived with a Polish count who, I think, was a diplomat. He had lipstick on his face but neither was aware of it. Anyway Betty and her count took over and I left them there [The count was probably Jerzy Polocki, Polish ambassador and an old friend of Betty's from her time in Spain when he was attaché at Madrid].[2]

In a subsequent interview Mrs Thorpe told me, "You only had to look at them to see that Betty and Charles were very in love with each other —it was the sort of love that everyone hopes will happen to them." Betty's future behaviour towards Charles would confirm that the feeling she had for him was special. Yet she never allowed her very strong feelings to distract her from her mission. As she went through that very exciting

184

period of new love, where lovers strive to learn all there is to know about each other in as short a time as possible, she mixed into all those questions of her own to which she wanted answers another set passed on to her by John Pepper Whatever she learned about Charles she dutifully passed back to New York. For example, that Charles's recall had been ordered about the time of her first meeting with him, but that Henry-Haye had intervened and insisted on his retention in Washington; that on the orders of Henry-Haye, Charles had maintained close contacts with first and second secretaries at the German embassy, "von Strempel, Heribert, von Roth and Ernst Ostermann."

Gradually the file on him was built up. Other intelligence agencies were also interested in Charles; according to an ONI report on him dated June 23, 1941, he "is reported as one of three men now leading underground work of Vichy in the United States and working under order of the French Ambassador Henry-Haye. . . ."[3]

From now on Charles Brousse, too, would be the subject of a round-the-clock surveillance. Soon both he and his wife would have their own dossiers with BSC, and almost identical ones with ONI who had close ties with the British Intelligence organization.

Information believed to be reliable reports that subject: ["Katherine Brousse alias Mrs. Charles E. Brousse"] allows herself to make violently anti-American statements. She and her husband own a villa in Saigon, Indo-China. In 1938 they had carefully built up a collection of Empire ornaments of which they were very proud; suddenly they disposed of the entire collection and announced the intention of leaving Paris, this plan never materialized. Subject and husband were reported as constant visitors at the apartment of Camille Chautemps. . . .[4]

Such is the bread-and-butter work of intelligence gathering. So Charles and Kay had a villa in Saigon. So they disposed of a favoured collection of ornaments and announced their intention to leave Paris, but then apparently changed their minds. So they had visited Camille Chautemps frequently. What could these things mean? By themselves, little. Nevertheless, the mass of seemingly irrelevant and insignificant facts are collected and duly recorded, all in the hope that one day one more seemingly irrelevant fact will come along and cast some prior bit of information in a new light, and maybe start to suggest the outlines of a picture puzzle. But it all starts with the day-to-day gathering and recording of scraps of information, a generally boring routine.

But Betty reported more than mere scraps of factual information. On June 15, Charles told her of two telegrams which had been transmitted that day. The first, number 4093, was from Admiral Jean François Darlan, the Vichy government's ambitious minister of marine. It asked Henry-Haye to transmit details of all British naval ships in U.S. dockyards for repair and his assessment of the type of repairs.[5] The French navy can have had little use for such information; patently, the information had been requested by Darlan for his German cohorts. For obvious reasons all British ships kept their departure dates totally secret; German knowledge of repair schedules could help plan U-boat ambushes as vessels left U.S. ports.

It is not easy to work out what Charles's feeling must have been when he learned of this cable. While he held grudges against the British that went back to their attack on the French fleet at Mers-el-Kébir and their championship of de Gaulle (in whom Charles had no faith at all), he did not look forward with any happiness to a total German victory. Prior to the war he had worked with British Air Intelligence and if driven to choose between the Germans and the British one supposes that his vote would have been cast, albeit marginally, for the British.

The ambassador's reply (cable no. 1236–1237) listing information obtained by the naval attaché, Captain Pierre Benech, went out on the same day. It advised that information "from a good source" revealed that there were three British naval ships in U.S. ports undergoing major work: the carrier *Illustrious* at Norfolk, Virginia; the battleship *Repulse* at Philadelphia; and two cruisers and the battleship *Malaya* (already notified) at New York. All these ships, the cable advised, were undergoing work of a long duration. The first to be ready for sea would be the *Malaya* but without doubt she would be immobilized for not less than a month.[6]

Some months later, after her refit in the United States, the *Repulse* was sent to the Pacific, where she was sunk with HMS *Prince of Wales* by the Japanese. "In all the war," Churchill wrote, "I never received a more profound shock."[7]

Charles told Betty about the cables that night. Somehow she persuaded him to obtain in-clear (decoded) copies which she passed on to New York. It was the first really important intelligence that Charles passed to Betty. Working on the premise that first acts of betrayal are always the most difficult to bring about, his willingness to provide the cables were an indication to her and to BSC that she had genuinely turned Charles.

As well as conveying important information such as this, Betty learned and reported how Charles, a loyal Frenchman, held Pétain and Laval in low regard; an opinion, he believed, that was shared by many Frenchmen. On a more personal note he saw Henry-Haye as less suitable to be France's ambassador to the United States than Charles himself. Charles's own father had been a member of the pre-war government, and the family had extensive holdings in France and were old-line and respected; Henry-Haye was parvenu. He also confided that his marriage was not a happy one. Katherine, "Kay," was subject to frequent bouts of ill temper and they often quarrelled. He told Betty with surprising candour that he would be prepared to divorce Kay but for the fact that she was a rich woman. Equally surprising was that Betty found no reason to comment unfavourably on such an attitude in him.

When Charles had been recalled by the government at Vichy, he revealed to Betty, Henry-Haye had offered to pay him a retainer from his own resources to enable Charles to stay in the United States and work for him. The amount, $600 a month, was only half the salary he had been paid by the Vichy government, but Charles had accepted because his wife wished him to remain in the United States. Now, he told Betty, he could not continue living on this pittance. Nor was he prepared to ask Kay to contribute. The only alternative was to return to France. Would Betty be prepared to go with him?

Betty was delighted with the idea. First, of course, she would not have wanted to face the prospect of separation from Charles. But as well the thought of serving British Intelligence in occupied Europe was thrilling to her. She reported the request to John Pepper, who suggested that this might be the right time to tell Charles about her intelligence work. But they agreed that she should not tell him the whole truth. Not that she worked for British Intelligence. Instead, she told Charles she would go with him if and when he had to leave and made her "confession": she was working for American intelligence, but with only one aim in mind —to help France.

Would Charles help her? She played particularly on his dislike of Laval, under whose leadership the Vichy government was not doing much to redeem French honour. It had refused to give the British an inch in the Middle East, and for all its bravado had suffered a quick and humiliating defeat of its forces there. Subsequently, it gave in meekly to Japanese demands in Indo-China, with the result that one of France's proudest and most beautiful pre-war colonies, including the exquisite city of Saigon, with its wide boulevards designed after those of Paris, was now in the hands of the Japanese. Socialist-turned-fascist Pierre Laval's pro-Nazi policies were so extreme that even his Vichy colleagues could not stomach them. With active Nazi support he began to introduce drastic measures against French Jews in the unoccupied zone, causing a furor among Americans.

There was more than a germ of truth to Betty's quiet assertions that France was no better fed and supplied than Holland or Belgium, which were wholly occupied. Nor could it be denied that were the remains of the French fleet, now scattered between Martinique and Alexandria, to stand alongside the British navy, it could contribute substantially to the defeat of the Germans. And how long, she asked Charles, would Rommel be able to fight on in North Africa if French North Africa at his back became unfriendly territory? Arguments that France was honour bound to respect the deal Hitler had forced on her while her army lay defeated and helpless were beginning to sound hollow. Helping the Americans was surely the most reasonable course of action for any proud and patriotic Frenchman to follow; ultimately, it was the only way to defeat the Germans and remove the stain of defeat from French honour.

Nevertheless, it is certain that Charles would not have chosen the path he subsequently did choose had he not been so besotted with Betty. Despite Betty's arguments, the Vichy government was, even if miserably wrong-headed, the legitimate government of France, and it was no easy step for Charles, who had an impressive background of service to his country, to betray it. The present regime might be a poor one, but unless and until changed it was entitled to the support of all Frenchmen.

Charles Brousse was fond of wine and food and the good things in life. He was not a poor man but his assets were in France and his wealth was not in cash. The life-style he enjoyed in America had clearly not been financed out of the small salary he was paid by Henry-Haye, suggesting that for some months he had either been living on savings or had in fact been subsidized by his wife. FBI checks on his bank account confirmed end-of-month balances of about $100. He could not therefore have been too unhappy when Betty offered to arrange that he be paid through the U.S. Treasury for the work he was doing for the Americans. While Charles would not have betrayed his country simply for money, considering the contributions he would be making to the American cause, accepting a small subsidy to his meagre income must have seemed justified.

From the end of July 1941 Charles provided daily intelligence reports that Betty fed straight to BSC in New York. As the weeks went by, he produced more and more information, so that actually there were very few top-level happenings inside the Vichy embassy of which BSC were not informed. Brousse had a good memory for conversation and at some personal risk took stenographic notes as the ambassador read out cables to his senior staff each day. The results were considered important enough for Betty to make two or three trips a week to New York to deliver them in person to Marion or Mr. Howard.

It was on one of these shopping trips, on August 28, coincidentally the very day of an assassination attempt on Laval, that Betty met Harford Montgomery Hyde, a fellow worker in Stephenson's organization. Although this meeting seemed an unimportant one at the time it was to have important repercussions for both many years later.

Hyde had previously worked at Bermuda in the British postal censorship office which was located there throughout the war. From Stephenson he had heard about Betty and her exploits in Spain, Poland and Chile, as well as her more recent success in connection with Admiral Lais. Intrigued, Hyde asked Marion to introduce him to Betty, who was working under the code name "Cynthia" at the time. Though Betty used many names in her career, Hyde always called her by that name, and it is because of this and the fact that he was the first writer to break silence on her story that she is often referred to as Cynthia.[8]

Betty was waiting for them at the Ritz-Carlton Hotel on Madison Avenue at the appointed time and Marion introduced Hyde as "Mr. Montgomery." Hyde recalled that Betty wore a simple, close-fitting grey suit which showed off her perfect figure to advantage; no hat on her shining amber-coloured hair, which she wore in a short, fashionable style. From the stories Hyde had heard circulating about Betty he expected to meet a woman with movie-star glamour. Instead, he found a quiet, intelligent woman who "looked smart and attractive." But as they talked he found himself astonished. The thought that flashed across his mind was, "What is this pacing tiger doing in this wholesome All-American conventional disguise?"

She had a force, or magnetism, to a terrifying degree. It leapt like light from the whole of her, not just from her green eyes or wide smile. Many a man, I think, read this force as warmth; as a concentrated and passionate interest in himself. The trick of making a man feel he is her entire universe is an old feminine wile, but Cynthia had it to the *nth* degree. I felt the impact at once.[9]

Marion de Chastellaine, Betty's chief contact in those days, also remembers this meeting, but her recollections of Betty were notably less stage-struck than Hyde's. She began working with Betty after the Italian affair, so did not yet know her very well at this time:

She could be an extremely *entertaining* person but she could also be very depressed, I gathered that this stemmed from her mother's dominance. The mother was always wanting Betty to do things she didn't want to do which annoyed her. Of course Betty enjoyed the *glamour* of the thing. She had got herself involved with Enigma in Poland in '37 and '38 and came into the service of her own volition . . . I think she came across some information and then set about finding someone to pass it on to . . .[10]

At that meeting Betty discussed with Hyde her infiltration of the Vichy embassy and her relationship with Charles Brousse. Hyde himself had recently scored several hits on the Vichyites by intercepting mail found to contain all manner of vital data, and even on one occasion had searched the luggage belonging to the daughter of Pierre Laval, an act which yielded to the British important correspondence linking members of the Vichy administration with Hitler's lieutenants. By coincidence, in the previous October Hyde had confiscated letters from Charles Brousse, then the new press attaché, on his way to Washington. This had enabled Brousse to make vigorous protests through the American newspapers about gross violations of diplomatic privilege, but it had also provided the British with a certain amount of useful information. Hyde subsequently issued an instruction that *all* mail to and from Brousse was to be intercepted.

On her next visit Betty asked Marion if she could see Hyde again but was told that he had left New York. This was not true, or at least it was not true that he had left permanently. He remained stationed at the New York office for another eighteen months but it was well known that Stephenson did not approve of too much cross-fertilization and as a deliberate policy kept his people very much in separate compartments.[11]

Meanwhile, though Betty was not aware of it, BSC had two other woman agents working *inside* the Vichy embassy. One of them, Madame Andrée Cadet, had worked for the commercial attaché in New York. Contacted by a BSC agent there, she fell in love with the agent, was "recruited" and persuaded to provide information. John Pepper, who "handled all French contacts in the United States during the war period,"[12] assigned Donald Downes as her controller, and she received $300 a month for her services. She brought out the commercial attaché's papers by the simple expedient of hiding extra carbon copies in her ample bosom and delivering them to her go-between "Mr. MacDonald" or mailing them if they did not seem important. The amount of money she wanted was considered relatively modest by Pepper, but Mme Cadet wanted love too; her amorous appetite was immense and was said by Downes to have taken a good deal of "Mr. MacDonald's" time.[13] SIS was an equal opportunity employer; both men and women agents were expected to use physical charms in the pursuit of information.

Mme Cadet had a friend, an excellent secretary who was also recruited to serve BSC's cause. When the commercial attaché moved to Washington as the financial attaché, Andrée Cadet and her friend accompanied him; the friend subsequently became secretary to Ambassador Henry-Haye. [14]

From August 1941 Andrée Cadet provided copies of all cables and correspondence that came within her competence. Her friend, the ambassador's secretary, provided cables and information from the ambassador's office, including in-clear copies of all the naval attaché's cables to Vichy, which were not always available to Charles. Meanwhile, Charles Brousse was feeding *his* series of cables, many classified beyond the cleared level of the ambassador's secretary and some duplicating those supplied by the other two. This meant that a great deal of the intelligence coming out of the embassy could be counter-checked.

The amount of material flowing into BSC's New York office became considerable; up to six people working under John Pepper were employed scrutinizing it each day, cabling the more important items in code through the FBI to London and summarizing the remainder for dispatch by diplomatic bag. Through the two women employed inside the embassy, BSC obtained other valuable materials; for example, rubber stamps, blank passports and details of the secret marks made upon visas issued by the embassy and its New York consulate. These marks were intended to indicate to examiners the degree of reliability of the passport holder. Knowledge of these marks could be used to great effect in creating papers for agents being sent into Europe through Vichy France. [15]

Among the reports submitted by the ambassador's secretary was one in September comprising minutes of a top-level meeting between Henry-Haye, Charles Brousse, several senior members of staff and Jean-Louis Musa, an agent of Vichy working as a businessman in New York. BSC had been on to Musa for many months and the concatenated results of the work of many agents (including Betty and Charles) resulted in a dossier about his affairs, including his sexual activities, and the work of the Vichy officials in the United States. Backed up by photostated documents and transcripts of recorded telephone conversations, it showed how Musa had bought passports and visas from German agents, and how he hired a defector from the British Purchasing Commission (part of BSC) to run a pro-Nazi propaganda sheet and set up a Vichy French news service called Téléradio Havas, all for the purpose of distributing propaganda throughout the Western Hemisphere. He also

. . . did a little pimping on the side and found himself working with French girls willing to pass along information useful to Vichy's economic-intelligence unit. He had a scheme for chartering ships that would carry refugees from Europe to Mexico, returning to ports in Unoccupied France with cargoes that could not be shipped directly to Germany because of trade controls.[16]

Stephenson took a copy of this dossier to England in July 1941 and arranged for another copy to be sent to President Roosevelt, who read it "as a bedtime story" and described it as "The most fascinating reading I have had for a long time . . . the best piece of comprehensive intelligence I have come across since the last war."[17]

Meanwhile, BSC were busily engaged in organizing a press campaign to discredit Musa in particular, and Vichy in general. Several leading American journalists, sympathetic to Stephenson, and in favour of an Anglo-American alliance, co-operated in this. On August 31, the *New York Herald Tribune* broke what was to be a series of stories under headlines such as VICHY MEN PLAY NAZIS' GAME HERE IN SHELTER OF EMBASSY and VICHY EMBASSY HEADING CLIQUE OF AGENTS AIDING NAZIS. The stories accused Musa of a variety of offences: involvement with smuggling the advance plans of de Gaulle's ill-fated Dakar expedition to Vichy; being the originator of plans to erect a powerful radio station on Saint-Pierre, a French island off Canada; and plotting to acquire secret plans of a lightweight Bren gun, "the mainstay of British invasion defenses," using German money. In addition, the newspaper pictured letters to Musa from Georges Bertrand-Vigne regarding his lavish expenses:

The Ambassador has at his disposal from now on an average of $1,000 a month for remuneration of services for "information" such as you are giving (without counting $1,000 for travelling). So cheer up.

The articles pointed out that these accusations were backed with documentary and photographic evidence which the hapless Musa, "a shadowy figure who signs himself 'secretary to Ambassador Henry-Haye' " could not refute. Nor could Henry-Haye refute the fact that Musa was on his payroll; photographic evidence of payments by him into Musa's bank account had been supplied to the press.[18]

In exposing Musa, the articles, which were nationally syndicated, went on to mention two others who

> at present head the underground work of Vichy in the United States. One is Colonel Georges Bertrand-Vigne, the one-eyed war veteran officially listed as counsellor of the embassy . . . Another is Charles Brousse, the embassy's former press attaché, whose recall was ordered some time ago by Vichy. However Captain Brousse has remained in Washington through the intervention of Mr. Henry-Haye and has maintained contacts with . . . officials at the German embassy.[19]

An additional list of people who worked in various capacities as couriers and liaison agents on Vichy operations in the United States while operating under the protection of diplomatic status followed. The list included Josée de Chambrun, daughter of Pierre Laval, and wife of a Vichy diplomat; "tall, suave" Count Serge Fleury; and Camille Chautemps. The whole was tied up by citing links to Otto Abetz, Hitler's personal representative in France.

The overall effect of the articles was to change public opinion of the Vichy mission to America. Hitherto, the Vichy French had been regarded by many as a brave group of proud men attempting to put a bold face on defeat; now they were exposed as "Nazi hirelings" and potential enemies of the United States. Henry-Haye tried to minimize the damage by calling a press conference, but BSC arranged for a "friendly" reporter to be present, primed with questions the embarrassing answers to which he already had documentary proof. The result was another leading article in the *Herald Tribune*, stating that though Henry-Haye spoke on behalf of the French people, "a friendly power, the government he represents has repeatedly done everything within its power to promote a German victory . . . and to embarrass the British resistance to which the United States is pledged to render every aid in its power."[20] An infuriated Henry-Haye blamed the situation on a "de Gaullist-Jewish-British-FBI intrigue."

At the meeting in Washington on September 8, minuted by Henry-Haye's secretary (she was clearly unaware that Brousse was "friendly," since her reports on him are as condemnatory as those on the others), feelings ran high; it was the unanimous opinion of those present that a great mistake had been made in failing to register Musa with the State Department as a foreign agent. His salary and expenses were confirmed as amounting to $1,000 a month and for the time being would continue, on Henry-Haye's insistence, but it was the consensus that he had been totally compromised and was no longer of any use to them.

Later in this same meeting Brousse reported that there were between "17 and 21 American agents at work in Dakar operating as vice-consuls."[21] In commenting on the copy of the report sent to him, the chief of naval operations stated, "This . . . shows very clearly that M. Brousse is extremely ill-informed on this phase of American activities. . . ."[22] More likely, Charles was *intentionally* misleading Henry-Haye with information fed him by BSC through Betty.

As for the media attacks on Charles Brousse, they continued, along with the attacks on Henry-Haye and Bertrand-Vigne. The three were the subject of intense, vitriolic publicity, although, notably, no specific accusations other than his liaison with the German embassy officials were ever made about Charles. It could not have been pleasant for him, for it resulted in his being given a cold shoulder by Washington society, but the attacks and the company into which they put him gave him a certain cachet—and some protection—within Vichy circles. Charles, who believed he was working for the Americans, was not in on the fact that the British were behind the campaign. If he ever suspected it he was one of a very few. Indeed, even SIS London seemed not to know, for a few weeks after the series of articles appeared Stephenson received a cable calling his attention to them which, ran the message, "we expect you will have seen in the *New York Herald Tribune* . . . Please comment."[23]

However, senior State Department and FBI officials suspected the British of planting the series of stories and in varying degrees were annoyed by it, in particular Adolf Berle, assistant secretary of state. Stephenson had made a bad enemy in Berle and this enmity would later have serious repercussions for Stephenson.* But the Americans were not slow in information gathering on their own account and had discovered equally damaging information on the Vichy French, such as the fact that the demagogue Laval, operating through his son-in-law René de Chambrun, had been active in transactions involving the purchase of large blocks of stock in American-owned French corporations at depreciated prices for resale to Germans, and that he had also been active in purchasing French francs for conversion into dollars at 250 francs for a dollar instead of the normal rate. It was known that he had a large personal fortune in America.

Betty's role during all this kerfuffle, apart from acting as the courier for information supplied by Charles, was to offer him a strong base of love and unqualified support. Kay was completely unnerved by the unpleasant publicity; soon after her picture appeared in newspaper articles alongside that of her husband she went off to spend time with her family in the South.

Using information provided by Charles, Betty provided a comprehensive report on all senior French personnel and the present situation regarding their activities.

> Bertrand-Vigne, Georges: . . . in disrepute by the Ambassador. He . . . is still receiving the sum of $1125 per month from a special fund authorised by Pierre Laval. Prior to the recent exposé in the Herald Tribune, the Ambassador communicated to Laval and Darlan his complete

---

* Adolf Berle appears often in this story in his role as a sort of assistant secretary of state in charge of keeping the British from leading the United States into war, but he had another life earlier on in the New Deal. When FDR first came into office he assembled around him a group of generally young advisors from academia to help him deal with the Great Depression and construct the new economic order he envisioned for the country. The group came to be known as FDR's Brain Trust and Adolf Berle, from Columbia, was one of them. Political cartoonists portrayed the group derisively, with oversized ovoid-shaped heads; pundits mocked their generally good intentions but lack of common sense and practical experience. They epitomized the stereotype of the better-educated bleeding-heart liberal whose complex solutions created more social problems than they solved.

As the Hitler threat became clear in Europe, most of these braintrusters became staunch internationalists, but Adolf Berle evolved into a super-practical, super-cautious advocate of not rocking the boat with Vichy France or even with Hitler.

confidence in Bertrand-Vigne and recommended the continuance of the special appropriation for his salary. . . .

Following the exposé . . . Bertrand-Vigne personally submitted his resignation which, however, was not accepted. The Ambassador feels he cannot at this time release Bertrand-Vigne and Musa following so closely the sensational newspaper stories, but [intends] to do so after a reasonable amount of time. He has instructed Bertrand-Vigne to do nothing and see no one in the Embassy.

Henry-Haye, Gaston . . . as an indication of the disfavour in which [he] holds B-V it was related that at a recent dinner party attended by the French and Brazilian ambassadors B-V made a general statement that Henry-Haye was going on a picnic with a young French girl he brought from New York. The Ambassador later stated to Brousse "What can you do with a fool like that."

Further information followed on the ambassador's affairs with several women, providing dates and details of the relationships. One of these women had been secretary to a former vice-president of the United States. In reporting on Charles Brousse Betty advised that he "expected to be given Musa's salary of $300 per month [and if he could] successfully expedite the recall of Bertrand-Vigne he will receive an additional amount from the special fund set up to pay for [his] services. . . ." She also provided details of names, addresses and telephone numbers she had copied from Charles's address book, which included those of known Nazis, and stated that he had told her that "by now Germany has 252 submarines" and that a sum of $1,000,000 was available per year for German propaganda in the Western Hemisphere but that much of that figure was being used to maintain consulates and legations in South America.

The effect on Betty of this double-game was great strain. Her mother noticed it and put it down to her relationship with a married man; while not disliking Charles himself she disapproved of the relationship. In late September, when Arthur arrived in Washington for his delayed discussions with Ambassador Halifax,[24] he found Betty very bright and brittle, clearly under stress. Not knowing the reason he was inclined to put her attitude down to sexual excitement. She told him she was no longer seeing Paul

Fairly but had fallen in love with a Frenchman whom she could not marry because he was already married and could not, yet, see any way to obtain a divorce. Arthur made an impatient half-hearted suggestion that they might yet attempt a reconciliation; under English law it was necessary, in any case, for him to make the suggestion. However, Betty insisted that Arthur should go ahead and divorce her, using the letter she had provided admitting adultery with Fairly. Clearly it was not going to be possible for Arthur to begin divorce proceedings until after the war, because any divorce would have to be obtained under English law; Arthur insisted on that.

With regard to Denise, Betty recognized that it was impossible for her to have the child with her during the war. But after the war, she told Arthur, she would expect to see her daughter for a short time each year. They parted amicably enough, though Arthur came away with no very great opinion of his wife, whom he now regarded as "impossible." There is a possibility that Betty attempted to tell him about her work for the Secret Service, for he wrote, later (without explaining the statement), that she appeared to exist in a world of make-believe.[25]

But Charles, too, was keeping his options open and there were things he did not tell Betty. BSC learned through their other agents at the embassy that he had sent to his newspaper in France "a complete and detailed report on the present strength of U.S. Armed Forces . . . subject is again reported to be outspoken in vituperous attacks against the British and Americans. . . ."[26] "Subject still owns . . . *L'Indépendant*, [despite] its relative unimportance, and contrary to all usage for provincial papers, a Berlin correspondent is maintained."[27]

In November Betty persuaded Charles to pass to her in-clear copies of *all* cipher telegrams being dispatched and received by the chancery. In addition, he produced a daily written report that "written as it was in great detail, filled in many gaps" arising out of intelligence gained from other sources, such as mail intercepted by the British Censorship Office at Bermuda, etc.[28]

By now Charles had made himself indispensable to the beleaguered Henry-Haye and had gained his trust, not least because of the "trial by media" they had shared. But Charles had become totally disillusioned at

Vichy's support of Japanese actions in the Pacific. As the Japanese threat mounted towards the end of November 1941, he "came over" completely.

The importance of the information he provided cannot be overestimated; a researcher scanning these files today can find fullest details of all day-to-day embassy matters, including diplomatic exchanges with the president and senior officials of the State Department; contacts with French possessions in the region of South America, in particular those with Admiral Robert, governor of the vital island of Martinique; the position of the French fleet; messages between Washington and other French diplomatic missions in the Pacific (especially important those to and from Tokyo); the placing of agents in the United States with their real names, code-names and addresses; knowledge of the identities and activities of personnel from the Office of Strategic Services; even a thousand-page embassy report on the president's budget speech. [29]

There is no doubt that Charles took enormous risks both in obtaining this information and, in many cases, in removing it from the embassy for photographic copying before returning it on the following day. He was fully aware of the danger of detection and always anxious that he might be under surveillance by what he called "the Vichy secret police." He constantly warned Betty that if he were exposed this group would not hesitate to have him killed—and if a link was suspected, Betty too. It is a great credit to Betty's powers of persuasion that she was able to keep Charles active and motivated as her sub-agent.

On December 7 the Japanese attacked Pearl Harbor and on the following day an estimated sixty million Americans heard Roosevelt's demands for a congressional declaration of war against the Axis powers. Three days later America declared war on Germany. Churchill reports that on hearing of the Japanese attack on Pearl Harbor (he first heard it on the radio and had to telephone Roosevelt for confirmation) his reaction was one of great joy:

England would live; Britain would live; the Commonwealth of Nations and the Empire would live . . . How long the war would last or in what fashion it would end no man could tell, nor did I at this moment care.

Hitler's fate was sealed. . . . I went to bed and slept the sleep of the saved and thankful. [30]

Nevertheless it was a bittersweet time for Churchill, for the Japanese had also attacked British forces in the Far East. With the sinking of HMS *Prince of Wales* and *Repulse* in the South China Sea by Japanese aircraft, Britain had lost command of every ocean except the Atlantic. A week later Prime Minister Churchill sailed for the United States and discussions with President Roosevelt. [31]

The importance of Betty's work, as part of BSC's overall infiltration of the Vichy French activities at many levels, can be gauged from Churchill's own words at that point:

> The most acute issue however that lay in our minds in foreign relations at this moment was France. What would be the effect on Vichy France of the American declaration of war between the United States and Germany? In Britain we had our relations with de Gaulle. The United States Government—particularly the State Department—were in close and helpful touch with Vichy.
>
> . . . Auchinleck's success in Libya and beyond opened on the highest level all questions about French North Africa. Would Hitler, rebuffed in the desert and halted in Russia insist upon sending German forces, not now through Spain, but by sea and air into Tunis, Algeria, Morocco, and Dakar? Would this, or some of it be a rejoinder to the entry of America into the war? . . . These baffling possibilities involved our whole naval position—the Toulon [French] fleet, the two unfinished battleships at Casablanca and Dakar, the blockade and much else . . . [32]

Given the strategic importance of Vichy-controlled North Africa, and the priority given the matter by both Churchill and Roosevelt, the intelligence obtained and supplied to Betty by Charles assumes a new level of interest. The extent of his power within the embassy hierarchy is illustrated in an FBI report which states that while interviewing Mme Chautemps, one of their agents had learned that Ambassador Henry-Haye was so preoccupied with his mistress (the wife of an embassy official)

> that he leaves the affairs of the Embassy in the hands of Brousse. Baron Baeyens, First Secretary, confirmed this and says that Haye actually allows

Brousse to send telegraphed reports to Vichy without seeing them. He adds that Brousse is the most evil element in the embassy and has a bad influence on the Ambassador. Haye is completely committed to the Laval/Darlan policy and Brousse works closely with him, as does Colonel Bertrand-Vigne, who however is said to be motivated by conviction rather than malice. Haye has direct personal contact with the German Chargé-d'Affaires.[33]

Throughout that winter during which Churchill and Roosevelt coined the term "United Nations" for the new alliance,[34] relations between the diplomats of both countries came under considerable strain because of Churchill's support of de Gaulle, whom the Vichy government saw as a threat to their own legitimacy as the government of France. On Christmas Eve, de Gaulle ordered a small force of Free French to forcibly occupy the islands of Saint-Pierre (the site of a powerful radio station) and Miquelon off the Newfoundland coast. Formerly these islands had been under the jurisdiction of Governor Robert of Martinique. While openly supporting de Gaulle and vilifying the Vichy government, to the annoyance of Secretary of State Hull Churchill was looking ahead to the planned North African landings and was most insistent that the United States retain their close diplomatic links with Vichy. For many weeks after the landings diplomatic activity between Britain, Canada, the United States and Vichy was intense, as pleas, suggestions and protests surged between them. Indeed, the matter almost brought about Hull's resignation, but at last Churchill was persuaded to prevail upon de Gaulle to withdraw his men from the island and the turmoil subsided.[35]

Throughout this crisis, the State Department had the benefit of knowing every instruction communicated to Henry-Haye from Vichy, and the ambassador's interpretation of the series of discussions he was having with Secretary Hull.[36] Hull did not know, nor did other senior State Department officials who were soon to join a witch-hunt against BSC, that most of the information they were finding so valuable was being passed to the FBI and ONI after being generated by agents working for the British Security Coordination. But the president knew; he received his daily crop of Vichy cables within hours of their transmission, directly from the naval intelligence officer to whom Betty delivered them.[37]

Chapter 11

*I*n March 1942 according to BSC records, Stephenson received a request directly from "C" stating that the Admiralty "wished to obtain a copy of the French naval cipher, a copy of which was used by the Naval Attaché in Washington."[1] At the time there was still considerable doubt about the intentions of what remained of the French fleet in the Mediterranean and the possession of this cipher would enable "those concerned" to keep informed of the fleet's intended movements. Attempts to persuade Laval to send the ships to Martinique "for the duration" had been met with flat refusals, and both the British and Americans were

203

convinced that given the opportunity and enough time the Germans would eventually seize them.

At this point BSC became wary of intelligence supplied by Andrée Cadet. They learned that Mr. Louis Cadet had written to the State Department complaining that his wife was working for British Intelligence, who had been paying her for information concerning the activities of the Vichy embassy:

A few months ago Mr Howard came from New York with Mr MacDonald, who was supposed to be from the State Department. Mrs Cadet told me on several occasions that she had no information to give them but she made up some information in order to remain on the payroll. When Mr MacDonald came to Washington he would contact Mrs Cadet and they would meet at some rendezvous for lunch or dinner and remain out until late at night . . .

Since she has been receiving this money she has made my life unbearable. She has been drinking excessively and buying expensive furs and clothes and while under the influence of liquor she would tell all her personal affairs to the neighbours . . .[2]

Both Mme Cadet and her friend, the ambassador's secretary, continued to supply intelligence for some time after this date but their unsupported reports undoubtedly received more careful scrutiny.

During one of her regular "shopping trips" Betty received a message that John Pepper wished to discuss several matters with her and would call on her in her room at the Ritz-Carlton hotel. He acquainted her with the request from London and asked if she could get the naval ciphers for them. Did she consider her hold over Charles Brousse strong enough to be able to count on his co-operation for a job of this importance? At no point did Pepper suggest how she might or should go about the assignment. He left it entirely to her.

Betty considered the matter, rolling it around in her head before, characteristically, reaching the only decision she ever reached—yes, she'd try it. She knew enough about the workings of an embassy to know that what Pepper was asking was no easy job. Nevertheless, she felt that with Charles's help she could somehow achieve it. If Charles would not help, well . . . she'd try to get the ciphers anyway, using any method she needed to employ. The challenge of another major job after the mundane intelligence gathering that been her role since Lais's departure was irresistible. She told Pepper she'd take the assignment.

His next statement was something of a surprise. From now on she would have a permanent liaison "contact for operational purposes" from the Office of Strategic Services (OSS), America's equivalent of BSC, and the embryo CIA. His name would be "Mr. Hunter." Though she did not know it then, her direct chain of reporting led from Colonel Ellery C. Huntington, Jr. (whom she knew initially as Mr. Hunter) through James R. Murphy, head of the OSS branch of counter-espionage, to Colonel William Donovan, head of the agency, himself.[3] The new arrangement would serve two purposes, Pepper told her: first, she would have an on-the-spot contact, and second, Pepper had to leave New York for several months; until mid-June Betty would have had to report to someone else in any event.[4] In fact, though BSC's reason for attempting to obtain the Vichy ciphers lay in a request from London, the OSS had a similar objective and made this a priority operation at a staff meeting held in April 1942.

Betty said she would give the assignment some thought and arrive at a strategy for achieving her objective; Pepper said that "Mr. Hunter" would contact her and give her any help she needed.

Now it was Betty's turn to air her problems. She was certain she was being continually followed by two FBI agents; not always the same men, of course, but she was often aware of being shadowed and her house in O Street was always under surveillance. It was essential that Charles should not be implicated in anything suspicious because of the danger to his diplomatic status and, ultimately, his usefulness to them. If her tails were not "G-men," then she was even more concerned; they may have been Vichy secret police. Charles had often warned her about this shadowy force and of the dangers if either he or she were detected. A speeding car as they crossed the street or a long dive into the Potomac one dark night—such things could not be ruled out, he told her.

She told Pepper that she had decided, since her lease had now expired, not to renew it but to move from O Street into an apartment in the residential section of Wardman Park Hotel [now Wardman Towers, part of the Sheraton Washington Hotel] in uptown Washington. Charles and Kay had an apartment there and it was a short distance, across the Connecticut Avenue bridge over Rock Creek Park, to the Vichy embassy. The hotel was a large establishment, originally nicknamed "Wardman's Folly" when it was built in 1928 because it seemed too far out in the suburbs for such a large hotel. But Washington had grown around it by 1942. The building had multiple entrances on both Woodley Road and Connecticut Avenue, so that with reasonable care Betty need never meet Kay Brousse; it also meant that Charles could visit Betty without being observed by outside surveillance teams.

Pepper approved the move and departed, leaving Betty to give her full attention to the problem in hand. How *would* she set about it? She decided to be frank with Charles on her return to Washington, but she worried about it during the flight back and several times asked herself why she had accepted the job. "I was apprehensive about what I had promised. Why had I said, "Yes, you can rely on me" when the assignment was proposed? I worried that I had led my chiefs into placing too much confidence in my capabilities. . . ."[5]

On the other hand she recognized the advantages that might be gained by the possession of such knowledge: the ability to read communications between Admiral Roberts on Martinique and the Vichy government, for example. The $300 million of French gold stashed there belonged rightfully to the French people. Stephenson had devised a scheme to "liberate" the gold from an old fort on the island, but had been stopped from carrying out his plan by opposition from the Americans; now his chief aim was to ensure the money was not used to promote Nazi interests, especially in the Americas. Knowledge of any plans the Vichy government had in respect to this gold would certainly be welcome. So too, would be any plans for the French fleet.

Charles Brousse's reaction to Betty's disclosure that she had agreed to get hold of the naval ciphers was perhaps predictable. He was taken aback that she had even considered such a proposal. It was an impossible task. His surprise turned to annoyance; she must be *mad* to have agreed.

Betty let him rant away. She knew that once having vented his Gallic

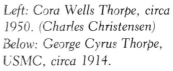

Left: Cora Wells Thorpe, circa 1950. (Charles Christensen) Below: George Cyrus Thorpe, USMC, circa 1914.

Left: Betty Thorpe Pack, aged eighteen, in 1929. (Bernadette Rivett)

Betty Thorpe Pack, aged twelve. (Churchill College, Cambridge)

Dust jacket of book written by Betty Thorpe Pack when she was eleven. (Churchill College, Cambridge)

Betty Thorpe Pack dressed for her presentation to the King at a court levee in 1933. (Rivett Collection)

INTERNATIONAL ENGAGEMENT

MISS BETTY THORPE.

Daughter of Col. and Mrs. George C. Thorpe, who today announce her engagement to Mr. Arthur Pack, commercial secretary of the British embassy, the wedding to take place in the Spring.
—Underwood, Photo

Left: Arthur J. Pack, Washington, 1930. (Rivett Collection)
Right: Engagement photograph of Betty Thorpe Pack in riding dress.

Wedding-day picture of Betty Thorpe Pack, 1930. (Library of Congress)

Captain Arthur J. Pack attached to U.S. Infantry as machine-gun instructor, 1917. (Eleanor, Lady Campbell-Orde)

Embassy staff at Santiago, Chile. Arthur J. Pack is on extreme right; the ambassador, Sir Henry Chilton, is third from right; Betty is fourth from left. (Rivett Collection)

Miss Jacobsen and two of her staff in the Scottish Ambulance Service. Betty stayed with her briefly during the Spanish civil war. (Rivett Collection)

Colonel Beck, Polish Minister of Foreign Affairs, 1934. (UPI/Bettmann)

Article written by Betty Thorpe Pack under the pseudonym Elizabeth Thomas. The map, which Betty stole from Konrad Henlein's office, shows the Nazis' intentions prior to 1940 when the Allies were still negotiating with Hitler.

Admiral Alberto Lais, 1941.
(UPI/Bettmann)

The house at 3327
O Street, Georgetown, where
Betty Thorpe Pack seduced
Admiral Lais and Charles
Brousse. (Mary Lovell)

Charles Brousse and his wife, Catherine, arriving in the United States in 1940 en route to Washington, where he was to serve as press attaché to the Vichy Embassy. (UPI/Bettmann)

Photograph sent by Betty Thorpe Pack to her uncle, a top U.S. official aware of her espionage activities. The mannequin was modeled on Betty herself.

To uncle Charlie —
Sh-h-h --
Cynthia

Gaston Henry-Haye,
Ambassador of the Vichy
Embassy in Washington.
(Library of Congress)

The Vichy French Embassy on
Wyoming Avenue, Washington,
in 1942. (Churchill College,
Cambridge)

Cover and a page from the Vichy Naval cipher book stolen and copied by Betty Thorpe Pack in 1942. (Churchill College, Cambridge)

OFFICE OF STRATEGIC SERVICES

~ • WASHINGTON, D. C.

December 22, 1942

Mr. Frederick B. Lyon
Executive Assistant to Assistant Secretary Berle
State Department
Washington, D. C.

Dear Mr. Lyon:

At my request, I understand that Mr. Kimbel has discus-

sed with you a matter concerning a certain young lady to be

permitted to go to Hershey and later to proceed with the

French to France in the diplomatic exchange. I should greatly

appreciate your making it possible for this to be accomplished.

Sincerely,

William J. Donovan
Director

Above: Letter of "Big Bill" Donovan recommending Betty Thorpe Pack for a mission in France. Left: General William J. Donovan.

Left and Below: Letter in Betty Thorpe Pack's handwriting to Special Agent Edwin Plitt, signing herself by the code name "Catherine Gordon."

Left: Colonel Ellery Huntington, Betty Thorpe Pack's controller in the OSS. (National Archives and Records Administration)

Sir William Stephenson, the man called "Intrepid," 1954. (AP/Wide World Photos)

Trust all goes well with the greatest unsung heroine of the — I was going to say — war — But, anyway, the more active part of a continuing warfare. Salutations   Bill.

Letter from Sir William Stephenson to Betty Thorpe Pack.

Left: Harford Montgomery Hyde, 1962. (Betty Thorpe Pack)
Right: Betty Thorpe Pack, 1962. (Harford M. Hyde)

Betty Thorpe Pack's son,
Anthony George Pack, in
1951. (Lady Campbell-Orde)

Above: Betty
Thorpe Pack's
daughter Denise,
aged eleven.

Top: *Charles Brousse and Betty Thorpe Pack on the ramparts of Chateau Castellnou. (Lady Campbell-Orde) Bottom: Chateau Castellnou, the fairy-tale home Charles Brousse bought for Betty in 1946.*

anger he would calm down and discuss the matter with her. By now he was too far committed to the cause to back down. First, he argued, she knew as well as he the security surrounding all ciphers, even non-military ones. During the day cipher clerks were allowed into the code-room to decode incoming cables and encode outgoing ones, but it was always under close scrutiny of the chief cipher officer. The only other people with authorized access to the code room were the ambassador, the naval attaché (who, by coincidence, had recently been reprimanded by the ambassador for visiting the code-room more often than seemed necessary), and the embassy counsellor who was personally responsible for handing the cables in raw cipher to the cipher officer.

At night the cipher books were locked in safes. The diplomatic cipher was locked in a safe in the code-room, and the naval cipher, contained in two thick, heavy volumes each about the size of a Victorian family Bible, was locked in a safe in the adjoining office of the naval attaché. The doors to both the code-room and the naval attaché's office were locked; the chancery was patrolled by an armed night-watchman with a trained guard-dog. In addition, Charles reminded Betty, there was the Vichy secret police force, who reported to the sinister military attaché, Bruno Daru. He did not know whether or not they had any security responsibility for the chancery.

Clearly there was no easy way to acquire the naval cipher. Betty had half-hoped that Charles would be able to secretly "borrow" the code books overnight, but after their talk she realized that this was not an option. On the following day she visited her mother, whose apartment was a few doors from the French chancery. Walking slowly past the chancery she made mental notes of its layout. Charles had drawn her a rough floor plan, and as she approached the building from the direction of Connecticut Avenue she could just see the windows of the code-room situated at the side of the building behind a wide portico. The ground sloped away from the street and there was an additional ground floor at the rear of the building. This meant that the window of the naval attaché's room was some ten feet or so above the ground. A paved path led down the side of a small lawn to the rear of the building, where there was a garage reached by a driveway which ran down the opposite side of the building.

For the next three weeks Betty thought of little else. On several occasions she met her latest contact "Mr. Hunter" at her new apartment at the Wardman Park Hotel to discuss possible methods of acquiring the ciphers. Colonel Ellery C. Huntington, Jr., was tall, well-built, and silver-haired. A former Wall Street attorney (and in 1913 an All-American Yale quarterback), he had been a chief fund-raiser for William Donovan in a gubernatorial campaign in 1932 and had been a close friend and confidant of Donovan ever since. Betty liked his confident, paternal manner and formed an immediate respect for him.

What Betty did not know was that the Special Activities division of OSS had plans to infiltrate the embassies of *every* neutral country, in order to obtain their military ciphers. Just as Stephenson had received a request "from the top" for the Vichy naval codes, so had OSS. The request to Donovan had come from "the highest possible military level. We have reason to believe they are handling information for the enemy. We want to be able to read their cables . . ." Donald Downes of the OSS Special Activities Branch was told. Downes and Huntington took on the job, which they recognized would in some cases mean their agents clandestinely entering foreign embassies to copy the cipher books.[6]

Because of their peculiarly close relationship (see Appendix) BSC and OSS decided to pool resources to obtain the Vichy naval ciphers, possibly because Charles Brousse seemed the best and safest method of achieving the objective at the Vichy embassy. A Presidential Directive on intelligence gave a limited power to OSS for subversive activities concerning neutral countries within the Western Hemisphere. "But," Downes wrote,

even under a Presidential Directive, an embassy is foreign territory . . . entering a foreign embassy clandestinely and "borrowing" code books . . . was full of risk for everyone concerned. Donovan, Kimbel, Allen Dulles, were justly nervous. True the joint chiefs of staff, through their intelligence liaison, had requested the information—the codes. But if we failed, if someone was caught inside the embassy and talked, an international incident of great moment would result.

While Americans were dying overseas, the calculated risk of our thievery did not seem too great. We had taken all imaginable precautions—that is

208

except one—the possibility of betrayal by someone high enough in the American Government to know what we were doing . . .[7]

It was in mid-April that an obvious opportunity presented itself to Betty. In Vichy France the aging World War I veteran Marshal Pétain became chief of state, an empty title with an essentially ceremonial function. Laval, with massive Nazi support, became premier, as chief of government thus assuming total direction of the Vichy administration. Darlan lost his former control and was moved sideways to head the French armed forces.[8] When this news broke five members of the Washington embassy staff resigned, on the grounds that they could no longer support Vichy policy. One of these men was Charles Benoit, the chief cipher officer. Betty decided that she should approach Benoit to see if she could persuade him to assist her.

The MID (Military Intelligence Department) file on Benoit added little to the information Charles had already given her.[9] Benoit was a few years older than Charles, a quiet, retiring man with little ambition beyond doing his job well in the cipher office. He was happily married and the only aspect favourable to Betty's plans that she could see was that her man was known to be a French patriot and anti-German. Charles warned her she would get nowhere with Benoit. "He has no needs, no ambition and no imagination. He arrives at the chancery, says good morning to no one and goes directly to the code room. . . . He is a bear." He was dedicated only to his work, Charles maintained; no arrangements could be made with him. Everything Betty learned indicated that the man would be impervious to sexual advances and to financial inducements.

Nevertheless, she called at Benoit's home at 4220 Chesapeake Street NW.[10] When he opened the door she told him she wished to speak to him on a matter of grave importance to France. He invited her in and his wife retired to another part of the house. Speaking in rapid French Betty told him that she worked for American intelligence. Her organization wished only to help France become reunited and free of German occupation, but in order to do this they needed to acquire the naval ciphers. Would he help them? She did not make the mistake of offering money, seeing the comfortable but humble manner in which he lived and accepting that he had no pretensions to anything better. It was a safe bet that he would have been affronted if bribery were even suggested.

Benoit considered the matter seriously. After a while he told her that while he was unhappy with the manner in which the Vichy leaders were running the affairs of France he could not help her. "I have built up a long record of loyalty to my chiefs," he said. "All of them have written me letters. The ciphers have been my own responsibility. To guard them has been my duty." He could not, morally, now betray what he had formerly protected. [11]

On the other hand he agreed to say nothing to anyone about Betty's conversation with him. Despite her disappointment Betty was impressed with the man and reported that she felt he deserved a better cause than the one he found himself unable to betray. [12] Some months later, in September 1942, Charles Benoit contacted the State Department saying that he wished to be of assistance to the United States. As a result he joined the Free French forces in America and after Vichy broke off diplomatic relations, Benoit resumed his duties as *chef du service du chiffre* for the Free French government at the Washington chancery. [13]

Betty's next move, made almost immediately without contacting Pepper or Huntington, and without discussing the matter with Charles, was not only stupidly impulsive but clearly dangerous. The result could easily have compromised her and, had the link been traced, her contacts. Having written off Benoit she decided to contact his replacement, Count Jean de la Grandville. De la Grandville had been appointed to Washington only a few months earlier as Benoit's assistant. When Benoit resigned, de la Grandville took over his former chief's job. As part of her research on Benoit, Betty had learned that the young attaché considered himself anti-Hitler and a patriot.

From what Charles had told her she thought de la Grandville might be amenable to a financial inducement since he was on a very low rate of pay and was known to have lavish tastes. His wife was in the last stages of pregnancy and had gone away to the country. Guessing that de la Grandville would be alone Betty rang him up, introduced herself as Mrs. Elizabeth Branch and asked if she could meet him to discuss a matter of great importance to France.

Such an approach must surely have generated immediate suspicion in the attaché's mind? This was 1942. America was now at war and Washington, like all cities, bristled with warning posters to citizens and members of the armed forces alike to beware of spies. Though America still retained its diplomatic relationship with Vichy, which was technically neutral, embassy officials had doubtless been well briefed regarding possible approaches by representatives of unsympathetic agencies. It seems surprising that Betty could have behaved in such a clumsy manner having already suffered one rebuff. Perhaps she was worried that Benoit, given time to consider the matter, might disclose her approach to the ambassador and therefore decided to make an immediate attempt to secure the ciphers before this could happen.

When Betty called at his apartment an hour after her phone call, Count de la Grandville greeted her with courteous gallantry. He was a few years younger than she but was obviously impressed with the physical attributes of his elegant visitor. Having accepted a drink, Betty sat down, crossed her slim, nylon-clad legs and came straight to the point. She had come to him, she said, as an agent of the American secret service working in the interests of France.

From her year-long liaison with Charles, Betty knew a great deal about Vichy France and the way a patriotic Frenchman regarded the Laval leadership. She knew which arguments to use and which not to use. She also knew how to flatter a man into believing that he was important. Therefore she launched into her attempt to win his co-operation with some confidence.

She felt that she had touched on a point of some significance to him from the count's agitation as he attempted to justify his allegiance to the Vichy mission in the United States. He was a career diplomat who took his orders from whatever government was in power; he might not always agree with the instructions, he said, but he was obligated for reasons of honour, family tradition and personal advancement to obey. Betty pressed what she took to be an advantage and suggested softly and sympathetically that she understood his attitude, naturally, but the future of France should surely rate above all other considerations.

Almost in passing she introduced the fact that she was empowered not

211

only to offer him a financial reward for providing her with access to the ciphers but also a regular monthly addition to his income if he would feed her occasionally with information. It ought to be remembered, here, that she had used this tactic successfully with Giulio to obtain the Italian naval ciphers. No doubt she thought she had correctly assessed her man but she ought to have been put on her guard when, instead of continuing the conversation in the same vein, the count turned it to a personal level. As it turned out, Count Jean de la Grandville may have been the only man who got the better of Betty.

Here Betty ought to have been the mistress of the situation. Skilled in the art of seduction, and faced with a man who by her own account was attractive and virile, she knew enough to clinch what she wanted before giving him what he wanted. But instead, when de la Grandville suggested she was too beautiful to be involved in such a serious matter and began to flirt with her, she hesitated.

Was the fact that she was so deeply in love with Charles a hindrance to her usual *modus operandi?* Or did she merely size up her quarry in a professional manner and decide that he would be more likely to acquiesce if she played him along for a day or so, as she had attempted to do with Charles before succumbing to his advances? My guess is that it was the former, for reasons which will be revealed later, but for once Betty did not come off best in a sexual encounter with a man. She allowed the count to flirt with her, and as he walked her back to the Wardman Park Hotel he suggested she meet him on the following night for dinner. Betty laughingly put him off with the rejoinder that he was welcome to contact her any evening at the telephone number she had given him at six-thirty, but only if he was prepared to be serious.

On the following day Betty flew to New York, reported to Marion and delivered a batch of routine cables and reports from Charles. Her return flight was delayed by bad weather and when she arrived back at the Wardman Park Hotel around eight o'clock she was taken aback to find Count de la Grandville waiting in the foyer. Tired and uncharacteristically flustered, she invited him to her apartment because she did not wish to be seen with him in public. As well, she did not want Charles to know that she was trying to deal with Grandville.

212

Once in her apartment the attaché told her he had discovered that her name was not Elizabeth Branch but that she was Mrs. Elizabeth Pack, the wife of a British diplomat. If she had lied to him about her name, he said, how could he trust her in the other matter they had spoken of? In seeking to soothe his apparent fears Betty allowed the situation to get out of hand. Over a drink she explained that she had been separated from Arthur for over a year. Her explanations did not entirely satisfy de la Grandville, who after he had seized her in his arms made it clear that the only way he could be sure of her was for her to let him make love to her. Reluctantly, for once, she allowed him to take her into the bedroom and make love to her. On this occasion she *was* actually sacrificing herself for her country, taking no pleasure from the sexual act at all and indeed revolted by it. Why? She had previously slept with men to further her work; de la Grandville was young, attractive, athletic. Certainly he was not physically repulsive. Her disgust can only have stemmed from her love for Charles. She recalled: "I closed my eyes and hoped that this, like so much else that I wanted to do, would be for England."[14]

While she sat on the bed and watched him dress, Betty quickly became suspicious that she had been used. There was something wrong with de la Grandville's attitude towards her. He looked at her reflection in the mirror and told her that he did not think he could help her to obtain the ciphers. He was, he said, "torn by doubts."[15] He may also have hinted that he felt it might be his duty to advise his ambassador of her approach to him. Or Betty may simply have guessed that this was what he was hinting at. She was still trying to retrieve the situation, and had just agreed to meet him again, when the telephone rang.

It was Charles with his usual brief message, "I'm coming right over." Without waiting for a response he hung up. Betty panicked, knowing that Charles would appear within a few minutes. Telling de la Grandville that he would have to leave right away she bundled him out of her apartment and begged him to hurry. She was already too late. The two men met in the corridor and when Charles blazed into the room seconds later she could see that he was not going to accept the explanation she had been framing. So she said nothing, walking towards the drinks cabinet and mixing a cocktail as a cover for her apprehension.

Charles meanwhile opened the door of the bedroom and saw at a glance the evidence of its recent activity. Knowing de la Grandville's position at the embassy he needed no further explanation. Had he been other than French he might have marched coldly from the room, or collapsed in despair. Instead he walked towards her with fury in every movement of his body. Taking hold of the arm which she held out towards him he slapped her across the face with a force that knocked her off her feet. Almost disbelievingly she attempted to rise but he attacked her again. Her attempts to fight him off were useless. Charles was heavily built and filled with anger which her struggles only served to fuel.

When at last he came to his senses and stopped his tirade she staggered to the sofa and sat with her head in her hands while he poured himself a drink. After a long silence he apologized for hurting her. By now she had regained control of herself and she told him with "cold, controlled fury" that she understood his point of view and knew that in his eyes she deserved the beating he had given her, but he should understand that though she loved him, she did not belong to him. She wanted more than anything to obtain the ciphers for her chief and as he, Charles, had not been able to help she had gone about it in her own way. "You were forewarned and anything that I have done was in the line of duty as I see it . . . When I think of the active warfare in Europe, all these personal preoccupations with self make me sick. For one reason or another no-one will help. . . ." He should understand that she would continue to try every method at her disposal to secure the ciphers and if he did not like it, then they might as well part now.

After Charles left, at her insistence, she left the hotel and walked across the Connecticut Avenue bridge to her mother's apartment in Wyoming Avenue. It was curious, this atavistic urge to run home to mother; for one thing, Cora was away from home and at any rate the relationship between them was hardly an ideal one. Perhaps Betty just needed to get away from her apartment. She was glad of the dark streets, for she was badly bruised and her lip was cut. As she neared her mother's apartment she had to pass the Vichy embassy; only a few yards separated her from her objective. Betty let herself in to her mother's apartment and, alone, indulged in a fit of sobbing. But her tears were not all self-pitying. She

214

was primarily angry that she had bungled the contact with de la Grandville, recognizing with hindsight that she had been a fool to allow him to make love to her without securing a promise of co-operation from him first. But she was also afraid that de la Grandville would go to the ambassador with his story; she would be compromised and lose all chance of getting the cipher. Worse, Charles might become involved and even the service might be implicated in the affair. These thoughts kept her awake most of the night.

Charles came for her early next morning expecting to have to mollify an aggrieved woman. He found Betty tensely plotting her next course of action. She did not even refer to the beating but over coffee told him everything that had happened between her and de la Grandville. Charles, presumably relieved that she was not carrying a grudge, also decided to be magnanimous and overlook her infidelity. He said he would try to defuse any damage de la Grandville might cause.

De la Grandville's statement to Betty on the previous night that he was "torn by doubts" was obviously untrue. He had no doubts at all. That morning, instead of attending at his office in the chancery he went straight to the ambassador's residence a few blocks away (the official "embassy" where Henry-Haye had his office and living accommodation) and told his story, considerably exaggerating—so the BSC official history claims —the amount of money he had been offered. It might be useful here to observe that earlier that same week BSC had discovered that there were moves within Vichy to take reprisals on the families in France of those five former diplomats who had resigned a month earlier. De la Grandville's actions could conceivably have been governed by this knowledge which through "leaks" to the American newspapers had been given wide exposure.

As the ambassador's most trusted aide, Charles was called in shortly after the de la Grandville interview. Since Charles lived at the Wardman Park Hotel it was natural that Henry-Haye should ask him if he knew this "Mrs. Elizabeth Branch alias Mrs. Elizabeth Pack." Charles admitted that he knew a little about her, that she was an American woman with an impressive family background who had friends in high places; her mother was known to be on friendly terms with senior statesmen, and her uncle

(Charles March) was federal trade commissioner and a personal friend of the president. He counselled care in taking the matter further in view of the delicate political situation then prevailing between the embassy and the American State Department. However, he countered, the ambassador ought to be aware that de la Grandville could not entirely be trusted or believed. As proof of this, Charles told the ambassador with apparent great reluctance, the young attaché had also been spreading stories of Henry-Haye's affairs with Mme Picot and the Baroness Zuylen.[16] Several times Charles himself had had to refute these stories that he knew had originated with de la Grandville.

The knowledge that his private affairs were known about astounded Henry-Haye, who believed he had acted with total discretion. Seeing the effect of his announcement Charles happily dropped in some precise details of meetings between Henry-Haye and his mistresses as part of the "rumours" being spread by de la Grandville.

Charles then "admitted" that he himself had recently been approached by an American who might or might not have been a spy. Perhaps de la Grandville had mistaken the woman's intentions. He strongly advised against over-reacting; he suggested as one solution that de la Grandville be removed from the sensitive code-room. If what the attaché claimed was correct he would be of no further interest to the woman. Whatever Charles said clearly convinced the ambassador. The hapless attaché was called in to the ambassador's office later that day, reprimanded for spreading rumours, and informed that he was to be withdrawn from the code-room.[17]

The only other action taken by Henry-Haye was to write a stiff letter to James C. Dunn, political advisor to the secretary of state, drawing his attention to

. . . two incidents which, in normal times, would not deserve to be brought to the State Department, inasmuch as both of them result from deplorable methods often used with diplomatic missions abroad. But in these troubled times . . . I beg you to bring to the attention of . . . the Secretary of State the following incidents taken out of uncanny attempts made to the staff of this embassy . . .

216

1. The youngest of my attachés, now in charge of the code office, Count Jean de la Grandville, has been approached at various times, by a certain Mrs. Branch, known also under the name of Elizabeth Pack, who resides at the Wardman Park Hotel and who has insisted to obtain delivery of the secret codes of this embassy. Mrs. Branch, pretending to act on behalf of an official American Agency, hinted that if Mr. de la Grandville did not respond favourably to this request, he could not avoid reprisals. Mr. de la Grandville, of course, refused to consider this queer bargain.

2. The Press Attaché to this embassy, Mr. Charles Brousse, was unwise enough—and I have reprimanded him for having done so—to receive a visit at the Chancery . . . at a time when I was out of Washington, of one of his former comrades, an ex-American flyer of 1918. This friend of Mr. Brousse, Mr. E. J. Jones, now a manufacturer in New Jersey, displayed to him an unfinished gadget supposed to improve the stability of the colt pistol, a device which according to the inventor is not in use in the American army. . . .[18]

The above letter, preserved in the State Department archives, is interesting on two counts. First, it highlights the fact that Henry-Haye did not connect the woman who had approached de la Grandville with the journalist Elizabeth Thorpe he had met some months earlier (a fact which would be important at a later date). Second, the English translation differs slightly from the original letter written by the ambassador in French, which states more clearly what Betty had asked of de la Grandville: ". . . *lui a demandé la livraison du chiffre naval de l'Ambassade.*" It was definitely the *naval ciphers* that Betty was seeking and this too is important in view of later repercussions.

A copy of this letter was duly passed to the FBI and added to the file on Elizabeth Pack, which was being fattened up at that time because of a report by the woman receptionist at a Washington residential hotel that "Mrs. Pack, a cheap and promiscuous woman was regularly visiting [a navy officer] almost nightly and at weekends." The informant thought the officer was acting in a suspicious manner because he often "wore civilian clothes, had telephone calls with persons who had foreign sounding accents and refused to allow the bellhop to touch his luggage."[19]

Surveillance on Betty continued. The FBI had, at that time, no evidence of what she was up to but were subsequently able to confirm that the man she was visiting was an officer in the ONI.[20] The name of the officer in this report remains censored by the FBI, but it was almost certainly Paul Fairly.

During this period Betty was preoccupied by her plans to obtain the French naval ciphers. A meeting was held between the principals involved. Betty, Colonel Ellery Huntington, Jr., and Charles. It was the first time Charles had met any of Betty's contacts, but he had, anyway, always believed he had been working for the Americans. Betty watched Charles's face anxiously as he was advised that the project to obtain the Vichy ciphers would be a joint one between the American and British intelligence services. He did not react adversely, presumably accepting it as inevitable now that the United States was at war and allied to the British. Indeed, to her great surprise when they were chatting generally about the state of the war Charles volunteered information about Japan, explaining that he had been there on vacation in February 1939. He had even shot a cine film between Shimonoseki and Kōbe in the Interior Sea which clearly showed the various islands, bays and inlets, and this he offered to the U.S. Navy as proof that he was wholeheartedly with them. This "exceedingly interesting" intelligence was later acknowledged officially.[21]

After a great deal of discussion about the Vichy cipher project all four agreed that the best method remaining to them for obtaining the ciphers was to break in to the embassy at night, through the naval attaché's window.

Huntington allocated them code-names. Charles was to be known as B.10 and Betty as E.11.[22] Charles had now obtained copies of scale floor plans from the embassy files and he also provided details of the layout of the code-room and naval attaché's office, the type of safe in the attaché's office, and its exact position, based on his furtive visual observations.

Together with Ellery Huntington, he and Betty spent hours working out a plan of operation and endlessly running through it for snags.[23] Meanwhile, the background work essential to their operation was going on. Charles, for example, had made an excuse to visit the naval attaché in his office. He perched casually against the window sill while he talked;

after a while he complained of the heat and opened the window, noting with quiet satisfaction that it opened easily with little noise.

When Betty noticed increased surveillance of her movements around the city, Huntington's organization, the OSS, arranged for her apartment at the Wardman Park to be "swept" for recording devices. Her telephone was also taken apart and declared clear of bugs. Plans were made for photographing the cipher books, and in several rehearsals Huntington brought camera equipment to Betty's apartment at the Wardman Park and photographed batches of cables supplied by Charles to ensure the plan would work. Huntington's visits were reported by yet another vigilant hotel receptionist and reported to the FBI.[24]

Through the BSC New York office, Huntington arranged for an expert safecracker to be available on the night of the break-in. Both BSC and OSS (which closely modelled itself on BSC, in the early days) employed a number of former prisoners, granted early release from jail in exchange for providing their expert assistance. The man allocated to the Vichy embassy job was known as the "Georgia Cracker." He was a Canadian and as far as is known had no connection with the state of Georgia, unless he had once spent a term in prison there. He was a peterman, skilled in the art of safe-breaking and possessed an encyclopedic knowledge of locks and safes. Betty flew to New York to meet him and talk to him about the safe. She gave him a sketch from memory that Charles had made and he identified it immediately. "Yes," he said. "It's a Mosler with a click-click com lock, probably four wheels. I reckon I can crack it in about fifty-five minutes."[25]

As a matter of routine, now, Betty walked to her mother's apartment each evening after the embassy night watchman, André Chevalier[26] had started work. Sometimes he patrolled the outside of the building and she took to hanging back until she saw him emerge so that she could call out a cheery greeting in French. Gradually, a casual relationship started to build up. On a number of occasions she took soup or coffee to him late at night as she passed by the embassy again "on her way home from her mother's apartment."[27] When they spoke she told him her name was Miss Elizabeth Thomas, the name under which she was booking airline and train tickets at this time.[28] Her intention was to establish a reason for being in the vicinity should she be caught following the break-in.

Betty's attempt to "get to know" the night-watchman worked so well that Charles came up with another idea. Suppose he were to confide to the man that Betty was his girl-friend and that they had nowhere to meet? He could explain that discretion was essential as he did not wish his wife to become suspicious. A hotel room in over-crowded Washington was out of the question. His solution was to bring his young lady to his office occasionally, at night, so that they could be alone together. If Charles could persuade the night-watchman to allow them in, perhaps with the added inducement of a small tip, it might be possible to obtain the cipher books as an "inside job."

The feeling among his conspirators was that it was worth a try. The idea of a break-in was not appealing to any of them. Consequently, Charles worked late one evening in order to speak to the guard. Having explained his dilemma he waited for the guard's reaction, at the same time discreetly fingering some dollar bills. Perhaps because of the seniority of the proposer, or the unique French attitude towards *l'amour*, the guard agreed to turn a blind eye.

Throughout early June on two or three nights a week Charles and Betty spent several hours a night at the chancery, at first in Charles's office and later, moving out to the divan in one of the two ground-floor salons. Then they would leave, sometimes quietly, sometimes after a cheery word and a grateful "*merci*" to the guard who, after a while, probably began to feel like a godfather to the affair. By the sixteenth everyone felt that all preparations were complete. After confirming that the "tame" night-watchman would be on duty, the date was set for the job: June 19, 1942, the same day that Winston Churchill was due to arrive in Washington by plane. Hopefully the attention of the security agencies would be elsewhere.

Chapter 12

*B*ecause there were so many people involved, the plan was necessarily complex and this alone gave opportunities for problems to occur. Betty and Charles, armed with several bottles of champagne, would travel to the embassy in a "cab" driven by the safecracker. On arrival they would loudly ask the cab to "wait for them" and inside would confide to the guard that it was the anniversary of the day they had met. They would drink a celebratory glass or two, inviting the guard to join them. Betty had been provided with two small packets containing the sleep-inducing drug Nembutal, one measure for the man, another for the dog. The dog, an Alsatian, looked very alert and fierce and Betty was rather afraid of it. Apart from its ferocity it was a very vocal animal; some neighbours had recently raised a petition on account of its loud barking and the row had made the columns of the *Washington Evening Star*. If Betty were able to administer the drug, it should ensure that the dog created no difficulties tonight.

When they judged it right to do so they would repair to the salon behind the entrance hall until they were sure it was safe to move into the next phase of the plan. Charles's main role was to act as cover; to engage the guard in conversation if he came to check and explain Betty's absence as "a call of nature." If at any point they were discovered Charles would deny any knowledge of what Betty was doing and would act the part of a shocked and duped lover.[1]

The safecracker, who was waiting in the car outside the chancery for a signal, would be admitted by Charles through the front entrance. One of the doors leading off the salon was the locked door of the naval attaché's office and the safecracker's first task was to unlock it. Next he had to open the safe; they had only the Georgia Cracker's rough estimate about how long this would take. Betty would watch the safecracker because she would have to lock the safe again several hours later. Charles would remain in the salon and alert them if the watchman came their way. Having identified the cipher books, Betty would escort the safecracker to the front door (a dangerous time, for while Charles might possibly have explained away the "cab-driver's" presence, the cipher books were too large to be easily concealed).

Once out of the building the Georgia Cracker would deliver the books to Colonel Huntington at a room at the Wardman Park Hotel. There, the books would be copied by a photographic team;[2] there were several hundred pages to be photographed and this would take some hours. Come what may the books would be returned to the embassy at 4:00 A.M. precisely. Charles would be at the front door of the embassy to retrieve the books and Betty was to stand by to divert the guard if he came to investigate. Once the books were back in the safe Betty would lock it, spin the dial to the original setting (which she would have noted before the Georgia Cracker started work), and clean the whole surface of fingerprints. The office door would be re-locked and the two lovers could leave.[3]

At first everything went according to plan. The guard was offered a drink while the three chatted amicably; his second drink contained the Nembutal and the guard drank it without apparently noticing anything amiss.

This aspect of the plan seemed weak to me when I read of it. Would the guard not see undissolved powder in his glass, and would he not, on the following morning, suspect he had been drugged? I checked this with a physician familiar with such drugs, Dr. Peter Bishop, and learned that

Nembutal is a hypnotic barbiturate and is both quick-acting and short-lived. Betty's story of how she drugged the guard with Nembutal mixed in champagne is entirely feasible assuming he had already had a drink or two and that they were standing in a not-too-bright light. There might have been a few small grains of undissolved powder in the glass but I doubt that they would be easily discernible unless one was actually looking for something.

The subject would have gone to sleep very quickly afterwards and would have slept for anything up to 6 hours. On waking he would have possibly felt a very slight headachey feeling such as one experiences after drinking too much before falling asleep.

The dog would be a different matter. Because of their different metabolic rate animals need much larger doses, up to six times the human quantity, to be effective.[4]

The dog's water bowl was similarly drugged and Betty and Charles retired to their divan to allow the guard to feel sleepy without embarrassment. After a short time Charles went, armed with champagne, to check. Both the guard and the dog were asleep. So far so good.

Charles's report of the next phase, written several months after the mission, and now part of the State Department archives, reads:

After many weeks of careful preparation under the supervision of Lt-Colonel Huntington . . . I have the 19 of June enter the naval room of

223

the French Embassy at 1 am, with Mrs Gordon [the name under which Betty subsequently worked—see chapter 13] and a specialist in safes brought from New York by the American Service . . . After three hours of work under the most dangerous conditions, the combination was solved and the safe open.

The combination formula was 4 Left 5
3 Right 20
2 Left 95
1 Right 2
Stop.[5]

The cipher books lay within Betty's grasp, and indeed she could not resist a natural urge to pick one up and glance inside it. Unfortunately, it was almost 4:00 A.M., far too late to allow an adequate margin for the ciphers to be photographed and returned before the guard awoke, or the early morning cleaning staff started arriving at the embassy. With utmost reluctance Betty abandoned the original plan, and allowed the Georgia Cracker to close the safe, removing all traces of their activity before the trio withdrew from the embassy.

At the Wardman Park Hotel both Betty and Charles were too exhausted and too keyed up to sleep. They showered and ate breakfast. Charles left to go to the embassy at eight o'clock and Betty telephoned John Pepper, recently returned to New York, and told him what had happened. She told him that she was sure she could obtain the ciphers if she got the go-ahead to try again. A short time later Pepper called back and agreed that she should make another attempt "tomorrow night," June 21. The photographic field unit would be in place, but there was a snag. The Georgia Cracker was not available. Having observed him only once could Betty open the door to the room, and the safe, without his help? Ever confident of her abilities, Betty thought she could. She had the combination written on a piece of paper given her by the Georgia Cracker and she had seen how he had removed the lock from the door of the naval attaché's office.

Charles came to see her at lunch time and reported with evident relief that everything was normal at the embassy and no one appeared to have noticed anything amiss. One can imagine his shock when Betty told him

224

that another break-in had been scheduled for the following night and that, this time, there would be no expert safecracker in attendance. He was extremely difficult but she soon brought him around as she always did. Using her best lines about "patriotic duty" she somehow managed to convince him, much against his better judgment, to regard the first attempt as a dress rehearsal. Charles was insistent, though, that they could not risk drugging the guard again.

On the night of the twenty-first Charles and Betty arrived at the embassy around midnight and spent almost an hour on the divan smoking cigarettes, talking and laughing softly and generally behaving as they thought the guard would expect. Given the state of nervous tension they were both feeling, this was a supreme piece of acting. When the guard and his dog had done a complete tour of the embassy Betty waited half an hour before rising and tiptoeing to the door of the naval attaché's office, where she began to remove the lock as she had seen the safecracker do two nights earlier. Instant success gave her confidence and she approached the safe without qualms and went to work.

She had learned the combination by heart and slowly dialled the numbers: 4 Left 5; 3 Right 20; 2 Left 95; 1 Right 2; Stop. When she had completed the sequence she attempted to open the door but it would not budge. She tried again, from scratch, with the note containing the combination propped up in front of her. Next, Charles tried reading out the numbers to her as she worked, but still the safe would not open. She tried over and over for what seemed like hours but she could not open the door. At last, upon Charles's insistence, she agreed to replace the door lock and leave. The pair stopped at the photographer's unlit car parked a little way from the embassy to tell them the job was "off" again.

She arrived home at 3:00 A.M. and rang Pepper immediately to report. He told her to get some sleep and fly to New York the following morning. In New York she was taken by Pepper to meet the Georgia Cracker, who took her to a deserted stretch of beach. He had taken out the back seats of his car and installed a safe similar in age and model to that at the French embassy. For the next few hours Betty was instructed in opening it, until she could literally do the job blindfolded. It wasn't enough to simply turn the combination lock, she learned. She had to wait, perhaps "feel" the dial slightly; listen for the tumblers dropping before going on to the next phase.

Afterwards she headed for Pepper's apartment on Fifty-seventh Street as they'd arranged. Pepper was fully in favour of Betty and Charles making one last attempt to obtain the codes and suggested that this should take place on the following night, but Betty said she could not do it unless the Georgia Cracker or another safe-breaker was there on call in case she ran into problems again. Pepper was initially reluctant to agree to this, but seeing Betty so uncharacteristically apprehensive he said it would be arranged. His hesitancy was possibly related to the fact that had Betty and Charles been caught they might have been able to talk their way out of it, and if not, do their best to protect their contacts. The Georgia Cracker would more surely have been traced to the BSC. It cannot have escaped Pepper that up to now the whole affair had many elements of a French farce about it.

If Betty's reluctance to plunge right ahead seems unlike her, it must be remembered that she knew Charles and that he would be in a state of nervous trauma about the whole affair. She was afraid that despite all she might say to persuade him, he would feel that they were pressing their luck too far and simply refuse to co-operate any further. Selling him on one more try would be very much helped if she could promise him that there would be an expert safecracker present as backup.

Oddly enough when in the company of Huntington that evening she told Charles of the "one final attempt" planned he seemed resigned to his fate, though he again vetoed a suggestion of drugging the guard on the grounds that the man's credulity was already in danger of being over-strained.

Just after midnight Betty and Charles walked to Wyoming Avenue from the Wardman Park Hotel. As they turned the corner from Connecticut Avenue Betty pointed out two cars parked a short distance away from the chancery. Each car had two occupants. She whispered to Charles that it was almost certainly the FBI and that she wouldn't put it past them to "burn them," knowing of the departmental jealousy that existed.

Charles opened the door with his own key and as they entered the building there was no sign of the guard. Charles had previously advised him that they would be spending one last night together at the chancery. Both found his absence odd but Charles thought the man might already be dozing. Betty, her senses stressfully alert, was deeply uneasy. She felt that at least the dog would have heard their arrival and made some noise. They went straight to the divan in the salon and began their act: smoking, talking, laughing softly. After twenty minutes or so they had still not heard a sound. The guard had not come to investigate and they had not even heard him in another part of the building. Betty grew even more concerned that his unusual behaviour was somehow connected with the presence of the FBI agents in cars outside the chancery.

Coming to a decision she sat up quickly, pulling her dress over her head and discarding her underclothes until she was left naked save for a pearl necklace. Cramming her bare feet into high-heeled shoes she stood up and tossed her clothes around the room. While this was happening Charles was fiercely demanding to know what she thought she was doing. In her hissed reply she told him to start undressing. If the guard came in to see if they were really lovers he would be less suspicious if he found them naked.[6]

Betty's instincts were not at fault. Hardly a minute had passed and Charles was still reluctantly undressing when, without warning, the door to the salon opened behind the couple. The blinding light of a powerful torch bathed Betty in light. She knew exactly what role to play in the circumstances. She turned towards the light and in the classic pose of surprised modesty attempted, vainly, to cover her nakedness with her hands, at the same time gasping "Oh, la la!" The torch beam faltered and swung towards Charles, catching him half-dressed on the divan. Clearly embarrassed and confused, the guard withdrew with loud apologies as he closed the door behind him.

The sudden appearance of the guard certainly justified Betty's unease but there is no report of this incident in the (open) FBI reports filed under her name. This would indicate that any suspicions the man entertained were his own and not connected with the presence of the FBI men outside the chancery. However, it cannot be ruled out that there are still many FBI papers appertaining to Betty's work which remain classified under agreements between the United States and foreign powers.

Relieved, Betty kissed Charles triumphantly and went to work, donning only a slip in case the guard should dare to return. She removed the lock on the naval attaché's office door with the aid of a torch held under her slip to veil the too-bright light. Inside the room she opened the window and flashed her torch. They had changed the plan to avoid having to lead the safecracker through the building from the front door. The Georgia Cracker was already in place with a ladder. He climbed in immediately. This time the cipher books were in their hands within minutes. The Cracker then climbed out of the window with the books. Betty listened to hear a car start up and drive off and closed the window. She spent some time cleaning the safe door of fingerprints and reassembled the lock on the office door. After that there was nothing to do for three long hours.

Both Betty and Charles mentioned the apprehension and fear during the long wait. Betty recalled:

> I was not afraid of going to prison, or being shot or being bitten by the dog. I was afraid of making a mess [of the job], especially as we knew there were two FBI cars sitting down the street . . . watching every move. If anything had gone wrong there would have been repercussions on the SIS, on the State Department and all over the place . . .[7]

At one point Betty noticed a "dark shape" flitting between the bushes around the embassy. She hoped it was an OSS man keeping watch and not the FBI; standing by the window she shivered despite the sultry heat of a Washington June night. Charles's fears, detailed in a letter to Admirable Leahy, were more self-centered: "I do not wish to underline the physical danger coming from two armed janitors on the spot if I had been caught."[8] The second man was undoubtedly the caretaker who lived over the garage behind the chancery building.[9]

The long wait provided Betty with ample time to magnify her personal concerns. The FBI could hardly fail to have seen the car pick up the safecracker and leave. Would they realize it was OSS and remain quiet, or might they knock at the door and alert the guards? She had prepared a story totally protective of Charles and her chiefs in BSC and OSS, and "would have no other consequence than a rest-cure [for Betty] in the District gaol or in the Psychiatric Ward of St Elizabeth's Insane Asylum."[10]

228

Chain-smoking cigarettes, their long wait broken only by Betty's occasional silent prowling to the window of the naval attaché's office and back, the couple passed the time, ears straining for the slightest sound and ready to spring into the role of lovers at the merest footfall. The time passed slowly. Betty was back in her station by the window at 3:55 A.M. The deadline—4:00 A.M.—came and went with no sign of anyone. After half an hour of nonappearance both Betty and Charles were desperately worried. Something must have gone wrong. This scenario, although covered in their plans, was one they hoped would not occur.

It was not until 4:40 A.M., nearly forty minutes late, that Betty was able to hiss to Charles that their man was back. After the long wait it was good to have something to do, though both Betty and Charles were in a highly stressed state, the flood of relief at the reappearance of the cipher books having worn off quickly. The precious volumes were handed through the window and replaced in the safe, the window closed and wiped for prints, the safe locked and the combination reset to the position in which Betty had found it that evening, a final polish here too, to remove any trace of fingerprints. The attaché's office door was closed and checked to make sure it was locked. The couple dressed, probably with as much haste as they had undressed almost four hours earlier. It was not quite 5:00 A.M. when Charles and Betty went down the chancery steps together, for the last time, hand in hand. There was still no sign of the guard.

They went directly to apartment 215B at the Wardman Park Hotel where they had spent so many hours with Ellery Huntington planning the project. Paul Fairly opened the door to them. Although he is hardly mentioned in Betty's memoirs, he crops up unexpectedly every now and then, indicating that a close professional relationship continued long after their romance petered out.

It seemed as though the entire apartment was filled with tables and photographic equipment, lights, cameras, tripods, cables; and people. But most important were the photographs of the ciphers spread around the room, apparently to dry, on the tables, on the furniture, on the floor.

There was a marvellous release from tension and a feeling almost of disbelief that they had finally done the job and got away with it. Huntington congratulated them both. Charles went off to get a few hours' sleep before going in to the embassy to check that everything was well. A few hours later, John Pepper arrived and was provided with a set of copies of the ciphers for Stephenson, but it was Huntington, dressed immaculately in the summer uniform of a colonel in the U.S. Army who was most satisfied with the night's work, as a result of which he would shortly be appointed head of SO (Special Operations).[11] Huntington was already deeply involved in preparations for the North African landings code-named TORCH (during the summer of 1942 this operation was still known as GYMNAST). Although this was to be an Allied project, the OSS took prime responsibility for subversion in the first of several wartime delineations of "spheres of influence" concerning clandestine activities.[12] Over the next few months the Vichy naval ciphers were to prove invaluable to Huntington.

Stephenson claimed, both in the BSC official history and in several interviews, that the photographs of the ciphers were sent to London "within twenty-four hours" of Betty's having obtained them. Professor Sir Harry Hinsley told me that though Vichy naval codes were used by the Allies in the landings which took place in November 1943, and for decryption purposes at Bletchley, they were obtained by the British in another manner. He pointed out that this does not rule out the possibility that BSC may also have supplied a copy of Vichy ciphers. He did not check out the BSC claim when writing the official history of espionage during the war because it was not necessary for him to do.[13] It was not unusual, of course, for work to be duplicated within the intelligence service. Some four months passed between the request to Stephenson and Betty's obtaining the ciphers. Another agency may well have had the same assignment; perhaps SIS obtained a copy directly from OSS in London. We can be sure, though, that had the British obtained the ciphers much earlier than July, Betty would have been called off the assignment. The gravest risks in intelligence are those to and caused by the human operator. It does not seem reasonable that Betty would have been allowed to continue her dangerous assignment, with its increasing risk of discovery after two failed attempts and the attendant dangers to the service that would have followed discovery, if the ciphers were already in Allied hands.

However, from my research it appears that the Americans were the more likely prime beneficiaries of the Vichy ciphers obtained by Betty and Charles. OSS used the codes to good purpose prior to and during the landings; before that, and long afterward, they were used to decode intercepted messages between the Vichy government in France, Admiral Robert at Martinique and Vichy diplomatic missions throughout the Western Hemisphere. Charles had previously been providing the contents of military communications to and from the Washington embassy but now all Vichy communications, world-wide, were open to OSS. The results, called the Vichy Intercepts, can be seen today in several public collections in the United States.[14]

The completion of this mission might have left Charles in the position of being superfluous. Not at all. OSS had further plans for both Charles and Betty.

During the summer months Betty continued to make her regular trips to New York to deliver intelligence produced by Charles, but plans were afoot for a more exciting adventure. Stephenson suggested to Donovan that Betty should be sent to England for training and subsequently parachuted into occupied France to work for the OSS Special Operations Executive.[15] This proposal went no further, for Donovan had plans of his own for getting Betty into France. By now Huntington was solely involved with the North African situation and the imminent Allied landings there. Betty's new OSS contact was Donald Downes.

Downes was a thirty-seven-year-old stocky graduate of Phillips Exeter and Yale. A former school teacher, he worked for the American Office of Naval Intelligence in the Balkans and Middle East in 1940 and in early 1941 as an amateur agent. On his return to the United States he was recruited by Donovan and seconded to BSC where under John Pepper he headed a team investigating the connections between German agents and the America First committee. Early in 1942 he transferred to Allen Dulles's intelligence staff in New York, where he worked on Special Activities for the OSS. He had his own important OSS responsibilities at the time that he came into contact with Betty, chiefly to recruit a team of twenty Spanish Americans and take them to North Africa after the TORCH landings. The fear was that as soon as the Allies landed in North

Africa, Franco would enter the war on the side of Hitler. The job assigned to Downes's team, called operation BANANA, was to get into Spain and gather information on the frequent reports to Donovan regarding Franco's intentions. Downes alerted Betty to the fact that a proposal was "on the table" whereby she and Charles would return to France and work there in close co-operation with an OSS agent already *in situ.*

Charles's background in France would provide an impeccable cover for their activities. Although his family home was in the Perpignan region of France's southland, now under Vichy control, he had lived for thirty-eight years in Paris. His father had been a member of France's parliament, twice minister of finance and leader of the majorities under Poincaré and Clemenceau. And of course there was his own excellent record, culminating in such strong, open support of the Vichy regime that the American media had vilified him for it. Not least in his favour was the ownership of several newspapers which covered "all the south of France . . . a wide network of correspondents . . . [and the fact that he knew] everybody in politics, press, business, etc."[16]

There remained the question of a cover for Betty. If Charles were to return it would not be in a quiet way; his pre-war connections and his service as a Vichy diplomat would dictate a high-profile return. Betty's French was excellent but could she pass for a native Frenchwoman? There had to be a subtle way of explaining her presence and this exercised the minds of BSC and the OSS for some weeks. At last they came up with a suggestion that was put to the couple by Colonel Huntington and Donald Downes. If nothing else it shows that they had been doing some homework into Charles Brousse's domestic background.

Betty, not yet thirty-two, had kept her youthful figure and could easily pass for five years younger. Charles and Kay were fifty, old enough to have a daughter in her mid-twenties. Kay had been married several times before her marriage to Charles Brousse and, as a matter of fact, on January 28, 1913, a year after her first marriage to a Lieutenant Shaw T. Waterbury, she had given birth to a daughter, named Catherine, who unfortunately died in childhood. Had the child lived she would be just past twenty-eight—only two years younger than Betty. The question put to a startled Charles Brousse was: Would he be able to "recruit" Kay to help

232

them? More specifically, could he persuade her to allow them to use the identity of her dead daughter?

Poor Charles. A myriad of objections must have flitted through his mind when the scheme was proposed. His relationship with Kay was already strained, though she was not yet aware of his relationship with Betty. How was he to explain Betty's presence to a woman who was already obsessively jealous?

He was empowered to tell Kay he had been working as an agent for American intelligence for the past year. He could easily prove this if necessary; Huntington himself would meet with Kay and back Charles's story. Surely as an American Kay would be pleased to know that her husband was not, after all, an ally of her country's enemies? Betty would be introduced to her as an American secret agent whom the service wished to infiltrate into France. If necessary Kay would be recruited to work as Betty's sub-agent.

Still resisting, Charles argued that he did not know how his wife would react to the idea of using the identity of her long-dead daughter (of whom he had, incidentally, never heard until now). As usual, his first inclination was to turn the entire proposal down flat. As usual, Betty prevailed upon him to "think about it."

Somewhat surprisingly Kay Brousse bit for this story, hook, line and sinker. She was extremely flattered to be asked to work for the intelligence service and did not demur when the plan was put to her. Over the next two months or so, it was agreed, Charles and she would gradually introduce Betty into their circle as her daughter and Charles's step-daughter, "Catherine Waterbury Gordon." Initially this would merely involve mentioning her to their acquaintances and Charles's colleagues, following which Betty, alias Catherine (whose cover story would be that she had been recently widowed), would come to live in Washington to be near her parents.[17]

The Special Activities office of the OSS had already been to work on the matter of Catherine's widowhood and had isolated a recent casualty of the war, a Lieutenant John Gordon of the United States Navy who was a man without living relatives.

What could go wrong?

Chapter 13

AUGUST 1942 –
FEBRUARY 1943

*T*he following letter is one of many in Betty's file at the FBI headquarters in Washington, D.C.:

FEDERAL BUREAU OF INVESTIGATION
UNITED STATES DEPARTMENT OF JUSTICE
1437 K Street Northwest
Washington, D.C.

August 20 1942

TO: *RE:*

Director   Mrs. ARTHUR PACK, *with aliases*
Federal Bureau of Investigation   ESPIONAGE—F
Washington DC   *Bureau File No.* 65–43539

235

Dear Sir,

. . . On August 20th 1942 Special Agent [name censored] of this office was advised . . . that the Military Intelligence Division is presently conducting an investigation on Mrs PACK at the Wardman Park Hotel. He said that in connection with this investigation the Military Intelligence Division has a plain-clothed man staying at the hotel, and also that every day or so a Colonel of that Division visits the hotel in connection with the same matter.

Military Intelligence Division has on occasion brought photographic equipment into the hotel apparently for the purpose of photographing documents which [agent] believes Mrs PACK has probably obtained from CHARLES BROUSSE, Press Attaché, French Embassy.

In furnishing this information the informant explained that he did not wish to cause the Hotel, the Military Intelligence Division or the Federal Bureau of Investigation any embarrassment whatsoever, since it appeared that the two organizations would be duplicating their efforts.

In view of this new development it is requested that the Bureau take steps to verify the investigation apparently being conducted by the Military Intelligence Division and instruct this office as to what further action should be taken in regard to this case. . . .

> S. K. McKee
> Special Agent in Charge[1]

No information is available on other work that Betty did during the summer of 1942 but it is known that she was employed briefly on several assignments in which she operated under the code-names Mrs. Charles Bennett,[2] Miss Carson, Miss Newhaven,[3] and Mrs. Powers. These assignments were clearly on behalf of BSC; documents that refer to them, though indexed, have been removed from the United States' National Archives with the bald statement: "Security Classified information; withdrawn at the request of a foreign government." An application for access to the documents concerned, made under the United States Freedom of Information Act, has met with a polite refusal for the same reasons. Perhaps they were not important jobs; they are not mentioned in the BSC official history. Probably they concerned merely the bread-and-butter gathering of information, possibly involving other foreign diplomats.

Prior to Pearl Harbor the FBI had forged an uneasy alliance with British Intelligence. Stephenson's organization was prepared to, and did, perform illegal acts to obtain intelligence, to which J. Edgar Hoover turned a blind eye because he was often a recipient of the results. For example, the FBI tried unsuccessfully to decode Vichy cables throughout 1941 and 1942;[4] BSC shared with the FBI certain Vichy decrypts. In the very early days of the war Adolf Berle noted in his diary that it had been suggested to Hoover that the two services "should co-ordinate and conduct a continuous exchange of information without passing through the State Department." It can only have been through Hoover that Adolf Berle learned of this.[5] It is easy to sympathize with Berle's opposition to this suggestion: "Apart from all other considerations, it would not seem likely to be well-accepted by American public opinion that this country's intelligence service was being guided by the advice of one of the belligerents. . . ." Even after America entered the war Berle saw no reason to change his views. He remained deeply suspicious of Stephenson and the British Secret Service presence in the United States. By then Hoover's position had changed; the FBI now had much greater power and Hoover no longer needed Stephenson, though he maintained his contact for his own reasons. However, the activities in the United States of foreign agents, even those of friendly powers, were regarded by senior State Department officials (Assistant Secretary Adolf Berle in particular) as being not necessarily in the best interests of the country. "Why should anybody have a spy system in the United States?" Berle wrote in his diary. "And what will anyone look like a little later when someone finds out about it?"[6] So, while Hoover did not attempt to hamper BSC openly, neither did he support Stephenson when the matter of BSC's extensive activities came up for discussion.

By now the FBI had discovered that Betty was "acting as a British Intelligence Agent in this country [and that] if any information is required on Mrs. Pack by the Washington Field office it should be obtained through MID. . . ." FBI archives note that limits had been placed by the ONI on FBI contacts with Mrs. Pack.[7] Yet despite their liaison with BSC and notification that Betty was involved with other United States security agencies, the Bureau continued to regard her activities with utmost suspicion.

Several times a week throughout this period new reports came in on Betty's movements. ". . . She has moved to a room [at the Wardman Hotel] other than the one she formerly occupied and is now living under an assumed name. . . ." "Confidential information has just been received that Mrs. Pack is using the name of Mrs. Powers. . . ." That in connection with her present activity "the MIS presently . . . has a plainclothesman staying at the hotel . . .: The Washington field office advised that [their agent] is rather reticent in complying . . . in an inquiry of Mrs. Pack, stating that inasmuch as MIS [is involved] there appears to be a danger of exposing the inquiries and of a duplication of effort. . . ." "It appears there is something fishy about the whole matter."[8]

In September the FBI put a tap on Betty's phone. Transcripts of her conversations are still classified but indexes to those still-closed documents reveal that the conversations were mainly between her and Charles.[9] The two may have discussed the plan to infiltrate her into the Vichy community as his step-daughter, since FBI reports shortly thereafter were wise to the fact that Mrs. Catherine Waterbury Gordon, who had an apartment at the Roosevelt Hotel was better known to them as Mrs. Pack, who also had an apartment at the Wardman Park Hotel.

Betty's sister, Mrs. Jane Thorpe Powell, was married to the owner of the Roosevelt Hotel, and was happy to accommodate Betty's request without asking too many questions.[10] Betty had already told her mother and sister that she was engaged in secret war work, but at this time they did not know the extent of this work or for whom she was working.

The plan was going well. Betty, in simple disguise, had already been introduced to several of Charles's colleagues by Kay. Wearing no make-up, sporting a pair of plain-glass spectacles, her hair darkened to a mouse-brown shade and cut in a simple, unfashionable style, dressed—as the badge of her recent widowhood—in modest black and wearing flat shoes, Mrs. Catherine Gordon appeared unfortunately plain and made no attempt to make a special impression upon those she met. The poor young widow, speaking perfect French in a soft, girlish voice, was really rather boring and attracted little attention beyond the politeness demanded of a first introduction. The close attachment between the girl and her mother and step-father, however, was truly commendable.

By November plans were well advanced for Charles's return to France with Betty. Charles had informed Henry-Haye that he could not continue to live on the small salary paid him by the ambassador, and the necessary permission to leave had been granted. Kay was to stay in the United States where she would be allocated a palliative job by OSS. Having no particular wish to suffer either the discomforts of living in an occupied country or the risk of discovery by the Nazis, with all the attendant horrors implicit in that prospect, Kay was, presumably, content with the arrangement.

At this point history intervened.

During the night of November 7–8, 1942, TORCH was launched. The Allied forces, in what was to be one of the greatest amphibian operations in history, landed along hundreds of miles of the coast of French North Africa. Based on a strategic need to deny Germany control of the West African coast and create a southern base for the Allied invasion of occupied Europe, the plan's first objectives were Algiers, Oran and Casablanca, all governed by Vichy France. Algiers fell by nightfall and though there were heavy casualties at Casablanca (one force lost 242 landing ships—64 percent of its fleet), the port was soon under Allied control. But opposition was stronger at Oran. Pro-Vichy French units there, who had fought the British in Syria and who retained, as did Charles Brousse, bitter memories of the naval attack at Mers-el-Kébir in 1940, put up strong resistance, with the result that it took more than two days of fighting before the French capitulated.[11]

The Allied success in this operation prompted one of Churchill's great wartime speeches: "This is not the end. It is not even the beginning of the end. But it is, perhaps, the end of the beginning. . . ."[12] Marshal Pétain told President Roosevelt: "It is with stupor and sadness that I learned tonight of the aggression of your troops against North Africa . . . France and her honour are at stake. We shall defend ourselves, this is the order I am giving."[13]

Betty met Colonel Ellery Huntington several days after the North African landings. In her memoirs she recorded her sense of pride and achievement when Huntington told her that possession of the Vichy naval ciphers had been of the greatest possible value to the OSS during operation TORCH. Thanks to their ability to read Vichy cables the OSS apparently knew that the Vichy government and the French intelligence service had no idea that the Allies intended to invade North Africa. Outside of the main objectives, Huntington told Betty, "Allied forces met with practically no enemy resistance. The reason is . . . a military secret. But I think that *you* should know that it is due to your ciphers. They have changed the whole course of the war."[14]

Predictably, Laval broke off diplomatic relations with the United States (having so openly accepted German military assistance during the North African landings he could, in any case, no longer claim neutrality). Secretary Hull immediately "sent Ambassador Henry-Haye his passports" and Roosevelt addressed the nation describing Laval's action as having been "prescribed by Hitler." No act of Hitler, the president said, could sever relations between the French people and the people of the United States. "We have not broken relations with the French people. We never will."

The fall-out from these acts of world-wide significance directly affected Betty's personal life and the plans to get her into Europe. There was no longer any question of the Vichy diplomats and their families being allowed to travel back to France. For one thing, American diplomats in France had already been interned (in what would later be discovered were harsh, primitive conditions); the State Department decided to follow suit and hold the French diplomats in the country until an exchange could be effected. One problem was to find a suitable internment location.

It was a delicate matter. The Americans had no desire to deal particularly severely with the former Vichy diplomats. Despite the fact that relations between the countries had been severed, State Department personnel were determined to treat the detainees with dignity. They would be somewhat pampered prisoners. Too, there was the hope (misguided as it turned out) that if the Vichy people were well treated, their American counterparts would be dealt with on equal terms. At the same time, in a period of wartime sacrifice, the internees could not be seen to be living lavishly at taxpayers' expense. The State Department settled on a large hotel in Hershey, Pennsylvania, that would accommodate "Adults at $7.50 a day; children up to and including 12 years, $4.00; guards $4.00. Incidental expenses, incurred by the State Department, will be billed at cost."[15]

Hotel Hershey was however, by the standards of many Americans, a luxury hotel, set in the rolling foothills of the Blue Ridge Mountains. It had been described by the traveller/writer Lowell Thomas as "a palace . . . that outpalaces the palaces of the Maharajahs of India."[16] Even discounting such public relations hype, it was a pleasant, self-contained world, some miles from the nearby town of Hershey, with its own golf course, horse riding, swimming pool and beautifully landscaped gardens surrounding the Mediterranean-style building. It was assumed that its isolation would make it easier to guard, but it would be found that this was not as easy as envisaged; the sheer amount of acreage and the number of unco-operative people would create many unforeseen problems for the thirty-six guards assigned to the job.

The changed situation was discussed by Betty, Charles, and Donald Downes at a meeting held in "Catherine Gordon's" apartment at the Roosevelt Hotel. Ellery Huntington had now become head of Special Operations[17] and would shortly depart for North Africa. Donald Downes, of the Special Activities department of OSS, was assigned as Betty's temporary contact. He, too, would shortly be on his way to North Africa to head up project BANANA. Downes informed Betty and Charles that the plan to place Charles and Betty in France was still being considered. Quite apart from anything else, it was generally thought at the time that any future Allied invasion of France was likely to take place along the Mediterranean coast. Charles's newspapers served the entire regions of Pyrénées-Orientales, Aude, Hérault and Gard; he could help to swing public opinion in this large area in favour of the Allies.[18]

However, under present circumstances Charles and Betty could not hope to get to France, as previously planned. It was believed by all those present that the incarceration of Vichyites would last no longer than six months. If Charles now attempted to evade internment it would undermine the credibility he had built up with his Vichy masters and thus risk the cover he and Betty would need in Paris. On the other hand, neither Charles nor Betty were happy about being separated for an indefinite period. It was decided that Charles and Kay should go to Hershey with the other diplomats and apply to the State Department for permission to have their "daughter" join them. Until such time as they were repatriated along with the other Vichy diplomats, Charles and Betty would work as inside agents, keeping the OSS informed about everything that was said among the internees.

Downes stressed that while he might be able to pull a few strings, the application for "Catherine Gordon" to join the Brousses at Hershey would have to be done formally, through the State Department. They could not ask for special favours; it was essential for the longer-term plan that as few people as possible know about the real identity of Mrs. Gordon. Therefore they could not risk a leak by advising those who ran the administrative machinery at the State Department of the special status of Charles and Betty. Other relatives of diplomats living in the United States and finding themselves unable to get work because of their Vichy record had been refused permission to join the group; the United States had no intention of supporting free-loaders. Clearly, it would not necessarily be easy to get Betty into Hershey but if they were successful, a spell at Hershey would undeniably help to establish Catherine Gordon's provenance and might also, because of the inescapable intimacy of the small group, provide useful information about Betty's fellow internees.

In the meantime, Betty and Charles underwent the bitter-sweet sorrow of an imminent parting, made more bitter by Betty's suspicion that she was pregnant.

At the Vichy embassy Henry-Haye pointed out that because Charles had remained in the United States on Henry-Haye's private payroll, and had officially been removed from the official diplomatic lists some months previously, he might, if he wished, avoid internment. Charles, fast becoming as good an actor as Betty, replied heatedly to his chief that he would not desert him, proclaiming that he wished to share Henry-Haye's imprisonment. Furthermore, Charles said, he utterly deplored the act of some of his colleagues who had sworn allegiance to the United States. He was referring to the fact that when diplomatic relations were broken off between France and the United States, six Vichy diplomats—including Count Jean de la Grandville and Guillaume Georges-Picot (the husband of Henry-Haye's mistress)—submitted their resignations and promised the State Department "that they desired to aid this government and the Allies in any way possible."[19] By this quixotic act Charles reinforced a picture of his firm loyalty to the Vichy government and to Henry-Haye personally.

On November 16, the eve of Charles and Kay's departure to Hershey, a further meeting between Charles, Betty and Downes took place. Charles's report of this meeting survives in the State Department archives and also details "the presence of an elderly gentleman Mr. Clark . . . a member of the Army Intelligence."

We agreed

1. That I would do no declaration of allegiance to the State Department of the kind that members of the Diplomatic French Staff were giving . . .
2. That I would, of course, be interned at Hershey.
3. That I would, in the meantime obtain the agreement of Henry-Haye to have my "daughter" coming with us to France, under the excellent . . . pretext that she has nobody here; we are her only support; she has no money; refuses to live without us as we refuse to live without her; has recently lost her husband; etc., etc.
4. That in France she and I will resume our work, highly facilitated by the fact that . . . [she] speaks French almost without an accent and is extremely cultured . . . Moreover I shall be received with full honours having apparently shown full loyalty to the Ambassador and to Pétain.
5. That I will employ a system of [contact], extremely simple, agreed with Mr Downes, to have our *agent de liaison* with the outside, coming to us.
6. That "Mrs Catherine Gordon" would [join us] in a very few days. [This being essential due to] the general and mutinous atmosphere . . . and the technicalities of such a dangerous matter; and my wife knowing nothing of the work done by "her daughter" and I.
7. That I would not make the official demand for her to come through the Swiss Legation as it was unnecessary to have the Swiss knowing her address.[20]

With this agreement comfortably between them, Charles and Betty parted. Hershey was, in any case, only a three-hour drive from Washington and for the short time they would be parted they hoped to communicate by telephone. Knowing that the press corps would be present in force and displaying her usual shyness about being photographed, Betty stayed away from the leave-taking of the French party on November 17. She was able to read later that day in the Washington newspapers that it had

the air of a wealthy group of fashionable people setting out for a weekend in the country. The warm autumn sun shone brightly on the castle-like [ambassador's residence] at 221 Kalorama Road . . . a row of limousines had pulled up in the driveway. White jacketed servants bustled about stowing away luggage. For a quarter of an hour Ambassador Henry-Haye, members of his staff, their wives and children . . . wandered leisurely in and out through the beautiful wrought-iron entrance doors, supervising the servants and chatting pleasantly . . . Among the group were . . . Charles Brousse, Press Attaché, and his Georgia-born wife. In his lapel Mr. Brousse wore the rosette of the Legion of Honour awarded him with gold leaves for valour in World War I.[21]

Although the State Department was not formally advised of the OSS plans for Charles and Betty, Assistant Secretary of State Breckinridge Long was obliquely informed that Charles Brousse "was decidedly a supporter of the Allied Cause" and that this information should be used "in considering the case of Mr. Brousse among those of the other French officials who are being sent to Hershey."[22] Secretary Long imparted the information in an internal memo, upon which a puzzled assistant scrawled "I do not know Mr. Brousse personally but I had always been under the impression that he was the reverse of what [Mr. Long] says."[23]

A week after Charles left Washington, Betty was admitted to the Garfield Hospital as an emergency case. She was suffering a severe haemorrhage, probably the result of a miscarriage. She was hospitalized for eight days and received two blood transfusions.[24]

That she spoke to Charles by phone during this period is known from indexed phone intercepts, but—again—the content of those conversations remains classified information. Both would, however, have been aware that phone calls from Hershey would have been tapped. Charles had begun to display signs of agitation at the separation, especially in view of Betty's hospitalization and his own realization that their reunion was not to be immediate. Huntington had departed for North Africa, and Downes had already received his orders to depart in connection with project BA-

NANA. But Betty's new contact at OSS, William A. Kimbel, Donovan's personal liaison man, agreed to obtain Donovan's personal intervention in the matter. He was as good as his word. Within a few days an extraordinary personal request was sent from William J. Donovan, director of the Office of Strategic Services to Frederick B. Lyon, executive assistant to Adolf Berle:

December 22nd 1942

Dear Mr. Lyon:

At my request, I understand that Mr. Kimbel has discussed with you a matter concerning a certain young lady to be permitted to go to Hershey and later to proceed with the French to France in the diplomatic exchange. I should greatly appreciate your making it possible for this to be accomplished.

Sincerely,

William J. Donovan[25]

Although Betty is not mentioned by name in this letter, it is clearly she to whom the letter refers; it is archived in the National Archives along with a large amount of correspondence regarding Catherine Gordon's application to be admitted to Hershey, and other documentary evidence that Catherine Gordon was in reality Betty Pack.[26]

Confident that Donovan's letter would secure her entry to Hershey, Betty packed her suitcases. On December 23, at a meeting with William Kimbel at OSS headquarters, known as "Q" building, Kimbel told her that there had been no immediate response to the letter sent by Donovan (Donovan was known to OSS employees as "Wild Bill" and later "Big Bill" to distinguish him from William Stephenson who was "Little Bill"). The State Department's last reply to Kimbel had advised that they could do nothing unless a formal application was made by Charles and Kay Brousse through the official channels of the Swiss legation.

Donovan's letter to Berle's office may have hindered rather than helped the attempt to get Betty into Hershey. Those State Department officials most closely concerned in the matter of Catherine Gordon were opposed to Donovan's organization and disinclined to go to any special lengths to help. Breckinridge Long wrote in his diary:

One of the most important things to be controlled is Donovan. His organization is composed of inexperienced people—inexperienced in so far as dealing with high powered information is concerned. They get all our information and use it ad lib. Sometimes there is a definite flare-back because of lack of judgement in its use . . .

Donovan has been a thorn in the side of a number of the regular agencies of the government for some time, including the Department of State. . . . he is into everybody's business, knows no bounds of jurisdiction, tries to fill the shoes of each agency charged with the responsibility for a war activity. He has almost unlimited money and a regular army at work and agents all over the world.[27]

Long might have added that Donovan also had the ear and the open support of the president, another cause for resentment. Adolf Berle felt much the same as Long and so did many other State Department officials at senior and junior levels. One, Mrs. Ruth Shipley, who ran the United States's passport division, attempted to insist that all OSS agents were described as such in their visas. It took all of Donovan's high-level connections to bring the message home to her that to thus identify secret agents would be incompatible with the aims of OSS.[28]

Perhaps sensing a lengthy delay in their objective of getting Betty into Hershey, Kimbel suggested that they perhaps ought to proceed along the lines demanded by the State Department and make a formal application through the Swiss embassy. Any other course might, in any case, lay her open to suspicion by the Vichy internees.

Uncharacteristically, Betty became difficult at this hint of a bureauocratic hitch; she told Kimbel that she was going to Hershey on the following day and would talk her way in to the compound somehow or other. Surely, she reasoned, the guards would not keep a daughter from visiting her mother on Christmas Eve? Kimbel recognized her determination and said he could do nothing to prevent her from going to Hershey. But he asked her to wait a few days to see if "Big Bill's" letter brought some action. Above all he urged caution, reminding her that if she were too aggressive she could ruin their plan. Her mind was already made up, however.

On arrival at the Roosevelt Hotel after this unpromising meeting, Betty was greeted by her sister, who advised her that "two men had called and asked questions about her." Betty surmised that it was the FBI. She was tired and felt ill and dispirited, but she was also angry and frustrated. She telephoned the Washington field office of the FBI and introduced herself, saying that she knew they had been following her for some time and that if they cared to call on her on the following day at her mother's apartment at 2139 Wyoming Avenue she would see them.[29]

Next morning she took a cab to her mother's apartment. The FBI agents were already there and were being entertained by a Cora obviously puzzled that Betty should invite these men to her apartment; she refused to leave the room while her daughter talked to the men. At length, out of exasperation, Betty gave in and allowed Cora to remain. According to the FBI letter describing the meeting, she told her fascinated listeners that she was a British agent attached to the Office of Strategic Services working in America's interests, and provided sufficient information to enable the FBI to check her story. Almost certainly she told them that she was being infiltrated into Hershey, since still-closed sections of the letter refer to the Vichy detainees. She finished by expressing her irritation at being shadowed at every turn and hampered from carrying out her assignments.[30]

In reporting the meeting the special agent in charge, S. K. McKee, also gossiped that Betty

was very well dressed and well groomed and that she appeared to have been well educated. It was also noted that her mother's apartment was expensively furnished in good taste. It is known that Mrs. PACK resided at the Wardman Park Hotel and latterly at the Roosevelt Hotel. Mr. Brousse visited her regularly at both places. It is also known that she kept a maid at the Roosevelt Hotel.[31]

Betty was not the only BSC agent to be put under such pressure by the FBI. It was a recurring problem, causing one BSC official to ask Downes, "Does J. Edgar think he's fighting on Bunker Hill against us

247

Redcoats or hasn't he heard of Pearl Harbor?"[32] After the FBI agents left, Betty was subjected to a long and uncomfortable interview by Cora, during which Betty evidently told her mother of her work. She also showed her mother a cyanide pill which she claimed had been given to her during the training she had received for her mission in France. Where this training took place is not known. It is possible that Betty spent a short period at "Camp X," BSC's training camp near Ottawa in Canada, though no one I spoke with knew of such a visit. Cora subsequently confided Betty's secret to her daughter-in-law, Shirlee Thorpe. When I expressed surprise that Betty had talked, Shirlee said: "Why? I imagine Betty thought something might happen to her and so someone ought to know. . . ."[33]

I mentioned the incident to Marion de Chastellaine, Betty's former contact at the New York office of BSC. Her reaction was mainly one of surprise that Betty would have told her mother, adding: "I can't think why she would have needed a cyanide pill in the United States. . . ." But "Marion" had not been aware of the OSS plan to send Betty to France.[34]

After the long interview with Cora, Betty left Washington and drove to Pennsylvania, arriving in the dark at seven o'clock. She presented herself at the gates of Hotel Hershey as Mrs. Catherine Gordon, the daughter of M. and Mme Charles Brousse, and asked to see her parents. She was referred to Edgar A. Innes, the special agent of the State Department assigned to Hershey to oversee the task of guarding the Vichy diplomats. She told her sad story, that she was "the widow of a United States naval officer, recently reported missing in action in the Pacific; that she is in a pregnant condition . . ." and that she desperately needed the support of her parents over Christmas. Indeed, she said, she had no other living relatives.[35] It is almost certain that she was no longer pregnant; she must have thought it a useful addition to her story.

Innes was personally sympathetic to the young woman. Widowed by the war, pregnant and lonely; wanting no more than to be with her mother on Christmas Eve. No wonder Betty thought the sheer pathos of her story would get her into Hershey. Yet Innes was not empowered to admit her and he was too experienced an agent to take Betty's story at face value. He telephoned Henry-Haye at the hotel to ascertain what the former ambassador might know of the young woman. Haye confirmed that Mrs.

Gordon was Brousse's step-daughter by a previous marriage of Mme Brousse and that his former attaché had, indeed, mentioned that he wished to have his step-daughter with him in internment and that permission had been sought through the official channel of the Swiss embassy to the State Department. Henry-Haye then promptly advised Charles that Betty was at the gates begging to be admitted.

Unable to leave the hotel because of the curfew imposed on the internees, Charles immediately telephoned Agent Innes and spoke heatedly to him. No official permission had been sought? Very well then, he was officially applying *now*. He tried everything to have Betty admitted, from begging to righteous indignation, all backed heartily by Henry-Haye. Innes said he would see what could be done.

Innes subsequently made phone calls to officials of the Foreign Activities branch of the State Department, and to a member of Assistant Secretary Berle's staff, but despite the fact that those on the spot "could sympathise with the wish of such close relatives to be together during the holidays," at such an hour on Christmas Eve it was not easy to contact anyone prepared to make a decision.[36] To her annoyance, and probably genuine distress, Betty was eventually turned away until after the holiday.

From memoranda reporting the matter that flew about for the next few weeks, it is safe to assume that Charles, frustrated in his attempts to see Betty, had his holiday utterly ruined. Furthermore, his fellow internees were incensed at the cavalier way the United States government treated the desires of the Brousse family to be together at this holy time of the year. All agreed it was wicked.

Intending to make a few phone calls of her own which might resolve the matter Betty checked in to the Community Inn in the town of Hershey. No evidence exists that she contacted Kimbel, or that she attempted to bring pressure through her old contacts at BSC, but it would have been out of character for her not to have done so. Meanwhile, Henry-Haye telephoned many former diplomatic contacts and continued to exert considerable pressure on Agent Innes throughout the Christmas period.

On December 26, Innes referred the case up, the matter eventually working its way to Adolf Berle himself. Notwithstanding Donovan's pre-Christmas request to Berle's executive assistant, and the obscure hints to

Breckinridge Long about Brousse's real loyalties, Berle and the other State Department officials retained grave suspicions regarding Catherine Gordon. Indeed, though most of those involved were fully aware that in some way she was linked with Donovan's organization they apparently could not see how it all fitted together. After some thought, Secretary Berle's cautious decision was that "it might be preferable to have Mrs. Brousse meet Mrs. Gordon outside the hotel premises until all the facts surrounding this case can be more definitely ascertained."[37]

On December 27, in a cruelly ironic twist, Kay Brousse was driven by Special Agent Edgar Innes to the Community Inn, where she was allowed to spend two hours in conversation with her "daughter," hardly the arrangement Betty and Charles had been clamouring for. In Kay's presence, Betty was allowed to take a telephone call from Henry-Haye, who assured Betty that he would "do everything possible to effect a reunion and that if the question of passports is a difficulty he [would] give me a French passport."[38] Betty then returned to Washington and met William Kimbel to decide on a new course of action. They decided that despite their earlier plan to stay low-profile there was no option now but to make all the formal official applications necessary.

Betty submitted her application to join the Brousses the same day.

December 28, 1942

I Catherine Waterbury Gordon, widow, herewith submit pertinent information about myself in connection with the request made on December 24th by my mother and foster-father, M. and Mme Charles Emmanuel Brousse to the Minister of Switzerland and the Department of State.

MOTHER: Catherine Calhoun Graves Brousse
FATHER: Shaw T. Waterbury
DATE OF BIRTH: January 28th 1913
PLACE OF BIRTH: Washington D.C. Columbia Hospital

I have recently been widowed and have also lost my mother and foster-father through their internment at Hershey. We have always been very close and this separation has come as a great shock to the three of us. My mother is not in good health, depends on me for many services that I have long been accustomed to do for her. I, in turn, depend upon my parents for material and moral support.

. . . It would I feel, be out of place to appeal to the human sentiments of whosoever may make a final decision, but I think that I should say that the happiness or despair of three people are involved, that these three people are devoted to the United States and that no possible harm could be done in permitting their reunion as soon as possible. I have fear for the consequences of a continued strain on nerves that have not been relaxed over a long period of anxious waiting.

Catherine Waterbury Gordon.[39]

What happened next gives us one more glimpse into that special psyche of Betty's, which could not allow any sense of caution to thwart her need to move things along. We must remember that the ultimate plan was for her to be sent into German-held Europe with Charles. Compromise of Catherine Gordon's real identity with any person outside of the smallest circles would surely have increased the already enormous risk that as the matter was talked about it would finally fall upon the ears of someone who would put the truth together and give or sell the information to those sympathetic to the German cause.

Yet though she was well known in Washington circles as the daughter of George and Cora Thorpe, and the wife of the British diplomat Arthur Pack, and could easily have run into someone she had known in those other lives, she actually chose to hand-carry her letter through the halls of the State Department and, in her "disguise" as Catherine Gordon, deliver it in person to Edwin Plitt and Frederick B. Lyon. On the following day she confirmed this meeting in writing to Plitt and enclosed a letter from her "parents" supporting her claim and begging that Mrs. Gordon be allowed to join them.

There are two interesting points to be made about the short covering letter Betty included with the one from Charles and Kay. One is that despite the fact that before Christmas she had gone to considerable pains to establish the fact that "Catherine Gordon" lived at the Roosevelt Hotel, she addressed this letter from 2139 Wyoming Avenue, her mother's apartment and an address known to the FBI and others as the some-time residence of Elizabeth Pack. Further, she made no attempt whatsoever to disguise her handwriting. Although this has been confirmed by a graphologist, one need not be an expert to recognize that the stylized signatures of Betty Pack and Catherine Gordon were executed by the same hand.[40]

All this suggests that in her eagerness to get in to see Charles, she may have told Plitt and Lyon either the whole story, or at least a part of it. A wry comment on a note Plitt attached to the letter from the Brousses reads:

Dear Freddy,

Here you are. Add or subtract as much as you want.

Ed.[41]

Charles, meanwhile, seemed prepared to match both Betty's impatience and her impulsiveness. In a series of astonishing, very lengthy letters to President Roosevelt, Admiral Leahy, and Cordell Hull, he outlined his background, detailing the work he had done for the OSS, and provided names, personal addresses and telephone numbers of his contacts within the organization so that his statements could be substantiated. Each letter was a personal plea for help in getting Betty into Hotel Hershey. He was able to have the Leahy letter delivered in person. A diplomatic visitor was acquainted with the admiral's aide, Commander Freseman, whom Charles also knew from the time when Admiral Leahy had had a lengthy series of meetings with Henry-Haye. The letter was hand-carried from Hershey and given to Commander Freseman in early January. The other letters were sent through the Swiss legation. Charles was aware that—with the exception of the letter to Leahy—the letters would be read on the way to their intended recipients, by censors, FBI agents, State Department special agents and members of the recipient's administrative staff.

He dared not compromise Betty but referred to her always as "my daughter." He was correct; the letters were passed along the lines of communication accumulating notes as they passed upward. One such note, from a member of Freddy Lyon's staff reads: ". . . if the contents of this letter are true it is practically *dynamite*."[42]

The letters are all similar in content, with only slight variations; some are countersigned and approved by Kay Brousse, and they run to over two thousand words each. In them Charles details his family background and adds a few interesting tidbits: that he had been personally recommended for the position of press attaché to Henry-Haye by Robert Murphy (at the time of these letters, Murphy, the State Department's political representative in North Africa and also Roosevelt's personal representative, was a powerful name to drop). He also listed a number of important American diplomats who formerly served in France and offered them as references regarding his long-term pro-American sentiments; during the early days of the war, he said, he had been personally selected by Premier Edouard Daladier as liaison officer to the American Press Corps and in this connection he had escorted Walter Lippmann, Dorothy Thompson, Clare Boothe and Henry Luce "of Time, Life and Fortune" to the front, and had acted as an interpreter in interviews between Mr. Mandell of the American embassy and Daladier; that it was under arrangements made by him that the American legation had enjoyed 2,000 litres of gasoline per month in Vichy "during the last two years, despite the acute shortage . . . when Maréchal Pétain himself had only 200 litres"; that he was "financially rather independent, being co-owner with my family of two very important newspapers: L'Indépendant des Pyrénées-Orientales (daily circulation 170,000) and Midi-Soir (daily circulation 70,000)":

> . . . My *secret* record is such that my statue in solid gold should be errected after the war. The mission of . . . General Clark* to North Africa [is] child's play compared to what I did . . .

---

* The reference is to General Dwight Eisenhower's sending General Mark Clark to Algeria by submarine to try to persuade the French forces to collaborate with the impending invasion of North Africa.

During the past two years I have sent to . . . Donovan's Office, namely to Mr. James Murphy, second in command of the Office of Strategic Services (Telephone: Executive 6100 ext 6. Personal address: 3731 North Glebe Road, Arlington, Va.) *all* the diplomatic secret telegrams received or sent by our embassy. My daily reports were transmitted by the daughter of my wife, Mrs Catherine Gordon, acting as my confidential secretary and *agent de liaison*. We worked under the denomination of B.10 for me and E.11 for her. The reports have been made until the day I left for Hershey.

. . . After many weeks of the most careful preparation, under the supervision of Lt-Col Huntington . . . I have, on the 19th, of June last, in the most dangerous conditions entered the naval room of the French Embassy between 1am and 4am with my daughter Mrs Gordon and a specialist in safes brought from New York by the American Service . . .

. . . as it was too late, the 21st of June I went again, alone with my daughter who vainly tried to open the safe, during which time I was [her cover]. Against my demand the specialist had gone back to New York under the orders of the Service.

. . . after many hours of work we found the secret of the safe and on the 23rd, my daughter and I delivered the naval cipher books to an agent who came to the [window] of the chancery. The pages were photostated and after three hours the books returned, was back in [their] hiding place and the safe closed. Never anybody has suspected anything.[43]

He went on to say that when he had accepted internment it had been on the understanding between himself "and Donald Downes, Chief of the French Section of OSS" [sic], that Catherine Gordon would be able to join him in a very few days. Permission had been granted but then suspended "because of some red tape." If it would help matters, he said, both his wife and daughter were prepared to give up their American nationality and become French citizens; he would meet all expenses which the American government could not cover. In the meantime, plans laid by himself with the OSS to return to France with his daughter, where they would spy for the Allies, were in danger. Furthermore, he was worried about the doubt that was being cast on the relationship; other sons and daughters had been permitted to join their parents at Hershey.

Without the humanity and intelligent comprehension of Mr Innes, the State Department representative here who permitted an interview between my wife and her daughter the loss of face would have been very damageable . . . my wife, who is very frail, has lost 8 pounds in the last few weeks under the constant worry. . . . what Catherine Gordon and I have done in the past is the guarantee of what we can do [in France]. I daresay that there is no limit to our possibilities in a country that we know to our fingertips.

I beg Your Excellency, most respectfully, to give immediate orders for the application of one of two solutions:

1. The Ideal One: Immediate arrival of Mrs Catherine Gordon and authorization to follow her parents wherever they will go (this is the solution planned with Mr Donald Downes of the Office of Strategic Services).

2. The Mediocre One: To let the Brousses free to go back to Washington under the sound pretext of the American citizenship of the wife and the illness of the daughter, it being understood that they will depart with their daughter if and when the French Embassy leave.

Our scheme will still be possible but I will lose my grip on Henry-Haye who is extremely flattered that we have come with him without any restriction; [also] we will appear less orthodox to the eyes of the Germans and to Laval than if we had remained in internment.[44]

Throughout January, Henry-Haye, the Swiss legation, Charles and Betty—Betty as Catherine Gordon—all bombarded the State Department with requests for her internment. Kay Brousse was quoted as being almost in a permanent state of swoon owing to the distress she was suffering at being parted from her daughter. So convincing was her act that Henry-Haye demanded an urgent medical examination of the poor woman. The doctor assigned by the State Department did not see through Kay's act but wrote her symptoms off as menopausal.[45]

On January 29, Charles wrote at length to Edwin A. Plitt, of the State Department, seeking help. Betty had previously met Plitt and had possibly suggested to Charles that he follow up on her request. Underlining his annoyance, Charles advised Plitt that several days earlier he had been visited by Colonel Paul Jacquin, formerly the Vichy air attaché and one of those Vichyites who renounced Vichy after Laval took ultimate power. Jacquin had been given permission to enter Hershey specifically to try to persuade Charles to "come over" to the Americans and go to North Africa to work with Robert Murphy as Press Corps liaison. Yet, Charles stressed, he had already been working for the Americans for nearly two years. Small wonder that Charles was exasperated at the "sheer stupidity" of it. It really did seem that there was no co-ordination between the various departments of State, Military, Security and Intelligence.

The jealousies and empire-building, present in each branch of administration, become obvious in examining this one incident. Everyone wanted to know everything there was to know, but they were all reluctant to pass on information to other departments and no one wanted to make a decision that would help one of the other departments. This muddleheaded attitude, Charles said, did not encourage his confidence to undertake the grave risks in going back to France, while the various American security agencies seemed to be "victims of inefficiency, incompetency and incomprehension."[46]

However, it becomes obvious that Charles's fury was not merely professional. Throughout his letter to Agent Plitt are hints that his anxiety for Betty is the overriding concern. By now all telephone calls between the Vichyites and the outside world had been stopped by order of the State Department. Only Henry-Haye was allowed to make and take outside phone calls and those had to go through the Swiss legation. Charles had received one letter from Catherine Gordon, but "the fact that I cannot speak with her drives me absolutely furious!" "I ask only one thing; to have Catherine Gordon here or to be free. . . . I have reached the *last limits* of suffering." He finished his letter with a formal application to be allowed to return to Washington, through the Swiss legation, on the grounds that he wished to join the diplomats who had formerly resigned

256

from Vichy. This application was to be filed if Catherine Gordon was not allowed to join him at Hershey.[47]

To be strictly fair the problem was not entirely caused by inter-agency politics. A main factor in the delay was the illness of Frederick B. Lyon, the ultimate recipient of all the data and applications made to the State Department on behalf of "Catherine Gordon." All of the papers, including Donovan's letter, were in his personal files and he had taken to his bed shortly after Betty visited him and Plitt at the State Department on December 28. On his return he acted swiftly, jotting a note to Edwin Plitt:

Mar 9, 1943

Dear Eddy,

While fumbling around in my unanswered file I unearthed this little package—it came in while I was ill! Hope no harm has been done . . .

FBL[48]

By then Betty had been at Hershey almost a month, but Lyon's note does explain certain aspects of the delays that caused so much annoyance to Betty and Charles. On February 8, the State Department issued a memorandum giving permission for Mrs. Gordon to join the Brousses at Hershey on the understanding that all hotel expenses were to be met by her, and that she undertook not to leave the hotel without permission. Two days later Betty, alias Catherine, was reunited with her beloved "parents" at the Hotel Hershey. Their obvious happiness was noted and approved by their fellow internees, who shared the French respect for family ties.

One of Betty's biggest fears had been that Henry-Haye would recognize her as the woman journalist who had interviewed him more than a year earlier. However, he made no connection between the chic, blond American reporter of that meeting and the pathetic, ill-looking young widow now before him. He accepted and wholeheartedly welcomed her into the community of internees.

Chapter 14

*B*etty earned her place at the Hotel Hershey. It appears that for a few weeks she *was* ill, possibly suffering the after-effects of her earlier miscarriage (on the other hand the illness could have been feigned to explain away the pregnancy she had claimed at Christmas),[1] but the archives indexes record that she submitted regular reports on activities and conversations between the diplomats. In addition she wrote, through Agent Lee H. Seward (successor to Edgar Innes), to State Department officials such as Frederick Lyon. Since these letters and reports are still classified we do not know what they contained, and it is something of a mystery that she should be writing to Lyon at all. One of the first rules in espionage is that an agent reports to only one contact. Perhaps some agreement had been made between OSS and the State Department in return for co-operation in getting Catherine Gordon into Hershey, for it is clear that Lyon was instrumental in passing letters to Betty's contact, William Kimbel. On her letter to Lyon dated June 14, 1943, Lyon scribbled the note, "letter handed to Mr. Kimbel (OSS) 12 noon—6/15/43."[2]

What is certain is that during this period she was completely divorced from her old organization, the BSC, though it is known that on several occasions she met her contact from the OSS. The letters from Betty to Lyon that are declassified are requests for her to leave Hershey in order to meet this person.[3] She was scheduled to go to Harrisburg in mid-May for debriefing and discussions, and she wrote Lyon asking that Brousse be allowed to accompany her. The request was held for several weeks pending a decision from higher levels and it appears that she continued to make her excursions alone.

On two afternoons a month all the internees were allowed to go shopping at the Hershey Department Store. It may be that Betty was somehow able to slip away and meet a contact from the OSS during these brief interludes, but she also made longer visits away from the hotel about twice a month. How this was managed is not clear. It must have been done in a way that would not arouse the suspicions of Henry-Haye and his cohorts. From the detailed knowledge of the back-lanes around the hotel estate Betty later displayed, it seems most likely that she was picked up some distance away from the hotel and that Charles and Kay "covered" for her long absences in some way.

She must also have used her brief periods of freedom to see to personal matters, for Arthur Pack, still in Chile, received a letter from her during the time of her internment, following which he wrote to his sister Rosie that "Betty is beyond redemption and now has a person whom she refers to as her fiancé whom she intends to marry. It is a nuisance and a bore but I cannot let things go on this way!"[4] Betty would never have risked writing to Arthur from the hotel, but it is interesting that she had started referring to Charles as her fiancé when he was still very much married to Kay. It may have been Betty's way of pushing Arthur into proceeding with the divorce.

At Hershey, as the months went by, the atmosphere became strained. There was a great deal of bickering among the internees themselves and between the French and their American guards. The latter complained to Frederick Lyon that the French considered themselves "more as privileged guests than detainees." At every possible opportunity the French violated rules and minor restrictions; even their children acted with an arrogance that must have had the guards clenching teeth and fists. From Nazi salutes and swastikas etched on furniture to abuse of the privileges —for instance shopping while being allowed to visit (under guard) the nearby town for dental work—they did everything possible to make the life of the guards intolerable.

There had never been any idea that the internment would last through such a long period, and Betty became uneasy at maintaining her cover in such trying conditions. After a visit to Harrisburg to meet her contact in June, she wrote—presumably having agreed to do so with her contact—to Agent Plitt advising him that Charles was suffering from a chronic digestive ailment which needed prolonged treatment in Washington. "We feel very strongly that he should be examined," she hinted, requesting permission to accompany Charles because, "I too require a physical check-up following the illness that I had a few weeks after my arrival at Hershey. We have been hoping to have a visit from you and Mr Lyon but perhaps we shall meet in Washington in the office of which I have a happy and grateful remembrance."[5] She was now signing herself Catherine W. Gordon-Brousse.

The question of whether Kay was buying the story that the relationship between Charles and Betty was only professional, or simply giving Charles an open-marriage opportunity, is settled by what happened next. In the midst of all this tension and confusion, Kay strayed into her "daughter's" room one morning and was confronted by the sight of Betty and Charles in bed together. Kay's first reaction was to try to kill Betty, but Charles somehow managed to get his wife out of Betty's room and tried to hurry her along the corridor to their suite. Here she hurled abuse, presumably overheard, that she intended to tell Henry-Haye that Betty was a spy.

The fracas was violent enough to send Agent Seward scuttling to telephone his chief, who in turn reported to various State Department officials. Memoranda recording the conversation state:

> Mr and Mrs Brousse had a bout which lasted for several rounds. Unlike most French arguments, it was more than verbal. Rocks were hurled. Apparently it was scandalous. The noise . . . was heard throughout the hotel. If [this can be confined to] rocks and bits of furniture I would not worry but I have fears that real weapons might possibly be employed and we are apt to have something serious on our hands . . .
>
> There are several other rather lurid details which it seems not necessary to record but none of which reflect credit upon . . . the participants.[6]

From Assistant Secretary of State Long's office came the immediate handwritten instruction to "get Mrs. Brousse, an American citizen, out of the hotel immediately . . . Mr. Lyon was informed accordingly and said he would clear her release with the FBI."[7]

Betty had already left, bundled out of the hotel for her own safety by Agent Seward. From her mother's apartment in Washington that evening, Betty telephoned Frederick Lyon at his home and asked for permission to telephone Charles at Hershey.

"I asked Mrs. Gordon why this matter was of such great importance and she replied that she had heard that feelings were very tense at Hershey, perhaps caused by her absence. . . ." Betty explained to Lyon (who had yet to be informed of the reason for the domestic trauma) that she had tried contacting the agent in charge, Bob Bannerman, but had been told he was unavailable. This sounds like a man who knows when not to take a call. She had tried to telephone Charles in the afternoon when she arrived in Washington but Agent Seward had told her, politely but firmly, that he did not think it a good idea in view of the prevailing atmosphere. He was still waiting for instructions on how to handle this delicate and potentially explosive matter.

Having heard Betty's story, Lyon telephoned several colleagues, including Bob Bannerman, who had not been available to Betty. After he had learned the facts, Lyon telephoned Betty and told her that he could not sanction her request.

> She became quite upset and . . . threatened to bring about a crisis of some sort at Hershey within the next day or so. It is my personal observation that something must be done immediately to avoid a real scandal that might possibly call for *PM* headlines—or worse.[8]

Kay remained at Hershey but was being kept apart from Charles in a small cottage in the grounds, pending her departure upon receipt of the sum of $2,000 from Charles to cover her expenses. He had "no objection to her departure" and needed a few days to arrange the sum in cash.[9] Henry-Haye could not have helped hearing about the accusations Kay hurled at Charles, about her threats to expose Betty as a spy, about the virtual imprisonment of Kay, directly afterwards, and the mysterious disappearance of Catherine Gordon. He called Charles in and demanded an explanation.

Charles was still striving to maintain his cover with the longer-term assignment in mind. How he answered the charges levelled at him, charges that must have looked strongly like incest to Henry-Haye and their fellow detainees, without blowing Betty's cover, is not recorded. What is known is that he defended himself by taking the offensive in his interview with Henry-Haye. Agent Seward reported, "the Ambassador and Mr. Brousse are in the midst of a violent personal controversy in which Mr. Brousse is the aggressor . . . there are a lot of antagonisms and animosities and some rather lurid details which appeared. . . ."[10] Breckinridge Long, to whom Seward reported the conversation, drafted a memo containing a transcript of this incident which details how Charles tried to turn the situation by rounding on Henry-Haye, accusing the ambassador of being pro-American "to a traitorous extent," and of being involved "in machinations with American officials to the detriment of France." All of this, Charles screamed, he was putting into a memorandum for eventual delivery to the French authorities. The Long memo observed that "the Ambassador does not look with equanimity on the delivery of this document to the French."[11]

Agent-in-charge Robert L. Bannerman, reporting this cleverly staged attack, warned his superiors to expect a request from Mr. Brousse that he be allowed to go to Washington "to consult certain doctors for treatment of a stomach ailment. The real purpose of this visit is, of course . . ." he commented sagely, "to see Mrs. Gordon." In the margin of this memo are scribbled the reactions of State Department chiefs. There is a cynical, "Stomach ailment!!!!!" from Frederick Lyon, and a more practical "I think he should see a doctor in Hershey or Harrisburg; under guard" from George Brandt.[12]

As predicted, Charles wrote formally to Cordell Hull, requesting permission to leave Hershey on medical grounds. This letter in the State Department archives is endorsed by Frederick Lyon: "The attached letter has NOT been handed to the Secretary. I am in touch with Mr. Murphy of the OSS. Mrs. Brousse left Hershey yesterday (with funds) and is now parked in the Waldorf in N.Y.C."[13]

Having been refused permission to telephone Charles, or to see him, Betty somehow managed to get word to him that she would meet him in a small wood behind the golf course bordering a public road. There were insufficient guards to patrol the entire perimeter of the hotel grounds; though there was some danger of being discovered it was a remote chance, and provided Charles was back at the hotel by 11:00 P.M., the risk of discovery was small.

For some weeks Betty lived at a local hotel and met Charles each evening to learn what was happening inside the hotel and to "keep up his morale"[14] while his release was being arranged. Charles was no longer sure of his standing within the group of Vichyites. He thought he might have fooled them, but they were extremely unsure and suspicious of him and he was very much left alone. The situation at Hershey was intolerable, he complained hotly, asking Betty why the OSS were not *doing* anything. She did not know why it was taking so long to get him out any more than he did, and could only assure him that she was doing everything possible. The problem was that both the State Department and the FBI were responsible for the French detainees and the OSS seemed to have little leverage. It was almost certain, Charles felt, that the detainees would be returned to France in early August. Because there no longer seemed any possibility of Betty accompanying him he did not wish to be of that party.

One night when she arrived for their rendezvous Betty was caught by one of the guards, who warned her to stay away, backed up with the threat that if she were caught again she would be arrested and imprisoned. The man did not recognize her as a former detainee but it meant the end of the secret trysts and she returned to Washington to continue the fight there.

By now it had become obvious to State Department officials, from the plethora of memoranda, letters and telephone calls that they had a potential crisis on their hands. By early July they had agreed to allow Charles to go to Washington for some weeks on medical grounds. As a demonstration of how well Charles had acted his part, when Agent Seward (who, having overheard the fight between Charles and Henry-Haye, clearly believed Charles to be a staunch Nazi) was advised, he replied that it would be an ideal opportunity to search Brousse's rooms for weapons. Meanwhile, Betty was still lobbying anyone at the State Department who would see her. Edwin Plitt, who had listened with apparent sympathy in the past, and had been a prime mover in getting her into Hershey, was one such target. In an attempt to set the record straight she told him that most of the agents, including himself, were aware of some aspects of the case but not all. Now that her cover had been compromised it was imperative that Charles was got out of Hershey and not forced to accompany Henry-Haye and the other French officials back to France.

During the entire conversation Mrs. Gordon seemed considerably agitated and in her remarks implied that there were many angles to the case with which I might not be familiar and in this connection referred to some special activity in which Mr. Brousse had been engaged in behalf of American interests.[15]

She pointed out that the department had secured Kay Brousse's release from Hershey within twelve hours when it seemed advisable to do so.[16] Charles, meanwhile, had met with Agent Seward and informed him

that since he had heard nothing definite concerning his release he was, beginning this morning, undertaking a hunger strike until such time as he heard some definite word . . . I tried to persuade him to be patient but this time it was to no avail.[17]

The reply urged the agent to relax. "The hunger strike will end on Sunday when he leaves for N.Y.C."[18]

For the guards and agents at Hershey the worst of it was nearly over, but the exasperated inter-departmental memoranda continued during these last days. "Good heavens! Are we running a hotel for these people?! I give up!" and the retort: "Mr. Lyon: Try doubling the amount of gin in your next martini and see how much better you feel. . . ." Scrawled underneath is the wry rejoinder by Lyon's assistant, "If this doesn't work try leaving the vermouth out!"[19]

On July 25, 1943, at 8:05 A.M., Charles left Hershey. His destination was the Gotham Hotel, New York City, where Betty was waiting for him. In what must have caused a universal sigh of relief among the agents and officials of the State Department, Frederick Lyon wrote a few days later that "Brousse is in hospital in New York. It isn't planned for him to return to Hershey."[20] Though Charles *was* suffering from ulcer-like symptoms that had been exacerbated by his hunger-strike, he made a rapid recovery once he was in New York and reunited with Betty.

After a few weeks in New York all traces of Charles and Betty vanish, with very brief exceptions, for almost a year. In all probability, having been compromised, they were useless as agents. Two writers on the subject of espionage claim that Betty was sent to the SOE in England at her own request. Her assignment was one she herself had proposed, according to William Stevenson, author of *A Man Called Intrepid*, the biography of William Stephenson. Stevenson had access to field reports of Betty's which may have either been subsequently destroyed, or taken into Foreign Office and Commonwealth Office archives and classified "closed." These documents in which Betty highlights her hatred for Hitler and what she condemned as his "psychological terrorism . . . which paralysed the will"[21] apparently revealed that she proposed to assassinate Dr. Gerhard Alois Westrick.

Certainly Betty had come across Westrick in her work for BSC. He had been a supporter of Hitler since the early 1930s and had bolstered German industrialists to join the Nazi cause. At the outbreak of war he had been sent to America to whip up support for Germany there. Exposed by BSC and expelled from the United States, Westrick had returned to

266

Germany where, according to reports, he lived a life of sybaritic luxury in Langenstein Castle where he entertained rich hangers-on from Vichy France. Even Stevenson queried whether Westrick was important enough to be made the subject of assassination, but records that Betty,

> nevertheless, went to Canada, where she was instructed in the ways of an assassin. She was flown to London. There she passed through a modest terraced house at 1 Dorset Square, Marylebone . . . [which housed] a reservoir of experts to whom hand-picked Baker Street Irregulars [SOE agents] came for information.

> She studied the files on prominent Vichy French collaborators, comparing them with knowledge she had gained in Washington. She reported to BSC that when Westrick caught Stephenson's attention in the 1930s, he was already employed in reality by Hitler's favourite intelligence chief, Heydrich.

> She left Dorset Square persuaded that it might be better to keep Westrick under secret observation until France was liberated. Such men would be needed to reconstruct the shameful story of collaboration at the top. [22]

The writer Richard Deacon, who also had access to Sir William Stephenson's personal papers, makes a similar statement. Both writers state that Betty's work in London was, in the end, confined to research. There is one small piece of evidence to support these stories. On November 22, 1943, four months after Charles's release from Hershey, Mrs. Catherine Gordon was granted a visa to leave the United States. This coincided with several telephone and mail intercepts (still classified but indexed) recorded for Mrs. Amy Elizabeth Pack. [23]

I could find no other documentary evidence supporting the claim that Betty worked in England, but this is not surprising in the circumstances; her mission would scarcely have been advertised. Maurice Buckmaster, who controlled the French section from Baker Street, the organization which would have been the obvious home for Betty, had never heard of her presence in London; but, again, this does not rule out the fact that she was not sent to Dorset Square.

Yet, after what had happened at Hershey, and with the imminent repatriation of Vichy French diplomats surely it would have been foolhardy to have sent Betty into occupied Europe. Charles is said to have worked for some months for the Free French and during the period that Betty was in London spent some time in Mexico. There is a further clue that Betty was involved in another BSC assignment. In letters to her after the war Sir William Stephenson adopted the familiarity of deeper friendship than might have been expected, had their relationship been restricted to that one meeting in Washington that Betty described as having occurred just prior to the Vichy embassy job.

Meanwhile, Kay Brousse was causing problems for the OSS's James Murphy, who made her his special responsibility. It was to Murphy that Frederick Lyon wearily turned for enlightenment when he received a peremptory cable from Kay:

> Please get me immediate release from Federal Reserve Bank here who have blocked my safe-box at the Waldorf-Astoria. Please note and inform Bank that I am American born and American citizen. Bank can examine box or any other baggage but I resent this. Hershey, where I went voluntarily was enough.[24]

Subsequently Agent Plitt was sent to interview the wronged Mrs. Brousse at the Waldorf-Astoria. He found her "in a very nervous state, sobbing occasionally." She "asked if the closing of her box meant that her husband Charles Brousse was in trouble. She said she had heard nothing from him for over two months and knew nothing of his whereabouts."[25]

She told Plitt that she had access to very little money; all that she had was in her safety deposit box. It was ridiculous, she said, when she had "a fortune in jewellery" in her luggage which had been impounded by the State Department and placed in storage when she went to Hershey.

James Murphy made a rapid decision. Kay Brousse was interviewed by an OSS agent, flattered into believing that the OSS wanted her to work for them, and sent to Mexico City to await further instructions. All was silent until February 1944 when Frederick Lyon wrote to a friend, Raleigh Gibson, first secretary at Mexico City's American embassy, to ask him to do him a favour of an unusual character.

In Mexico City staying at the Hotel Emporio at Paseo de la Reforma No. 124 is an American lady named Mrs. C. E. Brousse. She and her husband, who was formerly Press Attaché of the Vichy Embassy, . . . have been the cause of great confusion and bewilderment. In an attempt to assist a certain agency of this government to solve their problem they have asked me to to [write to you].

The problem was that Charles Brousse's French diplomatic passport was locked in one of Mrs. Brousse's twenty-nine large trunks and they needed to know which one. "Our friends feel," Lyon continued, that if Mr. Gibson were to make the request of Mrs. Brousse she might cooperate and give Gibson the key. Lyon, however, was not so sure.

To be perfectly frank, I personally fear she may smell a rat and catch the first plane back to New York. . . . If you are able to obtain her authorization and the keys I am sure you will obtain the blessing of our friends. Of course this letter should not be displayed to anyone, and certainly not to Mrs. Brousse. "Our friends" happen to be the O.S.S.[26]

Lyon was correct. When interviewed Mrs. Brousse informed Gibson that she had an open ticket to New York and intended returning at once. She refused to authorize examination of her trunks and became very agitated when the subject was raised. She was ultimately dissuaded from returning to New York City by her "controller" in Mexico City, who persuaded her that her reports were very helpful to American interests.

Meanwhile, Lyon received a note from an attaché at the embassy in Mexico describing disturbing reports he had heard; that Kay had confessed to some women in a powder room that she was a secret agent working for the American government. The informant had stated as her opinion, that if Kay Brousse was actually working for the United States Secret Service "she is operating [in] a very poor manner and was leaving a poor impression."[27] Called into the American embassy for interview the attaché noted:

The subject is alone in Mexico and is very vague in her conversation about the whereabouts of her husband. . . . She stated that she had heard that her husband was in Mexico and wanted to know if the Embassy had any information . . .

She claims to be employed by the New York Office of the secret service and is paid $300 a month for her work in Mexico. She wanted to return to New York but her superiors had advised her that her work here was not finished.

. . . She was married six times and as a result of such marriages presently has a considerable fortune, stated to consist of four million dollars in jewels which are presently blocked by the United States Government, in the United States. When she arrived in Mexico City she had four $100 bills . . . thirty-six thousand francs and $1,000 in traveller's cheques. She advises that her superior is Sherman Hall, Jackson Heights, New York City.[28]

In reply Lyon confessed that the contents were not a surprise to him. "For your own secret information . . . I may tell you that Mrs. Brousse, for convenience' sake, is spending some time in Mexico. She is not, repeat not, engaged in any secret activities for this government. She has a misconceived idea that she is on a mission for this government. *This is not altogether her fault* . . . It would be better for all concerned if she were to stay in Mexico at least for a month or two longer."[29]

Kay was still in Mexico six months later when Charles and Betty resurfaced in Washington. Quietly walking down Kalorama Road looking at his old haunt, the French *residence*, he turned the corner on to Wyoming and wandered down towards Betty's mother's apartment. He was spotted and followed by a curious reporter, Evelyn Peyton Gordon (coincidentally, a distant cousin of Cora's, though she knew nothing of Charles's liaison with Betty). She had, she wrote, seen him "walking just there a good many times in past years."

. . . But formerly he laughed and his round face was pink and happy. Yesterday he wore sun glasses—tho there was no sun—and his pink cheeks were pale . . . I was very curious about the presence in Washington of Charles Brousse . . . I had thought that the Embassy staff went, *in toto*, to Hershey for internment two years ago. And I knew for a fact that Ambassador Henry-Haye had returned to France. But Charles Brousse is living back in Washington just a stone's throw from the Chancery where he worked, just around the corner from the [ambassador's residence and embassy] where he lunched nearly every day with Henry-Haye . . .[30]

Perhaps, conjectured Miss Gordon, Brousse hoped to be reinstated when the French embassy was again established.[31] By now the Allied invasion of Europe had been successfully accomplished and though there was still fighting in many parts of France, Paris had been liberated and the ultimate outcome of the war could only be total defeat for the Germans.

In fact Betty and Charles had come to Washington to clear up a few loose ends before leaving for Europe. Arrangements had been made with the State Department for passports and visas.[32] Betty's sister-in-law, Shirlee, did not know that Betty and Charles were in town. Cora told her about them from time to time and Shirlee knew that the couple were together, somewhere. One morning "I opened the Washington Daily News and there was this article by Evelyn Peyton Gordon saying Charles was in Washington. I knew from things Mrs. Thorpe had told me that he wasn't supposed to be there, so I immediately telephoned Mrs. Thorpe and told her about the newspaper article. She was quite shocked and said, 'Betty and Charles are over at the State Department in Ruth Shipley's office getting passports. Rush over there right away and tell them about it.' But they had already left when I got there."

Mrs. Thorpe later told Shirlee that Charles and Betty were staying with her for a few weeks before leaving for Europe and that during this period Betty had gone to the White House for drinks with President Roosevelt.

Cora's cousin, Colonel Charles March, was chairman of the Federal Trade Commission. To Betty he was "Uncle Charlie" and he, like Cora, was aware of Betty's espionage activities according to surviving family members. Colonel March was a close friend of both J. Edgar Hoover and President Roosevelt and it is believed that it was through this link that Betty was invited to the White House. At what point Colonel March was let in on Betty's secret is not known; it may have been comparatively late in the war for it does not seem that she requested assistance of him when she was faced with the effects of bureaucracy. However, before she left for France she presented him with a photograph, a representation of herself which she inscribed with the message "Shhh-h-h Cynthia."

Soon after that they went to France. I saw them before they left at a drinks party that Mrs. Thorpe had arranged. They were obviously very much in

271

love . . . Mrs. Thorpe called Charles over and said, "Show her Betty's diamonds, Charles." He took out a cloth wallet and opened it and inside was a fabulous bracelet made of huge stones. It was breathtaking. I don't recall Betty ever wearing jewellery except for a emerald that she was very fond of that she got in Spain from one of Franco's men. But I think the diamonds were the way that Betty and Charles got their money out of the U.S. and into France.[33]

The $4 million, which Kay Brousse had told various people about, was possibly exaggerated, though she was indeed a very wealthy woman. Charles had astutely foreseen the war in the Far East, hence his disposal of his assets there, and the couple had hit on the idea of taking money into the United States in the form of jewellery. That some of this money belonged to Charles was indisputable, but while it had been locked away in Kay's luggage under the seal of the United States government it had remained inaccessible to both of them. Kay's nervousness when it was suggested that she should provide a key to a certain trunk may have been simply mistrust of Charles. How, why and where the couple's assets were eventually divided and what agreement was reached between them regarding a divorce is not known. But Charles obviously came away with an equitable share of the joint holding in jewels.

Charles and Betty sailed from New Orleans on a Spanish ship and landed in Lisbon in the third week in October 1944. Travelling via Hendaye, scene of so many of Betty's long-ago adventures, they entered France. By early November they were living in Charles's old apartment at 8, rue des Marronniers in the sixteenth *arrondissement* of Paris. It was from there that Tony Pack's foster-parents received the first letter in over a year from his mother. Tony had heard regularly from Arthur throughout the war. His letters were thoughtful, kind and even affectionate notes that attempted to make Tony feel that he had a family who thought of him, albeit on the other side of the world:

It is good to be chosen to represent the school at rowing. I used to do a lot before the war but my favourite sport was rugger at which I played in some big games . . . Glad you are settling down at Shrewsbury, I will write to your housemaster . . . I did want to send Denise to a good school in England but I cannot afford it so she will have to go to a boarding school here in Santiago. Her Spanish is so much better than her English and she is not keen to go away to school as she likes it here where she is thoroughly spoiled by the servants, but her English is improving.[34]

Shortly after Betty reached Paris the teenager wrote anxiously to Arthur that his mother had written a disturbing letter to his foster-mother explaining that she was divorced and remarried and she should now be addressed as Madame Charles Emmanuel Brousse. Arthur replied, exasperated:

What Mummy has written to Aunty about divorce and remarriage is all nonsense. She is neither divorced nor remarried. That is all part of her world of make-believe. Thank you for your thought of me though. I have been very lonely since my illness but I am relying on you and Denise to look after me in my old age![35]

Betty and Charles took up living in liberated Paris during the winter of 1944–45 while Charles re-established his contacts and Betty met old friends at the newly opened diplomatic embassies. Despite her love for the cosmopolitan society of Paris, Betty found the cold and rain depressing and longed for the sun of southern France or Spain. Any ambitions that Betty and Charles harboured of working with the still active resistance movements in France upon their return were disappointed. The war continued but there was little work for them to do.

In February Charles's sister-in-law visited Paris and lunched with them. Betty did not like their guest, having learned from Charles that she had been the mistress of the Gestapo officer in charge of the Perpignan region during the latter period of the war. But Betty was interested to learn from the woman that Kay Brousse had written to Charles's family after the Hershey incident and told them everything. Of the woman spy who had seduced Charles and persuaded him to infiltrate her into the Vichy legation as their daughter. Of the time they spent at Hershey and of her discovery of the couple *in flagrante delicto*. Versions of the story had also reached relatives of other diplomats interned at Hershey. The Hershey escapade reflected badly on the Brousse family and had created a few minor difficulties, which they were fortunately able to overcome.

273

It is certain, though, that the Germans fully expected Betty to be sent to France, had a full description of her and were waiting for her. Had Betty and Charles attempted to return to France during the occupation they would have been arrested. Indeed, according to Charles's sister-in-law, a trap had been set for Betty. What is less clear is whether the row following Kay's catching them in bed gave them away or if someone else at Hershey worked out Betty's cover and somehow got word to the Germans. If the latter, the ruckus Kay raised may well have saved the life of both Betty and Charles, a result we can be sure Kay would not have intended.

A few weeks later William Stephenson wrote in a Christmas card to Betty:

. . . I trust all goes well with the greatest unsung heroine of the—I was going to say—war. But anyway, the more active part of a continuing warfare. Salutations, Bill

Chapter 15

1 9 4 5 - 1 9 4 6

*I*n the spring of 1945 Betty and Charles spent a month in the south
of France looking at properties. When Betty saw the old chateau at
Castellnou she was enchanted. It was virtually uninhabitable as it
stood, but with a great deal of work part of it could be made into a splendid
home. Members of both the Pack and Thorpe families told me that Charles
could not refuse Betty anything: "He spent a small fortune, making it
beautiful for her. . . ."[1]

Castellnou was then a small village (population 33) set in the Pyrenees
mountains some 20 miles from Perpignan and a few miles from the

Spanish border. Today it still retains an air of magnificent isolation in wild, mountainous countryside, and the entire telephone directory consists of under half a page. The chateau itself was originally a hilltop fortress dating back to the tenth century with broad terraces and crenellated walls from which spectacular scenery of two countries could be gazed upon. The village had sprung up centuries earlier in the shadow of the chateau's ramparts, hugging the sleep slopes. To the adoring Charles it seemed a fittingly romantic setting for Betty, so he bought it and set about renovating the living quarters. It was to take a year or more before they could move in, and by then, many things had happened.

While Betty was house-hunting, Arthur Pack was in England enjoying his first home leave since the outbreak of war. For part of the time he stayed with his sister Rosina and her family in Woking and from there, on May 8, 1945, the day that came to be known as V-E Day, he wrote to Rex Doublet:

Here I am in England on Victory night. All alone. My sister and her family have gone to a Victory celebration in Woking but I did not care to go. I had a feeling that I did not belong. I have not shared in their trials and I cannot share in their justified jubilation. "Domine non sum dignus."

Doublet later said "it was characteristic of Arthur that although he had served his country loyally, energetically and intelligently for more than thirty years and that although he fought throughout the [previous] war he should consider that he had no right to share in a celebration when by his own standards he had not shared in the trials and tribulations. He had a great sense of humility. . . ."[2]

In an interview on April 27, 1990, Rosina's daughters Maureen and Bernadette remembered that they were shy with their uncle during his visit; this was the famous uncle Arthur of whom their mother was so inordinately proud and who had done so well. "He was a huge man and I was over-awed, especially as the family held him in such esteem and we had been brought up to think that he and Betty were such *important* people."

Bernadette was deputed to meet Arthur at the train station. She was twenty and young for her age, wearing a civil defence trenchcoat that reached her ankles. She felt self-conscious and very nervous about how to keep him entertained on the journey home and sensed that her uncle was

privately disappointed with us! We were 20 and 16 at the time, convent educated and perhaps rather conventional. Our childhood and youth had been swallowed up by the war without the excitement of serving in the forces so we were not particularly lively. (This changed later!) Anyhow, our mother encouraged us to entertain our sophisticated uncle but Betty was a hard act to follow . . .[3]

Possibly his nieces were wrong about Arthur's feelings about them, for Rex Doublet testified to Arthur's "affection, amounting almost to love, for young people" and perhaps this is the explanation behind a special memory which Bernadette retains of her uncle:

A friend was selling two beautiful pre-war evening dresses which no longer fitted her. One was lace over white satin and the other was eau-de-nil brocade with silver threads. She was asking ten pounds each for them. As my weekly wage was £2.5.0d (I was in the Civil Defence Ambulance Service) they were beyond my means though they fitted me and were so beautiful. Arthur noticed my disappointment and the wistful way I looked at the dresses and without any hesitation offered to buy them both as a twenty-first birthday present. It was a most generous gift because twenty pounds was a very large sum in those days. I wore the dresses until they fell to pieces . . .[4]

And towards the end of the visit she noted that although he appeared large, awe-inspiring and distant to her, when he spoke on the telephone to his friends "he became a different person—highly animated and very amusing." And once at dinner he mimicked a family friend: "It was terribly good and very funny but I was amazed that the great Uncle Arthur had a sense of humour."[5]

As a Catholic family the Rivetts and particularly Rosina were shocked and saddened when Arthur told them that his marriage had ended and that one of the purposes of his visit was to divorce Betty. He obviously confided to a certain extent in Rosina. This was the occasion on which he told her how he had found Betty in his bed at the house party in the

277

winter of 1930, and had asked of his sister, "What could I do?" He told Rosina, too, of his unhappiness at Betty's consistent adultery. He did not tell her about Tony and the family were totally unaware of Tony's existence. Clearly a divorce application had been made some time earlier through London solicitors, for the case was heard on May 14, 1945 (divorce in those days was not the simple matter it is now) and a decree nisi was granted. Paul Fairly was named as the co-respondent and the grounds of adultery, admitted in writing by Betty, were not contested by Fairly.[6]

For some years, pre-dating Betty's departure from Santiago, Arthur had been friendly with a "charming Anglo-Chilean woman," Violetta Muñoz. The friendship had deepened into love and it was their intention to marry sometime around Christmas 1945 after his divorce became "absolute" under British law. A friend later wrote to Rosina about Arthur's relationship with Violetta: ". . . he fell in love in a sensible, friendly sort of way . . . it doesn't seem to have been one of those tiresome and rather unpleasant infatuations of a man on the verge of old age, but a calm realization that she was the sort of woman who would be a pleasant companion for the rest of his life."[7]

Arthur had many friends in London and he spent some weeks there visiting and catching up on the lost years of the war. Notwithstanding his sadness over having been away from the scene of action he appeared at the time content with the way his life was turning and "blissfully happy with his life in Chile." The climate there suited him and his career was as successful as he could hope given his mild disability. One of these friends was Eleanor Campbell-Orde, his first love of many years earlier. She had lost touch with Arthur during the war but toward the end of 1944 she happened to hear on the radio the old ballad "Eleanor" that he used to sing to her. On a whim she wrote to him care of his London club (The St. James) and he answered some time later that he was in Chile but would see her in the spring when he came to England. The news of Arthur and Betty's divorce was not entirely unexpected by Eleanor; when she had last seen Arthur in 1938 he had told her he did not know whether he could stand Betty's infidelity and that there had been a major row about it. "I am quite sure Arthur knew nothing about her espionage activities. He just thought she was having affairs with all these men." But when, during the course of their conversation, he mentioned Tony,

> I was very surprised, having been totally unaware of his existence. Arthur said that he had been born four months too early [for convention] and it would have been a major set-back in his career. We stayed up all night talking about it. I saw him once more before he went back to Chile. As we were saying goodbye he looked at me in a very odd manner—very pointedly—though I couldn't quite pinpoint what was odd about it at the time, and he said "You will keep an eye on Tony for me, won't you?"[8]

Arthur then travelled north to visit Tony, who was fourteen years old by then. Tall and slim, his patrician good looks very much resembled a young version of Betty's father and brother. He was an intelligent boy who had been emotionally confused by his parents' rejection of him. Arthur either could not, or did not, see this as a valid reason for Tony's uncooperative attitude towards him; nor was he understanding that the youth might find it difficult to confide in a man whom he knew only by letter. Tony had last seen his father seven years earlier when Arthur had stayed for a week or so with the Cassells while still recovering from the aftermath of his stroke. For his part Arthur found Tony arrogant and difficult, and though he certainly intended at some time to have Tony join him in Chile he insisted that Tony should first complete his time at school and go on to university before this plan could be implemented. It was probably Arthur's own experience that without money and social backing, a good education was the only advantage worth having, which made him so adamant.

On learning that his parents were now divorced Tony was distressed. Possibly he had always cherished a dream that one day he would be gathered up by his beautiful mother and worldly father and taken off into an exciting life within that world of his own family—his sister, grandmother, aunts, cousins. The divorce was yet another manifestation of the rejection he had always known from his parents. Tony was not unhappy with the Cassells, indeed he was spoiled and petted by his foster-parents, which may have contributed to his apparent arrogance. He had always felt he was set apart from them somehow, though perhaps without analysing why. The feeling may have stemmed from the fact that on the few occasions when his parents had deigned to visit they had swept into the Cassells' quiet lives bringing with them an aura of almost visiting royalty. This, Tony clearly felt, was his birthright, and letters from his grandmother Thorpe only encouraged this attitude.

The meeting between father and son did not go well. After Arthur returned to Chile, he told Violetta (the only person to whom he had hitherto confided about Tony's existence), that he "was a little disappointed" in his son during the interview.[9]

While visiting the Foreign Office, Arthur was given a startling piece of news. There were plans to promote him and transfer him from Santiago to Buenos Aires. It was a much bigger job and carried the rank of Commercial Minister, a position to which he had long aspired. Had he been able to enjoy this rank in Santiago Arthur would have been overjoyed, but he knew Buenos Aires and disliked the hot and humid climate.

Accepting the offer would entail persuading Violetta to leave her native Chile. It would mean parting from a host of good friends who meant a great deal to him. "No man in Santiago had more friends than Arthur," said one,[10] and here was a man who leaned a good deal on his friends. He was also concerned about his ability to cope physically with the demands of the position. But he knew that if he refused it would, at best, cause him to be passed over in the future. At worst he might be asked to consider retirement on a pension.

There was one additional factor. One which staff at the Foreign Office—because of the well-greased diplomatic gossip machine—may well have taken into consideration in deciding Arthur's transfer. The ambassador at Chile had been for some years Sir Charles Orde. Orde was due to retire from the Santiago embassy and his replacement was to be none other than Betty's old lover, John Leche, C.M.G., O.B.E.[11] It may have seemed to someone at the Foreign Office that it would be asking too much of Arthur to have him work under Leche.

When he returned to Chile, Arthur had already made his decision to accept the job in Buenos Aires, but told Violetta she must come and see for herself what his life there would be like before they could marry. To Rex Doublet he confided his personal worries: about his health and Denise. He wrote to Betty at this point. She described it as "a happy letter, in which he expressed his delight and satisfaction at the new post"; he outlined some of his concerns but stated that he had now achieved a certain tranquillity. The increase in rank was one he had long sought. Betty replied, saying how glad she was for him. She and Charles would care for and love the children whenever they might come to them, she told him, and wished him luck. "Have confidence in yourself," she counselled.[12]

Denise was now ten years old, pretty and much spoiled by Arthur's Spanish servants. Until he could decide what to do for the long term, Arthur sent her, much against her wishes, to board at the American College in Santiago "to learn English as much as anything." His ultimate aim was to send her to a good convent boarding school in England; Betty had already expressed a wish to have the girl stay with her in France for some months each year. Because Arthur felt that Betty had at last settled down, this possibility was certainly in his mind, though he could not have seen it as a perfect solution.[13] But Denise was a difficult child, extremely sensitive and nervous, given to alternating bouts of hyper-activity and sulks. Her nurse, Juanquita, who had been with her all her life, was the only person who could really handle her. Given this background it is not surprising that Denise did not mix well at the school, and ran away several times.

Arthur arrived in Buenos Aires in August, expecting to dislike it; he found it every bit as difficult and distasteful as he had expected. It was a busy post requiring at least seven hours a day at the office, added to which was a heavy round of formal social duties which "just can't be dodged if one is to do the job properly." He found it all exhausting.[14] He knew very few people at a personal level and started to have difficulty sleeping. A colleague added that, "more serious from Pack's point of view . . . like a good many other people he found the climate of Buenos Aires very depressing. It is damp and relaxing and pretty hot in summer; liver complaints are common."[15]

Arthur seemed to cope well enough during his first month in the city, but during October he became increasingly depressed, "complaining of insomnia, depression and of how much he disliked B.A."[16] At the back of all this was the knowledge that he could not return to the embassy at Santiago, even at his former rank, because this meant serving under John Leche. On the ninth of October he consulted a doctor who confirmed to him that his blood pressure was dangerously high. He went home and wrote to the Foreign Office requesting a transfer to another post:

I fear a tragic mistake has been made by my promotion here. My health which was so marvellously good in Chile has deteriorated rapidly and I have had a frightening repetition of the troubles which ended in my stroke in Warsaw. My blood pressure problems which subsided in Chile have cropped up again and my doctor is very concerned. I fear that the summer heat here may bring on another stroke which may be fatal.

. . . Unless I can [transfer] I doubt whether my projected marriage should take place as it would be unfair to any woman to allow her to marry a man of 55 years whose health is liable to crack up at any moment and leave her stranded with a paralytic husband . . . I have too many responsibilities to retire on a sick pension. . . .

It is a terrible tragedy for me as I was looking forward to a happy married life after 5 years of loneliness but I dare not marry with the present risk of collapse over my head . . . I deeply regret all this but I was deceived by my long period of good health and hard work in Chile, into believing that I could do the same here—which I am deeply afraid will not be the case.[17]

Unfortunately the post-war mails were very erratic and the letter did not arrive in London for six weeks.[18]

In the meantime Arthur decided to take some sick leave and went to stay at an *estancia* belonging to a colleague in the Córdoba Hills, where he hoped the clear, drier air would cheer him up and reduce his blood pressure prior to Violetta's arrival in early November. Before he left he visited his doctor again and while in the city purchased a revolver. He stayed away for two weeks, during which time he wrote to Violetta saying that he was unwell and lonely and was looking forward to seeing her. Returning to Buenos Aires again on November 1, a national holiday, he looked in at the embassy to make sure there were no pressing problems needing his attention before lunching with his assistant, William N. Storey, and some young colleagues at a country club outside the city. He then went home to his apartment where he wrote some letters and ate a light supper before retiring to bed.

At some time during the night, he shot himself.

He was found next morning, his right arm outstretched, with the revolver clutched in his hand and a bullet hole through the right temple. His papers were found perfectly arranged along with a "calm and logical explanation of just why he couldn't face life any longer."[19]

His colleagues were as stunned as one would expect. During the previous day it was noted that he had seemed better for his short leave. ". . . he was smiling and joking in the office on the day of November 1st . . . I'll swear there was nothing in his manner to suggest his mind was in such a desperate state."[20] This is not unusual, of course; having reached a decision, the would-be suicide often seems to achieve a measure of mental tranquility and can appear perfectly normal for hours, days and sometimes even weeks, lulling otherwise watchful friends and family into a false sense of security. Arthur had possibly intended to kill himself in the *estancia* but decided it would be "tidier" for all concerned if he returned to Buenos Aires to do it. Violetta would not yet have left Santiago by the time word reached her and would have her family to support her.

In Shrewsbury, England, on the morning of Saturday, November 3, 1945, Margaret Cassells was shopping. At some point she stopped to have a coffee and picked up the *Daily Telegraph*. Idly scanning the front page her eyes lighted on a small headline in the bottom corner, MINISTER FOUND SHOT.

I rang mother immediately. Tony was a boarder at "the Schools." It was seven miles from Dorrington and there was no transport during the war so there was no option really. My one thought was how terrible it would be if Tony learned of his father's death in a newspaper.

. . . The news was broken to him, quietly, by Mr Binney the Churchill's housemaster. Tony was told he could go home if he wished but he stayed on and came home at the weekend. It was difficult for us as we did not know how he felt about his father so we tried to leave him alone but were there if he wanted us. He seemed rather depressed and mooched about and went up the Longbarrow (a nearby beauty spot) for long walks. I think he felt it rather deeply. We never heard the reason why Arthur committed suicide.[21]

Eleanor Campbell-Orde had already received the news of Arthur's death when she received his last letter to her, explaining his problems, that he had heard nothing from the Foreign Office and that he intended to take his own life. A week or so earlier Sir Charles Orde had received a letter from Arthur asking him to try to use his influence to get him transferred; by almost the same post as the letter received by Eleanor, Sir Charles had another from Arthur telling him "not to bother, events would sort themselves out." Arthur died without knowing that Sir Charles had recently recommended him for the C.M.G.[22] "He would have been thrilled," Eleanor Campbell-Orde told me. "Arthur was a very independent person," she continued, "and the first stroke had cost him a lot in courage and determination. He just couldn't face another with the possibility of being totally dependent on someone else for the remainder of his life . . . I think it takes a special kind of courage to take your own life."[23]

Betty's first reaction on hearing the news was to write to Rex Doublet to instruct that Denise be sent to her grandmother in Washington, with the intention of getting the child to France as soon as it was possible to do so. She also wrote to Rosina expressing her sadness at Arthur's suicide, saying "I will always love him . . . he was a great man:[24]

In the circumstances you must think very harshly of me for having left him but I did not do so until he was well-installed in Chile, in a well-run house and with well-trained servants. And even then I waited until he was really completely independent of me. My own health and nerves were deteriorating rapidly, and . . . I was finally obliged to take account of myself and decided that unless I did something positive to remedy the situation both Arthur and myself might disappear and leave our two children orphaned . . .

I have wept bitter tears and wrung my heart dry for him, but I cannot wish him back to continue his calvary for I know how heavy it was for him to bear. Surely, surely, somewhere he is at peace. . . . delivered from circumstances which even God found were too much for him. Denise is on her way to my mother in Washington, whence she will come to us as fast as possible. I long, with all my being to give her the material and spiritual advantages that will make her forget her bewilderment and despair at losing her Daddy . . . We will educate Denise into a little Englishwoman (at the age of 16, or thereabouts, we will send her to school in England), and in the meantime she will have the most guarded kind of life . . . I promise you that she will emerge a cultured, and at the same time, a practical young woman and that in the process she will be surrounded by love and understanding, with all the memory and fineness of her Daddy being kept alive . . . And there is young Anthony, a most darling lad, who would derive great benefit from his Aunt and Uncle and cousins. He is coming to us at Easter for the holidays.

I know it is not within your tender heart to hate or reproach me with Arthur's fate, which was never in my hands but in those of God. I always did what I could, within my limitations—the real thing with which I chide myself is that I was neither older nor wiser, but [even so] I could not have given him more comfort and understanding than I did, instinctively, during our life together. He kept a happy memory of it.[25]

Rosina must have read this letter many times with considerable puzzlement and distress. Who was this Anthony to whom Betty had twice referred, and what did the references to "our two children" and the "darling lad" who would benefit from contact with his relatives, mean? She could not make it out and wrote for enlightenment to Rex Doublet, Arthur's executor. Doublet had already written several long letters about Denise, about Betty and about Arthur's funeral. In none of them had he mentioned Tony. Rosina also wrote to Eleanor Campbell-Orde who replied at once:

I nearly wrote to you about Tony, but Arthur had said he thought the news would be a shock to you . . . I put it off, thinking it would be so much easier to talk about it than to write. I think only Mr Millis [a good friend of Arthur and Betty's with whom they often stayed when in London] and I, and the Cassells knew about Tony—even Sir Adrian [Arthur's oldest friend dating from before his time in Washington] did not know and he was quite astounded.[26]

Rex Doublet was able to provide further information in his response to Rosina's bewildered inquiry:

I believe it to be a fact that Arthur and Betty had a son who was conceived before their marriage and this child is . . . Anthony George Pack. From correspondence with Mrs Cassell I believe the child was delivered to his foster parents ten days after his birth in London. Arthur . . . never discussed the existence of this child with any of his friends and, for obvious reasons, I have not mentioned the matter to anybody. Betty told me about Anthony some years ago, but I kept my own counsel. . . . only when I opened the Will did I have confirmation of Anthony's existence. . . . Nothing I write must be construed as criticism on Arthur, for I am firmly convinced that "to know all is to forgive all" . . . knowing Arthur's sense of sincerity and fairness I am able to understand his attitude to Anthony George which, in strict confidence, I believe was merely a reflection of his feeling that Betty had not treated him with strict fairness . . . it is most unfortunate for the poor little boy that the sins of the mother should have perhaps been visited upon him . . .[27]

Other sections of the long letter make it clear that Arthur had told Violetta about Tony and his last meeting with the boy. Meanwhile, Doublet said, Denise was already on her way to Washington to stay with her grandmother, since Arthur had left a letter for his friend stating that "Denise had better go to her mother." Arthur's will was an unhappy document written some weeks before his death and leaving everything apart from £500 to Denise. It was not a huge amount and he apologised to his "beloved fiancée" that he had not been able to leave anything to her "owing to the need to conserve as much as possible for my daughter, Denise." The single other bequest was couched coldly, asking that a sum of £500 should be made available from the estate and paid to:

Mrs M. B. Cassell of Dorrington House, Shrewsbury for the use of my son Anthony George Pack who is in her charge. As I have maintained him for 15 years, in the future responsibility after the exhaustion of these five hundred pounds, should be assured by his mother Mme Charles Emmanuel Brousse of 8 Rue des Marronniers, Paris.[28]

Doublet was later to tell Rosina that Arthur had "married Betty out of duty" when she had confessed to him that she was pregnant and had never been entirely sure that the boy was, in fact, his son, especially in the light of Betty's adulterous behaviour after their marriage; equally though, he had never been certain that he wasn't. Doublet must have had this from Violetta since Arthur had never confided in him about Tony. Violetta was later to write to Rosina that Arthur had several times wanted to tell his family about Tony, "then his courage failed him, poor dear. Every hour is miserable without him."[29]

At some point after Arthur's death, possibly when he had sight of the will, similar doubts must have occurred to Tony, for he queried his parentage with Eleanor Campbell-Orde who was "able to assure him that he was Arthur's son." Unlike many of Arthur's friends who subsequently found out about Tony with astonishment, Eleanor never doubted that Tony was Arthur's son and with an artist's gift of observation noted that "neither Tony nor Arthur had any ear lobes," though she admits that Arthur "had the odd doubt, I think."[30]

Denise, missing her father and happier speaking Spanish than English, spent a few unhappy weeks in Washington despite Cora's best attempts to cheer the child. She was taken to the opera and the ballet, bought a new wardrobe, made a traditional Christmas and given lots of expensive toys. It was to no avail; Denise was unco-operative to all Cora's attempts at making emotional contact. In mid-January the girl flew to England to "meet her brother." She was to stay with the Howard Millises in London, where she would meet Tony, various friends of Arthur's and her Pack relatives, while she waited for the necessary documents to travel to France. Rosina had been warned by Doublet:

Denise is suffering from a natural preoccupation about the future. She is not yet eleven years of age and her upbringing has been in many ways, I consider, not a proper one for a child. Arthur had to rely so much on his servants who, whilst very good were not fit companions for a child born and brought up in comfortable and cultured surroundings. Whilst they were good to her and lavished every affection on the child, you will realise that the atmosphere of the servant's hall was not too fortunate . . . Denise

287

is very old for her age, too old, in fact, and I hope so much that she will now be restored to those joys natural to children and will be happy . . .[31]

The little girl arrived in England to the unaccustomed "bitter cold" of an English winter. She had been terrified on the flight over[32] and seemed to be under great stress according to her temporary guardian, Howard Millis. Her circumstances evoked a natural sympathy and an urge to comfort her, but she antagonized many with whom she came into contact by her outspoken disapproval of the weather, the lack of good food, clothes and household effects (England was still in the grip of fierce rationing), and this sounds suspiciously similar to the opinions expressed by Cora Thorpe during her visit to the Cassells.

Denise bottled up her personal feelings, allowing no one the opportunity to get close to her, possibly unable to find the appropriate words in English; however, she did convey to Millis that she was afraid that there was some conspiracy to keep her from her mother whom she hardly remembered but who was "just across the Channel." She seemed not to understand that travel was still restricted and that she had to wait for a visa.[33] She strongly resisted meeting the Cassells, and dismissed her aunt and cousins as "strangers!" though she seemed to enjoy their company when she was at last constrained to see them.

Her cousin, Maureen Rivett, recalls:

I went with my mother to London and met Denise . . . My impression was of a self-possessed little girl of medium height with blondish, straight hair; not pretty but not plain, favouring Arthur rather than Betty and with his long upper lip. She was obviously rich—her room was not large but was full of luxurious white cuddly toys. [We all] went to a matinée at the Windmill Theatre and I remember thinking how unsuitable it was— obviously the grown ups had not researched the outing very well! In the theatre Denise cuddled up to me, a wordless plea for the affection she was so obviously seeking . . .[34]

Betty continued to write to Rosina, clearly excited both at the prospect of seeing her daughter and at the forthcoming visit of Tony; they would be together for the first time in nearly ten years. For some unexplained reason she was against having Tony live with them permanently, and opposed every suggestion by Rosina and Rex Doublet that in the circumstances it might be a good thing. Betty wrote long screeds describing the bedroom she had decorated for the little girl which, when Rosina showed it to Lady Campbell-Orde who had known both Denise and Betty, prompted the cynical response that such matters were "quite beside the point . . . for the moment she does seem full of affection and one can only pray that it is sincere. What the child needs most of all is love and *stability!* . . . I always felt angry with Betty that she abandoned Denise so completely . . . and never even wrote, so Arthur told me."[35]

The meeting between Denise and Tony was not a success. It took place at Eleanor Campbell-Orde's penthouse apartment on the top floor of Harrods [there were apartments on the higher floors at that time; at each expansion Harrods simply took over another floor and converted the apartments into more store space]. Tony was appalled at Denise's precocity, apparent lack of manners and her outspokenness on any subject which came into her head. She openly criticized adults (something Tony would never have dreamed of doing) and spoke with venom about Violetta, of whom she was deeply jealous. A member of the Pack family who met her at the same time said of her, "she had an insoucient air of wealth and grandeur, very sophisticated, and old for her age in many ways."[36] In short, she was everything that a well-brought-up English girl was not.

The Pack family established a relationship with Tony, however. Though Rosina was to write to him for many years, his cousin Bernadette did not especially like him, sensing the arrogance that had often irritated his foster-sister Margaret. Eleanor Campbell-Orde liked him immediately: "He was a handsome boy with deep green eyes and thick lashes like Betty's. I think he was a nice boy too, though the Cassells tended to monopolize him and were a bit reluctant to let him mix with anyone— even me. . . ."[37]

When Denise joined her mother at the end of January, Betty was shocked at her daughter's vivid nightmares, talk of ghosts and superstitions, and her general condemnation of "society." For example, Juanquita had told the girl that Arthur had "gone to eternal perdition" because he had divorced Betty, something which spilled out one night when the child was screaming with one of her frequent headaches. "I blame the Spaniards," Betty wrote, referring to Arthur's former servants, "but what else could one expect from such an association with people who are almost illiterate and . . . ignorant. They have faithful hearts but ill-directed affection."[38]

As for Tony, whom she described as a worthy bearer of the family name, ". . . I am tremendously glad that Arthur has left this additional bit of himself behind. I am going to make Tony absolutely worship the memory of his Daddy—which is no more than right. I *worshipped* Arthur, Rosie, up to the end, probably in much the same way as you did.

I am very worried about Tony's future. Arthur left only £500 for him; we have no sterling or dollar account and have no possibility of transferring funds from France to UK . . . Denise tells me that Tony was "very shabby" when he came to London. Was this your impression . . . There is no question of his being homeless or starving etc, but I want to keep him in England as France is no place for a boy of 16 . . . and he would be lost in a country whose language he does not speak.[39]

Tony had told Denise he wanted to be a vet and Betty was coldly against this. "Why not a real doctor?" It was such a waste of good material, she wrote, though she had not seen her son since he was a small child and knew virtually nothing about his interests and aptitudes. She knew little of his marvellous ability to ride and handle horses. Or that he would work in someone's stableyard all day and hang around for hours on the off chance of being given a ride on a good horse. Occasionally he would get the chance to borrow a hunter and would go out with the local pack of hounds; those were red-letter days for the boy who had a great love of animals. Did Betty know of Tony's athletic prowess; that it was this more than anything that had enabled the Cassells to get him into Shrewsbury? Or that, often money for Tony's keep and school fees had not arrived at the Cassells' home because of the erratic mail service or some other reason and Dr. Cassells made up the deficit. In fact, Betty knew so little about her son, she could not have guessed at his hopes, fears or aspirations. If she saw herself in any maternal role towards him it can only have been from a distance and in some roseate version of motherhood concocted out of her own imagination. Tony could count the letters he received from his mother during his entire life on the fingers of one hand and he had seen her precisely three times.

Nor did he see his mother in spring 1946 as planned, for Betty was preoccupied with Denise and her new chateau; Tony's trip was postponed until the following year. The Brousses' had only just moved in to Chateau Castellnou following their quiet wedding in Paris when he arrived. Betty found Tony rather narrow-minded and introverted, blaming the Cassells for having instilled the morals of middle-class conventionality in the boy. As for Tony, he reported to Eleanor Campbell-Orde that he did not like Betty very much, either:

> Her idea of enjoyment was to drive into Perpignan every evening and go from club to club where there were loud jazz bands and parties. Tony had been brought up in rural Shropshire. The Cassells were very upright, even straight-laced people and I think he was rather shocked by his mother's behaviour. He was not a small-minded person though, far from it—he was game for anything . . .[40]

Chapter 16
1946 - 1962

*F*or the next half-decade Betty lived in happy obscurity, chatelaine of her castle, wife to Charles and mother to Denise. It was probably this last role which came hardest to her. She was not naturally maternal and though she had occasionally suffered sentimental pangs at her separation from her children she does not seem to have felt any sense of either loss or guilt. She had been content to love them, in her fashion, from a distance. Perhaps her own life-long, deep-seated need for periods of solitude, and her own mother's attempt at domination affected her perception of the mother-child relationship. She certainly found full-time motherhood more difficult; her relationship with Cora had provided her with no model, or not one that she cared to emulate.

Nevertheless, at Castellnou Denise grew less outspoken and less given to the violent tantrums which had so worried those who had cared for her after Arthur's death. The tantrums were replaced to a certain degree by occasional depressions, but apart from these the child grew into an attractive, intelligent and thoughtful young woman. Given her early up-bringing it was too much to expect that she would be entirely "normal" in her outlook. For instance, having always been treated like an adult, she found difficulty in relationships with contemporaries.

It is difficult to know how Betty passed her time, for although both she and Charles were popular the location of their home did not lend itself to frequent social outings. Furthermore, Betty was not the type to enjoy daily domestic chores. They entertained a great deal in the first years at Castellnou but the numbers of guests dwindled over the years. Betty wrote regularly to her mother, who visited occasionally, and to her sister Jane (now married for the third time), who also visited at Castellnou, but there are no clues in her letters to how she spent her days. Sometimes she composed a topical poem and a few were published in local papers.[1] Her only written complaint was that she and Charles did not travel often enough but once or twice a year they would go to Paris or Rome or Madrid or to S'Agaro, a favourite resort on the Costa Brava. She was never allowed to holiday without Charles; he could not bear to be parted from her.

One thing we can be sure of is that her marriage to Charles was happy. Though she occasionally found Charles's obsessive jealousy restrictive, she basked in his adoration of her. That she loved him is confirmed by the pleasure she obtained from performing many small tasks for his comfort. For instance, if she saw him sitting outside reading a book she would take out a cushion for his back, or a rug to throw across his knees if there was a cool breeze. The only reservation to this happy-ever-after chapter of her life was the nagging sense of entrapment she felt. This may have been connected with their respective ages. Betty was not yet forty; Charles was sixty and settling into early retirement. Though he went into Perpignan several times a week in connection with the family newspaper business he was content with his rural retreat and the sense of tranquillity their lives at Castellnou had achieved. Two world wars had provided Charles with all the excitement he would ever crave.

Tony seemed to have sorted out his life at last. He had hoped to go to university and Eleanor Campbell-Orde secured him a place at St. John's College, Cambridge, chiefly on account of his record as an oarsman. Unfortunately, he could not afford to take it up. In the immediate aftermath of the war everything was just as scarce in England as during the worst years of fighting, sometimes more so. The Cassells had no money to spare. His foster-sister, Margaret, who had married and was struggling to build up a home, as were all young couples at the time, had to refuse Tony's request for a loan.[2] Shortly after Arthur's death, Tony's grandmother had written offering to put him through university in America, but for some reason this did not appeal to him.[3] He may have turned to his mother but if so she had not been able to provide any help. Currency regulations of the day were very restrictive in respect of international transfer of funds. Eventually it was decided that Tony would fulfil his compulsory National Service and go to university when he had finished the two-year period of conscription.

Tony joined the King's Shropshire Light Infantry in 1949 and somewhat to the surprise of his foster-family he dropped into military life as a round peg will find its position in a round hole. Within a short time he was commissioned as a National Service officer (second lieutenant) and shortly after the outbreak of the Korean War shipped out for the Far East. He was very popular, striking an "instant rapport" with his brother officers. The fact that in his first months at the front he had at considerable personal risk rescued a wounded officer and several members of his platoon on the battlefield helped establish him as "the right sort." He was also a good horseman, an athlete and a willing volunteer, and these attributes were all to his credit. On one occasion, for example, a notice was posted asking for volunteers to represent the regiment in an inter-service boxing match. Though having never boxed before, Tony volunteered and gave a good account of himself.[4] He found himself "at home" in the army and enjoyed the easy camaraderie.

Long before his two years' conscription had expired he decided to make the army his career. His acceptability to the regiment, says a brother officer, "was a foregone conclusion in his case,"[5] and he returned to England in the autumn of 1951 for the Regimental Commission Board assessment. By February 1952 he was back in Korea, promoted to the rank of lieutenant and as happy as he had ever been in his life. During his home leave he had taken time out to visit his mother at Castellnou.

His previous visit had been a strained one, but he felt that he had grown up in the three intervening years. Possibly he thought he might see his mother in a different light now that he had his own life and a secure future. He travelled by train through France, standing most of the way because the few trains which ran were so packed. Betty met him at Perpignan and even before they reached the chateau he decided that his mother was "slightly odd in the attic" when she confided that she could speak with the two huge dogs which were her shadows. Not speak to them but with them. She claimed to understand them and to be able to speak to them in a dog language that they could understand. Tony could hardly do more than affect a polite interest.[6]

Betty's idea of an evening's entertainment had not changed but Tony was now disposed to be tolerant of her flirtatious behaviour. She had lost all power to hurt him.

Not that Tony ever expressed the idea that she had ever set out to hurt him, but he must have sensed that all the rationalizations offered him by the Cassells, and all those he created for himself, could not erase the fact that the woman who had borne him had found him so unappealing as a son that she was able to ignore his existence through huge tracts of his life, through virtually all of his growing-up years.

We do not know the rationalizations Betty made for herself in her most private moments, if ever Tony came into them. Tony's real paternity must have been known to Betty, though to no one else I have been able to find. Perhaps Tony had been fathered by a man who had rejected her; or one in whom she later found disgust (as expressed in her poem written nine months before Tony's birth); or perhaps he really was Arthur's child, but the timing of his birth had created an overwhelming need to erase from her conscious memory the difficulties his embarrassingly early debut into the world would have caused her and Arthur. Or perhaps there was more truth than seems feasible in the reason she gave the writer Harford Montgomery Hyde for denying her maternal instincts:

> . . . that a wholesome, happy life with his foster parents should not be shattered; that the emotional stability that Tony *had* was more important than her [own] emotional longings. Continuity and a calm family climate must take precedence . . . she felt humbly grateful for his existence . . .[7]

Much as I should like to take Betty at her word here, this all sounds too thought-out, too devoid of that mercurial quality, that impertinent impetuosity, that all remember as being such an important part of Betty's character. With all her talents one wonders what level of success she might have achieved in public life had she, in fact, been capable of putting practical considerations above her own emotional longings. More likely, by the time she came to explain Tony to Harford Hyde, she had allowed the Scarlett O'Hara in her make-up (so aptly recognized by Michal Lubienski) to recolour unpalatable truths.

If one believes that every good and decent woman should have strong instincts to do right by her children, someone like Betty would immediately be branded a most unpleasant type. The reverse is true. She always was, and remained, a delightful companion, charming and entertaining; she could be equally frivolous and serious, with a quick wit and a good head for international affairs. She understood human nature and to a remarkable degree was able to predict the reactions of people with whom she interacted. Well into middle age she retained this ability to attract, to charm, and to manipulate people without apparent effort, and usually without their resenting it.

During Tony's visit she was certainly too intelligent and maybe too proud to make the mistake of pretending that there was a great emotional bond between the handsome young subaltern and herself, and treated her son with the same casual affection she offered any visitor to Castellnou. He found himself enjoying her company in a distant way; given time he might have come to like her.

In his relationship with sixteen-year-old Denise, however, he found a great improvement from his prior visit. Though she was somewhat too "fey" for Tony's taste, they were able to take long walks together while she showed him around. She was a serious, often introverted girl, two characteristics he shared. Almost as tall as Tony, reed slim, and with naturally pale blond hair, she had the same finely chiselled Thorpe features; it must have given Betty a pang of pride to see the handsome pair together. Denise, however, lacked two features which their grandmother had noted in Tony: his wonderful eyes "with the bit of hurt in them, and the sweet sensitive mouth."[8]

Denise had been well educated in an exclusive girl's school and soon she, too, would be leaving Castellnou. In the summer she would sail for America to live with her grandmother in Washington, where she would attend Georgetown University.

Tony had only a few days with his family before he took the train back to northern France, again having to stand for the entire journey which took about fifteen hours. He saw Eleanor Campbell-Orde in London afterwards and confessed to her his doubts of surviving another spell of fighting in Korea. At the same time he told her that he had left several large trunks of china and linen in Hong Kong "to be called for," so there were also in him some hopes of returning. He spent his last weekend in England with the Cassells and while there took the precaution of making a will. It mentioned Denise, briefly, but not his mother. His possessions—such as they were—were willed to his real family, the Cassells.[9] Shortly afterwards he returned to the Far East. Within weeks he was in the front line, fighting with "conspicuous gallantry" for which he was awarded the Military Cross:

On the night of 25th March 1952 Lt. Pack led a fighting patrol of 9 O.R's [other ranks] to destroy a known enemy section post in front of his Company position. It was an extremely dark night and at 0330 hours the patrol was 50 yards from the objective and an N.C.O. and 4 O.R.'s were placed in a position to give supporting fire should this be necessary. Lt. Pack then led 4 O.R.'s forward to assault the enemy post. When some 10 yards from the post Lt. Pack was fired on by a sentry and wounded, the bullet passing straight through his thigh. He immediately killed the sentry with his Sten gun. The assault group at once came under close range fire from at

298

least five automatic weapons. Lt. Pack engaged the nearest enemy post and moved his assault group up the flank to engage the other posts.

The support group also engaged the enemy posts which were slightly to a flank. The assault group with Lt. Pack though under heavy fire continued to engage the enemy for some ten minutes with grenades and small arms fire. He only ordered them to withdraw when all all their grenades were expended. The withdrawal was covered by the fire of the support group, by tank fire and later by artillery fire, calmly called for by Lt. Pack. During the withdrawal by a different route the patrol was engaged by another sentry. Lt. Pack was wounded a second time in the face but again killed the sentry with Sten gun fire.

There is little doubt that while the patrol was organised to deal with a small enemy post, on this occasion they encountered enemy in platoon strength, alert and organised. It was due to Lt. Pack's aggressiveness and his cool handling of the situation in the face of heavy enemy fire that the patrol was able to inflict casualties and to subdue, to a great extent, the fire of the enemy. Although wounded at the outset of the action he set a magnificent example to his patrol to which they responded in full measure. [10]

Hospitalized in a base hospital in Japan Tony met and was very attracted to a young nurse. This relationship had hardly a chance to develop. Tony could have accepted a period of home leave on medical grounds, but when news of his MC came through it spurred him on to an early return to the front. Before his departure for Korea he wrote to his grandmother, with whom he corresponded regularly. She had invited him to come to her in the United States as soon as he finished his tour of duty. She was sure she could get him appointed to the British embassy in Washington in some capacity. Cora still had many influential friends and, being constitutionally unable to avoid interfering in the lives of members of her family, had been lobbying a friend on the British Joint Chiefs of Staff on Tony's behalf. Meanwhile, she had written to various American generals in the Far East asking them to contact Tony and entertain him, and also to the "future [Japanese] Empress's mother," whom she had met on several occasions, asking her to call on him in hospital. The succession of distinguished guests to his bedside did Tony's reputation no harm and the flurry of activity amused him; it was so typical of his grandmother. He wrote back politely thanking her and telling her, modestly, about his Military Cross.[11] There is no evidence in these letters of the arrogance attributed to him during his adolescence. Perhaps it had been a protective shell, his way of coping with the emotional effects of what must have always appeared to him as rejection by his parents.

Betty's brother, Tony's uncle George, had written congratulating him and predicting future promotion, and Tony also wrote and received letters from Lady Campbell-Orde, his aunt Rosina and Mrs. Cassell. It is not known whether or not he corresponded with his mother. But it is sad that it took an incident of publicly recognized exemplary military conduct to finally earn for him that which he must have longed for all his life—the approval and support of his glamorous blood relatives.

Bravery, an ethereal quality if there ever was one, ran strongly in the Thorpe family. Tony's grandfather, Colonel George Thorpe, had made himself conspicuous on numerous occasions during his service in the USMC. Betty's brother, George, had once plunged into the burning wreckage of a bomb-laden aircraft which had crash-landed in front of him while he was visiting the control tower of an airfield in England. First to arrive on the scene and without any thought for his own safety he pulled the crew out. His wife, Shirlee, asked him whether he had been scared and he had replied, "You don't stop to think about the danger; when there's something to do you get on and do it."[12]

Betty had it, too, this splendid quality which has fired legends from the times of earliest civilizations; many people I interviewed testified to Betty's coolness in tense and dangerous situations.

Tony was shot on July 10, 1952, while commanding Number 3 Platoon of A Company, and died almost immediately. Again he had placed himself in a position where he could provide maximum encouragement, by example, to his men. His death was felt deeply by the regiment. They buried him with full military honours at Pusan, under a pine tree. There had been no opportunity for him to receive his MC.[13]

Betty was informed by a cable from the Cassells. She had been planning to leave on the following day for Spain with Charles to accompany Denise to the ship which would take her to America and on to her grandmother.

Considering how little she knew her son, Betty mourned hard, mourned the tragic waste of the handsome young man she hardly knew but of whom she treasured a small maternal memory of his looking, as a child, like a "young Rupert Brooke." Among her papers is a small plastic photograph wallet on which she had written, "My Tony." Charles and Denise went together to Spain[14] and Betty stayed at the chateau, dispirited and suffering agonies of desolation, no doubt fed by guilt.

I must be content that he died doing what he wanted to do. You don't bargain with death if you are doing what you passionately want to do. Death is a mere hazard in the gains. I thank God for letting me have him here at Castellnou for those few days before we parted for the last time.[15]

But it was chiefly Tony's foster-mother and grandmother who mourned his loss. Mrs. Cassell had lost her only son. A son to be proud of, and the son she adored. Cora Thorpe felt much the same way, already planning Tony's career in Washington: "It was easy to have dreams about a grandson like that and I had plenty . . . I still can't believe it . . . it seems like a cruel dream. Life will never be the same. . . ."[16] Cora's only consolation was that Betty's other child was, at that moment, on her way to America. Eleanor Campbell-Orde, who had so taken to Arthur's son, is a prolific and much respected artist. She produced a portrait of Tony which she later presented to Margaret Cassell Owen's daughter (Tony's god-daughter).

Although devoted to Charles, Betty now felt her life tedious and dull. With Denise gone the chateau seemed quiet and the lack of fulfilment in her life caused Betty great frustration. She was filled with a sense of wandering restlessness. Nevertheless she felt she had made a bargain with Charles and for his sake she tried to content herself with the life of a chatelaine, spiced only by the occasional holidays which brought her briefly to life. There was no denying, however, that Charles, almost twenty years Betty's senior, carried his years heavily, while Betty had hardly aged at all. In her forties, she was just coming into the prime of her life; in spirit she was even younger.

It was on one of these holidays to Madrid that she was reunited with Carlos Sartorious. She had last seen him in the hall of a prison outside

Valencia twenty years earlier, after she had pleaded with Indalecio Prieto for his release. It was odd to see him and not feel the old surge of sexual attraction. They were simply old friends, meeting after a long period of absence, and when they embraced fondly it was the embrace of old companions who have shared something precious, once, a long time ago. Subsequently, Carlos was to write many letters to her; fond, cheery letters, and she came to know his children.

Another ghost came out of her past when she heard from John (by then he was Sir John) Leche. Retired and feeling lonely and bitter after the death of his second wife, he had obtained Betty's address from somewhere and wrote asking if he might visit her. Betty never replied, apparently feeling that it was an old wound that she had no desire to re-open. Her memories of the intensity of his passion may have persuaded her that it was not a wise thing to do at this point in her life. She may never have learned that he later married for a third time, though she made it clear in her memoir that her time with him was one of the most memorable and thrilling chapters in her life.

A minor skirmish of excitement occurred when Betty was contacted by the French security service (*Direction Surveillance de Territoire*) and asked to work as an agent, obtaining information on the activities of local communists. An assignment was suggested. In the town of Valladolid, which lies about a hundred miles northwest of Madrid in Spain's heartland, there was man named Sicre, a communist known to be a Soviet agent. It was proposed that Betty should go to Spain, make contact with this man and report on his activities. There was probably nothing that Betty had ever wanted more in her life than to escape the cossetted boredom of her days at Castellnou. But Charles, for once adamant in the face of her pleading, cajoling and finally outrage, refused to allow her even to consider it. This incident suggests that Betty's previous record in intelligence work was known about by those currently active in security. The Brousses certainly had a large number of friends in diplomatic circles and possibly they had let it be known that they had worked in the great game.

When Charles had bought Castellnou it had seemed like a fairy-tale place in which to live and Betty did, indeed, love it. One of the oldest inhabited castles in France, she had made it a comfortable home where huge log fires crackled and blazed for nine months of the year, where exquisitely faded tapestries covered ancient stone walls, where dogs almost dictated where guests could sit in the massive deep, velvet-covered sofas. But Betty's bright fairy-tale had withered to a mundane humdrumness. As the years rolled on she was to hint at her disillusionment, in oblique terms, to friends. "For the most part we are always here and never in London or Paris as Charles, now 71, dislikes postwar life in cities. . . ." Her chief consolation was their occasional trips to S'Agaro on the Costa Brava, ". . . pure paradise."[17]

Meanwhile the only thing which altered the measured tenor of her days was news from "outside." In 1954 her mother died. Cora was seventy-three and had, to the end, remained active in social and civic affairs. Her estate, which was substantial, was divided between her children and De-nise. Betty felt no sense of loss when Cora died; indeed there was perhaps a sense of release from the domineering influence of her mother, which had continued on occasion to pressure her from across the ocean. Betty wrote:

> She disapproved of me, and I disapproved of her. You might say that she was a Persian cat and I was a Siamese . . . She thought men were basically rather brutes and that sex was frankly disgusting. Still, to be honest, she was a good wife to my father—whom I loved with all my heart—and he seemed to love her.[18]

Cora's death precipitated the division of family trusts between the children of Cora and those of her sister Aimée. These assets chiefly consisted of Canadian farmland and at Betty's insistence the land was sold so that she could have her share of the inheritance in cash, a stand which made her unpopular with her cousins. In retrospect they are grateful to her, for they invested in stocks just prior to a boom and made far more money than had they left the money in land. However, the incident hints at financial need by Betty.

Denise would go on to finish college and find work as a journalist for *Newsweek* magazine. She was not entirely alone in the United States; her aunts, Jane (Betty's sister) and Shirlee (Betty's sister-in-law), and uncle kept in touch. Shirlee recalls teaching Denise some simple tunes on the piano. "She was very pretty. She had no accent and spoke English perfectly." In the late 1950s she fell in love and became engaged. She and her Jewish fiancé visited her mother, who at first had opposed the marriage on religious grounds. Betty was not anti-Semitic, but she was concerned about the problems which would inevitably arise in a marriage between a member of the Jewish faith and a girl who had been raised as a Roman Catholic, a girl who, because of her contemplative nature, had taken her faith more seriously than most. Betty was completely won over by the young man and Denise returned to the United States and married.

Betty's daily escape was writing letters and keeping in touch with many friends throughout the world, among them many former diplomats and colleagues in the BSC and OSS. It was through a friend who had worked for BSC that she first heard of a book, written by H. Montgomery Hyde, which was the biography of her old chief, Sir William Stephenson. In this book some of Betty's own adventures were detailed and she was identified by one of her code names: Cynthia. In the autumn of 1962 the friend sent an extract of the book, *The Quiet Canadian*, which had appeared in the Sunday *Times*.[19] It told of Hyde's meeting with her in 1941 and her role in capturing the Italian and Vichy naval ciphers. Betty confessed to her friend Kathleen Taylor Cockburn:

In reply to your question as to how Mr Hyde's book was allowed to be published I am as non-plussed as you and can only surmise. In the extracts re "Cynthia" I recognise direct quotes from some of my reports. Therefore Mr Hyde must have had access to my dossiers. Insofar as he tells the tale it is true, he kindly makes me out to be a heroine, which I was not . . .

Charles had been cross with me because he never knew about my activities except where they concerned himself DIRECTLY. Men are really children —that is their weakness, I think, and also their charm.[20]

For Betty this glimpse into the past brought a tidal wave of memories, and an unbearable nostalgia for the days when she had felt alive and fulfilled. She wrote immediately to the author, care of his publishers.[21]

Apart from recording her immense pleasure that the story of "this remarkable man" had been written "instead of being buried in Foreign

Office dossiers," Betty wrote her own small tribute to Sir William Stephenson:

> . . . He is a rare human being, and I am completely honest in saying that without *him* and the magnificent organization that he created I, personally, could have achieved nothing.
>
> Another reaction to your book—I am already filled with nostalgia for the happiest days of my life [Hyde had written a similar statement to Stephenson two years earlier]. They were packed with all sorts of emotions; the supreme desire to help the Allied effort, anxieties lest I fail in the responsibility entrusted to me, lonely despair when my moves went wrong, satisfaction when things took a constructive form. And in the end (it is with me still) the real anguish of wondering if, with more experience and better judgement, I could not have worked faster and done more . . .[22]

Yours ever, most sincerely,
"Cynthia"
(Mme Charles Brousse)

By return Hyde sent her a copy of the book and a note explaining that he hoped she had not objected to being included in the book. He had not known how to contact her and so had used the code-name CYNTHIA which had been used in the BSC official history, and compiled from some of her field reports. In her reply, addressed to "Dear Mr. Montgomery," as she had known him in 1941, she hardly referred back to his letter but instead offered him a confession regarding their meeting on that hot August afternoon in New York in 1941. She had wanted very much to see him again but "Marion" had told her firmly "No! He has gone away."

> I have thought of you many times since, as one thinks of a ship passing at sea—anonymous and unlikely to be found in any port. Can you imagine therefore how happy I am to be in touch with you again?

She went on to tell him that she had seen a former "friend" since the war. "Henry-Haye who in Washington sported merely a saucy moustache now skulks around Paris behind a disguise of sideburns and goatee."[23]

Hyde was mildly interested in the latter for he had assumed Haye dead. Before long he was to learn his mistake when Haye successfully sued him for libel.

Betty went on to invite Hyde to visit her, since there was no chance of her being allowed to visit him and she "so" wanted to see him again: "*I want to be with you*, listen to you, absorb your presence . . ." she wrote. After she had mailed the letter she began to worry that her outspokenness would annoy him. It did not, but he did point out in his reply that he was married and that she must not in her letters cause his wife any anxiety. She agreed: "I may have overstepped myself with you in recent letters and . . . should have kept my thoughts . . . and feelings within bounds. Please, please, do not worry for I will *not* let you down or add to your worries. . . ."[24]

At this point the writer in Hyde sensed another book. Although *The Quiet Canadian* was causing him a certain nuisance value (it was the first book to break the story of BSC and there had been enormous press interest leading to questions in the House), there was no doubt that the publicity had done sales no harm and he needed a follow-up. Betty, and what could be told of her activities given the constraints of the Secrets Act, would make an ideal story and a natural sequel. He wrote to her during the third week in January suggesting that her story would make an ideal series of newspaper articles and asking her to think the matter over. Betty accepted without hesitation. For her the mere *diversion* was sufficient motivation to agree.

There was no need for her to think it over, she replied. His suggestion was "100% acceptable." But she did not think she could write the articles, for she had no leisure time for such concentrated effort; she had no writing experience and would lack the "zing" to make the material living and vibrant, and also ". . . I might be indiscreet, unwittingly of course, where the Foreign Office is concerned, for the F.O. and I sometimes collided locally through the stupidity of certain of its representatives. . . ." She suggested Hyde write the articles from information which she would provide but naturally this would mean his visiting her.[25] He agreed to come to Perpignan at the beginning of March and his projected visit gave her something to look forward to at a very difficult time.

Always healthy, she had recently been unwell and, always slim, she had recently lost a lot of weight. Her teeth and jaw gave her a lot of pain and for some time she had only been able to eat soft foods. A visit to the dentist had revealed no tooth decay or gum disease but some unidentified problem in the jaw. The dentist advised her to see a doctor. She had been worried by this, sensing something sinister. But now an adventure loomed; she could forget about the health problem and concentrate on something else. With her fantastic ability to shed unpleasant realities she turned as a moth to the light. Her only worry now was that Hyde might not come as promised. She had already explained that she could not have him stay at the chateau as "we have no staff" and they were therefore to meet him at the airport and drive immediately to S'Agaro and stay at her favourite hotel.

While she waited for Hyde's visit she began to record her memories and a week before his arrival was able to promise him between twenty-eight and thirty typewritten pages. She was also able to tell him that she had heard from her old chief from the early days of her work in Poland, Jack Shelley. Shelley was "entirely reassured" by whatever Hyde had written to him, presumably some sort of undertaking to steer well clear of anything contentious and perhaps the opportunity to scan a draft of the manuscript.[26]

Betty greeted Hyde at the airport wearing a fur coat and silk headscarf. Though she had worried that Hyde would find her "aged" he saw hardly any change in her from their first meeting, only that she had acquired an attractive maturity. She retained her sweetness of manner, her vibrancy and her good looks. He noted that Charles, whom he met briefly in 1941 when he detained him in Bermuda, had already accepted old age, but that he was a good-natured man with a ready smile. He was utterly devoted to Betty. On the journey Betty kept Hyde entertained by treating the border guards as though they were old friends, and pointing out various landmarks such as Figueroas Prison where her lover, Carlos, had spent the last few months of his imprisonment before he was released in fulfillment of Prieto's promise to her.

They spent four days at the hotel in S'Agaro and Hyde interviewed Betty with a tape recorder at her suggestion. At one point he asked her at what point she had first become aware of her sex appeal, which, he noted, she still possessed in abundance.

I'm not conscious of any sex appeal particularly . . . I like people and have been attracted to them. They must have felt it, seen it, responded to it, because I think it was always a mutual thing. Certainly sex came after some other form of attraction, such as mental compatibility, companionship and a common interest in other things. But no agent can accomplish things on sex alone.[27]

On the second day, while Charles was taking an afternoon nap, Betty went to Hyde's room and the two became lovers. The attraction they had both felt in 1941 had survived and their conversation, harking back as it necessarily did to a time when they had been young and involved in work of vital importance, rekindled the dormant spark. It was probably almost too piquant a situation for either of them to resist, an opportunity to recapture, briefly, a moment of youth. They made love on two further occasions before they left the resort.[28]

It is already clear beyond any need for explanation that Betty did not regard sexual fidelity as a requisite component of marriage nor as an illustrative measurement of her affection. Her love for Charles Brousse was unquestionable, his presence in her life a touchstone. Lacking any sense of guilt she could not resist a romance with Hyde.

On the return journey Hyde visited Chateau Castellnou and spent a few hours being shown around by Betty and taking photographs. Betty was loath to say good-bye to this link with another, happier time in her life. Before leaving, Hyde suggested that perhaps it might be possible to persuade Charles to allow her to come to England to talk with his agent and the newspaper people.

During the next month she hung on to this suggestion as a talisman. And she had need of comfort since after their trip to S'Agaro Charles insisted she see a specialist for the pain and discomfort she continued to experience in her lower jaw. The long series of tests, which she undertook with a certain amount of exasperation, included a biopsy. The results would take some time to come through but her doctors had no doubts what the biopsy would reveal. The diagnosis merely confirmed what she had suspected for some weeks.

She had cancer.

Chapter 17

As soon as Harford Hyde arrived in London he had his secretary transcribe the tapes of his conversations with Betty and went to see his agent, H. I. "Iain" Thompson of International Literary Management. He outlined his proposal to write a book about Betty and told him that he had her total co-operation, and indeed he had every right to assume he had. The arrangement was not entirely straightforward. The businessman in Charles Brousse had naturally wished to know what benefit his wife would gain from such a project and it had been agreed, broadly, that Hyde would prepare publishable work based on information provided by Betty; any resulting royalties would be divided between her and Hyde.[1]

Thompson, having read the material, was not slow to realize that this story was perfect for a series of articles in the popular Sunday press and had no trouble in opening negotiations with the *News of the World* and *The Sunday People*. Harford Hyde, a former barrister, had been putting some thought to the business end of his literary relationship with Betty and came up with the idea of forming a company, Cynmont, the amalgamation of the code-names Cynthia and Montgomery. It was important for him, in those days of punitive taxes, that income from this venture, which was to be shared with Betty, should be kept entirely separate from that of his other income. He wrote to Betty explaining the reasons for forming the company and how it would work. In essence their agreement would be that Betty would write her memoirs, set out in a suitable format for newspaper articles. His own work, he said, would be to rewrite them. If the material was adequate he would subsequently compile the articles and add work of his own, to produce a book.

Betty agreed to his suggestions, saying she wanted nothing in cash, but that his proposal to create for her "a small nestegg in London was a stroke of genius . . . You would be wise to leave a margin open to finance my travels to meet you as I personally have no way of doing this . . . Don't be alarmed! I shall not have many opportunities to get away to you but I shall have to be financed by Cynmont when I do. . . ."[2]

Hyde meanwhile went off to China, a trip he had always wanted to make, and did not return until early May. Then, in a further series of telephone calls and letters between himself and Betty, it was agreed that she would write a series of six articles about her work in intelligence; Hyde would edit and generally make them suitable for publication and he and Betty would share the sum of £12,500, which Iain Thompson had now negotiated with *The Sunday People*.

Despite the feudal grandeur of their home and her share of Cora's estate, Betty and Charles were not well off financially. They "managed," and it is at least a possibility that the reason they could not make more trips (Betty had ascribed it to Charles's dislike of post-war cities) was simply one of financial constraint. This would also explain the absence of servants at the chateau. There is no evidence that they were in straitened circumstances, but the upkeep of the chateau was a constant drain and they had to live carefully, harvesting their resources for the years ahead when they would doubtless require medical treatment, more heat in their vast home, and possibly nursing care. Betty, trying to face up to the hopeless prognosis of her cancer and aware of Charles's dependence on her, was also deeply concerned about his future.

She determined to fight. She would not give in to this repulsive malignancy attacking her body and simply give up on life. She would write her story, and if it was worth money so much the better. She was delighted when Hyde wrote to advise her that Sam Campbell of *The Sunday People* wished to meet her in London. Simultaneously, she saw an opportunity to fulfil a life-long wish. Just as Hyde had always wanted to see China, Betty had always wanted to visit Ireland. Hyde, who had Irish connections and many friends there, happily agreed to escort her on this whimsical wish-fulfilment. Not knowing of her cancer he may have been drawn to the prospect of resuming the physical side of their relationship.

Charles, who had taken the news of Betty's cancer badly, was now not disposed to deny her anything and drove her to Barcelona so that she could catch a direct flight to London.

Betty and Hyde spent a night in London before flying on to Dublin. She had taken with her the first-draft article. Hyde could not help but be impressed with her writing style and indeed was later to find that he could not improve on it a great deal. With this happy discovery the two went off on holiday.

Once, Betty had written that Spain was her "spiritual home." Yet in her heart she had always felt herself Irish, so perhaps she regarded Ireland as her natural home. On the day of their arrival she had to see a dentist over a tooth that had come loose. Shocked at what he saw, the dentist advised her to return home at once for treatment. Naturally she ignored him and embarked upon the planned week-long tour of Ireland.[3] She was entranced, as so many before her, by the sheer greenness of the country. The lushness, after the harsh grandeur of the Pyrenees, must have come almost as a shock to the senses.

"A gayer or more attentive companion could not be imagined," wrote

Hyde, and it is clear from his description of their time together, in his book, in correspondence and in conversation that there was a good deal of mutual happiness, almost—as it were—retrieved from a past when it had been denied them. Without the restrictions of Charles's presence they reminisced nonstop about mutual friends and their wartime experiences in BSC. Hyde introduced her to some literary friends, and drove her through the heart of Ireland to the stunningly lovely scenery of the west-coast counties of Sligo and Mayo. She particularly wished to see the house of a friend she had known for many years in the diplomatic service.[4] The house, a holiday home at that time, was empty apart from resident staff and it was a typically sweet gesture of Betty's that she should take time to pick a small posy of spring flowers from the garden, carefully package them in damp moss and send them to the owner, Owen O'Malley, in England with a descriptive note about her visit:

. . . The weather was wild Irish with mist and drizzle and white wavelets on Clew Bay. A brown hare hopped in the wind across the green grass outside the library, and the wind blew hard and strong. But spring was there too, in the apple blossoms trellissed against the wall near the front door and in the early flowers in the lawns. How glad I am to have seen it all . . .[5]

When they returned to London, Betty met Sam Campbell, to show him her original draft for the first article and to discuss the material that she could supply for the remainder. She would be identified in the series by the pseudonym "Cynthia Beresford." On another day the pair lunched with Colonel Charles "Dick" Ellis,[6] the former right-hand man of William Stephenson, in BSC. They talked of Sir William, who was said to be very ill, and Ellis was given a copy of Betty's manuscript. Ellis had been in charge of BSC's Washington office and responsible for facilitating liaison with OSS. As much as anyone, apart from Betty herself, he knew the background to her work at the Vichy embassy. He knew, too, of her role in obtaining the Italian ciphers and of her record prior to 1941. As he was still working for "the Firm" Ellis agreed to read the draft article and test its acceptability. Later he wrote that he could see no objections to its publication:

I suggest that more should be said about the help given to us by locals (police, harbour officials, G2 and ONI etc). We helped them, but got a lot of help from them.

The Vichy story *is* too good to miss out but there may be some hurt feelings about Cynthia's *modus operandi*. However you and Bill can best judge . . .[7]

In the short time since his return from China Hyde had spent some time checking out, as far as he was able, those who peopled Betty's story in an attempt to discover who was still alive. Most would need to be disguised for one reason or another. Neither knew, for example, whether John Leche was still alive when Betty started writing about her affair with him, but his death was easily traced. Jack Shelley could not be named but Hyde wrote to Iain Thompson that he had "squared him" regarding the Polish episode.[8]

To Betty's surprise, in the course of his enquiries Hyde discovered that Michal Lubienski, her great Polish love, was not only very much alive but living in London. Probably without giving a thought to his family, she telephoned him but was told that he would be out of the country on Foreign Office business for a period of time. By then Betty would be on her way home. She cheerily told Hyde that she would make contact with Michal in the autumn when she intended to return to England. Hyde had his doubts. Though she had not been honest with him about her illness he sensed rather than recognized the extent of it, which by unspoken agreement they had chosen to ignore during their holiday together.

He was therefore not surprised to get the letter she wrote immediately upon her arrival at Castellnou telling him that she had now received the results of a biopsy which confirmed the cancer. Nor did she set out to fool herself, now that the thing was confirmed. She wrote:

The treatment is merely to retard, you know, nothing more . . . I do hope I can live another year before the pain gets too bad. Anyhow I will stick it as long as possible before becoming too much of a screaming nuisance. . . . I was wise when I urged that we get together without waiting for the shadows of old age. It is always later than one thinks—you should find comfort in the knowledge that you have given me my last wonderful memories . . .[9]

Over the next weeks she embarked upon a painful course of treatment which to her dismay involved the extraction of all her teeth. The radium treatment caused such pain she could not sleep, eat or speak but she was still driving herself to Perpignan to her doctors and could even find humour in her situation.

> . . . the other day a cousin of Charles saw me emerging from the doctor's and asked me what was the matter. She is a dreadful cat and a busybody and kept nagging me to tell her my trouble, although I kept saying it was a personal thing.

> Finally she exasperated me and I said, "Well, if you must know I have been making love three times a day and am now in the family way!"

> Since then five people have telephoned congratulations . . .[10]

She assured Hyde and Iain Thompson of her ability to meet the deadlines she had agreed to in London. She had found an excellent secretary who could take English dictation and now that the course of treatment was over she would get down to work. She wrote that she was fighting a *"terrific"* battle with all her stubborn will-power. She would not let the cancer get her down. Not yet.

News that Betty was to tell her story was mentioned in a London evening newspaper and Dick Ellis wrote warningly to Hyde,

> I was asked by "C"s secretary if I knew anything about the Evening Standard's reference to "Cynthia's" memoirs. I said I knew nothing beyond what I had read. The secretary said the F.O. hoped (if Cynthia wrote her memoirs), she would not say anything *embarrassing* to H.M.G. (Italian?) or elaborate on the Vichy Embassy incident which had upset the French! I said I understood the lady was [now] French and presumably could do what she liked.[11]

At this point Hyde innocently forwarded to Betty a copy of a legal contract he had prepared concerning Cynmont, in order to place the

314

arrangement between them on a proper footing. In a covering letter he also suggested he would include a clause in his will so that should he die before she any money due him under his half of the contract would automatically be returned to her. He assumed she would do likewise. The contract outlined the company Cynmont and its two directors, Hyde and his secretary/housekeeper Rosalind Brown (later Hyde's third wife), who were to hold 51 percent of the company.

Betty's carefully worded formal reply, made after she had seen the edited draft of the article—so close to her own original work that she bridled at sharing the proceeds—stated in unequivocal terms that she would not "under any circumstances" be associated with an undertaking in which she was not

absolute mistress of assets coming to me through my own earning power . . . In short, all things considered, I want to keep any moneys . . . from my articles, a book, a film, or TV or anything else based on my life story, clear of restrictive devices, partnerships or suchlike.

. . . as I understand it *The People* have proposed £12,500 for six articles of about four thousand words each, based on my experiences as an intelligence agent. Of this amount Mr Iain Thompson is entitled to £1,500 this being his fee as literary agent. This leaves you and myself, and as you point out you have incurred some expenses on account of my proposed articles: your travel expenses to and from Perpignan, my trip to London and Ireland with the subsistence this entailed etc. This of course must be straightened out . . .

As to the articles themselves I believe I am capable of writing them, and indeed would prefer to do so, as there is much more in my head than I have committed to tape, and I feel that I could tell the story better than anyone, it being so completely personal. (I feel that the Ciphers article which I left with you in England was a creditable job even if it may need pruning) Finally it is I who carry the responsibility for possible libel. [12]

She signed her letter "Cynthia Beresford/Elizabeth Brousse." Increasingly now, she referred to herself as Elizabeth rather than Betty, and she attempted to soften the severity of the more formal letter with a personal note thanking him for offering to name her in his will but saying she could not accept as she could not reciprocate, "my obligations being elsewhere. But please realize that I am very touched. . . . the enclosed letter being a business one does not include all the expressions of gratitude I feel."[13]

Hyde was clearly stunned at what he saw as this volte-face. Not only had Betty broadly agreed in writing to everything he had done, but she had been present at discussions with Campbell and Thompson in London at which the matter was agreed. He had committed a considerable amount of time and expense to the project on this understanding. He replied firmly, explaining that her letters and conversations already committed her to the existing contract, that of providing the material for (though not necessarily writing) the remaining articles, and his right to share in the proceeds. He had been concerned that her illness might not allow her to write the remaining articles and he was proposing to do this.

Betty had reached a critical point in her illness and was now in a clinic in Perpignan where she was receiving daily treatment and regular blood transfusions. With her secretary in attendance she worked each morning on her articles for as long as she could manage, trying not to allow her pain and tiredness to affect her fighting spirit. Deeply unhappy with the arrangements she claimed Hyde had made "over her head," she wrote angrily reminding him that she had already produced the first article which, if nothing else, ". . . was a work of great precision and hardly the slap-dash effort of someone throwing a few notes together," as he implied. Their intention had been, surely, that she would write the articles; he would edit them for publication and write an introduction.

When I returned to France in May you said that I should continue with the remaining articles, working along the same lines as I did the Vichy French one. But now you tell me that you are to write the articles so I presume this is no longer a matter for confusion. There is, nevertheless, a question that remains unanswered; are they to be signed Cynthia Beresford or H. Montgomery Hyde?

. . . I became slightly uneasy when you began sending me papers to sign which amounted to outright surrender of my rights in connection with

316

my life story. In the accompanying letters I looked for some personal word of reassurance, and of course there was none . . . in fact you were forming a company destined to exploit things that belonged to *me*.

. . . If as you say Iain Thompson and Mrs Roberts are "mystified" it might be as well to tell them that the only document that I have ever had from you (until recently a draft agreement) was a Memorandum of Association, and the papers for signature that would lock me up in a company controlled by you and for your convenience. I am greatly at fault for having permitted myself to be lulled into such confidence, but you are even more so for not having explained in a more straightforward way at its inception what the "Cynmont" device meant to you, quite apart from "tax considerations."

I was entitled to this minor courtesy I think for without my life story, my experiences and my basic materials you would have had to create the company from your own efforts. And should there remain additional ground for bewilderment you might say that you asked me to draw up a document to be incorporated in my will, or as a codicil to it, leaving you my shares in "Cynmont"! . . .

If Mr Thompson agrees it might be preferable for him to act as intermediary between you and me. [14]

What Betty could not know was that Hyde had recently had a bitter experience in his relationship with Sir William Stephenson after having produced the best-selling book *The Quiet Canadian* (In the United States, *Room 3603*). Sir William had obviously bowed to pressure from contacts still active in intelligence circles[15] and had insisted that the book should not be reprinted once existing copies were sold. No foreign rights could be sold, nor would he allow any film or TV rights to be marketed. Stephenson had been party to the book throughout its production, and this was a shabby way to treat Hyde. Hyde's actions in respect of Betty seem clearly an attempt to ensure that he did not lose control of this project as well.

Iain Thompson, at Hyde's request, then wrote to Betty and his calm, objective approach seemed to introduce a note of reason into the dispute.[16] Betty still refused to sign the offending document but accepted that she was bound by her earlier agreement to share the proceeds from the articles. Nevertheless, she insisted that the articles were to be published under her name and that substantially they must remain her work. Her subsequent letters to Hyde are short and businesslike.

She was to remain in the clinic for almost three months, punctiliously writing her memoirs whenever she felt well enough. Her handwritten drafts were typed by her secretary on Betty's own typewriter with its distinctive blue-ink ribbon, on which all Betty's letters during this period were also produced. The manuscripts she had produced for the Vichy episodes and her time in Spain amounted to three full-length articles. Knowing that she was not capable of sustained work she gave in and provided notes for Hyde to write the introductory article which was needed almost immediately to enable *The Sunday People* to start the series in early October. Meanwhile Betty worked on her fourth article: the Polish episode. Hyde's agent in Paris negotiated an agreement with a French newspaper, *France Dimanche*, which ran a French—slightly more *risqué*—version of the series, in parallel with *The People*.

In the last week in September 1963, reporter Peter Forbes of *The People* arrived at Castellnou. Without informing Hyde, Forbes had done some research to identify the real woman behind "Cynthia Beresford." His mission was to interview Betty and to try to persuade her to appear in a television advertisement for the forthcoming series. The story was potentially explosive with its sexual overtones involving the two worlds of diplomacy and espionage.

Betty was at home for a few days recuperating from surgery and trying to gain her strength for the next round of treatment. She was resting when Forbes arrived, unannounced. He had not been told how ill Betty was and was shocked at her appearance. He saw immediately that she could not appear in the film. Nevertheless he recognized the courage of this fatally ill woman as she pretended that "everything was fine"; he had no alternative but to play along with her. He explained why he had come and Betty insisted on appearing in the advertisement. Dates were made for the filming and Forbes, against his better judgment, agreed to send a team. Perhaps if she were shot mysteriously shadowed, against the ramparts of her castle . . . Charles opened champagne. It seems that each of the three was acting for the benefit of the others.[17]

Betty was unable to speak properly but wrote replies to the reporter's lengthy questions. "No, I have no objection to revealing my real name . . . the time has come to "tell everything" . . . Why should I care what narrow-minded people say? I did my duty as I saw it. It involved me in situations from which respectable women draw back. But wars are not won by 'respectable' methods. . . . I was not a loose woman. I hope and believe I was a patriot."[18]

Three weeks later the camera team arrived at Perpignan. Betty had by then undergone another operation but "Incredibly, against the advice of her despairing, admiring doctors she insisted on being taken home to shoot the film."[19] The advertisement went out early in October, just as the series began, by which time Betty was in hospital having undergone further surgery which, "went wrong . . . I am now waiting to hear whether they will remove my tongue. It would be a shock but anyway I am alive and grateful for that . . ." she wrote to Kathleen Cockburn (daughter of a former colleague at BSC), on October 20.

> Oh Kathleen, NEVER let the children smoke. In my case cigarettes are the direct, unquestioned cause. I suppose you have been following the shady career of one "Cynthia"! The articles have all been rewritten by "The People" to conform to their style. I never wrote anything so bragging and conceited . . . it makes me blush.[20]

Betty was released from hospital at about this time and as the first three articles had already appeared she wrote to Hyde asking what he thought of the series so far. "I've lived with the articles for so long that I've lost my objectivity. Also do you know how they are being received by the reading public? What, for instance, does Mrs Roberts think? And does Mary (Hyde's second wife) read them surreptitiously?"[21]

There *were* reactions to the series. Dick Ellis wrote to Hyde that, "The first Cynthia article is not exactly exciting but may catch the female reader's eye." Presumably he found the second a little nearer the bone for after reading it he wrote a little more anxiously, "Re the Cynthia articles, I trust *my* name will be kept out of the story!"[22]

319

Possibly Betty had no conception of the house-style of *The People* in the early 1960s. Brash and lively, it was not a newspaper likely to be taken by those who moved in her circles. Subtle changes had been made to the manuscript, and her story of seduction across three continents appeared under lurid headlines such as "I had to stage a strip scene at the French Embassy." The articles were eagerly devoured by the newspaper's regular readers. What seems surprising, though, is that Betty apparently did not stop to think that her story might cause her daughter distress. The sixties (which are now seen as the start of a new sexual revolution) were revolutionary more in word than deed; the order of the day among "nice girls" was still that they "didn't"! Despite her cosmopolitan upbringing Denise was very upset, according to her aunt Rosina.[23] There is proof here of Betty's attitude to her work—or more particularly to her MO. She saw nothing whatever reprehensible about the latter and nothing to be ashamed of. Why not tell the world? And if her daughter heard of it why should anyone be embarrassed?

As Dick Ellis predicted, the articles caused "hurt feelings," despite the fact that many names had been disguised. Michal, for instance, was given a pseudonym in the articles, but he was easily recognizable to the Polish community in England; Beck had had no other *chef de cabinet* during the period Betty wrote about.[24] The Pack family were deeply shocked, especially when Arthur's picture appeared in the articles, and must have been mortified to read that he "had been posted to one European capital so that his wife could use her power to fascinate on its leading officials."[25]

A number of her regular correspondents wrote to Betty on the subject of "Cynthia," whose escapades had first been revealed in Hyde's book on Stephenson, and were now elaborated. One wrote that he "must admit to being considerably 'shook up' " but was applying the admonition "judge not. . . ."[26] Another, a woman friend, wrote with humour; ". . . it occurs to me to ask which side of your activities you enjoyed most!?"[27] Sir Piersson Dix wrote from the British embassy in Paris, "It was such a pleasure . . . to be let into the secret of Cynthia. . . . I am lost with admiration of your exploits. When will you and Charles be here? You know how much we should enjoy seeing you and talking about our many friends in common. . . ."[28]

There was no question of Betty ever seeing Paris again. In permanent and terrible pain, which she always attempted to rise above for Charles's sake, she limped agonizingly through each day. Never was her personal courage displayed more directly than during this period. When her doctors said there was one final possibility of extending her life, which involved more surgery, she did not hesitate. While she was in the hospital at Montpellier her daughter, Denise, and her sister, Jane (both women accompanied by their husbands), flew to France at Charles's urging. Betty was thrilled to see them, though she could communicate only by means of scribbled notes.

On the day Betty was released from the hospital and sent home they helped her prepare for the journey back to Castellnou. Jane later told Shirlee Thorpe (her former sister-in-law) how they had driven back from the hospital in convoy.

> Betty was in the ambulance in front and Jane and Denise and their husbands were in a car following. Betty kept looking out of the rear window and pulling faces to make them laugh. And she was still smoking too. I would say that was typical of Betty . . .[29]

Her family did not stay long—a few days; Betty told them she wished them to leave before she re-entered the hospital for follow-up treatment. No one had any illusions. The end was clearly very close and Betty now seemed reconciled to the fact that her fight was almost over.

In the last week in November 1963 she left Castellnou for a Perpignan clinic. During the night of December 1 she died there. The news was telephoned to Charles and he asked that her body be brought home immediately.

"They brought her here at 4 o'clock in the morning," he wrote. "I cannot get over the shock . . . [she] is buried in the park of the castle due to a special authorisation of the representative in Perpignan of the French Government."[30] To the many letters he received from Betty's friends, Charles replied that he intended to stay on in the chateau, surrounded by the souvenirs he and Betty had collected during their twenty-three happy years together.

Over and over he used the same phrase:

"My heart is broken to pieces."

Epilogue

arford Hyde wrote immediately to Charles saying that he still wished to go ahead with the proposed book on Betty based on her memoirs. Charles agreed, "Your idea about a book on her is splendid," he said, apparently absently; a brief sentence among detailed descriptions of Betty's death and her grave. Thereafter, he hardly referred to the matter again, writing on rare occasions, usually in three-line notes, mere acknowledgements of Hyde's letters to him.

Betty died without making a will and Hyde was reluctant to put too much work into the project which he feared might carry potential copyright

323

problems, especially as Charles gave him no specific answers in his letters. But in March 1966 Hyde finally published *Cynthia*, quoting directly from her memoirs, clearly edited with the Secrets Act and the laws of libel in mind. On his American agent's advice Hyde played down Betty's sexual activities. Her adventures would be too much for some readers, he was counseled: "The principal need . . . is to avoid the impression that we are dealing with a nymphomaniac. She was obviously much more interesting than that . . . gifted with the sex appeal of Marilyn Monroe [and] the intelligence, tenacity and guts of a heroine."[1] Likewise, Hyde was not able to mention Betty's work in connection with Enigma in Poland though he later wrote that he was aware of it. It would be almost another decade before the existence of Enigma would be publicly revealed.[2]

Uncharacteristically, Harford Hyde, a noted biographer, appears to have taken Betty's memoirs at face value and did little additional research beyond checking on Betty's birth and her early years. He contacted Shirlee Thorpe and, through her, attempted to contact Betty's brother. George was not disposed to co-operate. He had been annoyed by Hyde's statements in *The Quiet Canadian* that Betty was "rather ordinary . . . neither beautiful nor even pretty in the conventional sense, though she had pleasing blonde hair."[3]

"Contrary to Hyde's statements," George growled, in a letter to his former wife, Shirlee,

> she was considered one of the most beautiful debutantes who ever "came out" in Washington [and] far from being of "ordinary" personality she was highly intellectual . . .

> With the entrance of England into World War II she was consumed with a desire to aid the Allied cause, so she became associated with British Intelligence—and the rest you know, as confided by Mother . . .

> I know I can trust you to handle the subject delicately . . . if her story is to be told, it must be told in its true perspective.[4]

Nor did Hyde attempt to speak to the Pack family or any of Arthur's friends. As a consequence Arthur was portrayed as a complaisant bore, a patently inaccurate portrait. When she was shown a copy of *Cynthia*, Rosina was deeply upset that her brother should have been described so inaccurately.

That Betty could have confided her betrayal of Arthur to Hyde, could have said that she had never loved him, could have claimed that he had "forced her" her to attempt to abort her first child; these items were a source of great distress and shame to the entire family. But Rosina was bewildered too; she had a drawer full of letters from Betty, full of expressed love and admiration for Arthur to the point of being gushing.

"Perhaps I failed her," Rosina wrote sadly, explaining to an enquirer that she had last heard from her sister-in-law in January 1963 when Betty had written that she was ill and on very expensive daily drugs. "She complained of being tired and said she would rather like to find an apartment in the sun . . . as the castle was too cold for her. Perhaps she was distressed that I did not reply to her letter, so causing her to write so unkindly of Arthur. Who is to know?"[5]

I do not think Betty thought unkindly of Arthur; he hardly came into her memoirs at all, which consisted of four separate sections of manuscript. They were not written in consecutive order and do not necessarily link, although Betty often backtracks, or brings in a memory from another period to illustrate a point, and these form the few mentions of her former husband. Hyde had no alternative but to fill in gaps from things which Betty might have told him during their time together in S'Agaro or in Ireland (but would probably not have written), or to leave lacunae in the story which could only reflect poorly on Arthur.

Apart from those people directly affected by the book, it was well received. It has a distinctly different style from Hyde's normal technique; throughout the book he used Betty's written memoirs almost as though they were her replies to his questions during interview. But Betty's literary voice is so beguiling that it is difficult to resist writing the story as she wished it written.

Coinciding with the publication of the book, the magazine *Reveille* published extracts in a weekly series accompanied by artists' impressions of Betty in the most intimate situations with her various lovers, clad usually in diaphanous négligée and posed alluringly.[6]

Hyde's claim that Betty's work had "changed the course of the war," stemmed from the remark made to Betty by Ellery Huntington after the North African landings. It was not generally taken too seriously and whether Huntington ever said this cannot of course be proven. But it is a historical fact that Huntington was involved at the highest levels, heading OSS Special Operations for TORCH. Certainly he was in a good position to know how useful the information gained by Betty was, to the Americans—if not to the British.

Notably it is members of the British Intelligence *establishment* who have been the most stubborn sceptics of Betty's story. Coming, as it did, so soon after the Profumo affair ("what a commotion over a couple of weekends with a tart," Dick Ellis wrote),[7] Betty's revelations caused new panic in political and diplomatic circles. There was a faint swishing sound, like that of skirts being drawn aside, from members of "the firm" who wished to disassociate themselves from any connection with Betty's story. Notably, most of the sceptics were inside workers, not those who had worked in the field.

But, due to the openness of American State Department files, there is no longer any question that Betty obtained the material she claimed to have obtained. There is ample official documentary support, amounting to thousands of documents, to the parts of her memoirs which detail her period in the United States with BSC and OSS. The still-classified document which is the official history of the BSC also details Betty's work. There is also the verbal confirmation by former colleagues and connections, some of whom wish to remain anonymous for various reasons. The only question open to discussion is whether the Italian and Vichy ciphers were as useful to the British as trained and experienced MI6 officers (such as Ellis) at BSC claimed they were. I repeat that only when the relevant British files are opened to the public will the full value of Betty's work be made known.

Cynthia gave the reviewers a treat. "More alluring than Mata Hari" wrote one, while John Raymond of the *Sunday Times* was, more than anything, puzzled at "this brief, startling and (for a writer of Mr Hyde's competence and resource) surprisingly slipshod memoir of a remarkable woman."[8] Headline writers had some fun with "Spy with a Tiger in her Blood"; "Secret Bedroom Agent"; "Cynthia The Spy Slept Here"; "Scented

Spy"; "The Playgirl Spy," etc. While one reviewer looked beyond the frivolous side of the story to ask a few serious questions: "Why did the British *Chargé D'Affaires* take an active part in a plot to free a Franco supporter . . . when this was contrary to British Government instructions? Why was Cynthia put in contact with British Intelligence in Warsaw when she had just proved in Spain that she was a dangerous security risk, both politically and morally?"[9] It is just such second guessing that makes intelligence people reluctant to have anything revealed to the general public, even so many years after the event.

Still, the point raised in the last question—Why was Betty drawn into intelligence work after her experiences in Spain seemed to label her undisciplined and likely uncontrollable?—had occurred to me during my own research. The answer has to do with the state of the art of intelligence work at the time. Prior to 1939, there was no serious co-ordination between the low-grade intelligence work going on under the cover of an embassy in one country, and that going on in another country. The only thing generally known about Betty was that she had had love affairs and in these she had been fairly discreet. The John Leche and Michal Lubienski affairs, where she ran afoul of gossip, were exceptions, but even here the affairs were seen as romantic liaisons and nothing more. British Intelligence was an old industry but in 1937 and 1938 it was neither so sophisticated nor well-staffed as readers of espionage novels are entitled to imagine it is today. It was carried out on the smallest, most begrudged, budget. It is true to say that there was a great deal of naïveté and a large number of errors were made by well-meaning operators.

This was not confined to British Intelligence. An American ambassador complained to the political advisor to the State Department that prior to the formation of OSS some of the agents sent to Lisbon "terrified me. They had the mentality of Hollywood comic sleuths, seemed bent on a rousing good game of cops and robbers and were about as confidential as a foghorn." Both British and American intelligence agencies had, too, significant difficulties due to jealousies and friction from other state services which hampered their work.[10] The intelligence service "grew up" as a result of the Second World War and started to achieve a measure of sophistication only in the post-war period.

What Charles Brousse thought of the book is not known. There are no letters from him on the subject. For the ten years after Betty's death he lived in virtual seclusion. A sad and pathetic figure, he had been ailing even before Betty died[11] and her loss robbed his life of everything he valued. He was found dead in 1972 in his burned-out bed, among the charred remains of the living quarters at Castellnou. It seems that he had taken a sleeping pill before retiring and had fallen asleep without switching off his electric blanket, which caught fire during the night.

Denise died a few years later. The cause of her death is not precisely known either by the Thorpes or the Packs. Both sides of the family lost touch with her after 1962. A former colleague of hers on *Newsweek* told me that she had committed suicide.

All that is left, now, is Betty's story. Thrilling and often hilarious; sometimes brave, sometimes indecorous, but always interesting. And the memory of a woman who took life as she found it, happily meeting challenge after challenge head-on, no matter what the consequences of the collision. She was not perfect—few of us are. She frequently viewed life in the manner of that fictional Irish-American Scarlett O'Hara, whom she resembled in so many ways. For Betty too, there was always "another day" to deal with life's problems, though her strong sense of loyalty and a need to get things done sometimes conflicted with this attitude.

She was a dreadful parent, and after that is said there is a natural tendency to proclaim that nothing else needs to be said or can be said of a woman's life. But there were many men of history, many, many men, great men and boulder pushers, who were equally poor parents, whose lives as they lived them impacted in equally destructive ways on their children. While we don't excuse this failing in them, neither do we refuse to recognize the professional accomplishments of these men because of it. Betty's work is surely entitled to the same consideration.

There was a natural gaiety about her (particularly evident during her final, agonizing illness when she refused to capitulate to pain), that was irresistible. Her friends were legion. She enjoyed life. She did not let down the side in a time of great crisis. What more needs to be said?

Appendix

Sir William Stephenson and British Security Coordination

Sir William Stephenson was later to become famous as the man called Intrepid. In the past few years—particularly since his death in 1989—a number of attacks have been made on his reputation by former members of the British espionage "establishment." It is fair to say that these attacks are rooted in apparent discrepancies contained in A Man Called Intrepid, the best-selling biography of him.

It would be equally fair to say that Sir William himself was partially responsible for these discrepancies. After he suffered the first of his strokes shortly after The Quiet Canadian was published, his memory was affected; it appeared to some of his close friends and former colleagues that he "remembered" being involved in things that he had only heard or read about. This would not have mattered but for the fact that he began giving interviews to journalists. Harford Montgomery-Hyde, the author of The Quiet Canadian, who was also a close friend and former colleague, was especially worried about this. He confided in his wife, Rosalind, that without inside knowledge it was impossible for an interviewer to differentiate between Sir William's actual experiences and those he thought he had experienced.

All the former BSC operatives that I have spoken to agree that what was written in Hyde's biography was entirely factual, though not comprehensive due to the Secrets Act. "Within hailing distance of the truth" was how Sir William's attackers have described it. Undoubtedly in the subsequent biography *of Sir William and newspaper articles about him there were errors of fact, and it is certain that these occurred because he told journalists things which were not true. For instance, he had no connection with the assassination of senior Nazi Reinhard Heydrich. This was noted by Hugh Trevor-Roper in his article in the* Sunday Telegraph *of February 19, 1989. But the same article also stated that Sir William had made false claims about "the glamorous spy Cynthia," yet my research has shown that the short account of "Cynthia's" work for BSC which appeared in the biographies of Sir William can be substantiated by documentary evidence from a variety of independent sources. So one cannot automatically accept the criticisms themselves, even from such an important source, as being totally accurate. And of course one must not neglect to note that the writer of this debunking article was also capable of making significant gaffes himself, for did he not confirm the authenticity of the Hitler diaries which were later proved to be fake?*

Sir William never made any secret of the fact that he regarded much of the SIS's Broadway administration as incompetent. Perhaps the recent revelations of double agents who were able to infiltrate its higher echelons vindicate his opinion. Nevertheless, this did not earn him any friends among SIS administrators in London. And it cannot be overlooked that, discounting journalists who are always on the lookout for a controversial story, his detractors seem to be, in the main, establishment figures.

What we know for sure is that Sir William Stephenson was a remarkable man and fully deserved the decorations heaped on him after the war. He had played a significant part in helping to win it. That there are minor—and they are minor, given what we know to be fact—inconsistencies in the legend of Intrepid cannot be denied. It is doubtful that he had any direct influence over intelligence matters in Europe after 1939, other than through his close connection with Donovan's OSS. The full story of his activities in the United States during those desperate days before the United States entered the war has yet to be told in full; there are at least two researchers working on it at present. It does not need embroidery; the story of how he manipulated the United States into the war is surely enough to prove that here was an intrepid man. Whether one approves of his methods is another matter. War is total. He succeeded. Viewed against the backdrop of Stephenson's life and achievements, the objective reader might feel justified in seeing many of the points raised by his attackers as petty and the attacks more personally vindictive than called for. Yet they have cast a shadow on the reputation of a man still revered by those who knew and worked for him.

Few Englishmen arriving in the cold climate of isolationism that existed in 1940 in America could have done what he did and operated as he operated. It was Stephenson's dynamism and flair (and not a little of his own money) that created BSC, which became a huge organization during the war. It hummed with efficiency and achievement under his dominating direction. No one can doubt the value of BSC's early work to sway public opinion in the United States away from the policy of isolationism and towards helping Britain to defeat the Nazis. He also helped to engineer the appointment of William "Big Bill" Donovan to head-up the new American intelligence agency known as OSS, forerunner of the CIA whose historians freely admit Stephenson was the architect of both agencies.

Sir William's principal wartime secretary, Grace Garner, dismisses the attackers as "pygmies trying to bring down a giant," and during the course of my researches I have certainly found more evidence to support Sir William's emminence than the views of his detractors suggest. It might be useful to readers to know more of the organization for which Betty Pack worked, and the remarkable man who was its founder and chief. The following is merely a précis of his recruitment and early work as head of BSC, based on sourced documentary evidence that I found during the course of my research on Betty Pack, but it is relevant to her story.

Regarding the name "Intrepid," this was never Stephenson's official wartime code name. Stemming from a conversation with Churchill, it was later to become Stephenson's cable address in New York. It was therefore natural enough for those sending a cable to instruct a secretary, "Send this to Intrepid," and easy for the name to stick to the man who was chief of the organization and seemed to those within it to embody the description. Certainly the name appealed to Sir William and was mentioned in both biographies. It did not occur to his first biographer, H. Montgomery Hyde, a former senior officer of BSC, that it was out of place in a serious work.

On April 2, 1940,[1] a representative of the British Secret Intelligence Service (SIS) acting on instructions from that organization's chief, Stewart Menzies (otherwise known as "C"), arrived in New York. The man was William Samuel Stephenson who, according to Kim Philby, was "a friend of Churchill's [and] wielded more real political power than any other British Intelligence Officer."[2] Stephenson's brief was "to establish relations of the highest possible level between the British SIS and the U.S. Federal Bureau of Investigation."[3]

The mission resulted from a letter written by President Roosevelt to Menzies stating that he would welcome such collaboration. As a consequence, Stephenson, "a true top level operator" not accustomed to "footling around at lower levels,"[4] effected a meeting with Bureau Director J. Edgar Hoover through a mutual friend, the boxer Gene Tunney. Stephenson was then forty-four, Hoover was forty-five; both were powerful men with enigmatic personalities, at the height of their abilities. Between them (Hoover having first ascertained FDR's wishes, which ran contrary to those of State Department officials), they worked out a mutually acceptable arrangement enabling Stephenson to return to England in early May to report favourably:

> The President has laid down the secret ruling for the closest possible marriage between the FBI and British Intelligence. The fact that this cooperation was agreed upon is striking evidence of President Roosevelt's clarity of vision. The fact that it has to be kept secret even from the State Department is a measure of the strength of American neutrality. It is an essential first step towards combating enemy operations but it is insufficient to meet the demands of the situation. The Nazis in America are already well organized and well entrenched. They realize the extent of British dependence on American material aid, and so direct their subversive propaganda towards buttressing the wall of traditional isolationism by which the President is encompassed.[5]

On May 10, 1940, following their success in Norway, Hitler's armies attacked Holland, Belgium and Luxembourg, easily defeating the British and French forces that rushed in to confront the enemy. Chamberlain resigned and Churchill became prime minister. According to Stephenson and his two biographers he was then asked by Churchill, during a dinner party, to return to New York and replace Captain Sir James F. Paget, Bart., R.N., who had formerly been MI6's representative there, under the title Passport Control Officer.[6]

Stephenson's claim requires qualification since his precise connection with Churchill has been questioned by several eminent historians who dispute that Stephenson *ever* actually met Churchill and that it was historically impossible that he was with Churchill on the evening of May 10th. Indeed, Stephenson's entire version of the events described in the two biographies of him has been called into question. It is true that little documentary evidence of any meeting between Churchill and Stephenson exists in the public sector, apart from a written account by Ernest Cuneo (one of Roosevelt's confidential advisors), who was introduced to Churchill by Stephenson in December 1943.[7]

Apart from the evidence of this first-hand testimony, however, would Churchill not have needed to meet and talk with the man who, even his detractors have to admit, headed up every branch of British Intelligence in the Western Hemisphere until 1945?[8] Stephenson made many (documented) trips to England during the crucial period between June 1940 and December 1941, during which Churchill's chief ambition was to bring the United States into the war. It is inconceivable that Churchill would not have summoned Stephenson, on at least one of these trips, to discuss at first-hand the matter that was the core of his aspirations.

Nor can one overlook circumstantial evidence that Churchill and Stephenson were acquainted prior to 1940. For instance, it is known that "C" was opposed to the appointment of Stephenson as PCO at New York but that Churchill overrode these objections.[9] Would Churchill have risked open conflict at such a sensitive time with the chief of his secret service over a man he had never met but had only heard of? It seems unlikely. Then, too, Stephenson claimed that he dined with Churchill in the presence of Lord Beaverbrook and others. After the first biography of Stephenson was published,[10] Beaverbrook wrote to the author and thanked him, ". . . I like the references to myself," he said. These references included a description of the incident where he played host to Churchill, Stephenson et al. Yet Beaverbrook, the pedant, did not question the account as it stood. This would seem to indicate that while Stephenson may have mistaken the date of the dinner party, it had occurred.[11]

Furthermore, there is no doubt that Stephenson was involved in pre-war intelligence gathering, reporting his findings to Major Desmond Morton. It is an acknowledged fact that Churchill would befriend anyone who could be of use to him[12] but Stephenson knew, personally, so many people who were part of Churchill's set that it would be more remarkable if he had *not* been introduced to the great man.

Stephenson's detractors place a great deal of emphasis on the fact that Churchill's private secretary, John Colville, did not remember any meeting between Churchill and Stephenson and could not recall Stephenson ever calling at 10 Downing Street. Stephenson's reply to this (made shortly before his death when he had been the victim of several major strokes), was that his visits to Churchill were inevitably nocturnal when day-time staff were off-duty and he pointed out that Colville was away on active service for two years from October 1941.

Another factor frequently dredged up is that none of Churchill's biographers give Stephenson more than a passing mention. In view of Stephenson's role, though, is it surprising that his still-secret activities were not documented in the public sector? That his name is absent from those papers of Churchill's which are open to the public will come as no surprise to any researcher on the subject of British espionage. We know of his visits to England during these years only because of United States administrative processes and the Freedom of Information Act there. Among the private papers of William Donovan, head of OSS, is a note in his own handwriting which states that it was Stephenson who arranged for him to meet Churchill in July 1940. Could Stephenson have done this (so soon after his own appointment) without some direct contact with Churchill? Was it within the remit of all Passport Control Officers to set up appointments with a wartime prime minister? I doubt it.

Stephenson recalled that it was at a meeting which he had requested, at the Admiralty offices, that Churchill first told him that it was his duty to go to New York and bring the Americans into the war. It was some days later, at the disputed dinner party, in a further discussion on the subject that Churchill apparently told Stephenson that he would be his "personal representative" in the United States. It is not beyond the bounds of credibility that Churchill used this phrase in an unofficial capacity; given his origins and talents it certainly seems that Stephenson was the ideal man for the task Churchill had in mind.

A Canadian by birth, Stephenson had served with distinction in World War I, initially in the trenches, where he was gassed and invalided home. Following this he learned to fly, joined the Royal Flying Corps and was returned to France. There seems to be some contention about the number of enemy aircraft he actually accounted for; there is certainly evidence for six definite kills, twelve probables plus two dirigibles. He was awarded the Military Cross and DFC by his own government and, his biographers claim, the croix de guerre by the French in 1918. This is another fact disputed by the anti-Stephenson faction, who claim that there is no record of the honor in French archives. Yet, contemporary French newspapers reported the award in an article praising the young airman when he was declared missing.[13] Shot down (and badly wounded) by an RFC observer who mistook his airplane for an enemy craft (this fact alone surely highlights the difficulties in precisely identifying enemy "kills"), Stephenson was captured and as a prisoner of war learned at first-hand to dislike the Germans.

With the design of a can-opener purloined from his captors, he escaped back to his own lines. After the war he patented and manufactured the device, which formed the basis of his personal fortune.[14] Branching into communications, he invented the transmission of pictures by radio and was responsible for the first mass-production radio sets in England through his company, the General Radio Company Ltd. By the time he was thirty he was a millionaire (the term millionaire really meant something in those days). Stephenson was a short, well-built man, purposeful and economical in his actions and speech. In his spare time he boxed to keep fit and though his biographers described him as the amateur lightweight boxing champion of the world he was in fact a flyweight and there is no formal record of a world title. He was established in a smart London address by the early thirties, happily married and at pains to cultivate those who made up London's power center.

Company House archives in London reveal that Stephenson's companies included: Earl's Court Ltd., which constructed the great exhibition hall (then the world's largest), Sound City Films (Shepperton) Ltd., Catalina Ltd.— one of the first British companies involved in the manufacture of plastics, and Pressed Steel Ltd., who provided virtually all the car bodies for leading car manufacturers such as Morris, Humber, Hillman and Austin. In addition he was associated with many other companies whose concerns ranged from aggregates to engineering and aviation. One of his companies produced the Monospar airplane, and it was with one of these that Stephenson entered the Kings Cup air race in 1934. Although Stephenson was a pilot he was no air racer and for this important promotion he hired Flight Lieutenant H. M. Schofield to fly his plane, registration number G–ACTS. It won at an average speed of 134.16 miles per hour in extremely poor weather conditions, and just as in horse racing, it was Stephenson, as the owner, who received the gold cup from His Majesty King George V.

It was not entirely due to his wealth and success that Stephenson made powerful friends such as fellow-Canadian Max Beaverbrook, for he was a man of considerable charisma and astuteness. As he travelled around Europe on his various business concerns Stephenson was not slow to notice that Germany was quietly but efficiently turning over the production of her factories from items of a domestic nature to military ones. At home he voiced these observations to a few well-placed friends and it was almost certainly as a result of this that Beaverbrook introduced Stephenson to Major Desmond Morton. Later, Stephenson's friend Ralph Glyn (later Lord Glyn), a member of Parliament, introduced him to "C." Stephenson and 'C' never liked each other but from the mid-1930s Stephenson was acting as an amateur agent, or intelligence-gatherer for SIS.[15] In the course of this work he claimed to have learned about the German interest in Enigma cipher machines and, in 1938, their mass-manufacture of a new portable version.[16]

Desmond Morton was Churchill's personal assistant throughout the war but in the years before Churchill came to power Morton operated as chief of an organization known as The Imperial Defence's Industrial Intelligence Centre (IIC) whose brief was to discover and report plans for the manufacture of armaments and war stores in foreign countries. From 1936, representing IIC, Morton was a member of the Joint Intelligence Sub-Committee (JIC), a body which brought together representatives of the other branches of British Secret Intelligence Services. A neighbour at Chartwell and a close friend, he had been supplying Churchill with confidential information since 1933, when it first became known that the Germans had begun secret production of military aircraft.

Morton was not unique; all manner of people, including senior officials in the military and civil services, frustrated by the Chamberlain government's refusal to face the horrible truth about Hitler, reported and rallied to Churchill's intelligence network, enabling him to harry the government with accurate facts and figures which could only have come from documents classified "Most Secret." But it was to Morton that Stephenson reported his informed observations[17] and with his immense and well-established business interests Stephenson had the entrée to the highest levels in German industry. Thus was Churchill able to write with confidence in the *Strand* magazine as early as November 1935 that Hitler had "sprung forward armed to the teeth, with his munitions factories roaring night and day, his aeroplane squadrons forming in ceaseless succession, his submarine crews exercising in the Baltic, and his armed hosts trampling from one end of the broad Reich to the other. . . ."

Nor is there any doubt that Stephenson had played an *active* role in intelligence activities prior to the war, for he was certainly deeply involved in an SIS-backed plan to sabotage shipments of high-grade steel from Sweden to Germany in September 1939. The operation misfired when Sweden's King Gustav learned of it, and—convinced that if it succeeded it would cause the Nazis to invade his country—he made a personal appeal to King George to

336

put a stop to the project. It is on record that Stephenson put forward a plan in which he himself would assassinate Hitler with a high-powered hunting rifle, but was prevented from carrying it out because Lord Halifax at the Foreign Office felt it preferable to bring Hitler round by means of diplomacy.[18] But Stephenson really came into his own when he was sent to New York as Passport Control Officer.

Lord Beaverbrook actively recommended that Churchill attempt to draw the United States away from its policy of isolation. He knew that this could not be accomplished quickly but he felt a closer, more sympathetic relationship between the two countries was a possible first step. In order to encourage the United States towards supporting Britain, Beaverbrook advocated the use of fifth column activities.[19] One way of achieving this, he suggested, was to stir up Scandinavian citizens of the United States against the encroaching Nazi and Russian threat to their mother countries, using semi-military demonstrations and collections of money for a "Scandinavian Defence Fund."

. . . If the Scandinavian demonstrations were successful the movement should extend to the Czech population and also the Poles . . . the responsibility for the project must not rest with the Foreign Office or any other Government department. If there is any difficulty, there must be complete and absolute repudiation . . .

In a remarkable letter to Churchill he urged that in order to initiate this plan, "a competent man should be encouraged to go to the United States. . . ."[20]

Churchill had already reached the conclusion that Britain's only way of defeating Hitler was to bring the United States into the war,[21] but Beaverbrook's suggestions, advancing so well his own ideas about the need to draw the United States into active belligerency, fermented fruitfully in his mind. Indeed, within weeks of his appointment to the premiership, thanks to his mutually admiring relationship with the U.S. president, such a man was in place. On June 21, 1940, Stephenson arrived in the United States to take over British SIS interests there.[22]

At Churchill's insistence and to "C"'s chagrin Stephenson replaced Sir James Paget, who was an archetypal officer and gentleman, thoroughly decent and a highly competent diplomat.[23] What Churchill needed *in situ* at this point, however, was a buccaneer, a man used to taking bold decisions on a grand scale and with the nerve and wherewithal to implement them, and—

moreover—one who could "deal" with Americans. As a Canadian Stephenson was less obviously "a foreigner" than Paget, but he was also not afraid of implementing Churchill's concept of "ungentlemanly warfare." It seems likely that Churchill had Stephenson installed either because he knew him personally, or because Beaverbrook (who was on first-name terms with Stephenson, whom he called "Bill"; Stephenson called him "Beaver")[24] had pushed him forward as a suitable candidate. Possibly it was both. Either way it was a shrewd choice.

At the time of Stephenson's arrival in New York most Americans thought that Britain was already defeated. Newspapers carried daily reports on German successes and the evacuation of the British Expeditionary Force from Dunkirk. France had collapsed. Influential men such as the U.S. ambassador to Britain, Mr. Joseph Kennedy, who had the ear of the president, and Charles Lindbergh, who held the affection of the American public almost to a point of idolatry, made no secret of their opinions that the Allies—even under Churchill—could not prevail against Hitler's massive war machine. Britain's defeat, they said, was inevitable. No one wanted to back a loser.

Stephenson started by spurning the cramped, inconspicuous space Paget had used as offices in favour of a plush apartment in Hampshire House overlooking Central Park. Later, he would move to Rockefeller Center at 630 Fifth Avenue, opposite Saint Patrick's Cathedral, where for a peppercorn rent courtesy of Nelson Rockefeller, British Security Coordination would occupy two entire floors of the skyscraper for the duration of the war. The brass plaque on the lower of these floors identified the office as that of British Passport Control. Callers to the upper floor found a similar plaque identifying the offices of an organization called, appropriately enough, "Rough Diamonds Ltd."[25]

Within days of his arrival Stephenson flew to Washington to meet Lord Lothian, the British ambassador, through whom he claims he met Roosevelt. The meeting was said to have taken place at the suggestion of Vincent Astor (Roosevelt's intelligence advisor and a close friend of Paget's) at Roosevelt's home at Hyde Park. Again there is no documentary proof that this meeting ever took place but it is extremely unlikely that Stephenson would not have met the president given his position and contacts. Grace Garner cannot recall any specific meetings but is convinced from the way senior American politicians and State Department officials referred to her boss that he had met Roosevelt on a number of occasions. It is recognized historical fact that Roosevelt sent his son to Stephenson in November 1941 to deliver personally

338

a message that negotiations with the Japanese had broken down. But it must be remembered that Stephenson quite deliberately made himself the "faceless man" during the war,[26] and those to whom the delicacy of his position was known would have felt a natural hesitation to mention him in daily journals and appointment diaries.

Even the foreign secretary, Anthony Eden, did not recognize Stephenson, though he certainly knew of him. In December 1943 Stephenson lunched with Lord Louis Mountbatten and his wife at their Hyde Park penthouse. Eden was a fellow guest, as was Ernest Cuneo. After lunch Eden asked Mountbatten who Stephenson was. "Oh, don't you know?" Mountbatten asked. "He's your man in New York."[27]

That Winston Churchill thought highly of Stephenson and his work was confirmed by a former senior BBC executive, Ron Robbins, who dined with the great man in the House of Commons. Churchill spoke to him of Stephenson "in the highest terms."[28] One of the principal problems is that those who know the truth about Stephenson—his closest associates at BSC—still take very seriously their vow of secrecy. They bridle at the occasional knocks against Stephenson and write angrily among themselves: "Shall we jump in or rally the troops to jump in?"[29] So far no one has jumped in. Yet there is evidence among Churchill's private papers of the importance both he and President Roosevelt gave to Stephenson's work. In an assessment written in September 1941, Desmond Morton stated:

. . . Another most secret fact of which the Prime Minister is aware but not the other persons concerned, is that to all intents and purposes U.S. Security is being run for them *at the President's request* by the British. A British officer sits in Washington with Mr Edgar Hoover and General Bill Donovan for this purpose and reports regularly to the President. It is of course essential that this fact should not be known in view of the furious uproar it would cause if known to the isolationists.[30]

With his considerable organizational ability and immense personal drive, Stephenson took on the three prongs of isolationism: pacifism, fascism, and communism. The powerful and well-intentioned "America First" organization (it attracted a million members within six months of being formed in the fall of 1940) had been infiltrated by elements from all three. Advocating non-intervention in the European war, it was one of Stephenson's main protagonists. In addition, Stephenson fended the scarcely veiled enmity of the State Department, and the FBI whose chief, despite an apparent amiability, undoubtedly co-operated for motives which were at best protective of his country and at worst self-seeking.

As far as the U.S. State Department was concerned, Stephenson's role as Passport Control Officer was a closely defined one, limited to anti-sabotage protection at ports and the protection of British shipments from American factories to the docks. There was some concern, therefore, when it was noticed that some six months after Stephenson's arrival in New York not only had his organization grown to somewhat larger proportions than seemed necessary for its ostensible duties, but Stephenson was now operating under the title "Director of British Security Coordination" responsible for all matters of British Intelligence in the Western Hemisphere. The suggestion for this title had come from J. Edgar Hoover when he learned of Stephenson's true role. [31]

Eventually BSC's operations precipitated a high-level meeting attended by Attorney General Francis Biddle, J. Edgar Hoover, Adolf Berle, Admiral Wilkinson and General Raymond Lee. Likely because Stephenson's organization was working under "an informal agreement between Churchill and the President before the war . . ."[32] the discussions produced more impotent irritation than anything else.

But the concern of State Department officials was not misplaced. The British Security Coordination (BSC) consisted of more than 2,000 employees at its most active point, including probably a thousand agents in the field. No country could happily countenance such an army working covertly in the interests of a foreign power (even a friendly power) under the apparent protection of the host government. Little was known about BSC at first beyond the fact that in some way it enjoyed the patronage of the president. State Department officials were justifiably uneasy at the "full size secret police and intelligence service [that] is rapidly evolving"[33] in consequence they were wary and unhelpful towards BSC and they remained so, unless specifically directed to be otherwise.

The United States had no well-established intelligence service when war broke out in 1939. Such intelligence activities as were carried out were fragmented and unco-ordinated. Inter-departmental jealousy pervaded, just as it did in the British SIS (where it was, and apparently remains, rife), but Hoover did not even enjoy the protection of a well-defined structure for his counter-espionage activities. Before America entered the war the FBI was constrained by U.S. law from using the doubtlessly illegal methods in which BSC engaged in the course of intelligence gathering. So it was in Hoover's interests to co-operate, up to a point, with Stephenson, for in this way the FBI gained a great deal in the way of information through counter-espionage techniques: clandestine mail-opening, for example, and valuable leads on enemy aliens. The FBI arrested forty-two German agents between 1941 and 1942; thirty-six of them were identified through information derived from BSC's files. BSC, in turn, gained an aura of "respectability" through this symbiotic relationship, but Hoover resented BSC and the fact that as the representative of a foreign government Stephenson had such power within the United States. The extent of Stephenson's recognition of the wary alliance may be gauged from the sentence buried within the official history of the BSC: ". . . Hoover is a man of great singleness of purpose, and his purpose is the welfare of the Federal Bureau of Investigation. . . ."

Eventually the State Department called in the British ambassador, Lord Halifax (appointed after Lothian's sudden death in December 1940), to query BSC's tactics and objectives. Hoover, also present at the interview, pretended an innocence of BSC's operations that he almost certainly did not possess. When questioned he confirmed that the FBI was sending some 300 messages a week "in secret code for the British Intelligence here to the British Intelligence in London." This, Berle pointed out to Halifax, ". . . argued a considerable sub-structure, and no one knew anything about it. . . ." Halifax said he was not party to BSC's secrets and had the impression that Stephenson's employees numbered only 137. He knew that BSC transmitted a number of cables in cipher and had asked Stephenson whether the reason for the secret cipher messages was that they reflected correspondence between the president and Churchill. Stephenson had replied that he had never made such a claim. "The Attorney General thereupon pulled out a report by Mr. Hoover, dated last July, in which Stephenson had given this reason as an excuse for not permitting any American official to know the code. . . ."[34] After Halifax had left, Biddle observed sagely that it was clear the ambassador was "fuzzy" in his knowledge and had been fed inaccurate information by Stephenson; summing up, he told Berle, ". . . someone has been doing some tall lying here."[35]

Clearly Stephenson was paddling around in deep water, making potent enemies who would eventually fight even the president to restrict the scope of BSC's operations. Indeed, it was the same aggressive, ram-through tactics, the refusal to be bound by conventional methods, that made his operation such a success but simultaneously created opposition to him personally both at SIS in London and in the U.S. State Department in Washington. Only the shelter of an implied support by both Churchill and Roosevelt, constantly confirmed by Donovan, enabled Stephenson to continue his work until the end of the war.

Agents in the field, such as Betty Pack, were not part of such political machinations but still felt the effects, reflected in FBI surveillance of their activities, which potentially called unwelcome attention to them. Such agents obtained the intelligence that fuelled and armed the BSC machine; using this vast amount of information gathered in the field as ammunition, Stephenson set about the Herculean task of changing American public opinion on the European war.

His propaganda program was described by the *Washington Post* as "arguably the most effective in history. And by drawing the United States out of iso-lationism and into the web of British secret operations in a global war, it changed America forever."[36] Needless to say, it changed the world as well.

He began by cultivating friendships with the most powerful publishers, editors and columnists of the day, among whom were: George Backer, pub-lisher of the *New York Post*; Helen Ogden Reid, owner of the *New York Herald-Tribune*; Paul Patterson, who published the *Baltimore Sun*; A. H. Sulzberger, president of the *New York Times*; and Walter Lippmann and Walter Winchell, two of the country's most respected and widely read col-umnists. "The British Spymasters played this media network like a mighty Wurlitzer," said the *Washington Post*, acknowledging Stephenson's success.[37] In addition to promoting propaganda, media contacts were used to discredit politicians with isolationist sympathies, such as by exposing one who was misusing congressional postal franking facilities.

Nor was the powerful medium of radio ignored by BSC. One New York radio station, WRUL, which had a 50,000-watt shortwave transmitter and an established international audience, was virtually taken over. BSC subsi-dized it financially, recruited foreign news editors, translators and announcers, furnished it with material for news bulletins and scripts for talks and political commentaries. "The station's nominal commitment to journalistic ethics was easily subverted"[38] and although WRUL's policy was not to broadcast material unless it had already appeared in the American press, BSC got around this by planting material in co-operative newspapers and then quoting it in broadcasts.

On the ground, agents and sub-agents were dispatched to every meeting of America First (there were 700 chapters by the summer of 1941) to disrupt, harass and where possible discredit the speakers. When Senator Gerald Nye spoke in Boston in September 1941, for example, a group called "Fight for

Freedom," supportive of Britain's stance and connected with BSC, passed out 25,000 handbills calling the senator a "Nazi lover and appeaser." Hamilton Fish addressed a meeting in Milwaukee and faced barracking from the same group; while he was speaking he was handed a large card which read, "Der Führer thanks you for your loyalty." Photographs of Fish holding the card with its discernible message were quickly taken and appeared nationally in reports of the rally. It is known that at least three women agents were instructed to get to know senior American politicians who supported isolationist policy, and to use whatever means were necessary to change their views. Stephenson overstepped the mark, though, when he instructed an agent to "get some dirt" on Adolf Berle, one of BSC's sternest opponents. The worst that the agent could find on Berle was that his bathroom housed two bathtubs so that he and his wife could bathe together. "It would be amusing," Berle wrote in his diary, "if it did not illustrate the danger which is run from having these foreigners operate. . . ."[39] The agent, Denis Paine, was hastily sent to Canada when Berle discovered the surveillance; formal complaints were made to the British ambassador and Berle became an implacable opponent of Stephenson. After the United States entered the war he would press for the implementation of the McKellar Bill to curtail BSC's activities by making it mandatory for all foreign agents to be registered as such. When the bill was passed Stephenson merely went underground; BSC agents, whose work altered not one jot, were told that henceforward they were working for OSS.

BSC's "dirty tricks" campaigns included personal harassment of known Axis agents; telephone calls to the person's home throughout the night, automobile tires punctured, huge shipments of luxury goods delivered to the person's house "cash on delivery," letters sent without stamps so that the person was constantly being bothered to pay out petty sums of money. "His lady friend can receive anonymous letters stating that he is suffering from mysterious diseases or that he is keeping a woman and children in Detroit. He can be cabled apparently genuine instruction to make long expensive journeys; a rat might die in his water tank; a street band might play 'God Save the King' outside his house all night; his favourite dog might get lost; with a little thought," BSC instructed its operatives, "it should be possible to invent at least 500 ways of persecuting a victim without the persecutor compromising himself. . . ."[40]

Stephenson believed firmly in the maxim that the end justified the means. If ever an end called out for any means possible the defeat of Nazism was that end. So the press campaign, the rumour factories, the dirty tricks, the discrediting of politicians, the wire-tapping, the shanghaiing of Axis sailors, the infiltration of foreign embassies, the propaganda feature movies directed by Alexander Korda (a Stephenson recruit), the technique of fostering resentment among specific groups: the Irish, the Arabs, the Catholics, against the Germans, the entire gamut of BSC's stratagems must be regarded as acceptable. What is more, viewed against these activities, Betty's *modus operandi* might appear almost unobjectionable. The result of all these activities was that American public opinion was brought round; isolationism was seen to be cowardly, pro-Nazi and anti-American. Even before Pearl Harbor, Americans universally wanted to help the British defeat Hitler.

It was a well-conceived strategy. Stephenson orchestrated it brilliantly. Only a faint unease tugs at the reader of the BSC official history. Perhaps it is due to the hint of arrogant self-satisfaction evident in the document (probably natural coming as it did at the end of a hard-fought war) at BSC's success in so demonstrably manipulating Britain's closest ally. For his work Stephenson was personally recommended for a knighthood by Churchill. It is said that on the list of candidates prepared for the King, Churchill wrote in the margin alongside Stephenson's name "This one is dear to my heart."

Sources and Acknowledgments

Harford Montgomery Hyde, Betty Pack's first biographer, knew a great deal about her work since Hyde served in British Security Coordination during the same period and without doubt knew more than he was able to reveal in *Cynthia*. However, when he wrote that book, only twenty years after the end of the war and amidst almost daily revelations of treachery within senior ranks of the MI6, security was even tighter than it is now. Enigma, for example, was still a closely guarded secret in both the United Kingdom and the United States, and there were other things he was not allowed to write about without running the risk of being arraigned for breaking his oath under the Secrets Act. He sailed pretty close to the wind anyway and his book on Sir William Stephenson, *The Quiet Canadian*, which first revealed BSC's work and touched on Betty's story, was passed for publication only through a series of misunderstandings at MI6 which left them unable to withdraw it from publication, or to prosecute its author. It was Colonel Charles "Dick" Ellis who engineered the book past the scrutiny of MI6's security officer, as he explained in a letter to Hyde on November 5, 1962:

You may have seen this clipping from the *[London Evening] Standard*. It is not *strictly accurate* to say that the proofs were submitted to MI6 and returned with a few corrections. MI6's SO saw the first draft (mine) and passed it, and when I offered the final version, he said he did not want to see it but trusted me to scrutinise it for possible security lapses. I gather

"C" is being harassed but I think it extremely doubtful that the DPP will take action as the book was offered for clearance.

Ellis, who had earlier written a very "watered-down" biography of Stephenson with whom he had worked closely in New York throughout the war, and who has been suspected of being "The Fifth Man" by Chapman Pincher, subsequently lost his job at MI6, almost certainly as a result of the publication of Hyde's books.

One of my chief sources was Betty's memoirs, written while she was undergoing painful surgical treatment for the cancer that killed her a short time later; and her letters, many of which survive, are lively, amusing and sometimes moving, but always entertaining. Her memoirs are sensational. What a pity she did not take to writing as a career. She might easily have done so; indeed as an eleven-year-old she had a book published. However, as I was to discover, there were elements of her story that she did not include in her memoirs—perhaps due to the fact that she never lived to complete them. These events came to light only after extensive research in the U.S. National Archives holdings on the Office of Strategic Services (predecessor of the CIA), the U.S. State Department and the FBI.

By far the most intriguing prime source of my research was the *Official History of the British Security Coordination*, written in 1945. This document, bound in leather, less than 500 pages in length, is still classified "top secret" by MI6 and was made available to me by an informant to whom I have promised "absolute discretion and anonymity."

Often referred to by former BSC operatives as "the bible," the official history was compiled on the instructions of William Stephenson (later Sir William) as the war was ending, using the thousands of tons of reports and contemporary documents which the organization's records comprised. A number of writers (all employees of BSC) worked on the project, including, somewhat surprisingly, the late Roald Dahl who told me that he quickly became bored with the task of distilling hundreds of thousands of documents into what Stephenson wanted: a lively, dramatic and readable record of BSC activities and achievements. Other writers were Gilbert Highet, a professor of classics at Columbia University; Tom Hill, a Canadian journalist; and Giles Playfair, a broadcaster who had provided dramatic eye-witness accounts of the fall of Singapore. Stephenson's two private secretaries, Grace Garner and Eleanor Fleming, typed the manuscript. The operation was carried out in the closing months of the war at BSC's spy training centre, Camp X, Oshawa, near Toronto.

The BSC papers were then burned under careful supervision, so that this history remains the chief source of official information on BSC. How such a mass of documents *can* be accurately compressed into less than 500 pages must remain a mystery but Rupert Allason, a British Member of Parliament and a leading writer on the subject of espionage under the name Nigel West, told the *Washington Post* that the document was "one of the most astounding documents in history."

Not all BSC papers were destroyed, however. Sir William retained a number of the more important documents and some of these were given or shown to his biographers, H. Montgomery Hyde in 1963, and William Stevenson (no relation) in 1976. After Mr. Hyde's death his papers were opened to researchers at Churchill College, Cambridge, but only after Intelligence service "weeders" had combed them and removed anything sensitive. As the first researcher given access after Hyde's papers had been cleared I was disappointed, but amused, to find that while large parts of the collection were "closed indefinitely," some files remained partially open. Individual documents removed from these had been replaced with slips helpfully advising the researcher that the withdrawn papers were "closed until the year 2041." "Indefinitely" is therefore, presumably, some time after 2041. One can only wonder, in these days of *glasnost*, about the nature of such information which must remain classified for one hundred years—and more—after the events took place. Fortunately a number of researchers were given access to Hyde's unweeded papers during his lifetime, so we know the nature of the papers which were removed that concern BSC.

The documents given to the writer William Stevenson for his two best-selling biographical accounts of Sir William are now housed at the University of Regina, Canada, available to approved researchers. The ultimate fate of the papers retained by Sir William himself was revealed to me by Professor Hugh Trevor-Roper:

> . . . after the publication of . . . *The Quiet Canadian*, the Head of the Security Service ordered Stephenson to return all his documents (which he had illegally kept) to London. . . . Stephenson replied by burning all the papers—but not before he had written what he called a summary of them, of which he presented one copy to William J. Donovan and kept

one copy himself. So I presume [that] what is now available as Stephenson's papers is this document which is not authentic but is Stephenson's own retrospective version of his "achievements" designed to confirm his own claims.

When I first received this letter I jumped to the conclusion that Professor Roper was referring to the BSC official history. However, further research established conclusively that this is not so; I subsequently interviewed a number of people who worked on the official history and have no further doubts that the document I saw was written as the war ended, by writers who had access to BSC archives and who used them as the basis for the work I saw. Since *The Quiet Canadian* was not written until 1962 Professor Roper clearly referred to some other document.

According to the writer David Stafford, who researched the history of the document itself, ten leather-bound copies of the book were circulated. One, Sir William kept for himself. The other nine were distributed to Sir Winston Churchill, William Donovan (head of OSS) and the heads of the services which BSC had represented, such as General Sir Colin Gubbins of SOE and Norman Robertson of the Canadian Department of State. A copy was undoubtedly sent to "C" (head of the Secret Intelligence Service) but this, like all SIS documents, remains "permanently unavailable and officially non-existent" according to Stafford. No copy of the BSC official history has ever been made publicly available (though one surfaced briefly during 1989, seen by a *Washington Post* reporter), and I invite the reader to imagine the level of interest with which I examined the copy made available to me.

In a very few cases it has not been possible to identify a source because my informant requested total anonymity. In other cases, while not being able to identify the prime source for my information, I have been able to provide the source of counter-checked information that verifies it. All documents (mostly photocopies of originals) in my possession will be handed to a public facility upon completion of this book and will be made available to other researchers.

I am always humbled when I come to acknowledge those who have helped me in the production of a book. This book is no exception and I wish to record my most grateful thanks to everyone listed below, and also to those who (at their own request) are not listed here, but who nevertheless provided me with a great deal of help and information.

As usual I have met, through my research, a large number of interesting persons, and I have a new crop of pleasant memories; of lunches with Colonel Maurice Buckmaster, Margaret Owen and Eleanor Campbell-Orde; tea at the House of Lords with Lord Hankey; a mid-summer walk in the rose garden at the home of Sir David and Lady Hunt; a lunch at the home of Miss Grace Garner (Sir William Stephenson's wartime secretary) which went on until after 7 o'clock (among the guests was Bill Ross-Smith who also worked in BSC's New York office). Arthur Pack's niece was kind enough to welcome me into her home, allow me to browse through his papers, and subsequently read relevant sections of the manuscript for accuracy, while Mrs. Shirlee Christian Thorpe (Betty Pack's former sister-in-law) entertained me royally at her lovely apartment in the now famous Watergate Building in Washington. Mr. Hans Wyss kindly allowed me to wander around his Georgetown house, which in 1941–42 was Betty's home. Perhaps, after all, it will be easier to simply list alphabetically all those kind people who helped, and thank them for their various contributions:

Rupert Allason, M.P. (the writer Nigel West); Dr. Peter Bishop; Colonel Maurice Buckmaster; Eleanor, Lady Campbell-Orde; Peter Chapman; Marion de Chastellaine; Charles M. Christensen; Mrs. Kathleen Cockburn; John Costello; Lord Dacre (Hugh Trevor-Roper); the late Roald Dahl; Miss Elizabeth Doublet; Baptiste André Fitzroy; Miss Grace Garner; Major C. B. Grundy, M.C. (K.S.L.I.); Lord Hankey; Lieutenant Colonel Keith Heard, M.C.; Professor Sir Francis H. Hinsley; Sir David Hunt; Mrs. Rosalind Hyde; Ms. Stella King; Mme M. Lubienski; Donald McCormick (the writer Richard Deacon); Bill MacDonald; George Millar; Ms. Hope Ridings Miller; James Murphy; Timothy Naphtali; Lieutenant Colonel Richard Osborne; Mrs. C. B. Owen; Miss Bernadette Rivett; Bradley Smith; David Stafford; Miss Elizabeth Stephenson; William Stevenson; Mrs. Barbara Stransky; Mrs. Shirlee Christian Thorpe; Thomas Troy; Hans Wyss; Ms. Rebecca Wyss.

On the administration side of things I should like to thank Katy Belcher, who helped with early research, and Susan Rabiner, who set me on the trail of women in espionage and—having read the first draft—made many pertinent suggestions as to how I might improve it.

Many organizations provided access to special collections of documents, materials and facilities. I wish to acknowledge this help and thank those individuals who were especially helpful to me. In particular I should like to mention the long-suffering staff at Salisbury (Wiltshire) Public Library who patiently cope with my numerous requests for obscure, out-of-print and rare books, often at very short notice:

British Library Reading Room, London.

Butler Library and Oral History Research Room, Columbia University, New York. Collection: W. J. Donovan, "A History of Espionage."

Churchill College, Cambridge, England. (Miss Elizabeth Bennett). Collection: The Hyde Papers/Cynthia Papers.

Federal Bureau of Investigation, Washington, D.C. File: Mrs. Elizabeth Pack.

Foreign and Commonwealth Office, London. (I. S. Lockhart).

Library of Congress, Washington, D.C. Reading Room.
LC Manuscripts Division, Madison Building. Collection: Cordell Hull Papers.
LC Prints and Photos Division.
LC Newspaper & Periodicals Room, Collections: *Washington Post, Washington Evening Star*;

Martin Luther King Library, Washington, D.C. Collection: Washingtonia.

National Archives and Records Administration, Washington, D.C.
(Mr. John Taylor), Military Records, OSS Papers.
(Ms. Sally Marks), Diplomatic History and Records.
(Mr. Eddie Barnes) Room 6E3 Archives.
(Mr. Richard von Doehoff), navy history.

Public Record Office, Kew, England.

Franklin D. Roosevelt Library, Hyde Park, New York. Berle Papers, etc.

Salisbury Public Library, Wiltshire, England.

University of London: Senate House Library.

United States Army Military History Institute, Carlisle Barracks, Pennsylvania. (Dr. Richard Sommers Archivist-Historian; David A. Keough Asst. Archivist-Historian). Collection: William J. Donovan Papers.

Washington [D.C.] Historical Society. Collection: Social History of Washington.

Prime Documentary Sources

Elizabeth Pack "Cynthia Papers," Churchill College Archives, Cambridge, England.

Arthur J. Pack Papers (no public repository as yet, currently in family possession and some with friends).

H. Montgomery Hyde Papers, Churchill College Archives, Cambridge, England.

William J. Donovan Papers, United States Army Historical Institute, Carlisle, Pennsylvania.

Adolf Berle Papers, Franklin D. Roosevelt Library, Hyde Park, New York.

Cordell Hull Papers, Library of Congress, Washington, D.C.

National Archives and Records Administration, Washington, D.C.
    Record Groups:
    The Office of Strategic Services Papers, Record Group 226.
    State Department Papers, Record Group 59.
    Thomas Troy Papers.

Foreign Office, Record Group 371, Public Records Office, Kew, England.

OSS Foreign Nationalities Branch Files. 1942–1945. Washington, D.C.: Index to National Archives.

Reading List

Unless otherwise stated all books listed were published in England.

Espionage (MI6; BSC; OSS) and General
Andrew, Christopher. *Top Secret Mission.* Evans Brothers, 1954.
———. *Secret Service.* Guild Publishing, 1985.

Baptiste, Fitzroy André. *War, Cooperation and Conflict*. New York: Greenwood Press, 1988.

Brinkley, David. *Washington Goes to War*. New York: Alfred A. Knopf, 1988.

Brown, Anthony Cave. New York: *"C" The Secret Life of Sir Stewart Menzies*. Macmillian, 1987.

Buckmaster, Maurice. *Specially Employed*. Batchworth Press, 1953.

———.*They Fought Alone*. Popular Book Club, 1958.

Calvocoressi, Peter. *Top Secret Ultra*. Cassell, 1980.

Campbell, Christy. *The World War II Fact Book*. Macdonald & Co. 1985.

Churchill, Winston S. *The Second World War*. Vols. 1–4. Cassell, 1951.

Colville, John. *The Fringes of Power*. Hodder & Stoughton, 1985.

———. *The Churchillians*. Weidenfeld & Nicolson, 1981.

Cookridge, E. H. *Inside SOE*. Arthur Barker, 1966.

Costello, John. *Love, Sex and War*. Collins, 1985.

Dalton, Hugh. *The Fateful Years*. Muller, 1957.

Deacon, Richard. *A History of the British Secret Service*. Granada, 1980.

———, and Nigel West. *Spy!* British Broadcasting Corp., 1980.

Downes, Donald. *The Scarlet Thread*. Verschoyle, 1953.

Dunlop, Richard. *Donovan*. New York: Rand McNally & Co., 1982.

Eccles, Sylvia and David. *By Safe Hand*. Bodley Head, 1982.

Farago, Ladislas. *The Game of the Foxes*. New York: David McKay, 1971.

Foot, M. R. D. *SOE: The Special Operations Executive, 1940–46*. B.B.C., 1984.

———. *Six Faces of Courage*. Methuen, 1978

———. *Official History of SOE*. Her Majesty's Stationery Office, 1966.

Ford, Corey. *Donovan of OSS*. Robert Hale & Co., 1971.

Goralski, Robert. *World War II Almanac, 1931–1945*. Hamish Hamilton, 1981.

Haswell, Jock. *Spies and Spymasters*. Thames & Hudson, 1977.

Hinsley, F. H., et al. *British Intelligence in the Second World War*. Vols. 1–5. HMSO, 1979–1990.

Howarth, Patrick. *Undercover*. Routledge, 1980.

Hull, Cordell. *Memoirs*. 2 vols. Hodder & Stoughton, 1948.

Hyde, H. Montgomery. *Cynthia*. Hamish Hamilton, 1966.

———. *Room 3603*. New York: (Published in England as *The Quiet Canadian*. Constable, 1962.) Farrar, Straus, 1962.

352

————. *Secret Intelligence Agent*. Constable, 1982.

Irving, David. *Churchill's War*. Vol 1. Australia: Veritas Publishing Co., 1987.

Jones, R. V. *Most Secret War*. Hamish Hamilton, 1978.

Kahn, David. *The Codebreakers*. New York: Macmillan, 1968.

Langley, J. M. *Fight Another Day*. Collins, 1974.

Lash, Joseph P. *Roosevelt and Churchill*. New York: Norton, 1976.

Lewin, Ronald. *Ultra Goes to War*. Hutchinson, 1978.

L'Heureux, Danielle. *Les Oublier de la Resistance*. Editions France-Empire, 1988.

Marshall, Bruce. *The White Rabbit*. Evans Brothers, 1952.

Millar, George. *Road to Resistance*. Bodley Head 1979.

————. *Maquis*. Pan, 1956.

Miller, Hope Ridings. *Embassy Row*. New York: Holt Rhinehart & Winston, 1969.

Pearson, John. *The Life of Ian Fleming*. Jonathan Cape Ltd, 1966.

Philby, Kim. *My Silent War*. MacGibbon & Kee 1968.

Pincher, Chapman. *Too Secret Too Long*. New York: St. Martin's Press, 1984.

————. *Their Trade is Treachery*. Sidgwick & Jackson, 1986.

Ruby, Marcel. *F Section—SOE*. Leo Cooper, 1985.

Singer, Kurt. *Three Thousand Years of Espionage*. New York: Prentice-Hall, 1948.

Smith, R. Harris. *OSS*. Berkeley, Calif.: USC Press Ltd, 1972.

Stafford, David. *Camp X*. New York: Viking Press, 1986.

Stevenson, William. *A Man Called Intrepid*. New York: Harcourt Brace Jovanovich, 1976.

————. *Intrepid's Last Case*. New York: Villard Books, 1983.

Sweet-Escott, Bickham. *Baker Street Irregular*. Methuen, 1965.

Troy, Thomas F. *Donovan and the CIA*. New York: University Press of America, 1981.

Tunney, Christopher. *A Biographical Dictionary of WWII*. Dent, 1972.

Welshman, Gordon. *The Hut Six Story*. Allen Lane, 1982.

West, Nigel. *Unreliable Witness*. Weidenfeld & Nicolson, 1986.

————. *GCHQ*. Weidenfeld & Nicolson, 1986.

Winterbotham, F. W. *The Ultra Secret*. Weidenfeld & Nicolson, 1974.

————. *The Ultra Spy*. Macmillan, 1989.

Books on Women in Espionage

Note: I began work on this book by reading about women who had worked in clandestine services such as SOE. I found it difficult, initially, to put a reading list together but the following might set readers on the same path of discovery:

Aline, Countess of Romanones. *The Spy Wore Red*. New York: Random House, 1989.

Babington Smith, Constance. *Evidence in Camera*. Chatto & Windus, 1958.

Braddon, Russell. *Nancy Wake*. Cassell, 1956.

Butler, Josephine. *Churchill's Secret Agent*. Blaketon Hall, 1983.

Duke, Madeleine. *Top Secret Mission*. Evans Brothers, 1954.

Duncan, Sylvia and Peter. *Anne Brusselmans*. Publisher unknown, 1959.

Fourcade, Marie-Madeleine. *Noah's Ark*. Allen & Unwin, 1973.

Fuller, Jean Overton. *Madelaine*. Gollantz, 1952.

———. *The Starr Affair*. Gollantz. 1954.

Gleeson, James. *They Feared No Evil*. Corgi, 1978.

Hutton, J. Bernard. *Women Spies*. W. H. Allen, 1971.

Jones, Liane. *A Quiet Courage*. Bantam Press, 1990.

King, Stella: *Jacqueline*. Arms and Armour Press, 1989.

Lomax, Judy. *Hanna Reitsch*. John Murray, 1988.

Marsden, A. *Resistance Nurse*. publisher unknown, 1961.

Masson, Madeleine. *The Search for Christine Granville*. Hamish Hamilton, 1975.

Miller, Joan. *One Girl's War*. Brandon, 1986.

Minney, R. J. *Carve Her Name with Pride*. Newnes, 1956.

Murray, John. *A Spy Called Swallow*. W. H. Allen, 1978.

Murray, Nora. *I Spied for Stalin*. W. H. Allen, 1950.

Muus, Fleming and Varinka. *Monica Winkfield*. Arco Publishers Ltd, 1955.

Neave, Airey. *Little Cyclone*. Coronet, 1954.

Newman, Bernard. *The World of Espionage*. Souvenir Press, 1962.

Nicholas, Elizabeth. *Death Be Not Proud*. Cresset Press Ltd, 1958.

Overton Fuller, Jean. *Madeleine*–the story of Noor Inayat Khan.

———. *Born for Sacrifice*. Pan, 1957.

Pitt, Roxanne. *Operation Double Life*. Bachman & Turner, 1975.

Reitsch, Hanna. *The Sky Is My Kingdom*. Publisher unknown 1955.

Senesh, Hannah. *The Summer That Bled*. Publisher unknown, 1972.

Thatcher, D. and Cross. *R:PIA NAA—The Story of Nona Baker*. Publisher unknown, 1959.

Ticknell, Jerrard. *Odette*. Chapman & Hall, 1949.

Turner, John Frayn. *A Girl Called Johnnie*. Publisher unknown, 1963.

Villiers, Jose. *Granny Was a Spy*. Quartet Books, 1988.

Walters, Anne Marie. *Moon Drop to Gascony*. Macmillan, 1956.

Ward, Dame Irene. *Fany—Invicta*. Hutchinson, 1955.

Reference Books

Who Was Who in America. Chicago: A. N. Marquis, 1942.

Notes

Abbreviations used in notes:

AET   Amy Elizabeth "Betty" Thorpe. Later known as Betty Pack (during first marriage), Elizabeth Brousse (during her second marriage), and various code-names, e.g., Cynthia, Catherine Gordon, et al.

In 1964 AET wrote her memoirs. These are housed in the Churchill College Library, Cambridge. Several versions are on file. The originals were written by AET and typed for her by an English-speaking secretary; they are recognized by a distinctive typeface and an equally distinctive blue-colour ink, as well as editing in AET's own handwriting. Other versions are those which were retyped after editing by H. Montgomery Hyde, AET's first biographer. In all cases I have used AET's original ms., unless otherwise stated.

AJP   Arthur Joseph Pack

BSCO   British Security Coordination Official History

CCC   Churchill College Library, Cambridge, England

DP   The papers of Colonel William J. Donovan held at the U.S. Army Military History Institute, Carlisle Barracks, Pennsylvania

ECO   Eleanor, Lady Campbell-Orde

FO   Foreign Office archives at the Public Record Office, Kew, London

HMH   Harford Montgomery Hyde. The author of *Cynthia*, a previous biography of AET. During the preparation of this work, AET, then known as Mme Elizabeth Brousse, supplied HMH with many personal documents and ms. These are housed at CCC in the "Cynthia Papers."

NARA   National Archives and Records Administration, Washington, D.C.

PP   Pack Papers

PRO   Public Record Office at Kew, London

BR   Bernadette Rivett—AJP's niece and the custodian of the Pack Papers

All interviews were conducted by the author unless otherwise stated.

Introduction

1. AET Memoir, sec. 3, p. xx, CCC; Hyde, *Cynthia*, p. 156.
2. Telephone interview with Marion de Chastellaine, June 11, 1990.
3. Interview with Howard Millis, a close family friend.
4. Interview with an anonymous friend.

Chapter 1 (1910–1929)

1. *Who Was Who in America*, 1942.
2. Obituary "George Cyrus Thorpe," *Washington Star*, July 28, 1936.
3. AET Diary, November 1922, Elizabeth Brousse Papers, File Hyde 2/1, CCC.
4. Ibid., June 19, 1921.
5. Told to HMH by ETB in Hyde, *Cynthia*, p. 16.
6. Betty Thorpe, *Fioretta* (Honolulu: Advertiser Publishing Co. Ltd., 1922), p. 1.
7. Obituary "George Cyrus Thorpe," *Washington Star*, July 28, 1936.
8. AET Diary, May 30, 1923, File Hyde 2/1, CCC.
9. Ibid., October 1, 1923.
10. Deacon and West, *Spy!*, p. 68.
11. Alicia Rose interview with Deacon, *Spy*, p. 68.
12. AET Diary, November 18, 1925, File Hyde 2/1, CCC.
   Note: Samples of Elizabeth's handwriting, analyzed by leading British graphologist

Lawrence Warner in 1990, brought forward the following unprompted comments upon the complexity of her flowering personality:

> I suggest that her sexuality was not intended as really promiscuous but was a way of drawing attention to herself. It was also possibly useful as a way of getting what she wanted because she needed to find constant challenge and have her own way even if that meant others getting hurt (albeit unintentionally) . . . She had felt rejected by her mother within a few weeks of birth (and therefore felt inflexible towards her mother) . . . More importantly I consider that she felt anger towards the father figure. Her feelings seem to have been wounded very deeply and her life was a continuous effort towards finding a father figure coupled almost with a need for revenge. This she could most nearly achieve by dominating relationships . . .

13. AET in *The People*, March 11, 1963, p. 4.
14. *Washington Post*, November 21, 1929, p. 8.
15. Deacon and West, *Spy!*, p. 69.
16. *Washington Post*, November 18, 1929, p. 8.

Chapter 2 (1930–1935)

1. Telephone interview with ECO, March 29, 1990; also interview with BR, April 27, Woking, Surrey.
2. Letter, AET to Rosina Rivett, February 26, 1946, PP.
3. Letter, ECO to author, May 17, 1990.
4. Telephone interview with ECO, March 29, 1990.
5. Interview with ECO, April 5, 1990, Dedham, Essex.
6. Interview with BR, April 27, 1990, Woking, Surrey.
7. Ibid.; also interview with ECO.
8. *Washington Post/New York Times*, February 8, 1930.
9. Hyde, *Cynthia*, p. 22.
10. Ibid.
11. Letter, AET to Rosina Rivett, February 26, 1946, PP.
12. *Washington Post*, April 30, 1930, p. 8; *Washington Evening Star*, April 29–30, 1930, p. 4.
13. *Washington Post*, April 30, 1930, p. 8.
14. Interview with Mrs. Margaret Cassell Owen, March 13, 1990, Longnor, Shrewsbury, Salop. See also letter, Rex Doublet to Rosina Rivett, January 11, 1946.
15. Interview with ECO, April 5, 1990.
16. Interview with BR, April 27, 1990.
17. Letter, BR to author, May 2, 1990.
18. *The Times*, London, September 13, 1930, p. 1.
19. AET to Rosina Rivett, February 26, 1946.

20. *The Times*, London, January 15, 1932, p. 11, col. 5.

21. Interview with Margaret Owen, March 13, 1990.

22. NARA Record Group 59 (U.S. State Department Papers) 701.4125/35.

23. There is a famous Irish family called Beresford Pack, a connection of the powerful Waterfords. It is known that without actually saying so AJP let people assume he may have been related to this family through his Irish grandparents. He was not. His decision to give his daughter the middle name Beresford and to tell her that it was "an old family name" may have been his way of giving the child some social advantage.

24. AET Memoir, Cynthia File 2/9, sec. 2, p. 1, CCC.

25. NARA RG59 701.4125/41.

Chapter 3 (1935–1936)

1. AET Memoir, File 2/8, sec. 2, p. 2, CCC.

2. Ibid. Also letter, Margaret Owen to author, May 12, 1990: " . . . Betty was due to dine with Beaverbrook. . . ."

3. Margaret Owen, March 13, 1990.

4. AET Memoir, File 2/8, sec. 2, CCC.

5. Ibid.

6. Ibid.

7. Johnson, NARA RG59 825.00/2386.

8. Henry Chilton report, PRO, FO 371/20525: 167151.

9. Ibid.

10. NARA RG59 825.00/2386.

11. Sir Henry Chilton report to Anthony Eden, August 4, 1936, PRO, FO 371/20525 W7618/62/41, p. 4.

12. Ibid., p. 2.

13. AET to Catherine Pack (her mother-in-law), October 6, 1936, PP.

14. Ibid.

15. PRO, FO 371/20525 (W7223).

16. Chilton, August 8, 1936, PRO, FO 371/20526 16751.

17. Chilton to Eden, August 4, 1936, PRO, FO 371/20525 7618/62/41, p. 1.

18. USS *Oklahoma* to State Department, NARA RG59 352.1115/89.

19. Chilton to Eden, August 4, 1936, PRO, FO 371/20525 7618/62/41; also, AJP to Chilton, PRO, FO 371/20527: 167151.

20. Chilton to Eden, August 5, 1936, PRO, FO 371/20528:167151, p. 2.

21. AET to Rosina Rivett, October 6, 1936, PP.

22. AET Memoir, sec. 2, CCC.

23. PRO, FO 371/21303.

24. AJP to Department of Trade, March 30, 1937, PRO, FO 371/21289:163822; also Chilton to Mountsey, March 25, 1937.

25. Chilton to Eden, PRO, FO 371/21292.
26. Mountsey to Chilton, PRO, FO 371/21289:163822 et seq.

Chapter 4 (1936–1937)

1. AET Memoir, File 2/8, sec. 2, CCC.
2. Deacon and West, *Spy!*, pp. 71–72.
3. Mountsey to Chilton, April 16, 1937, PRO, FO 371/21289:163822.
4. Chilton to Mountsey, June 14, 1937, PRO, FO 371/21298.
5. Ibid.
6. NARA, 701.4125/25, and 852.00/6621.
7. This is not unusual. Before I became involved in research I assumed like most people, naively as it turns out, that all government and official papers were sacrosanct and would—given different time spans to account for political or personal sensitivity—eventually be archived in the public domain to enable historians to discover the truth about events that might originally have been presented in a biased light. I had in mind a vague notion of the thirty-year rule. In practice, of course, this would be totally impractical. The paper generated by government and state departments is simply too voluminous to be archived intact. So, teams of people called "weeders" are employed to toil through the tons of papers due for declassification, and to discard or destroy administrative minutiae which they believe would be of no possible interest in the declassification process.

This also provides an opportunity to destroy or suppress (under the Secrets Act) sensitive items that might compromise or embarrass officials or government departments. Some weeders are more generous, or less thorough, than others and it is often possible to find documents within the Foreign Office archives which one would have thought would be still classified. But the experienced researcher in England, knowing that a certain document *did* exist and finding a lacuna in the appropriate file, becomes used to being told by a Public Record Office employee, "Sorry, it looks as if it didn't survive. . . ." Royal papers have their own archivist and set of rules. The Secret Service of course never release any documents, on the grounds that it could compromise their present operations, and their documents simply remain classified. This also applies to the papers, diaries and letters of individuals who have worked within or connected with the SIS where items can be removed and classified for a hundred years or more. So the absence of documentary evidence regarding the hand of the intelligence network in Arthur's transfer to Poland does not necessarily rule out the possibility that such a hand was involved. In addition, what possible reason could Betty have had for concealing such a dramatic incident in her career even later, when she was prepared to reveal so much of her life as a spy? The final answer, in this case, lies locked within the files of MI6.
8. Official pass dated Paris, June 2, 1937; Brousse Papers, AET, File 2/7.

9. Leche to Vansittart April 14, 1990, PRO, FO 371/21290.

10. AET Memoir, sec. 2, CCC.

11. Stephen O. Fuqua to Chief of Staff, Military Intelligence Div., Ref. 852.00/6249, NARA.

12. AET Memoir, part 2, p. 12, CCC.

13. AET in *The People*, October 20, 1963, p. 2.

14. AET Memoir, part 2, p. 12, CCC.

15. Ibid.

16. AET Memoir, sec. 2, CCC; and *The People*, October 20, 1963, pp. 2. Whether his blindness was due to injury or vitamin deficiency is unclear, but by sheer coincidence Carlos Sartorious was a fellow inmate for some weeks and it was from him that Betty subsequently learned the fate of the young officer.

17. AET Memoir, sec. 2, p. 14, CCC.

18. Ibid., pp. 20.

19. PRO, FO 371/21302–167151.

20. AET Memoir, sec. 2, p. 20, CCC; also, letter from Margaret Owen to author, April 12, 1990.

21. Martha Gellhorn, *The View from the Ground* (London: Granta Books, 1990), p. 42.

22. Leche to Vansittart, April 14, 1990, PRO, FO 371/21290.

23. Leche to Mountsey, June 1937, PRO, FO 371/21297.

24. Hyde, *Cynthia*, p. 65.

25. AET Memoir, sec. 2, p. 23, CCC.

26. Ibid.

27. Ibid., pp. 17–18.

28. Ibid.

29. AET Memoir, sec. 2, CCC.

30. G. H. Thompson dispatch to London, PRO, FO 371/21297. Also, Sir Arnold Wilson, M.P.: "50,000 non-combatants were murdered [by the Republicans] in Barcelona and Valencia alone, at the lowest estimate . . . and the total number of murders in the last 15 months on the Eastern side of Spain is put at 300,000. . . ."

31. AET to AJP, Brousse Papers, File 2/6, CCC.

32. NARA RG59 852.6249.

33. Leche, PRO, FO 371/21290:163822.

34. AET Memoir, sec. 2, pp. 25, CCC.

35. Leche to Vansittart, April 14, 1990, PRO, FO 371/21290:163822.

36. AET Memoir, sec. 2, pp. 29–30, CCC.

37. PRO, FO 371/21298, July 11, 1937.

38. As a general rule all real names were changed in the memoir except for those people who were dead when Betty wrote it; but she also provided the real names as footnotes.

Chapter 5 (1937–1938)

My chief sources for Betty's experiences in Poland were her own memoirs in Churchill College, Cambridge, and those listed below. But in addition I received considerable information during the course of several interviews at the Royal Overseas League (London) with two (unrelated) persons to whom I promised absolute confidentiality; one for personal reasons and one because disclosure might have affected pension income. Because I cannot thank them in the acknowledgments I hope that they will both accept my thanks, here, for their contribution.

1. Interview with Lord Hankey, at the House of Lords, April 19, 1990.
2. AET Memoir, File 2/9, sec. 3, p. 3, CCC.
3. ETB to RR, February 26, 1946, PP.
4. Interview with Lord Hankey.
5. AET Memoir, File 2/9, sec. 3, p. 3, CCC.
6. Ibid.
7. March 12, 1938.
8. £20 (sterling) a month. Current equivalent would be approximately $500 (U.S.) a month.
9. Irving, p. 111. Andrew, *Secret Service*, p. 448.
10. See: Deacon, *A History of the British Secret Service*, p. 380; Deacon and West, *Spy!*, p. 74; Costello, p. 255; Stevenson, *A Man Called Intrepid*, pp. 311–13.
11. Lewin, pp. 27–29.
12. According to General Gustave Bertrand, the French secret service was contacted in 1932 by a German named "Asche" who worked in the cypher branch of the German army and who offered information and documents in return for money. He was, apparently, in reality Hans Thilo-Schmidt and between 1932 and 1939 supplied the French with 303 documents about Enigma which included army Enigma keys for 1932, 1933 and part of 1934, as well as instructions for use of the machine and other key data. Bertrand claims that the key settings, when given to the Poles, enabled the breakthrough in reading Enigma traffic.

It is significant that in *British Intelligence in the Second World War* (the official history) vol. 1, p. 491, etc., F. H. Hinsley relies heavily in his sources on *published* personal recollections by Bertrand and other personalities involved in the Enigma project to chronicle the matter. This does not imply that no secret documents exist (for he was not able to quote those documents "which are unlikely ever to be opened in the Public Record Office"; see p. viii) but rather that the sources available to him more closely agreed with Bertrand's version than those of F. W. Winterbotham and other British writers on the subject.

13. Calvocoressi, pp. 31–35.

14. Hinsley, vol. 1, p. 487.

15. Lewin, p. 40.

16. Ibid., pp. 38–39.

machine. One is that when Denniston was staying in the Hotel Bristol in August 1939 a large bag containing an Enigma machine (a Polish replica) was left in the foyer. Denniston, whose luggage was identical, hastily exchanged one of his own bags leaving behind a collection of dirty shirts and heavy books, and departed for England with his prize.

Another story, told by General Bertrand, head of the French cryptanalyst unit, is that he was given two Enigma machines, that he brought one to London and personally handed it over to Stewart Menzies, later head of British SIS and known as "C."

Gordon Welshman, author of *Hut Six Story*, believes both stories to be true, theorizing that the Poles may well have covered their options by sending two machines by different routes, to ensure the safe arrival of at least one of them.

18. Remarkable though it may seem, the Germans were never aware that the Allies were able to read all of their top-grade secret communications. Churchill called his Ultra team at Bletchley, those who were responsible for the decoding of Enigma transmissions, his "geese that laid golden eggs and never cackled." Enigma gave the Allies Top Secret information in every theatre of war and arguably was a key factor in the defeat of Hitler's forces. Many hundreds of Allied personnel were involved in decoding Enigma traffic throughout the war and yet it was not until 1974 that the secret was disclosed.

19. Brown, "C."

20. Hyde, *Room 3603* (NY: Farrar, Strauss, 1962). In U.K. p. as *Quiet Canadian*; Constable, 1962 and Stevenson, *A Man Called Intrepid*.

21. Deacon, *A History of the British Secret Service*, p. 380; Kahn, pp. 486–88; Costello, pp. 255–58; Deacon and West, *Spy!*, p. 74.

22. Deacon and West, *Spy!*, p. 74.

23. William Stephenson to W. J. Donovan, memorandum entitled "British Recruiting and Handling of Agents," p. 3, Folder 929, Box 120B, DP.

24. Secret memorandum to Colonel William Donovan from Colonel Charles Ellis entitled, "Working of a Secret Service Organization," p. 8; copies in DP; and Folder Hyde 3/32, CCC.

25. NARA RG59 860C.002/252.

26. Churchill, vol. 1: *The Gathering Storm*, p. 290.

Chapter 6 (1938–1940)

1. Wilbur J. Carr, 123/37 RG59, NARA.

2. AET Memoir, Polish sec., File 2/8, CCC.

3. *Secret Service*, p. 343.

4. Interview with Lord Hankey at the House of Lords, April 19, 1990.

5. AET memoir, Polish sec., File 2/8, CCC.
6. Interview with Lord Hankey.
7. Biddle, December 2, 1938, File 860c. 00/762, NARA.
8. Interview with Margaret Owen.
9. Cora Thorpe to Rosina Rivett, July 16, 1952, PP.
10. Interview with Margaret Owen.
11. Hyde, *Cynthia*, p. 86.
12. AET Memoir, Polish sec., File 2/8, CCC.
13. Ibid.
14. Death certificate of Sophie Shelley: ORS 702249 (Registered with British consul at Bucharest). Also, PRO FO 371/23151. Letter, Lord Hankey to author, April 24, 1990.
15. Interview with Lord Hankey.
16. NARA RG59/860C.001.
17. AJP to Rosina Rivett, April 7, 1939, written on board the MV *Reina del Pacífico*.
18. Howard Millis to Rosina Rivett, November 28, 1945, PP.
19. PRO, FO 371/26182:16751.
20. AET to Rosina Rivett, December 15, 1945, PP.
21. From the transcript preserved by the International Military Tribunal. My source: *World War II Almanac, 1931–1945* by Robert Goralski, p. 87.
22. 2/14 Letter, AET undated; February 1963 File Hyde 2/6 to HMH.
23. Parry-Jones to AET, February 1, 1963, File Hyde 2/6. Also, AET Memoir, File 2/8, article 1, p. 9, CCC.
24. Interview with Margaret Owen.
25. AET Memoir, File 2/8 Article 1 op.cit. CCC.
26. *South Pacific Mail*, September 21, 1939, pp.14–15.
27. AET to Rosina Rivett, December 15, 1945, PP.
28. PRO, FO 371/26182:167151.
29. PRO, FO 371/24169:167151.
30. AET to Rosina Rivett, December 15, 1945, PP.

Chapter 7 (1940–1941)

1. AET to Rosina Rivett, December 15, 1945, PP.
2. Ruby, pp. 3–5.
3. Buckmaster, *They Fought Alone*, p. 22.
4. Ibid., p. 15.
5. Dalton, p. 368.
6. Foot, *SOE*, p. 62.
7. Ibid., p. 61.
8. Interview with Colonel Maurice Buckmaster at Forest Row, November 3, 1988.
9. Liane Jones, *A Quiet Courage*, p. 17.

10. William J. Donovan to President, April 12, 1945, Files 447–51, DP.
11. Interview with Maurice Buckmaster.
12 Letter, Pearl Cornielly to author, September 25, 1989.
1. Masson, *The Search for Christine Granville.*
14. Donovan Files 447–451, Folder 1, DP.
15. Ibid.
16. Report from Mrs. Elizabeth Pack enclosed in official letter, Bentinck to Halifax, PRO, FO 371/26182:16751.
17. Ibid.
18. Sir Charles Orde, FO 371/26182:16751.
19. AET in *The People,* November 3, 1963, p. 4.
20. The ticket stubs for this flight survive among her papers at CCC. File Hyde 2/5.
21. AET to HMH, File Hyde 2/6, CCC.
22. AET Memoir, File Hyde 2/8, CCC.
23. Lady Orde to Rosina Rivett, February 1946, PP.

Chapter 8 (January–April 1941)

1. AET Memoir, CCC. Section audio-taped by author without pagination; tape no. 2.
    Note: Betty was not alone in finding Courteney Forbes an unpleasant man even in this short association with him. The American chargé d'affaires, Henry Norweb, felt so strongly that he wrote a long memorandum to the secretary of state about Forbes, " . . . he frequently attacks me and the Embassy . . . because he is jealous of the prestige and influence that the United States enjoys in Peru . . . he often criticizes Americans and their customs and behaviour." Although Norweb recognized the mutual advantage and desirability of British-American co-operation he reported that he did not "place enough reliance on Mr Forbes tact and judgement to enable me to work with him on a close and confidential basis. . . . [his] exhibitions of tactlessness have alienated a goodly number of persons in Lima, including members of his own colony," NARA RG59 701.4123/16.
2. Ibid.
3. Ibid. Also, *The Reveille,* Cynthia articles, 1963, CCC.
4. Confirmed by Bill Ross-Smith. Interview at Chertsey, October 1990.
5. Stevenson, *A Man Called Intrepid.*
6. Downes, pp. 59–60.
7. Interview with Marion de Chastellaine, June 11, 1990.
8. NARA RG59 701.6511/1037.
9. NARA RG59 841.01b11.
10. Stafford, pp. 12–14. Also, WSS's precise duties as the head of SOE, SIS, MI6

and MI5 in the Western Hemisphere are confirmed in a Colonial Office telegram dated November 7, 1942. See File Hyde 3/23, CCC.

11. Troy, p. 83.

12. AET Memoir, sec. 3, CCC. Author's audio-tape no. 2.

13. Washingtonia collection of directories at the Martin Luther King Library.

14. Interview with Mrs. Shirlee Christian Thorpe, Washington, D.C., June 1990.

15. Senator Tom Connally, chairman of the Foreign Relations Committee, AET Memoir, sec. 3, CCC. Author's audio-tape no. 2.

16. BSCO, p. 167.

17. FBI File 100.3712.

18. NARA B12-2-12.

19. BSCO, p. 166.

20. Ibid.

21. Hyde, *Room 3603/The Quiet Canadian* op.cit.

22. The Sunday *Times*, London, November 11, 1962.

23. FBI File 100.3712 (sheets 44 and 45).

24. *Time*, December 20, 1963.

25. Goralski, *World War II Almanac 1931–1945*.

26. Letter, F. H. Hinsley to the author, dated September 12, 1990.

27. Ibid., March 15, 1991.

28. An Australian by birth, Ellis was "placed" in BSC's New York office by Sir Stewart Menzies ("C"). It has been alleged that this was to keep an eye on Stephenson, whom Menzies did not like but who had been imposed upon him by Churchill. After Ellis's death it was suggested by several writers (notably Chapman Pincher) that Ellis might have been a "mole" for the Russians, possibly even "the fifth man"; and that he betrayed Britain to the Nazis before the outbreak of World War II. His colleagues in BSC absolutely refute this.

29. BSCO, p. 167.

30. Sir David Hunt to the author, May 29, 1990. During a subsequent interview at Sir David's home in June 1990, at which I revealed some of my research materials, Sir David did accept that Betty alias "Cynthia" had existed.

31. R. V. Jones, *Most Secret War*, p. 73.

32. Anthony Cave Brown, p. 521. Quotes R. V. Jones's lecture on SIS to British Air Staff after the war: "It is difficult . . . to trust 'Dirty' work, although it may sometimes produce very valuable results. . . ."

33. R. V. Jones, *Most Secret War*, p. 354.

34. Smith, p. 42.

35. Maurice Buckmaster, in *The People*, October 28, 1962, p. 12.

36. R. V. Jones, *Most Secret War*, p. 351 et seq.

37. FBI File 100.3712; also FBI File 65.43539 JHW:AB, August 18, 1942.

38. *New York Times*, March 31, 1941, pp. 1–3.

39. Ibid., March 30, 1941, p. 1.
40. Breckinridge Long, NARA RG59 701.6511/1027, April 2, 1941. Communication handed to the Italian ambassador at noon on same day.
41. NARA RG59 701.6511/1012.
42. Hull, vol. 2, p. 927.
43. Sumner Welles to FDR, NARA 103.91802/308a.
44. NARA RG59 701.6511/1022 and 1023.
45. Hyde, *Cynthia*, p. 118.
46. NARA RG59 701.6511/1028.
47. Divorce papers, Pack *vs* Pack, May 14, 1945, Somerset House Archives, London Folder 188.
48. *Washington Evening Star*, April 4, 1941, p. A2.
49. BSCO, p. 167.
50. *Washington Evening Star*, May 21, 1941, p. 14.
51. AET Memoir, sec. 3, CCC. Author's audio-tape no. 2.
52. Downes, p. 60.

Chapter 9 (*April–May 1941*)

1. PRO, FO 371/25875.
2. Brian Blood to Sir Edward Wilshaw, FO 371/25875:165304.
3. PRO, FO 371/25875:165304.
4. Ibid.
5. Ibid.
6. NARA RG59 800.20210/1694, November 3, 1943.
7. AET Memoir, CCC, and Stevenson, *A Man Called Intrepid*, pp. 314–15.
8. Stevenson, *A Man Called Intrepid*, pp. 315–16.
9. Ibid.
10. Churchill to Ismay, August 5, 1947, PRO, CAB 120/746.
11. Bill Ross-Smith interview. Mr. Ross-Smith, who worked at Stephenson's head-quarters, found the story of this meeting difficult to believe. He recalled that Stephenson was extremely reticent about meeting field agents and made himself as "invisible" as possible, employing the "need to know" rule. However, Betty wrote about the meeting in her memoirs and in letters and Stephenson talked about it to his biographers. Perhaps Stephenson, having heard of Betty's powers as a super siren, simply cast aside his own rule and called on her to have a look at her for himself.
12. NARA RG59 701.5111/733.
13. Letter, Lawrence J. Warner to author, September 17, 1990.
14. NARA RG59 701.5111/766.
15. Ibid.
16. FBI report, Hoover to Berle, October 1940, NARA RG59 851.20211/16.
17. Hull, vol. 1, p. 847.

18. Hull Papers at Library of Congress; also *Memoirs*, vol. 2, pp. 959–60.
19. BSCO, p. 167
20. Ibid.
21. NARA RG59 740.0011 (1939)/4425.
22. Hull, vol. 1, p. 799; and Goralski, p. 125.

Chapter 10 (May 1941–March 1942)

1. Interview with Shirlee Thorpe in Washington, D.C., June 1990.
2. Ibid.
3. NARA RG59 701.5111/829.
4. NARA RG59 701.5111/934. Note: Chautemps was initially suspected by the British of being pro-German but by 1942 he was working for the OSS; see RG59 701.5111/900.
5. BSC official history, p. 156; also NARA OSS Papers RG457; Vichy Intercepts box; also DP; also Roosevelt Papers, Hyde Park, New York.
6. Ibid.
7. Lash, p. 490.
8. Hyde, *Room 3603/The Quiet Canadian.*
9. Hyde, *Cynthia*, p. 4.
10. Telephone interview with Marion de Chastellaine, June 11, 1990.
11. Letter from the late Roald Dahl to the author, May 2, 1990.
12. H. M. Hyde to Carter Ruck, January 23, 1964, CCC, File Hyde 1/11.
13. Louise D. Cadet to State Department, NARA RG59 701.5111. Also Downes, p. 60.
14. BSCO, p. 155.
15. Ibid.
16. Stevenson, *A Man Called Intrepid,* p. 328.
17. BSCO, p. 155.
18. *Herald-Tribune,* August 31, 1941 (p. 1), and September 1, 1941 (p. 1); also syndicated accounts in other newspapers.
19. Ibid.
20. Ibid.; also BSCO, p. 157.
21. NARA RG59 701.5111/835 ONI, September 4, 1941.
22. Ibid., 701.5111/836.
23. BSCO, p. 157.
24. NARA RG59 701.4125/61.
25. AJP to Tony Pack, November 21, 1944, ECO Papers.
26. NARA RG59 701.5111/876.
27. NARA RG59 701.5111/935.
28. BSCO, p. 155.
29. NARA. OSS Papers RG457, Vichy Cables and Intercepts box.

30. Churchill, vol. 3: *The Grand Alliance*, pp. 539–40.
31. Goralski, pp. 187–88.
32. Churchill, vol. 3: *The Grand Alliance*, pp. 560–61.
33. OSS Foreign Nationalities Branch Files, Report 262, December 16, 1941.
34. Hull, vol. 2, p. 1124.
35. Ibid., pp. 1127–37.
36. NARA OSS Papers RG457, Vichy Cables and Intercepts box.
37. NARA OSS Papers RG457, Vichy Intercepts box; also, DP; also, Roosevelt Papers, Hyde Park, New York.

Chapter 11 (March–June 1942)

1. BSCO, p. 159. NB: The diplomatic cipher had already been obtained through the Vichy French consulate in New York.
2. Louis J. Cadet to State Department, June 1941, NARA RG59 701.5111.
3. Discussion with Tim Naphtali and Bradley Smith, Washington, D.C., June 1990.
4. George Merton to Thomas Troy, September 3, 1972, NARA RG263 (CIA). Merton's detailed account confirms Pepper's extended absence from the New York office. Bill Ross-Smith, who was with Stephenson from the beginning ("There were only four of us at the start," he told me: William Stephenson, John Pepper, Bill Ross-Smith and a girl). Interviewed in 1990, he found it strange that Betty should be asked to report to another control (he had forgotten Pepper's absence during this period). "I doubt that Cynthia would have reported to Huntington other than through Pepper. . . . the one thing that was sacred was the link between agent and contact. . . ."

Tim Naphtali, a Harvard post-graduate researcher on the subject of espionage, pointed out that after the passing of the McKellar Bill at the beginning of 1942, OSS ostensibly took over a lot of BSC operations. From Betty's subsequent history she clearly worked directly through OSS contacts. Mr Naphtali's research showed that Betty had reported directly through Huntington and Murphy to Donovan. Source: Discussion with Tim Naphtali and Bradley Smith, Washington, D.C., June 11, 1990.
5. AET Memoir, sec. 3, CCC.
6. Downes, p. 33.
7. Ibid.
8. Goralski, p. 212.
9. Foreign Nationality Branch Files, NARA FR238/Benoit.
10. NARA RG59 701.5111/918.
11. BSCO, p. 160.
12. Ibid.
13. NARA RG59 811.2222/2162 and 851.01B/152.
14. AET Memoir, sec. 3, p. 13, CCC.
15. BSCO, p. 161.

16. Interview with Mme Camille Chautemps. Foreign Branch File at NARA, FR262/Chautemps; also Deacon and West, *SPY!*, p. 93.
17. BSCO, p. 161.
18. Henry-Haye to James Dunn, NARA RG59 701.5111/981.
19. D. M. Ladd (FBI agent) report to J. E. Hoover, FBI File 116–7648, p. 1.
20. Ibid.
21. Charles Brousse to Admiral Leahy, December 28, 1942, NARA RG59 701.5111/12–2842. Also, Captain W. A. Heard to Charles Brousse, April 7, 1942, OP. 16 F.10. A7 4QQ (also at NARA; in 701.5111/12).
22. Ibid.
23. Charles Brousse to Admiral Leahy, December 28, 1942, NARA RG59 701.5111/12–2842.
24. John H. Williams to D. M. Ladd, FBI File 65.43559.
25. Richard Deacon, *Spyclopedia* (London: MacDonald, 1987), p. 187.
26. Swiss Legation memo, November 17, 1942, NARA RG59 701.5111.
27. Interview with Shirlee Thorpe, Washington, D.C., June 1990.
28. NARA RG59 701.5111/12–2842.

Chapter 12 (June 1942)

1. Information on this plan and the chronology of the next week's activities is taken from three sources: The BSC official history; Betty's memoir; and Charles Brousse's reports in the State Department papers, Record Group 59, File 701.5111.
2. It is not known whether this was the BSC or OSS photographic team. Bill Ross-Smith thought it was BSC's: "We had our own field unit in Washington and would have used that. . . ." Interview with Ross-Smith, Chertsey, October 6, 1990. FBI files, though, contain reports that Huntington and other OSS operators were the occupants of the room used to photograph the material supplied by Betty.
3. Ibid.
4. Dr. Peter Bishop, September 28, 1990, Coleford, Glos.
5. NARA RG59 701.5111/12–2842.
6. Betty's Vichy Memoirs, p. 30, CCC.
7. Tape-recorded interview between H. M. Hyde and Elizabeth Thorpe Brousse (on file) in 1962, *Cynthia*, p. 169.
8. Brousse to Leahy, December 28, 1942, NARA RG59 701.5111/12–2842.
9. Charles need not have worried. According to Donald Downes the janitor was in the pay of the OSS.
10. AET Memoir, sec. 3, p. 32.
11. Donovan papers, NARA RG226 OSS E90, Folder 426. Formally notified August 11, 1942. SO in the OSS organization was responsible for Special Operations, Planning and Propaganda.

12. Smith, p. 52.

Secretly warned that Donovan's status and the future of his organization was under scrutiny at a "high level," SIS took a decision to set up a clandestine operation of their own in North Africa, in parallel with the American one, to be used only if Donovan was axed, and then at "C"s personal command. Donovan was not advised of this. In June 1942 his organization was redefined; formerly COI, it became the OSS with different command procedures, and military rather than civilian. The SIS set-up remained in place, however, and on the day the original "sphere of influence" arrangement ended (after TORCH), a fully organized SIS network sprang to work.

13. Hinsley to author, April 29, 1990.

14. NARA OSS Papers RG457; Vichy Intercepts box; also DP; also Roosevelt Papers, Hyde Park, New York.

15. Hyde, *Cynthia* p. 158.

16. Brousse to Roosevelt, NARA RG59 701.5111/1–743.

17. Elizabeth Pack, alias Catherine Gordon, to State Department, Declaration, December 28, 1942.

Chapter 13 (August 1942–February 1943)

1. FBI File "Elizabeth Pack."

2. NARA RG59 701.5111/9–544. *Note:* Mrs. Charles Bennett was also the name of Kay Brousse's mother, who had formerly worked for a business firm who published the Congressional Record in Washington.

3. Four-page memo from S. K. McKee (Special Agent in charge) to J. Edgar Hoover, August 8, 1942. FBI Ref: 65.3575.

4. NARA (Suitland): RG319 Box 456, January 13, 1942, Entry 47. Lee to Hoover: " . . . No solution has yet been affected."

5. Troy Papers (CIA) RG263, Box 10, Folder 14.

6. Berle Diary, February 2, 1942. Hyde Park.

7. FBI agent John H. Williams to Mr. Ladd, August 13, 1942, FBI File 65–43539–2.

8. Ibid , Williams to J. Edgar Hoover, August 27, 1942.

9. NARA RG59 701.5111/12–2842, report by C. E. Brousse.

10. NARA (Suitland): indexes to telephone intercepts, RG59 811.751.

11. Churchill, vol. 4: *The Hinge of Fate*, pp. 552–53.

12. Churchill, BBC Home Service Broadcast, November 10, 1942.

13. Pétain to FDR, FDR Library, Hyde Park, New York.

14. AET Memoir, sec. 3, p. XX, CCC; Hyde, *Cynthia*, p. 156.

15. NARA RG59 701.5111, Joseph Gassler to Cordell Hull, November 12, 1942.

16. Hershey Hotel brochure, 1942.

17. Donovan papers NARA RG226 OSS E90, Folder 426.

18. NARA, RG59 701.5111/1–2943.

19. FBI Archives: letter, Adolf Berle from J. Edgar Hoover, November 16, 1942; Also NARA RG59 701.5111/1019 1/2.

20. Charles Brousse to President Franklin D. Roosevelt. NARA RG59 701.5111/1–743.

21. *Washington Evening Star*, November 17, 1942, p. 1; event also covered extensively by the *Washington Post*, pp. 1–3.

22. Memo from the office of Breckinridge Long, November 16, 1942, NARA RG59 701.5111/1010 1/2.

23. Ibid.

24. NARA RG59 701.5111/12–2842, p. 3.

25. NARA RG59 701.5111/12–2242.

26. Ibid.

27. Fred Israel (editor), *The War Diary of Breckinridge Long* (Lincoln, Nebr.: University of Nebraska Press, 1966).

28. Smith, p. 24.

29. FBI File 65.3575: S. K. McKee to Hoover, January 22, 1943.

30. Ibid.

31. Ibid.

32. Downes, p. 96.

33. Interview with Shirlee C. Thorpe, June 3, 1990, The Watergate, Washington, D.C.

34. Interview with Marion de Chastellaine, June 11, 1990.

35. Edwin A. Plitt, writer of memo dated December 27, 1942, recording conversation between Betty and Edgar Innes, NARA RG59 701.5111/1080 1/2.

36. Ibid.

37. Ibid. Also, NARA RG59 701.5111/1089 1/2.

38. Catherine Gordon declaration to State Department, December 28, 1942, NARA RG59 701.5111/12–2942.

39. Ibid.

40. Lawrence Warner to author, October 1990.

41. December 31, 1942, Office of Foreign Activities Correlation, NARA RG59 701.5111/12–2842.

42. NARA RG59 701.5111/12–2842.

43. NARA RG59 701.5111/1–743, January 7, 1943, and 701.5111/12–2842.

44. NARA RG59. Letters from Charles Brousse to: Admiral Leahy, December 28, 1942, 701.5111/12–2842; Cordell Hull, January 5, 1943, 701.5111/12–2845; President F. D. Roosevelt, January 7, 1943, 701.5111/1–743.

45. Innes to Plitt, NARA RG59 701.5111/1–3043.

46. Brousse to Plitt, January 19, 1943, NARA RG59 701.5111/1–2943.

47. Swiss Legation to G2, NARA RG59 701.5111/1094.

48. NARA RG59 701.5111/1101.

Chapter 14 (1943–1944)

1. NARA RG59 701.5111/1167.
2. Catherine W. Gordon-Brousse to Frederick Lyons, NARA RG59 701.5111/6–1443.
3. NARA RG59 701.5111/5–2843 et seq.
4. AJP to Rosina Rivett, June 8, 1943, PP.
5. NARA RG59 701.5111/1167.
6. NARA RG59 701.5111/1168 and 1168 1/2, June 22, 1943.
7. George Brandt memo, Filed with NARA RG59 701.5111/1168.
8. Lyon to Brandt, Plitt & Bonbright, June 22, 1943, NARA RG59 701.5111/1168.
9. Bannerman to Fitch, June 24, 1943, NARA RG59 701.5111/1170.
10. Ibid.
11. B. Long, June 22, 1943, NARA RG59 701.5111/1168 1/2
12. NARA RG59 701.5111/1170, June 24, 1943.
13. Ibid.
14. Hyde, *Cynthia*, p. 158.
15. E. A. Plitt; précis of conversation, NARA RG59 701.5111/6–3043.
16. Ibid.
17. Lee H. Seward to Mr. Fitch, NARA RG59 701.5111/1180.
18. NARA RG59 701.5111/1180.
19. NARA RG59 701.5111/1181.
20. F. B. Lyon memo to Smith, circulated to Bonbright and Brandt, NARA RG59 701.5111/1178.
21. Stevenson, *A Man Called Intrepid*, p. 340.
22. Ibid., p. 341.
23. NARA RG59 811.111/19864, November 22, 1943, and 800.20210/1694.
24. NARA RG59 701.5111/8–2543. A handwritten note on the cable reads, "Jim Murphy is handling this 8/30/43."
25. NARA RG59 701.5111/2643.
26. NARA RG59 701.5111/5–244.
27. Ibid.
28. Birch O'Neil, civil attaché, to F. B. Lyon, April 29, 1944, NARA RG59 701.5111/5–244.
29. F. B. Lyon to Gibson, May 16, 1944, NARA RG59 701.5111/5–1644.
30. *Washington Daily News*, Friday, October 6, 1944, p. 34.
31. Ibid.
32. F. B. Lyon memo, NARA RG59 701.5111/9–544.
33. Interview with Shirlee Thorpe, June 1990, The Watergate, Washington, D.C.
34. AJP to Tony Pack, April 16, 1944, ECO Papers.
35. AJP to Tony Pack, November 21, 1944, ECO Papers.

Chapter 15 (1945–1946)

1. Interview with Shirlee C. Thorpe, The Watergate, June 1990, Washington, D.C.
2. *South Pacific Mail*, Obituary, November 8, 1945.
3. BR to author, May 2, 1990.
4. Ibid.
5. Interview with BR, Woking, Surrey, June 1990.
6. Decree Absolute issued November 26, 1945, Folio 188, Divorce Registry, Somerset House, London.
7. Howard Millis to Rosina Rivett, November 20, 1945, PP.
8. Interviews (in person) March 29, 1990, and (telephone) June 27, 1990.
9. Rex Doublet to Rosina Rivett, January 11, 1946, PP.
10. Lady Campbell-Orde to Rosina Rivett, January 30, 1946, PP.
11. *South Pacific Mail*, November 1, 1945.
12. AET to Rosina Rivett, December 15, 1945, PP.
13. Rex Doublet to Rosina Rivett, November 26, 1990, PP.
14. Howard Millis to Rosina Rivett, November 15, 1945, PP.
15. Ibid.
16. AET to Rosina Rivett, December 15, 1945, PP.
17. AJP to Foreign Office, related in letter to Rosina Rivett, November 16, 1945, PP.
18. Letter to Rosina Rivett from E. Edgecombe, November 16, 1945, PP.
19. Howard Millis to Rosina Rivett, November 15, 1945, PP.
20. Ibid.
21. Interview with Margaret Cassell Owen, Shropshire, March 13, 1990.
22. C.M.G.: Companion of the Order of St. Michael and St. George. ECO to author, April 4, 1990.
23. ECO to author, April 11, 1990.
24. January 24, 1946.
25. AET to Rosina Rivett, December 15, 1945, PP.
26. ECO to Rosina Rivett, January 2, 1946, PP.
27. Rex Doublet to Rosina Rivett, January 11, 1946, PP.
28. Last will and testament of AJP, October 2, 1945, Somerset House, London.
29. Violet Muñoz to Rosina Rivett, March 27, 1946, PP.
30. Interviews and letters.
31. Rex Doublet to Rosina Rivett, November 26, 1945, PP.
32. Interview with Margaret Cassell Owen, March 13, 1990, Shropshire.
33. Howard Millis to Rosina Rivett, January 17, 1945, PP.
34. Maureen Rivett to author after reading the draft ms.
35. Lady Campbell-Orde to Rosina Rivett, January 30, 1945, PP.
36. BR.

37. ECO to author, telephone conversation, June 27, 1990.
38. AET to Rosina Rivett, January 28, 1946, PP.
39. Ibid.
40. ECO to author, June 27, 1990.

Chapter 16 (1946–1962)

1. Not only local papers. A short poem she wrote about a cruel tradition involving a horse made the *Herald-Tribune* (Europe), August 4, 1947.
2. Interview with Margaret Cassell Owen, March 13, 1990.
3. Cora Welles Thorpe to Rosina Rivett, July 16, 1952, PP.
4. Interview with ECO, April 5, 1990.
5. Major C. B. Grundy, M.C., to author, April 5, 1990.
6. Interview with ECO, April 5, 1990.
7. Hyde, *Cynthia*, p. 162.
8. Cora Welles Thorpe to Rosina Rivett, July 16, 1952, PP.
9. Last Will and Testament of Anthony George Pack, November 24, 1951, Somerset House, London.
10. Citation of Award of Military Cross to Lieutenant Anthony George Pack, King's Shropshire Light Infantry archives; copy also in Hyde Papers, File 2/4, CCC.
11. Cora Welles Thorpe to Rosina Rivett, July 16, 1952, PP.
12. Interview with Shirlee Christian Thorpe, The Watergate, Washington, D.C., June 1990.
13. Letters to author from Major C. B. Grundy, M.C., March 28, 1990; Lt. Col. Richard Osborne, March 24, 1990; Lt. Col. Keith Heard, M.C., March 28, 1990. Telephone interview with Lt. Col. Richard Evans, M.C., March 20, 1990. A memorial to Tony was subsequently organized by family and brother officers in the chapel at Shrewsbury School.
14. Cora Welles Thorpe to Rosina Rivett, July 16, 1952, PP.
15. Hyde, *Cynthia*, p. 164.
16. Cora Welles Thorpe to Rosina Rivett, July 16, 1952, PP.
17. AET to HMH, December 12, 1962, File Hyde 2/7, CCC.
18. Hyde, *Cynthia*, p. 14.
19. The Sunday *Times Magazine* (London), October 21, 1962, p. 25 et seq.
20. AET to Kathleen Taylor Cockburn, November 14, 1962.
21. The chain of events leading up to this incident is remarkable. The entire community of former BSC operatives were amazed that Hyde had been able to obtain permission to write this book and it had, indeed, come about in a surprising manner given the security which then existed and still exists now, nearly thirty years later. According to letters from Ellis to Hyde in the CCC, it is obvious that a misunderstanding had occurred. MI6 approved Ellis's early (abandoned) manuscript, not Montgomery Hyde's much fuller account.

376

22. AET to HMH, November 15, 1962, File Hyde 2/7, CCC.
23. AET to HMH, December 12, 1962, File Hyde 2/7, CCC.
24. AET to HMH, February 21, 1963, File Hyde 2/7, CCC.
25. AET to HMH, January 28, 1963, File Hyde 2/7, CCC.
26. AET to HMH, February 23, 1963, File Hyde 2/7, CCC.
27. Hyde, *Cynthia*, p. 168.
28. Hyde papers, File 2/15, CCC (Betty has marked a newspaper account of a divorce case, underlining the times of the alleged adultery, and referred to two occasions "at S'Agarro . . . 10 am and 3 pm," which were the times when she and Hyde made love); also private information; also author's telephone conversation with Nigel West, who stated Hyde had told him of the affair which he described as "torrid"; March 30, 1990. Also, letter from Nigel West to author, August 6, 1990.

Chapter 17 (1962–1963)

1. Numerous letters in File Hyde 2/14, CCC, refer.
2. AET to HMH, March 24, 1963, File Hyde 2/14, CCC.
3. Hyde, *Cynthia*, p. 173.
4. Owen O'Malley, whom she had met in Biarritz after her return from Poland.
5. AET to Owen O'Malley, May 13, 1963. Reproduced in Hyde, *Cynthia*, p. 174.
6. AET to Kathleen Cockburn, June 13, 1963.
7. Ca. June 1962 (date indecipherable), File Hyde 1/6, CCC.
8. HMH to H. Iain Thompson, March 11, 1963, File Hyde 2/14, CCC.
9. AET to HMH, May 17, 1963, File Hyde 2/7, CCC.
10. AET to HMH, June 6, 1963, File Hyde 2/7, CCC.
11. Ellis to HMH, September 1962. Hyde files, CCC. The references to the Italian and French "annoyance" was in connection with Hyde's earlier disclosures in *The Quiet Canadian*. See also Appendix.
12. AET to HMH, July 10, 1963, File Hyde 2/14, CCC.
13. Ibid. (enclosure).
14. AET to HMH, July 28, 1963, Hyde File 2/14, CCC.
15. Numerous letters in File Hyde 1/10, CCC, refer.
16. H. Iain Thompson to AET, August 2, 1963, File Hyde 2/14, CCC.
17. *The People*, December 8, 1963, p. 1.
18. Ibid., September 29, 1963, p. 1.
19. Ibid.
20. AET to Kathleen Cockburn, October 20, 1963. Kindly loaned to the author by Mrs. Cockburn.
21. AET to HMH, October 23, 1963, File Hyde 2/7, CCC.
22. Ellis to HMH, October 1963, File Hyde 1/10, CCC.
23. Rosina Rivett to Sheila More, undated ca. 1966, PP.
24. Telephone conversation with Mme Lubienski, May 22, 1990.

25. *The People*, September 29, 1963.
26. Dr. Harvey Brinton Stone to AET, January 30, 1963.
27. Mrs. Robert Gillican to AET, undated ca. 1963, Cynthia Papers, CCC.
28. Sir Piersson Dix to AET, October 1963, Cynthia Papers, CCC.
29. Interview with Shirlee Thorpe, Washington, D.C., June 1990.
30. Charles E. Brousse to HMH, December 12, 1963, File Hyde 2/7, CCC.

Epilogue

1. Robert Lantz to HMH, December 5, 1964, File Hyde 2/14, CCC.
2. Winterbotham, *The Ultra Secret*.
3. Hyde, *The Quiet Canadian*, p. 105.
4. George Thorpe to Shirlee Christian Thorpe, October 1964, p. 2.
5. Rosina Rivett to Sheila More, undated ca. 1966, PP.
6. H. Montgomery Hyde articles in *Reveille*, May 1966: "She Gave her Love for Secrets," etc.
7. Ellis to HMH June 10, 1963, File Hyde 1/11, CCC.
8. John Raymond, "The Adventures of a Charming Lady Spy," The *Sunday Times*, London, April 3, 1966.
9. Len Deighton, "The Secret Life of a spy called Cynthia," *Glasgow Evening Citizen*, April 12, 1966.
10. NARA RG59 103.91802/796.
11. Howard Millis to HMH, November 1963, File Hyde 2/14, CCC.

Appendix

1. NARA 811/8111/Dip. 15254.
2. Philby, p. 53.
3. Troy, p. 34.
4. Philby, p. 54.
5. Lash, p. 140.
6. The date of this dinner party has come in for considerable scrutiny, for both Stephenson biographers have stated unequivocally that it took place on May 10, while historians point out that this was impossible as Churchill and Beaverbrook dined alone together that evening. However, in a cable among writer William Stevenson's papers in the University of Regina archives, Sir William advised (long before the date was queried) his uncertainty about whether the meeting took place on May 10 or 12.
7. Part of a handwritten account by Cuneo and first published in *The Quiet Canadian* in 1962. Cuneo was aware of the attacks later made on Stephenson and never deviated from his first recollection of the event. Hyde Papers, CCC. In December 1952 he told McKenzie Porter, feature writer for *Maclean's* magazine, "Stephenson is the only

man who enjoyed the unqualified confidence of both Churchill and Roosevelt." The story appeared in the December 1, 1952 issue.

8. The fact that Stephenson headed all British Intelligence activities in the Western Hemisphere is so well acknowledged that it seems almost unnecessary to cite documentary references. However, one—a Foreign Office cable referring to Stephenson as "D"—is of particular interest since it defines the agencies specifically and states that his authority is subject only to the "over-riding authority of the Chairman of the United Kingdom Security Executive." This may be found in File Hyde 3/23, CCC.

9. Anthony Cave Brown, "C," p. 263. Apart from all other considerations Stephenson had made it clear that he would only report directly to Churchill and would not be responsible to "that crowd at Broadway"; Paget had reported only to "C." Stephenson's ill-concealed dismissive opinion of the espionage establishment in London would not have helped his relationship with "C."

10. Hyde, *The Quiet Canadian*.

11. Beaverbrook to HMH, September 10, 1962, File Hyde 1/6, CCC.

12. William Manchester, *The Caged Lion* (Michael Joseph, 1988), p. 374.

13. *Avion* undated cutting but obviously contemporary from surrounding news, File Hyde 1/1, CCC. It states that Stephenson is the holder of the Military Cross, the DFC and croix de guerre. This is verified in a letter to Hyde from a fellow officer in RFC 73 Squadron. T. G. Drew-Brook to Hyde, December 12, 1961, Hyde File 1/5, CCC.

14. T. G. Drew-Brook to HMH, December 12, 1961, File Hyde 1/5, CCC.

15. Brown, "C," p. 262.

16. Hyde, *Secret Intelligence Agent*, pp. 80–81.

17. Interview with Bill Ross-Smith, Chertsey, 1990.

18. Anthony Cave Brown, "C," p. 195.

19. The designation "fifth column" stems from the Spanish civil war. Franco is reputed to have said he had five columns of soldiers: four marching on Madrid and a fifth waiting to strike within Madrid. The term has come to mean any element in the civil population, native or alien, who in any way contributes to the strength of the enemy.

20. Beaverbrook to Churchill, December 13, 1940, Beaverbrook Archives.

21. Martin Gilbert, *Winston S. Churchill* (William Heinemann, 1976), vol. 6, p. 358.

22. NARA RG59 702.4111/1608.

23. Technically, officials of the Passport Control department were not diplomats and although employed by the Foreign Office enjoyed no diplomatic status. Paget, though, had friends in high places in the United States (such as Vincent Astor) and his contacts subsequently helped Stephenson get established.

24. Interview with Grace Garner and phone conversation, September 27, 1990; Stephenson "loaned" Grace Garner to Beaverbrook in London after the war and she was an observer of their close personal relationship.

25. Downes, p. 63.
26. Interview with Ross-Smith, Chertsey, 1990.
27. Hyde, *Quiet Canadian*, p. 186, based on incident described in Cuneo/Mountbatten/Hyde correspondence in Hyde Papers, CCC.
28. *Globe and Mail*, Toronto, December 28, 1984.
29. Grace Garner to Sir William Stephenson and HMH, January 10, 1984.
30. Morton to Colonel E. I. Jacob, September 18, 1941, Churchill Papers, CCC, Box 145, Folder 463, Item 2; also quoted in CIA paper entitled, "Studies in Intelligence," p. 109, written in 1974.
31. R. B. Long memorandum of meeting, January 28, 1941, NARA 841.01 B11.
32. Biddle, Memorandum, February 26, 1942, Hyde Park, New York.
33. Berle to Sumner Welles, March 31, 1941, NARA 841.20211/23.
34. Berle diary VIII/2, pp. 139–40, March 10, 1942, Hyde Park, New York.
35. Ibid.
36. *Washington Post*, "Outlook Section" C1, September 17, 1989, pp. 1–2.
37. Ibid.
38. Ibid.
39. Berle Diaries, Hyde Park, New York, February and March 1942. In old age Berle admitted to an interviewer that he admired Stephenson greatly, though he thought he had taken some ill-advised risks prior to Pearl Harbor: "Bravely, but in defiance of the constitution." See Hyde File 1/10. Ogilvie to Hyde, February 25, 1963, and Hyde File, 1/6 February 19, 1962, CCC.
40. BSCO.

Note: General Reference Material on Sir William Stephenson

This list is not comprehensive but will give the reader all-round insight into the controversy.

BIOGRAPHY

Hyde, H. Montgomery. *Room 3603*. Farrar Straus, 1962. Published in England as *The Quiet Canadian*. Hamish Hamilton, 1962.
Stevenson, William. *A Man Called Intrepid*. Harcourt Brace Jovanovich, 1976.

ARTICLES

Hunt, David. "A Tepid Intrepid." *Times Literary Supplement*, London, September 3, 1982.
Ignatious, David. "Britain's War in America." *Washington Post* ("Outlook" section), Washington, D.C., September 17, 1989.
Mandrake. "Death of an Intrepid Fraud." *Sunday Telegraph*, London, February 12, 1989.

Stafford, David. "A Myth Called Intrepid." *Saturday Night*, Toronto, October 1989.

Trevor-Roper, Hugh. "The Faking of Intrepid." *Sunday Telegraph*, London, February 19, 1989.

Walker, David. "How Britain Hoodwinked Roosevelt." *The Times*, London, April 2, 1985.

Index

383